DRIVING DIGITAL TRANSFORMATION

Driving Digital Transformation

Lessons from building
the first ASEAN digital bank

DENNIS KHOO

© 2021 allDigitalfuture LLP

Reprinted 2021

Published in 2021 by Marshall Cavendish Business
An imprint of Marshall Cavendish International

A member of the
Times Publishing Group

Other Marshall Cavendish Offices:
Marshall Cavendish Corporation, 800 Westchester Ave, Suite N-641, Rye Brook, NY 10573, USA • Marshall Cavendish International (Thailand) Co Ltd, 253 Asoke, 16th Floor, Sukhumvit 21 Road, Klongtoey Nua, Wattana, Bangkok 10110, Thailand • Marshall Cavendish (Malaysia) Sdn Bhd, Times Subang, Lot 46, Subang Hi-Tech Industrial Park, Batu Tiga, 40000 Shah Alam, Selangor Darul Ehsan, Malaysia

Marshall Cavendish is a registered trademark of Times Publishing Limited

National Library Board, Singapore Cataloguing in Publication Data
Name(s): Khoo, Dennis, 1963-
Title: Driving digital transformation : lessons from building the first ASEAN digital bank / Dennis Khoo.
Description: Singapore : Marshall Cavendish Business, 2021. | Includes bibliographical references.
Identifier(s): ISBN 978-981-4974-58-5 (paperback)
Subject(s): LCSH: Internet banking--Southeast Asia. | Financial services industry--Technological innovations--Southeast Asia.
Classification: DDC 332.1202854678--dc23

Printed in Singapore

Contents

Foreword   11
Preface   13
Acknowledgements   15

Chapter 1: The journey to TMRW   **17**

Chapter 2: What the future holds   **28**
2.1 The future of banking   31
2.2 Difference between digital banking and digital bank   41
2.3 Disruptive Innovation vs Sustaining Innovation   50
2.4 Challenges facing legacy incumbent banks   59
2.5 Experience starts with engagement   66
2.6 What should legacy banks do?   71

Chapter 3: First, get the basics right   **77**
3.1 Is building a digital bank just about technology?   79
3.2 What's role of design in an experience business?   84
3.3 Start with the solution or the problem?   89
3.4 SME vs consumer banking as beachhead segments?   92
3.5 Data and its role in a digital bank   97
3.6 Alternative credit scoring and its role   102
3.7 Designing a seamless onboarding experience   106
3.8 Core banking and its evolution   109
3.9 What do we do with product?   115

Chapter 4: Building a digital bank   **124**
4.1 Designing it right   125
4.2 Selecting and understanding your segment   137
4.3 The path to profit   141
4.4 The role of service in a digital bank   150
4.5 How to differentiate?   157
4.6 Learning as a differentiator   163
4.7 Fostering an innovative culture   167
4.8 Talent: What to look for in key hires?   172

4.9 Ecosystem (its misuse) and partnerships   177
4.10 Biggest obstacles you will face   185

Chapter 5: The allDigitalfuture Playbook™:
A step-by-step guide for any digital transformation   191

5.1 Customer dimension   198
    5.1.1 Segment and gaps   199
    5.1.2 Insights, experience and process 204

5.2 Business dimension   218
    5.2.1 Differentiation   220
    5.2.2 Path to profit   225
    5.2.3 Scaling   232
    5.2.4 Core competence   234

5.3 Capabilities   241
    5.3.1 Design   244
    5.3.2 Methodology   249
    5.3.3 Data   253
    5.3.4 Technology   256
    5.3.5 Ecosystem   262
    5.3.6 New disciplines   267

5.4 People & leadership   275
    5.4.1 Mission-Values   278
    5.4.2 Leadership   291
    5.4.3 Talent gap   309
    5.4.4 Structure   317

Chapter 6: Beyond banking   331

References   347
About the Author   357

List of Figures

1. TMRW's markets by highest potential — 20
2. TMRW's ambition and new capabilities — 23
3. TMRW's vision: The world's most engaging bank for millennials — 23
4. TMRW Indonesia since launch in August 2020 — 24
5. What has TMRW achieved since launch — 25
6. TMRW app sign-in, main and account services screenshots — 26
7. Author receiving the 2019 Global Finance Award — 27
8. Evolution of consumer banking — 28
9. Charging the Apple wireless mouse — 32
10. The future of retail banking — 35
11. Vertical and horizontal integration in computing — 35
12. Vertical and horizontal integration in financial services — 37
13. How digital banks compete — 41
14. Nokia/Apple handset revenue 2010–2012 — 43
15. Leading digital banks in the world — 46
16. Sample of digital banks launched by incumbents — 50
17. Unbanked, underbanked and banked in Southeast Asia — 53
18. Satmetrix NICE 2018 average NPS® by industry report — 60
19. 2018 current account NPS® in the UK — 60
20. Legacy banks' biggest threat — 61
21. What should legacy banks do? — 73
22. Cost advantage of next-gen bank vs legacy banks — 81
23. Screenshots of TMRW Thailand — 86
24. Start with the problem vs start with the solution — 90
25. TMRW's ATGIE flywheel model — 98
26. Algorithms commonly used in credit scoring — 103
27. First to fourth generation of core banking — 111
28. TMRW savings game — 116
29. Design challenges in digital banks — 126
30. Proposed method to get from "concept to code" — 128
31. Normal spacebar vs shortened spacebar — 129
32. Understanding Design Thinking, Lean, and Agile by Jonny Schneider — 132
33. Propensity to switch banks — 137
34. Example of deep-linking screens within conversations — 152

35.	Tia's dual language capabilities	153
36.	How to differentiate?	158
37.	Launching a new TMRW brand	160
38.	How to properly accept failure	163
39.	Recommended assessment and hiring process	172
40.	Solution vs transaction ecosystem	177
41.	TMRW partnership model	181
42.	The first digital camera	185
43.	Circular Interactions cause severe complexity	193
44.	The allDigitalfuture Playbook™	195
45.	Dimensions, elements and considerations	197
46.	Designed for customers	199
47.	Most attractive ASEAN markets for digital bank	202
48.	CVP creation checklist	204
49.	How will you know if you have a great insight?	206
50.	Double-diamond method	207
51.	Design Thinking approach	208
52.	A sample of the biggest failures in innovation	209
53.	Customer dimension template	211
54.	Customer and business dimension interaction	214
55.	Interaction within and between the 4 dimensions	218
56.	Designing for business	220
57.	Ten types of innovation by Doblin	221
58.	Ten types of innovation in TMRW	222
59.	TMRW kiosk at BTS station in Bangkok	223
60.	Size vs adoption matrix	225
61.	Three-stage path-to-profit model	226
62.	Core competence gap	234
63.	Desirable, viable and feasible	235
64.	Customer, business and capability dimension interaction	237
65.	New capabilities needed	241
66.	The business value of design	244
67.	Business designer vs management consultant	245
68.	Business innovation designer	245
69.	The top 6 key design considerations in TMRW	246
70.	Sample design consideration cascade	248
71.	Design Thinking, Lean and Agile	249
72.	A pictorial checklist for scrum	252
73.	How to operationalise the software factory	252
74.	Four key considerations for leveraging data	253

75. Designing your data management lifecycle 254
76. 6 key design principles to embed data security into your company's core 255
77. Build, customise and configure analysis 257
78. Sample architecture diagram 258
79. Designing for modularity and scalability 260
80. Example of an ecosystem mapping exercise for a solution ecosystem 263
81. Airbnb platform business model canvas 264
82. Six-step evaluation of transaction ecosystem feasibility 265
83. All dimension interactions 269
84. The people & leadership dimension 278
85. Sample vision, mission, values and behaviour statements 281
86. Deepavali celebrations in October 2019 282
87. One-pager to get to know us better 283
88. How to design a balanced scorecard for a digital bank 286
89. Co-ordination vs depth 292
90. Innovation requires people, process and leadership 293
91. The innovation landscape map by Gary P. Pisano 295
92. Creating a high-performance environment 299
93. Linear vs systems thinking 300
94. Traits that enable systems thinking 301
95. "The balanced leader" using the Harrison paradox graphs 303
96. 360-degree feedback in the open 305
97. Cost and reporting alignment to TMRW across various units 311
98. How to inspire and attract talent 313
99. Important core attributes 314
100. Employee motivation vs company processes 320
101. The digital revolution 332
102. Years to reach a valuation of $1B or more 333
103. Types of digital transformation 334
104. Accenture's disruptability index by industry 335
105. Boston Dynamics robot improvements over time 338
106. Digital transformation complexity vs coverage 340

Foreword

I read *Driving Digital Transformation* and found it to be an excellent guide for anyone looking to build a digital bank. Dennis' belief in the virtual bank business model is commendable and as someone who has seen the banking industry over decades and experienced all the changes, I find the content extremely credible.

A comprehensive and structured playbook to build a digital bank was lacking in the industry, but thanks to Dennis' passion to share his experience on paper, I see this as a tremendous benefit to those who apply the principles, not only for incumbents starting on their journey but traditional bankers as well. This book will push the industry forward, so thank you, Dennis, for this contribution.

While reading the book, I would often pause to reflect on my own journey building a digital bank while being the CEO of a traditional bank. This unique perspective let me appreciate both the courage of virtual bankers bringing an idea to life, and the boldness of traditional bankers for always adapting to a rapidly changing industry with innovative solutions. A traditional bank has a franchise value and a proven track record, while a virtual bank as a concept is a lot harder to justify. So, I would often get asked why we were building a digital bank when we already had a successful and established traditional bank. I would always respond, "Why not?" And this "Why not?" mindset is necessary throughout the journey of building a digital bank.

The journey from traditional bank to a challenger model requires a cultural and mindset shift to have any chance at success. This shift is only possible if you truly believe in the power of the new model. If the "Why?" questions will test your belief, it is the "Why not?" answers that will strengthen your resolve.

A digital bank is a new business model, a new technology stack, and a new partnership. No one knows it all, not even a CEO. The reality of building a digital bank is that there will be chaos because you are building something completely new from the ground up. There is no roadmap to follow, rather you must figure it out as you go along. That is the power of this book. It provides a blueprint, where previously none existed.

Customer obsession is a mindset while technology is an enabler. These two elements combined are the secret sauce of digital banks' success. These differentiated customer experiences have helped raise the bar for the entire industry, to the benefit of the end customer. That is why the market has been very receptive of digital banks. Digital banks are a healthy development and bring a different oxygen to the banking ecosystem. The way they design client journeys is a great example of the "Why not?" mindset in action.

This book provides important lessons and a much-needed roadmap in a very practical way, while also calling out some of the unspoken dilemmas in building a digital bank. What makes this playbook particularly valuable is that it is written by Dennis Khoo, one of the sharpest minds in our industry.

Mary Huen
CEO, Standard Chartered Bank, Hong Kong
Chairperson of the Board, Mox Bank

Preface

This book contains all my learnings from the past decade, designing, building and running digital banks, and building and running consumer banks with digital banking as a channel. There is a big difference between the two, but we shan't get into that here. The first few chapters in this book will address this important point. When I was asked to build a separately branded digital bank from scratch in 2017, it required me to bring to bear all that I had learnt in my career in technology, my experience writing software (C++[1]), and my 19 years of experience in all aspects of consumer banking. Even then, it was a real journey of discovery. There was so much my team and I didn't know and so much we had to learn through trial and error.

I graduated with a major in computer engineering from NUS[2] in 1988 and spent the next decade in Hewlett-Packard (HP) supporting mini-computer systems hardware, then software. I got a chance to start a networking business from scratch, and fondly remember the days when I would go to the interop[3] networking conferences in the US to scout for potential networking solutions that were interesting enough to fit into our repertoire. After leaving HP, I was marketing director for a content management company for 9 months at the end of the dot-com era. The company was beginning to downsize when I was fortunate to be able to join Standard Chartered Bank as head of marketing in 2001.

In the 12 years I was there, I again had the good fortune to be given the opportunity to run every single product unit (investments, insurance, deposits, credit cards, personal loans, mortgages) in the consumer bank, before becoming the Singapore consumer head for Standard Chartered in October 2010. After leaving Standard Chartered, I joined United Overseas Bank (UOB) in a similar capacity as head of consumer banking for Singapore, albeit in a bigger business.

So, when in 2017 I was asked to set up TMRW (pronounced "tomorrow") by UOB, ASEAN's first digital bank, from scratch, I was as well prepared as anyone could be, having received the relevant training for almost 30 years. And yet, it still turned out to be a monumental challenge. It felt akin to searching for buried treasure

---

1. Believe it or not, it's still the fourth most popular programming language in the world, after so many years.

2. National University of Singapore (more correctly NTI, Nanyang Technology Institute, which issued degrees from NUS back then)

3. The first Interop was held in San Jose, California, in 1988. Vendors with TCP/IP products that could reliably interoperate were invited to participate. Fifty companies made the cut and 5,000 networking pros attended. Source: network computing.com

with only a compass. We had one good guide from a consulting firm who went along with us, but there was no map. Many times, we were travelling at night in the dark, and you had to get comfortable with the ambiguity. I often thought, "If only we had a map." We might still get lost from time to time, of course, but the map would at least provide a good guide and a bird's-eye view of the lay of the land and journey ahead.

This book is that map. It is written to guide senior executives who are starting a major digital initiative and to show a clear way through the challenges that lie ahead. By distilling the essence of what my team and I learnt building digital banks in Thailand and Indonesia, I hope to save the reader from repeating the mistakes we made. Whilst the examples are drawn mostly from banking, I believe the concepts and approaches are applicable in any industry.

Without a map, the chances of failure are overwhelmingly high. Research from BCG indicates that 70% of digital transformations fall short of their companies' expectations (BCG, 2020). Research from the Everest Group and many others corroborates this: only 22% achieve their desired business results (Bendor-Samuel, 2019; Wade, 2018; Solis, 2020; Rogers, 2016; Kitani, 2019; Sutcliff, Narsalay, and Sen, 2019; McKinsey & Company, 2016; Boutetière, Montagner, and Reich, 2018).

In my opinion, the reason for such a high failure rate is the overwhelmingly interconnected nature of digital transformation. While there is much literature out there on design, design thinking, innovation, Agile and business strategy, there is no single resource that puts all these myriad methods together in a comprehensive and coherent way. This book articulates the learnings as a result of my involvement in building TMRW by UOB, and how I leveraged these learnings to create a new approach to improve the probability of success of any digital transformation initiative. I believe that if you follow the steps prescribed, you will be able to avoid all the major pitfalls as well as reduce the design and implementation time of your digital initiative by half!

Chapter 1 of the book introduces TMRW, the digital bank my UOB colleagues and I built from the ground up. Chapter 2 talks about what the future holds for banking. Chapter 3 addresses the fundamental thinking you have to get right before you even start, and Chapter 4 condenses the learnings from building TMRW into 10 easy steps. Chapter 5 introduces The allDigitalfuture Playbook™, which has been created based on my experiences over the past 30 years. The strategies in the playbook are not limited to financial services, but are universally applicable to companies in any industry looking to undergo their own digital transformation journey.

This is my first book, and I'm hoping it won't be my last. I appreciate any feedback you have to improve the next version, which you can send to dennis@allDigitalfuture.com. Thank you for joining me as we take this journey together into an exciting new future.

Acknowledgements

There is an army of people to thank for making TMRW and this book possible. Firstly, TMRW would not have come to life without the support of UOB Group Deputy Chairman and Chief Executive Officer, Wee Ee Cheong, who gave me some of the best advice when I first set out as the architect of TMRW. Ee Cheong was instrumental in advising us to build something truly differentiated and not to rush. He also strongly encouraged the creation of TMRW as a separate brand and supported the pivotal decisions to invest in Personetics and adopt their solution in ASEAN. Without his strong support, TMRW would not have been born.

The initial thinking to create a digital bank came from UOB's former Head, Group Retail, Francis Lee, who was instrumental in gathering the support to initiate the programme. His shrewd insight and advice helped us to get many of the basic foundations of TMRW right from the beginning. Frederick Chin guided the TMRW programme as Head, Group Transformation, in addition to being the Group Head of Wholesale Banking, and he brought the relationships and perspectives that were extremely complementary and instrumental to the success of the programme.

Susan Hwee, who heads UOB's Group Technology and Operations, was a great partner and collaborator, without whom it would not have been possible to bring such a complex and difficult programme to fruition. I would also like to thank Lee Wai Fai, UOB Group Chief Financial Officer, and Chan Kok Seong, UOB Group Chief Risk Officer, for their help in refining the approach for TMRW. Country support came from Tan Choon Hin, Yuttachai Teyarachakul, Natee Srirussamee and Kevin Lam, whose close collaboration enabled everything to gel together well at launch.

My deepest appreciation to the pioneer team who joined me from the beginning not knowing what the path ahead was. In Singapore: Annie, Andrena, Aaron, Charmaine, Darren, Delwyn, Edrick, Gemma, Grace, Jamorn, Jill, Ju Han, Juan Jose, Karthik, Matthew, Michael, Min Yeow, Roy, Srivats, Stuart, Suzette and Wendy. In Thailand: Nantawan, Thanita, Chantarin, Theerawat, Arnupap. In Indonesia, Fajar, Arief, Aisha, Yanti. In Vietnam: Minh.

To all members of the Singapore, Thailand and Indonesia working teams: Brand and Marketing, Engagement Lab, Group Technology and Operations, Group Retail Business and Finance, Human Resource, Legal and Compliance, Onboarding, Partnership, Product, Program Management Office and Serve & Transact – I am extremely grateful for your dedication and commitment.

There are too many others left to thank beyond the TMRW team: Gan Ai Im, Maybelline, Nicolette Rappa, Richard Lowe, Stephen Lin, Vincent Lim, and those who worked tirelessly behind the scenes to make the near-impossible happen. Thank you for all the fond memories.

I am very grateful to my friends and colleagues who helped review and perfect the manuscript: Andrew Quake, Boon Kiat, Gemma Tay, Chen Kar Poh, Michael Koh, Steve Shipley, Stuart Kamp, Qian Xiao Dong, Wendy Ong, and many more, especially Mary Huen, who wrote the foreword and dedicated time to review the book despite her busy schedule.

I would like to thank David Sosna, CEO of Personetics; David Rogers, speaker and author of the best-selling book, *The Digital Transformation Playbook*, and faculty at Columbia Business School; Jungkiu Choi, partner and managing director, Boston Consulting Group; and Hsieh Tsun-Yan, Chairman of the Linhart Group and board member of Dyson, Manulife and Singapore Airlines, for their generous endorsement of the book.

Thanks also to Lillian Koh for introducing me to Marshall Cavendish, and Justin and Melvin from Marshall Cavendish, who were pivotal in editing and publishing this book.

Finally, a huge thank you to my wife, Soo Ping, whose encouragement and critique helped me write a better book.

CHAPTER 1

The journey to TMRW

In the final months of 2016, I was asked to spearhead a new initiative to design and create a pan-ASEAN bank from scratch. At that point, I had been with United Overseas Bank (UOB) for three years as managing director and head of consumer banking in Singapore. In 2015, we had launched UOB Mighty, a new mobile banking app that leveraged the native capabilities of mobile phones to make banking intuitive and simple. Now, given the latest mandate, I set out with a few staff to build a bank to serve the digital customers of tomorrow, to help ensure that UOB would thrive in a world where customers bank very differently from today.

UOB is the quintessential ASEAN bank. During the Asian Financial Crisis, it acquired banks in Thailand and Indonesia and thus has a network of locally incorporated bank subsidiaries that rivals other competitors in ASEAN. However, expanding regionally in the consumer banking business has always been very challenging, and today UOB still generates most of its retail income from Singapore. This is because gaining a bigger overseas presence has always meant expanding your physical footprint, and many countries impose restrictions on the expansion of foreign bank branches as well as higher fees to join the national ATM networks.

In this landscape, digital banks pose both **a threat and an opportunity**. A threat in the stronghold of Singapore, where UOB is a local bank, and where it generates a substantial share of its profits; and an opportunity outside Singapore, where UOB is a foreign bank, and where for the first time, being a digital bank gives it almost equal footing to expand its presence and capture a large share of the emerging segment of digital-savvy millennials who are young professionals.

Over the past decade, banking in Asia has undergone significant change. While most Asian banks did not directly feel the impact of the 2009 global financial crisis, intense competition, low interest rates and increased regulations have resulted in significant margin compression, increased costs and a lower return on equity. After the global financial crisis, start-ups in the West found reason to create **challenger banks** to face existing traditional banks. Challenger banks or neo-banks like Monzo, N26 and Nubank compete against the incumbents by providing customers with increased transparency, better app experience and better customer service. This strategy pits them against the incumbents' focus on growth through cross-selling and consistent profits quarter-on-quarter.

At the same time, well-funded start-ups or Fintech have leveraged technology to make non-bank payments and lending possible. Examples abound. Indonesia's

Akulaku offers card-less instalment shopping. FinAccel's Kredivo service helps Southeast Asia's unbanked make online payments. Ride-hailing platforms and unicorns Grab and Gojek are investing heavily to grow their digital wallets GrabPay and GoPay, and are also starting digital banks or buying into banks (Ang, 2020; Jiao, Sihombing, and Dahrul, 2012).

This climate has prompted the directors and major shareholders of banks to take notice. Thus, it has become an imperative for traditional banks to adapt to the fast-changing and increasingly competitive landscape to survive in the long-term.

TMRW is UOB's response to this uncertain climate. TMRW is the first mobile-only bank designed for young professionals (YP) and young professional families (YPF)[4] in ASEAN. It breaks away from the norms that guide traditional consumer banking, e.g., digital as a channel, product as a key focus rather than service and engagement, high advocacy, etc. Instead, it is shaped from the ground up by the needs, preferences and behaviours of the YP and YPF in ASEAN, representing a shift to a long-overdue rethink of the status quo.

TMRW differentiates itself from traditional consumer banks in two compelling ways. First, it is a **purely millennial-branded mobile bank** – the first of its kind in ASEAN. All transactions, from fund transfers, bill payments, credit card sign-ups, to reporting a lost or damaged card, or setting a new debit or credit card PIN, are made through the TMRW mobile app. While customers have the option of visiting a UOB branch to resolve any problems, TMRW is designed so they don't need to, so there are no long queues or paperwork to fill out. In Indonesia, the fully digital onboarding process takes just 7 minutes.

Second, TMRW is centred around an **engagement-focused business model**. Powered by Fintech solutions like Meniga[5], which categorises transactions, and Personetics[6], which takes these transactions and turns them into insights, TMRW generates a vast amount of data through banking transactions and gleans relevant insights from it. This allows the bank to learn to anticipate customer needs, personalise customer engagement, and continually improve the customer experience. By consistently offering a seamless and frictionless experience, it will be able to create long-term affinity with the YP and YPF segments in ASEAN. These YP and YPF, most of whom have good educations and jobs, are the affluent of the future.

In conceptualising TMRW, I had intentionally started with a **blank slate** to keep us from getting boxed into existing paradigms that could hamper our thinking and prevent us from crafting a truly unique approach. It helped that at the start, we were mostly Singaporeans building a digital bank in Thailand and Indonesia – the two

---

4. Young professionals who form a family and have children.

5. https://www.meniga.com/banks/story/uob

6. https://www.businesstimes.com.sg/companies-markets/uob-invests-and-partners-in-ai-firm-personetics

markets we chose to start in – as it removed any bias, gave us a fresh perspective, and forced us to do a lot more to understand customers. This ensured that TMRW started with a customer-centric approach from day one.

We spent the better part of 2017 studying leading global and local banks and talking to experts around the world to get an idea of how we could begin the journey. We held many workshops with the country teams to jointly digest and synthesise the common themes that were emerging from what customers were telling us. We experimented with different business models, conducted many rounds of discussions to extract relevant insights from observations about customers, and applied design thinking to create new customer journeys and experiences.

We learnt a lot through this process of discovery. If I had to distil the most pivotal insight we discovered, it would be that data-driven insights, rapid learning and feedback loops are very likely to significantly increase engagement amongst customers in tomorrow's consumer banking landscape (Khoo, 2020b). Rather than just being growth- and product-focused, the bank of tomorrow needs first to be **customer- and engagement-focused**. The new digital bank will coexist with traditional banks offering digital banking as part of their omni-channel strategy. We believed it wouldn't be about just digital banks or digital banking, but both would have their place and serve different segments and likely have different growth trajectories. We also believed progressive incumbent banks, neo-banks and Fintech would capitalise on this opportunity to drive unprecedented disruption globally. The capabilities to power these data-centric banks are emergent and will accelerate over the next 3 to 5 years.

The new data-driven banks with their superior cost-to-serve and ability to underwrite credit by leveraging alternative data will drive large-scale financial inclusion in ASEAN. While the challenges remain steep, the opportunity for digital banks is large in ASEAN. The main factor is the **big unbanked and underbanked opportunity in a region where smartphones abound**.

Sixty percent of the ASEAN population (400M out of 650M) is under 35 years of age (Wijeratne et al., 2019). This makes ASEAN home to the largest pool of millennials in the world outside China and India. In 2017, slightly over 50% of the ASEAN population had a smartphone (We are social, 2020). This number was projected to grow to 65% by 2020, adding 100M new smartphone-equipped consumers to the market. With entry smartphone prices now averaging US$50 and expected to become even cheaper, the day when most ASEAN consumers will be online on mobile is fast approaching.

Smartphone penetration in ASEAN exceeds credit card and even bank penetration. One in every two working adults in ASEAN is unbanked (Martinez, 2016). This is a significant statistic for banks to consider, as smartphone proliferation and low-cost data plans have essentially made it possible for banks to **onboard and**

serve customers without a physical presence, especially in transactional banking products like savings accounts, current accounts and credit and debit products. Customer insights from McKinsey's 2018 Asia Personal Financial Services (PFS) survey reveal that digital banking penetration has grown 1.5 times to 3 times in Emerging Asia[7] since the last survey in 2014 (Barquin, Vinayak & Shrikhande, 2018). The median penetration for developed Asia[8] is around 97%, and 52% for Emerging Asia. Smartphone banking penetration has grown at a faster pace than overall digital banking, jumping two- to four-fold in many emerging Asian markets.

With 30% to 50% of those not using digital banking expressing the likelihood that they will eventually make the switch, growth in digital banking penetration is expected to accelerate in Emerging Asia. McKinsey's PFS survey results highlight a significant opportunity as approximately 55% to 80% of customers in Asia would consider opening an account with a branchless digital-only bank; and those willing to bank digitally would be willing to shift between 35% to 40% of their total wallets to the digital account (Massi et al., 2019).

Figure 1 shows the consumer banking pool size in US$B set against the banking penetration growth potential and the population of the countries in ASEAN. **Thailand and Indonesia were selected as the first countries for TMRW because of their growth potential and the size of their markets.**

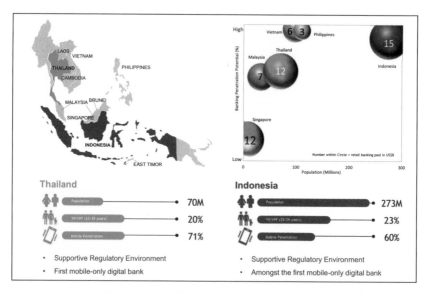

Figure 1 – TMRW markets by highest potential
(Source: UOB website: Investor Relations, 7 Dec 2020; BCG;
World Bank, 2017; We Are Social, 2019)

7. Emerging Asia: China, India, Indonesia, Malaysia, Myanmar, Philippines, Thailand, Vietnam
8. Developed Asia: Australia, Hong Kong, Japan, New Zealand, Singapore, South Korea, Taiwan

New regulations in ASEAN are very supportive of **non-face-to-face onboarding**. The banking industry has always been strictly regulated due to its importance to the economy and the emphasis on prevention of terrorism financing and money laundering. Therefore, banks that want to onboard customers without physical sighting of a customer's credentials need to comply strictly with the regulations and guidelines of the country's financial services regulating body. Southeast Asian regulators are responding positively to the concept of online or e-authentication and are adapting regulations to allow its implementation. They have different reasons to do so, but the most common one is to foster the growth of digital banks and digital banking, and promote financial inclusion.

Extending access to banking will also facilitate more efficient payments through increased use of cashless payments. This in turn reduces working capital requirements, as merchants get paid faster. In fact, research has shown that up to **1% of additional GDP growth** for mature economies and more than **3% for emergent economies** is possible with high adoption of cashless payments (Massi et al., 2019). Plus, the extension of credit will encourage consumption and GDP growth if managed appropriately. Regulators acknowledge these potential benefits and have been quick to adopt the proper regulations to ensure they are not left behind.

From the perspective of ASEAN's millennials, their service expectations are increasingly being shaped by fast-growing mobile platforms and are centred around three key dimensions of differentiation: simplicity, accessibility and proactiveness.

1. The expectation of **simplicity** comes from their experience with smartphones. Every digital service they subscribe to needs to replicate this ease of use, offering a frictionless experience on a relatively small screen with no unnecessary steps required to accomplish a task. Some examples of fast-growing platforms that do this well are Sendo.com[9] and Chatesat.com[10]. The former is a Vietnam-based social commerce platform that lets users sell products right away with just an email and a phone number. The latter is a Myanmar-based website where businesses and freelancers can collaborate on projects without passing any papers back and forth.

2. Mobile platforms are also innovating the ways customers **access and pay for their preferred services**. Instead of the usual subscription-based services paid with credit or with debit cards, customers have a variety of payment options to choose from. Akulaku, for example, offers online payments based on instalment

---

9. Sendo.com is a Vietnamese e-commerce retailer and online commerce platform. It is a subsidiary of Vietnamese software conglomerate FPT Corporation.

10. Chatesat.com is the leading freelancing platform in Myanmar bridging between businesses and talented freelancers. Source: Chatesat.com

payments. And Goama of Myanmar wants to be the Netflix of games – it offers 400 mobile games through a subscription that can be paid via mobile credits.

3. Lastly, mobile platforms are becoming more **proactive**. This means customers get a smarter, more seamless and more personalised experience. For instance, Grab and Gojek use data to make intelligent on-demand surge pricing. Grab, in support of tourism, has also introduced GrabChat, an in-app feature that auto-translates messages so foreigners have no problem booking a ride (PuReum & Chung, 2019).

All of these developments in mobile platforms are shaping the expectations of the millennial customer. Banks that want to keep up need to meet these criteria as well.

New technologies are already disrupting several facets of consumer banking and making operations cheaper, easier and more efficient. For example, developments in artificial intelligence (AI), machine learning (ML) and natural language processing (NLP) have made **intelligent chatbots** possible. These technologies lead to operational benefits and an alternative to call-centre service by providing immediate, round-the-clock support for mobile-savvy millennial clients.

Various security and authentication technologies have also evolved to enable users to perform almost any bank transaction digitally. Users can open bank accounts through video calls or biometric methods involving facial recognition. Singapore uses a login ID, password, and additional PIN or facial identification[11], and leverages a national identity database known as MyInfo. Thailand plans to operationalise peer-to-peer facial identity matching for bank onboarding from 2020 onwards. Indonesia has regulations to allow video onboarding using Dukcapil, a national registry. Malaysia is lab-testing various methods, but currently requires physical inked signatures, as does Vietnam, but that is expected to evolve quickly. Such measures reduce friction for customers and drive more mobile account openings for banks.

Lastly, data is transforming the banking industry in a compelling way. By learning more about a customer through his transactional data, financial institutions can create better customer experiences through intelligent engagement decisions, e.g., reminding customers who have forgotten to pay or letting customers know who has forgotten to pay them.

In August 2018, UOB announced that they were building a digital bank for this new future. The ambitions of this then-unnamed bank which would become TMRW are shown in Figure 2.

---

11. QR code scanning as a means of authentication was recently introduced.

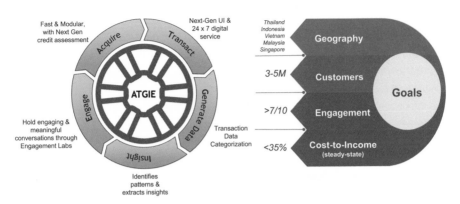

Figure 2 – TMRW ambition and new capabilities
(Source: UOB website, Investor Relations, 3 August 2018)

The prevailing thinking in consumer banking, especially amongst the market leaders, tends to be overly focused on cross-selling. This is because the industry's drive for revenue generation may not be sufficiently balanced by the desire to serve customers well. TMRW would address this and turn it on its head by **engaging to cross-sell rather than cross-selling to engage**. To achieve this, I created a unique flywheel model centred on data-driven insights called ATGIE (Figure 2) – which stands for Acquire, Transact, Generate data, Insights, and using these insights to Engage the customer – that would power TMRW's customer-centric vision. Figure 3 describes TMRW's vision as the world's most engaging bank for millennials.

Figure 3 – TMRW's vision: The world's most engaging bank for millennials
(Source: UOB website, Investor Relations, 7 Dec 2020; US$10B estimate by BCG)

Seven months later, on 1 March 2019, UOB launched the first pan-ASEAN digital bank in Thailand, called TMRW, a challenger bank with a **DNA focused on being simple, engaging and transparent.** What's unique about TMRW is its departure from the traditional business model of consumer banking. Its focus is on engagement and experience instead of just on products, on quality instead of quantity in terms of customers, and on driving the cost of acquisition down sharply by focusing on improving the Net Promoter Score[12] (NPS®). Early in 2020, TMRW Indonesia was beta-launched, and officially launched in August the same year.

Figure 4 – TMRW Indonesia since launch in August 2020
(Source: UOB website, Investor Relations, 7 Dec 2020; US$10B estimate by BCG)

In December 2020, UOB gave an update of the performance of TMRW, both the launch in Indonesia as well as how TMRW was doing overall, as shown in Figures 4 and 5. Unlike in Thailand, where TMRW had to launch with kiosks that would allow users to complete their onboarding by matching their biometric data (facial or fingerprint) with their Thai ID card[13], in Indonesia, TMRW designed an onboarding journey that took **less than 7 minutes** and worked well even when the network was congested.

---

12. To calculate NPS®, start with the ultimate question, "How likely are you to recommend us to a friend or colleague?" and score the answers on a zero-to-ten scale. Your Net Promoter Score is simply the percentage of customers who are promoters (those who scored 9 or 10) minus the percentage who are detractors (those who scored 0 to 6). The percentage is dropped and NPS® can range from -100 to +100. More info can be found at: https://www.netpromotersystem.com/about/measuring-your-net-promoter-score/

13. The Thailand National Digital Identity or NDID enables bank-to-bank identity authentication; it was not fully operational when TMRW was launched on 1 March 2019.

Figure 5 – What has TMRW achieved since launch
(Source: UOB website, Investor Relations, 7 Dec 2020; new
customer data – Nov 2020, NPS® and awards info – Oct 2020)

Aligned with a strategy of launching with a minimum experience score (using NPS® as a proxy) rather than a minimum viable product[14] (MVP), TMRW Indonesia took the best of TMRW Thailand and achieved a score of +60 in 2020. This likely places TMRW as the leading NPS bank in Indonesia, above BCA, Danamon, BRI, BNI and Mandiri.

In a 1 March 2021 interview with Fintech Futures, Kevin Lam, who succeeded me as Head of TMRW Digital Group at UOB, had this to say: "In just under two years of operations in Thailand, a market with one of the highest digital banking standards in ASEAN, our engagement-focused business model is bearing fruit. In the most recent survey conducted by Bain & Co in January 2021, TMRW (in Thailand) is now second in the market with an NPS of 40 and is ranked number one for credit cards and for current account/savings accounts" (Futures, 2021).

There are few incumbent banks that have successfully built and launched digital bank spinoffs within the same entity under a different brand. Two large banks, JP Morgan and RBS (later renamed NatWest in Feb 2020), shut down their digital bank units Finn and Bo within a year and six months, respectively. This makes the creation of TMRW within a traditional bank like UOB truly remarkable.

---

14. A minimum viable product (MVP) is a version of a product with just enough features to be usable by early customers who can then provide feedback for future product development.

One of the distinguishing features of TMRW is the app user experience (Figure 6). The design is colourful, and navigation of the bank accounts is done through a **horizontal scroll**, while the **vertical scroll** is a personalised insights feed generated from transactional data. Notice how more space is allocated to insights on the main screen, balancing the "invisible" part of banking (transactions) with the part of banking that can create value (insights) and become "visible".

Figure 6 – TMRW app sign-in, main and account services screenshots

This, I believe, will be the **blueprint for the bank of tomorrow**, balancing where you must get the transactional banking basic navigation and usability right and where you must get proactivity right. TMRW incorporated 500+ new features that were designed from scratch, including those you see on the right of Figure 6 (Warden, 2019b). These security and payment limit features were derived from the many observations we gathered. This allowed us to gain significant insights into what TMRW customers wanted.

TMRW was created by a tenacious bunch of pioneers, who didn't take no for an answer and dared to dream big. As a team we adopted many new methods like design thinking and Agile-at-scale, and ventured into unknown territory often, introducing new concepts like an engagement lab that would learn how to engage customers and over time leverage those learnings to improve TMRW's customer engagement. At times it was difficult, confusing and exasperating, but at times exhilarating, inspiring and awesome. The continued success of TMRW today is a testament to the team's talent, hard work and belief as we took a wild journey into the unknown.

Figure 7 – Author receiving the 2019 Global Finance Award

CHAPTER 2

What the future holds

To look at what the future holds, we have to start with the past. Banking has been a digital business ever since Bank of America installed the **world's first computer used in banking**, ERMA (Electronic Recording Method of Accounting), in 1955 (Fisher & McKenney, 1993). Today, banking relies almost totally on computers to record transactions and data around the clock and around the world. So, what's changed isn't the heart of banking, but how banks serve customers.

Branch Banking & Invention of the ATM
Channel
Banking is done in person at branches and automated teller machines
1967

Telephone Banking
Channel
First Direct launches telephone banking in the United Kingdom on
1 October 1989. There were no branches and 24-hr call center service
1984

Internet Banking
Channel
Internet banking allows customers to transact outside the physical
limitations of the branch, telephone and ATMs using personal computers
1994

Direct Banking
No-branch Channel
Pioneered by ING Direct in Canada in 1997, provided higher interest
rate savings account through internet-only banking
1997

Mobile Banking
Channel
Mobile allows banking via user-friendly mobile apps
2007

Digital Bank
Business Model
Obsessive focus on customers. Frictionless & intuitive mobile-only banking with
excellent service. Leverages data for insights to achieve deeper engagement
2018

All these channels still exist, creating an omni-channel approach that is very expensive for incumbent banks to manage

Figure 8 – Evolution of consumer banking

Until the advent of telephone banking in the 1980s, customers had to visit a branch to do their banking. First introduced by Girobank in the United Kingdom, which established a dedicated telephone banking service in 1984, phone banking has become as ubiquitous as branches, but has also drawn much criticism for long wait times, the need to navigate arcane telephone menus, poor staff retention and other service issues.

Then came internet banking in 1994, following widespread availability of internet connectivity and the commercialisation of the World Wide Web. Customers could now enter data directly into electronic forms and perform their bill payments and fund transfers online. In 1997, ING Group launched a "direct banking" concept under the trade name of ING Direct, with the aim of providing a value proposition through the use of cost-effective products, processes and distribution channels (only one location, no branch network for country-wide operations). Finally, with the introduction of the smartphone in 2007, consumers began to carry in their pockets their own branches, capable of performing a wide range of banking transactions when leveraging mobile banking.

With this development and the introduction of cashless transactions through QR codes, NFC[15] payments, online payments, etc., it has become possible for the first time since the introduction of modern banking in medieval Europe to have a **completely digital banking experience**, from accounting and statementing to transactions, payments and transfers. A new generation of customers may never visit a branch to perform transactional banking. And in the next 15 years, this will come to dominate consumer banking and make banking digitally the norm rather than the exception.

The impact of this development will upend consumer banking. Consumer banks that underestimate the forces at play and what this new business model entails **will become obsolete**. Making onboarding and transactional banking frictionless and intuitive is just the ante to play. No one will bank with you if you aren't excellent here. If you add great service on top of this, that can be a great delighter, especially if you leverage new technology solutions to improve service so that most problems are solved at the point of occurrence.

Chapter 2.1 is about the future of consumer banking. We look at how the competitive dynamics are changing and what banks must do to react and adjust to these changes. From the traditional six Ps of People, Product, Place, Promotion, Price and Process as factors of competition, I believe **Process will be the only P left**. Process excellence is the fundamental fabric of great experience, along with a focus on human-centred design.

What happens when all the leading banks wring out all the creases in their transaction banking experience? Where will the competition shift to? We will also discuss how the forces of vertical and horizontal integration change over time, and their influence on existing players in the industry. The discussion draws from examples in the computing industry to infer how the financial services industry could be affected by such forces. We also explore the impact of open standards on banking, and how such standards have forced changes in other industries.

Incumbent banks have been improving their digital banking over time. So, can digital banking be the defence against a digital bank entry into their markets? This

---

15. Near Field Communications; labelled as Visa payWave or Mastercard "Tap & Go" Contactless when used for in-store contactless payments.

is a question that has many different answers depending on who you speak to, and thus a single consensus has not yet developed. Since incumbent legacy banks have been building up their capabilities, **why can't they just compete status quo with the digital banks** like how incumbents compete with each other? What's holding them back and why is there a need for a new approach? This is the question that Chapter 2.4 tackles.

Chapter 2.5 discusses the role of engagement. Consumer bankers have always been schooled that cross-selling is the way to deepen relationships and engage the customer. To some extent this is true, as over the long term, you complete the relationship with the client as they consume more financial products in their journey through different life stages − from transactions using debit cards as a child with money from their parents, to having their own credit cards and personal loans when they graduate and find a job, then mortgages as they build a new home when they are married, and then accumulating insurance and investments after they start a family, and finally planning for their retirement.

However, detecting this **window of opportunity** when they are transitioning from one life stage to the next is mostly hit-and-miss, even with the predictive and machine learning capabilities today. To improve these odds in a world that's all digital, **engaging to cross-sell** might be a better path. Since banks currently don't have a high-enough frequency of visitation and depth of content to fuel meaningful engagements, there is a need to focus on identifying useful data that can be used to engage customers throughout their life stages. This will enable banks to focus on anticipating customer needs and actions, conversing with customers to nudge them into better saving and spending habits, and creating the feedback loops that enable rapid learning from what works and what doesn't.

A new capability to **extract useful insights from data** is the final ingredient. Whilst in the world of big tech and Fintech this is becoming the norm, it hasn't necessarily been the case in banking, where regulations, risk management and the drive for growth have resulted in organisations that are slower to react to the new forces at play. Traditional banks are not as obsessed with customers and have a higher tendency to be internally focused and siloed in their ability to collaborate. Therefore, almost everyone is still taking baby steps, learning and getting better by the day. This will become a major battleground for differentiation in the years ahead.

Finally, Chapter 2.6 discusses what incumbent or legacy[16] banks need to do to stay competitive and survive the inflection points brought about by the significant changes the industry is undergoing.

---

16. This book uses "traditional", "legacy" and "incumbent" interchangeably to mean existing banks who are not born digital.

The future of banking

It's clear **banking isn't about products anymore**. In the areas that lend themselves most to being digitised – e.g., transactional banking – products are commoditised. And so, the competition has long shifted to price competition and targeting sub-segments by tailoring benefits to their lifestyle and needs. The fundamental features that customers need to pay and transact, like fund transfers and bill payments, are still the most commonly used services in banking. Not everyone needs a private property home loan or is looking to make an investment all the time. Transactional services are the "broadband" set of services where participation rates are high, if the experience is great. Banks then cross-sell "narrowband" services like investments, home loans and personal loans to this broadband base by trying to insert the right conversation at the right time.

Competition among banks has made it difficult to generate decent profits by just charging for transactional services. Most customers today expect this to be free. Interestingly, we found that many young customers don't quite understand why banks charge them to access their own money. Hence banks have pivoted more and more to generating profits from lending, and lending needs deposits as banks must put at least 8–10% of their own capital at stake, while the rest can be backed by customer deposits.[17] Thus, providing transactional services today is not so much about generating fee income, but much more about **generating the deposits required for lending**. Lending is the key profit generator.

Legacy banks have in the past treated digital banking as another sub-segment, a segment of customers who prefer digital means of access and prefer not to visit the branch. As digital banking becomes more mainstream, and gradually becomes the preferred mode of banking, this segment has grown. Digital banks target a subset of this segment that **prefer never to visit a branch**. As more banks refine their processes and put all possible services online, this segment will grow bigger. Covid has also broken the barriers about getting advice over video. Making a big commitment on a home or other investments may still require in-person advice, but in the future, we should be seeing more integration of such advisory activities over video.

---

17. To provide a very simplified example, if a bank lends $100, then $10 must come from the bank's capital and the rest of the $90 must be backed by deposits. In reality it's a lot more complicated, but this suffices to illustrate the basic concept.

But just looking at the future as simply a result of more people banking online instead of face-to-face misses the actual transformation that is happening. The shift is from the traditional six Ps of People, Product, Place, Promotion, Price and Process into an **experience business**. You will need to get many, many small things right to make an experience great. In other words, Process is the only P left. For a clear parallel in the personal computer market, just look at how Apple can still command a premium and steal customers away because of its unique design capabilities that result in a **superior total experience** even though the industry is commoditised.

Most of the recent innovations in the financial services industry have been about price and promotion, and this has compressed margins for the industry as a whole. So, the future of banking isn't just about technology and innovation. It's about the use of technology to innovate the experience of banking so that everything is frictionless and easy-to-use. The capabilities required are **excellence in business process skills, design skills to create the best experience, an obsession with simplicity, and a great eye for detail that can spot sub-optimal experiences**. This is much harder than it sounds.

Seen through this lens, even a company like Apple may not always have the fussiness required! It would seem like the last thing you'd want to do is place the charging port of a wireless mouse on the underside, so that while it is charging, you can't use the mouse. But that's exactly what Apple did with their Mighty Mouse 2 (Figure 9). I'm sure the notoriously fussy Steve Jobs would have thrown this design out and not allowed the product to be launched. (In its defence, the Magic Mouse 2 can last a day on just a 2-minute charge, so they did think about the problem, but this wasn't made widely known.)

Figure 9 – Charging the Apple wireless mouse

So, if this is a problem even for Apple, imagine what it's like for a bank, where such details usually don't find their way to the top of the organisation. Indeed, **most**

process work occurs in the bottom one-third of incumbent banks. It isn't something that is currently top-of-mind for the upper management. And so, save for an exceptional few, banks will find it very hard to adapt to a world where superior process is paramount. In launching TMRW in Thailand, I personally reviewed hundreds of user interface screens to get the first launch right. It's all about getting to the fine details to make the experience perfect. Only then can you compete against the digital banks, who are using customer experience as their primary instrument of attack. Unfortunately, as I discuss in Chapter 2.4, this is very, very difficult to do, as it is ingrained in the culture and hierarchy of most banks to do the opposite.

Is there a diminishing return to continuous improvement in the everyday details of banking? There probably is. Once everyone has improved their basics significantly, will banking become largely undifferentiated? It will be some time before the majority of leading banks get their act together, but yes, I believe that eventually, a very high standard of basic transactional banking will be achieved. When that happens, banks need to prepare to **differentiate through advice**. Just doing the basics very well does make you invisible. The example I like to quote is the utilities business. It's so invisible that if someone from your electricity provider turns up at your door, it can't be good! It's likely some kind of disruption in service. So, it comes as no surprise that commoditised businesses need to get everything right as that's what customers expect, but at the same time, there may be little to go on to proactively engage the customer to differentiate your offering.

The key question here, therefore, is whether being invisible and intuitive is a **sufficient differentiator?** Or do banks also need to engage customers proactively over and above that in order to sufficiently differentiate themselves? The jury is out on this, but if great experience becomes a norm for most digital banks, then creating the **right engagement to further improve experience and advocacy** may become essential for differentiation.

I believe there are a few ways to go about this. One is to focus on those banking services that have **more advisory content**, such as mortgages and investments, where the big sums involved, affordability and risk appetite considerations warrant advice from a specialist. The upside is that many banks have both the core competence and the size of business to make this a reality. The downside is that the engagement will only be felt by a relatively smaller proportion of your banking customers at any one time. This is because mortgages and investments have a smaller window of opportunity than basic transactional services, which are evergreen.

An additional difficulty is that if persuasion is needed, the digital format may not be the best channel. Focusing on self-directed users would avoid this issue for investments, but this segment is very price-sensitive, hence margins will likely have to be sacrificed in return for volume. This takes us back to the point that the segment size must be large, otherwise no significant volume is likely to be achieved for this to make business sense. In Southeast Asia at present, **no country is sizeable enough** to make this viable, and hence anyone building such a business needs to penetrate North Asia as well. The difficulties are therefore not trivial.

The other area is to provide advice on **financial management**, for individuals as well as small businesses. Early versions of personal financial management (PFM) were not successful in attracting more than a small proportion of users. One of the first banks to attempt this was mBank in Poland. Even as they built a huge base of close to 5M customers, **only 5% subscribed to the PFM service**. The problem with this first version of PFM was that it required a lot of work on the users' part to track and reduce their expenses. Since then, newer versions of PFM – let's call them PFM 2.0 – are much more automated and less laborious. For example, Personetics can analyse all a customer's transactions and detect patterns and trends, allowing them to compare new transactions with past ones. Whilst this may not be as fine-grained as categorising transactions yourself and being able to slice and dice the transactions to make comparisons of your own, it requires much less work on your part.

Another problem with the early versions of PFM, as highlighted by the Council on Financial Competition[18], was that banks tended to give customers information without sufficiently getting them to act. In fact, in looking at this area more closely, you'll find that most PFM tools are **"after the fact"**, i.e., the money has already been spent and the user is looking at his past transactions. To increase actionability, it became apparent that PFM 2.0 needed to focus on **real-time ability** to influence purchase and savings decisions rather than give a post-mortem perspective.

My experience in banking and PFM led me to an early hypothesis that **most customers aren't that keen to do a lot of work to save money**. Thus, having simple starting points that draw users in and then working to help them over the hump on more complicated problems is critical to success.

Let's zoom back out to the macro view. Figure 10 (which was presented at UOB's 2018 first-half results announcement) illustrates UOB's view of the future of consumer banking. My belief is that both digital banking and digital banks will co-exist. It won't be a case of one or the other, but both, at least for some time to come. While the ante to play in both will be superb navigational and transactional experience, **data will play a pivotal role** in the digital bank's drive for superior engagement and experience. As one of the first to recognise this trend, I created a new acronym, ATGIE, to explain how data, starting with transactions, which are plentiful within banks, can be used for insights that can then be used to engage customers. Since engaged customers transact more and refer more friends and family, transactions grow, **creating a flywheel and triggering a virtuous cycle**.

---

18. A service offered by the Corporate Executive Board. Eventually the name was changed to CEB and in 2017 it was purchased by Gartner.

From Cross-selling to Engaging

- *Digital bank's advantage: Data-driven digital engagement*
- *Unique **ATGIE** business model: **A**cquire, **T**ransact, **G**enerate data, **I**nsights, **E**ngage*

Digital Banking & Digital Banks

- *Are distinct & will-coexist*
- *But data-driven digital banks*
- *Will drive unprecedented growth*
- *opportunities for progressive banks, big tech and Fintech*
- *Capabilities to power data-driven banks will accelerate*

Business Model

Future Focus

New Digital Banks

Future of Retail Banking

Simple, Engaging Transparent

- ***Simple**: Intuitive UI, remembers, provides fast & fully digital experience*
- ***Engaging**: Anticipates your needs & prompts you towards smarter spending & savings habits*
- ***Transparent**: Promotes openness and engenders trust*

Figure 10 – The Future of Retail Banking
(Source: UOB website, Invester Relations, 18 May 2020)

Another lens to explore the future of banking is the industry lens. Banking since its invention has mostly been tightly vertically integrated, with banks typically performing all the functions required to deliver on their value proposition. Industries undergo change over time as technological improvements drive competition. In some cases, the competition, together with the introduction of standards, allows new entrants to attack vertically integrated industries and create value by specialising in specific horizontal plays that can combine into a finished product. Over time, some of these successful horizontal players might expand upstream or downstream, becoming a vertically integrated player themselves.

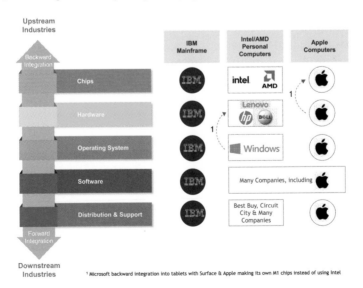

Figure 11 – Vertical and horizontal integration in computing

Figure 11 showcases some of these moves in the computing industry. Before the personal computer was invented, most computers were manufactured by large vertically integrated firms. These firms made the chips, the hardware, operating systems and software, and took care of all the sales, distribution and support. However, beginning in 1980, the industry went through a structural transformation (Baldwin, 2019). Over a roughly 20-year period, supported by the creation of open standards and platforms, a radical shift from a vertically integrated model to a horizontal platform-based model took place. This transformation happened before my eyes while I was working for Hewlett-Packard.

In 1985, IBM accounted for half the market value in the industry, alongside other vertically integrated manufacturers such as DEC, Unisys, Hitachi, NEC, etc. By 1995, however, as Carliss Baldwin explains, "horizontal players accounted for around three-quarters of the computing industry's total value. Microsoft was #1; a shrunken IBM was #2; and Intel #3" (Baldwin, 2019). During this time, "the industry as a whole also greatly expanded from a total market value of US$181B in 1990 to US$683B in 1995".

The IBM PC, released in 1981, was the first computing device made by IBM to feature a horizontal platform-based solution, with chips from Intel, the DOS operating system by Microsoft, and software from third-party providers. This was made possible by the industry's adoption of certain standards based on the initial IBM PC design, which had an open architecture and used off-the-shelf parts, as IBM was in a hurry to launch a product to counter Apple's success with the Apple II personal computer. The only component of the original PC architecture exclusive to IBM was the BIOS (Basic Input/Output System), which was not protected or patented.

The IBM PC was quickly reverse-engineered, and because Microsoft sold MS-DOS as a standalone version, clones quickly appeared. The IBM design became a standard with the introduction of the IBM PC/AT in 1984, in that the circuitry that interconnected the off-the-shelf components became an industry standard, allowing an entire industry to develop and flourish. The other driver of success for the PC was Moore's Law[19]. By doubling the number of transistors in a microprocessor every 24 months, the PC got more and more powerful, eventually making it very hard for the vertical incumbents to catch up. **The twin blows of standards and microprocessor power changed an industry**. Will they do the same for banking?

Over time, some of the horizontal players began to vertically integrate upstream and downstream. Microsoft went from DOS to Windows and then went downstream in 2000 by creating Microsoft Office and upstream in 2012 by launching the Surface tablet. Microsoft Office today still has a commanding share of the office productivity

---

19. A rule of thumb that has come to dominate computing, Moore's Law states that the number of transistors on a microprocessor chip will double every two years or so – which has generally meant that the chip's performance will, too. Source: Nature.com

business, with an estimated 40% Office 365 share as of October 2020 (Liu, 2020). This phenomenon is also witnessed in other industries, e.g., Netflix moving from distribution into producing its own original content, or Amazon developing its own cloud solution and eventually going upstream to become a provider. This constant unbundling and bundling is part of the cycle of renewal that keeps competition alive and incumbents on their toes.

Apple, on the other hand, has always manufactured its own hardware and operating systems while using chips from other companies like IBM and Motorola, and later Intel. Recently Apple has started to design its own chips, starting with the iPhone and iPad, leveraging the A14 custom Apple-designed chip. Most recently, Apple laptops now carry the Apple-designed M1 chip. Apple is a rare standout in the computing industry, having championed for 35 years a vertically integrated model. This gives Apple **very tight control of its entire experience**, from hardware to software, allowing it to engineer improved overall performance and experience for its customers, while at the same time outsourcing its manufacturing and supply chain to companies like Foxconn and TSMC. The ever-tighter integration of Apple's hardware and software has improved customer experience – for instance by allowing longer battery life without a significant performance penalty – which has so far allowed it to differentiate itself in a market of laptop clones and against intense price competition.

Figure 12 shows a possible future configuration of the financial services industry.

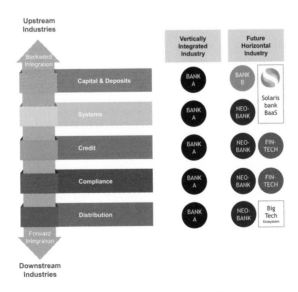

Figure 12 – Vertical and horizontal integration in financial services

Incumbent banks, illustrated by Bank A, are mostly **vertically integrated**. They perform all the core functions, such as raising capital and taking deposits, designing and building the systems required to operate the bank, and managing the credit risk, compliance risk and distribution and sales of its products and services. Distribution has in the past two decades experienced some horizontal unbundling, with partners that have large distribution abilities, such as supermarkets.

A potential **horizontal configuration** in the financial services industry is shown on the right of Figure 12. As the taking of deposits is likely to stay a regulated activity that can only be performed by a licensed bank, Bank B still performs this regulated activity, but for the rest of the systems, credit compliance and distribution, it **works with a neo-bank** that doesn't have a licence but is nimble and possesses the depth of technical, process, customer, credit, compliance and distribution design skills required to create a great banking experience. Bank B remains responsible for the quality of the credit and adherence to regulations to ensure no financial crime is being committed. It also has to subject the neo-bank to the same level of scrutiny that it is itself subjected to.

The neo-bank could in turn rely on other partners, for example partners specialising in superior credit algorithms, mixing and matching its own in-house developed algorithms with those of its partners to find the best solution. Solarisbank[20] offers another approach by coupling the systems needed to run a bank and a German bank licence for anyone who would like to start a bank in the EU. This allows them to run a "Banking as a Service" or BaaS offering. It comes complete with KYC offerings to onboard customers whilst staying compliant with EU anti-money-laundering laws. In my view, the big tech ecosystems are unlikely to enter banking directly, as they do not welcome the regulations that come with it, but they are happy to take on other horizontal roles like IT systems provision or distribution.

As we saw in the computing industry, the development of **industry standards** based on the open nature of the IBM PC allowed new entrants to quickly replicate the PC based on these standards. The standards were further enhanced by industry bodies like IEEE, ANSI, VESA, ISO, IEC, ITU[21], etc., which created a high degree of interoperability amongst components that made up the entire solution, allowing for modularity and thus the ability to sustain a horizontal platform-based model. Similar

20. Solarisbank is a Berlin-based Fintech company that offers Banking-as-a-Service Platform with its German banking licence.

21. ANSI is the American National Standards Institute, a private non-profit organisation that oversees the development of voluntary consensus standards. VESA supports and sets industry-wide interface standards for the PC, workstation, and consumer electronics industries. ISO is an independent, non-governmental international organisation with a membership of 165 national standards bodies. The IEC is a global, not-for-profit membership organisation that brings together more than 170 countries and co-ordinates the work of 20 000 experts globally. ITU, founded in 1865 to facilitate international connectivity in communications networks, allocates global radio spectrum and satellite orbits, develops the technical standards that ensure networks and technologies seamlessly interconnect, and strives to improve access to ICTs to under-served communities worldwide.

standards bodies in financial services would be FATF[22] for preventing financial crime, BCBS[23] for best practice in banking, and BIAN[24] for a common architectural framework for banking interoperability. More standards and standard bodies will need to be created to facilitate a horizontal unbundling of the traditional vertically integrated model for banking.

At the end of the day, banks will still be needed in the foreseeable future to collect and safeguard depositors' monies and to ensure compliance to laws, regulations and key policies. Currently, the financial services industry, given that it is regulated by country, has not reached the degree of standardisation that the computing industry did to create the conditions that allowed a horizontal takeover. This isn't just about open standards in payments or data or banking APIs. It must also include the way customer due diligence is done, how credit risk, reputational risk and operational risks are implemented and standardised so that the task can be performed by any suitably certified Fintech.

So, Bill Gates wasn't right when he said in 1994 that "Banking is necessary, but banks are not". In the same way that computing is necessary but so is the microprocessor, banks will continue to have a role; but if the standards that allow different members of the financial services ecosystem to interoperate continue to improve, banks may have a very different future. Those that want to stay vertically integrated will have to redesign themselves to be **the Apple of banking**, constantly focusing on the smallest of details to make the banking experience seamless and proactive. Other banks, such as those who have a DNA for control, risk management and compliance, could serve as the **microprocessors of banking**, providing adequate returns on capital and deposits but letting other neo-bank partners perform all the rest of the horizontal layers – very much like Bank B.

---

22. The Financial Action Task Force (FATF) is the global money laundering and terrorist financing watchdog. The inter-governmental body sets international standards that aim to prevent these illegal activities and the harm they cause to society. As a policy-making body, the FATF works to generate the necessary political will to bring about national legislative and regulatory reforms in these areas.

23. The BCBS formulates supervisory standards and guidelines and recommends statements of best practice in banking. In this regard, the BCBS is best known for its international standards on capital adequacy and the Core Principles for Effective Banking Supervision.

24. The Banking Industry Architecture Network was created to establish, promote and provide a common framework for banking interoperability issues and to become and be recognised as a world-class reference point for interoperability in the banking industry.

Key takeaways

- The future of banking is about the use of technology to innovate the experience of banking so that everything is frictionless and easy-to-use.

- The capabilities required are excellence in business process skills, an obsession with simplicity, and a great eye for detail to spot what could be a sub-optimal experience.

- If great experience becomes a norm for most digital banks, then creating the right engagement to further improve the experience and advocacy may become essential for differentiation.

- This will require banks to invest in the capability to leverage data for digital engagement.

- Cost advantages brought about by the cloud and other efficiencies of being truly digital will make financial non-inclusiveness a thing of the past.

- The entire industry is currently mostly vertically integrated, with banks performing most of the functions themselves.

- With the advent and pervasiveness of standards, new business models and lower cost of operations brought about by digital capabilities, one future scenario is the unbundling of financial services from a vertically integrated industry to a horizontal platform.

- This could represent a once-in-a-lifetime transfer of value from current incumbent banks to future horizontal players in the industry, similar to the great transfer of value between 1980 to 1995 in the computing industry.

- Further development of operating standards in customer due diligence, credit, reputational and operational risk management are needed so that the quality of work done by horizontal players can meet minimum required standards.

Difference between digital banking and digital bank

Some think it's the same thing, others don't. What really is the difference between them? Digital banking is a channel, amongst the many existing channels like ATMs, branches, call centres, etc., whereas a **digital bank is a business, where everything (e.g., technology, design, service, products, etc.) is put towards the pursuit of better customer experience**. This to me is the biggest threat of a digital bank: its ability to create great customer experience at-scale and produce a bank with very high advocacy scores, as indicated by measures like Net Promoter Score (NPS®) (Bain, 2018), at very low costs.

	Digital Bank Average	Traditional Bank Average
Net Promoter Score	62	19
Customer Growth Rate	150%	<2%
Operating Cost per Customer	US$25	US$208
Customer to Staff Ratio	c.3000	c.750

Figure 13 – How digital banks compete
(Source: Accenture market research)

As illustrated in Figure 13 (Leung & Gordon, 2019), two things stand out. Firstly, it shows a **very low variable cost per customer**, more than 8x less than a traditional bank, and secondly, **a very high NPS®**, more than 3x higher than a traditional bank. These two factors drive the high customer-per-staff count and the high customer growth rates, respectively. It's a business model that is superior to the traditional bank.

Digital banks – whether they are part of a bigger organisation, a standalone start-up not affiliated with a legacy bank, or part of a legacy bank but housed in a separate entity and sharing some common resources – are typically smaller in size and much less complex than legacy banks. This allows the digital bank to adopt a

different culture from the start. One that is more customer-centric, less hierarchical, more agile, suited to novel approaches and able to maintain a high level of collaboration across teams. Culture is paramount because the digital bank's main advantage is its ability to focus on its target customer and create an experience that is hard to replicate in terms of simplicity and ease of use.

Most digital banks, especially in countries with smaller populations, will still have to **compete by winning over customers in basic transactional banking first**. This will provide the base for them to engage and cross-sell more complex products like investments and mortgages. This of course doesn't prevent digital banks from focusing on just mortgages and investments in countries where the population size is sufficient for these segments to be a sizeable initial beachhead – for example, Wealthfront[25] and others focused on wealth advisory.

In the transactional banking arena, the key entry-point differentiation is in ease of use and reduction of friction in navigating the **payment and account management functionalities**. Based on observations of existing challenger digital banks around the world, most are focused on providing better and more transparent transactional banking and lending services to under-served or marginalised customers. Their clients tend to be younger and more tech-savvy but under-served. These are the clients who feel that traditional banking is opaque, unfriendly and hard to understand.

Digital banks are also more likely to focus on personal financial management (PFM) to help their customers manage their money better as their segments tend to be younger and have problems saving enough for the future. Another big difference is that digital banks are more likely to be mono-channel, leveraging the smartphone as **the main and only channel** to serve customers. This affords both a cost and simplicity advantage since it involves servicing a specific customer through a specific channel.

Banking was originally mono-channel, just focused on the branch. Omni-channel grew out of the evolution to serve customers better, with ATMs, call-centres, internet banking, cash-deposit machines, mobile banking, etc. added over the years. As illustrated in Figure 8, banks have added more channels but never removed any. Every channel that banks have created is still in use today. In reality, omni-channel is an expensive proposition, and almost all omni-channel initiatives **have not yielded the promise of being able to orchestrate activities seamlessly**. And if the future is a return to a mostly mono-channel model via the smartphone, this investment will impact fewer and fewer customers over time.

I predict that over that the next 10 to 15 years, more and more customers **will**

---

25. Wealthfront Inc. is an automated investment service firm based in Palo Alto, California, founded by Andy Rachleff and Dan Carroll in 2008. As of September 2019, Wealthfront had $21B AUM across 400,000 accounts.

desire a mostly mono-channel experience via their smartphones. The young professionals who will be affluent or mass affluent in the future thus become the natural target market in this scenario, since they are comfortable doing everything on the go with their mobile phones.

Many senior bankers fail to understand the threat posed by digital banks. It is true that most digital banks won't make a profit for some time to come, and their initial share gains will be small. So, unlike the case of Nokia and BlackBerry, the impact on the existing incumbents will happen over a much longer period of time, likely 10–15 years, whereas Nokia's peak market share **collapsed from 50% to 5% in just six years**.

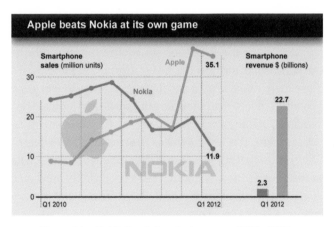

Figure 14 – Nokia/Apple handset revenue 2010–2012

(Source: Statista)

The iPhone was launched in 2007 when Nokia held a market share of 50% in mobile phone handsets. And as you can see from Figure 14[26], Nokia's sales continued to climb after 2007, hitting a peak in Q4 2010 (Krigsman, 2018). By 2013, however, its market share had cratered, collapsing to just 5% share, a 10x loss in 6 years. The same thing happened to BlackBerry. RIM's (Research in Motion, the maker of the BlackBerry) global market share began a downward spiral, going from 20% in 2009 to less than 5% in 2012, a 4x decline in just three years (Appolonia, 2019).

The story in both cases was the same: the incumbents failed to recognise the power that a single word gave to the phone: *smart*. They failed to understand that **a smartphone was smart first and not phone first**, and thus the digital capabilities around text and surfing the net came first.

---

26. Source: https://www.statista.com/chart/255/smartphone-sales-of-apple-and-nokia/

I expect the same result for digital banks vs the incumbents, just not in such a short timeframe. My view, as I have stated, is that the direction is very clear that transaction banking will one day in the near future, be it 10 or 15 years, be done primarily online, on the mobile, tablet or personal computing device. To me, that is a given; only the timeframe is unclear. It will be influenced by many factors such as internet access, demographics (preferences of the young vs old), governmental action, industry efforts, etc. In a way, though, this makes the **threat more insidious**. It is akin to the urban legend of how a frog will boil if you put it in cold water and slowly turn up the heat, as opposed to throwing it into boiling water, where it will jump out! This really is an urban legend, by the way (Obradovich, 2019).

Over time, the new digital banks' biggest threat is their ability to **radically improve customer experience**. Many in banking have forgotten that banking is first and foremost based on superior business process as a competitive advantage. What has changed is that the speed and ability of technology to be the enabler to support the deployment of superior business processes has improved dramatically.

Banks have many stakeholders and distractions. What takes centre stage are the regulatory requirements, risk management, growth and profits. These are important considerations, and thus not every bank will place customers and customer experience above them. This is the **Achilles heel** that the new digital bank entrants will aim for. They know that improving customer experience is **much harder for the incumbents** than it is for new entrants. That's because the new entrants have a simpler business model, whereas the incumbents are saddled with an omni-channel infrastructure, a legacy technology platform that makes it hard and expensive to test and roll out new changes and applications, and a large number of products to maintain.

Besides legacy technology challenges, the incumbents also have a culture tilted towards risk mitigation, and a business model that is still fundamentally product in orientation. Typical incumbent banks split their businesses and reporting lines into consumer, wholesale and global markets[27], with compliance, risk, technology, human resources, finance, etc. as supporting functions. In an experience-oriented digital company, the key competitive capabilities are to be found in the expertise around understanding customer problems, customer experience design, user interaction design, business process design and transformation, project management and technology implementation. In most banks today, these capabilities, if present, are **dispersed in the business units and serve to sell more products and manage risks** rather than focus on better customer experience as their primary motivation and objective.

---

27. For readers not familiar with banking, this is the unit within a bank that handles all the trading activities on primary and secondary markets (rates, credit, foreign exchange, fixed-income, treasury, etc.).

Many people ask why these banks can't just change. I think it's for the same reason why one word and five letters felled the giants of mobile. **Seemingly simple things aren't easy to change if they revolve around organisational and cultural change**.

The standalone challenger banks have challenges of their own. They may find it easier to lend than to raise deposits, especially if they don't have a parent share-holder that can imbue them with trustworthiness and ease of acquisition. Without deposits, they have to use their own expensive capital to lend, which is not viable. However, raising deposits doesn't make much money if you can't charge fees, and competition has reduced any bank's ability to charge significant fees. The revenue growth engine of a bank has also shifted more and more towards wealth fee income generation, where persuasion and education are required (and thus not something a digital bank does well today, unless it's about serving the self-directed, but that has other issues as discussed earlier), and lending.

Lending is a key factor in digital bank profitability, as witnessed by the con-trasting fortunes of Starling Bank with £2B in loans as of March 2021 vs Monzo with just £124M by early 2020 (Worthington, 2021). Starling, started by Anne Boden, understood that loans generate the profits; deposits and transactions simply pro-vide the deposits against which to lend. Thus far, the economics of banking for digital banks are such that no one is generating significant new income streams outside of traditional fee income and interest income from the difference between deposit and loan rates. The prize is long-term, and thus a lot of patience is needed in the sense that profits won't arrive quickly.

Banking looks easy from the outside, but it's hard. There is a large mismatch between initial cost outlay and revenue. **The prize is the strong annuity stream once you make the bank profitable.** Figure 15 illustrates this with a comparison of some of the leading digital banks in the world. All but four of those shown are unprofitable, with Starling Bank, a recent fifth, having turned a small profit of £0.8M for the month of October 2020.[28] The rest of the almost 200 digital banks around the world are mostly unprofitable. Of the banks shown, Starling's focus on quality customer growth, high NPS and lending as a key profit generator has the most parallels with TMRW. The key differences, in my view, are Starling's earlier start in 2014, its entry into SME banking in 2018, and significant cumulative funding of almost US$900M.

Of the profitable ones, Webank (Tencent owns 30%), MYbank (Ant Group owns 30%) and Kakao Bank (Kakao Corp owns just over 30%, and is the company behind KakaoTalk, which is used by 93% of smartphone users in South Korea) all have

---

28. Starling reported in March 2021 that it generated £12M of revenue in January 2021 and posted operating profits for a fourth consecutive month.

unique strengths imbued by their shareholder parentage, which have helped them acquire the necessary data and/or customer base very quickly. Their unique DNA is hard to copy and so their path-to-profit won't be the path most digital banks will take.

The fourth of the profitable digital banks, Tinkoff Bank, is different. It started in May 2007 pursuing a monoline credit card business in Russia from scratch (Rubinstein, 2021). Oleg Tinkov, the founder, had sold his Tinkoff beer business to the Belgian beer giant InBev in 2005 for US$260M, and thus became a multi-millionaire. He had always fancied running a bank, so he bought a banking licence by acquiring Khimmashbank, which wasn't really operational, and then spent $20M on the latest technology. From his biography, entitled *I'm Just Like Anyone Else*, Tinkov's **focus on the small details and customer-centricity** shines through. He describes how he would perform test-and-learn experiments on whose signature appeared on the credit card mailers they were sending out, to see which yielded better results (Tinkoff, 2010). So Tinkoff is more of a traditional bank that got digital right from day one. Whilst the opportunity to do so may be particular to Russia, Tinkoff is probably a **better model for digital banks setting up from scratch, compared to Webank, MYbank and Kakao Bank.** However, Tinkoff is now positioning itself to be the super-app of Russia by buying into the retail business needed to support this strategy, and this approach may not be replicable elsewhere.

Most people clump all start-ups into one category, but in reality, there are at least **two different ways to set up from scratch**. First you have those start-ups who are thoroughly breakthrough in nature; they have an approach that will create a 5x or larger product performance improvement over current alternatives that their customers value. The bicycle is a good example. When it was invented, it lacked brakes, but still prospered. The inventors chose to create the minimum needed to demonstrate the bicycle's 5x improvement – what we now call a minimum viable product or MVP. Then you have those start-ups for which no such single breakthrough is possible; the nature of their breakthrough is stringing together many small improvements to create a dramatically different experience.

Companies like Airbnb (stay in a home, not a hotel), Netflix (no rentals and returns, and a wide range that's always available) and SpaceX (reusable rockets) are able to generate that 5x performance improvement over the previous method of doing the same. It doesn't stop them from combining this singular breakthrough with great customer experience. Other innovative companies don't operate in such a space that has one powerful initial breakthrough. They can be equally successful, but it calls for a different DNA. Companies like HubSpot[29] (make every part of

---

29. HubSpot is an American developer and marketer of software products for inbound marketing, sales, and customer service. HubSpot was founded by Brian Halligan and Dharmesh Shah in 2006.

Digital Bank	Customers (Millions)	As of	NPS Score	Cumulative Losses/Profit (Millions)	Years to Profit	FY2019 Net Loss/Profit (Millions)	2019 cumulative funding (US$M)
WeBank	200	2019	n.a.	1016	2	602	182
NuBank	34	2020	highest in S. America	-90	unprofitable	-24	1500
MyBank	20	2019	n.a.	n.a.	2	198	n.a.
Revolut	15	2020	n.a.	-239	unprofitable	-147	906
Chime	12	2020	n.a.	n.a.	n.a.	n.a.	1500
Kakao	12	2020	top in S. Korea	-82.7	1.5	23	n.a.
N26	7	2020	n.a.	n.a.	unprofitable	-256	819
Tinkoff	7	2019	26	1436	5	472	90
Monzo	3.9	2020	+75	-278	unprofitable	-158	435
Starling	1.5	2019	+54	-127	unprofitable	-74	878

Source: Business of Apps, SFA, BCG Expand Report November 2020, Crunchbase, etc   n.a. = not available

Figure 15 – Leading digital banks in the world

the digital CRM journey great) and Zappos[30] (overnight delivery and 365-day return policy) focus on great attention to detail in order to identify the many small issues their customers face and to perfect a large number of them to make the experience great. Apple competes in the highly competitive arena of personal computing by doing the same.

Building a digital bank is in this latter category, unless the standard of banking in your target country is low, then there might be the possibility of creating a large singular breakthrough in one area of banking. What that means is that you need a great experience from the start, otherwise it's very hard to scale. In my view, digital banks don't operate on an MVP approach; instead they have to operate on a very high net promoter score (NPS®) difference with the competition. If you rush to launch and your NPS® is poor, that poor experience sticks in the customer's mind. One of the biggest things we did right in designing and building TMRW was following the advice

---

30. Zappos.com is an American online shoe and clothing retailer based in Las Vegas. The company was founded in 1999 by Nick Swinmurn and launched under the domain name Shoesite.com. In July 2009, Amazon acquired Zappos in an all-stock deal worth around $1.2B at the time.

that UOB's Group CEO gave us: since we weren't the first to launch a digital bank, we should **take the time to design and build something truly differentiated**. And that's exactly what we did.

Key takeaways

- A digital bank is a business where everything (technology, design, service, products, etc.) is put towards the pursuit of better customer experience, as evidenced by the 3x improvement in NPS scores of digital banks over incumbents.

- Culture is paramount because the digital bank's main advantage is its ability to focus on its target customer and create an experience that is hard to replicate in terms of simplicity and ease of use.

- Leveraging better-written applications and cloud infrastructure, digital banks can achieve an 8x differential in operating cost per customer.

- The digital bank has a different culture from the start – one that is more customer-centric, less hierarchical, more agile, suited to novel approaches, and able to maintain a high level of collaboration across teams.

- Most digital banks, especially in countries with smaller populations, will still have to compete by winning over customers in basic transactional banking first.

- In the transactional banking arena, the key entry-point differentiation is in ease of use and reduction of friction in navigating the payment and account management functionalities.

- Over the next 10 to 15 years, more and more customers will desire a mostly mono-channel experience via their smartphones.

- Webank, MYbank and Kakao Bank all have unique strengths imbued by their shareholder parentage, which have helped them acquire the necessary data and/or customer base very quickly.

- Digital banks don't operate on a minimum viable product (MVP) approach; instead, they have to operate on a very high NPS® difference with the competition.

Disruptive Innovation vs Sustaining Innovation

In the previous chapter, we explored how digital challenger banks and digital banking channels of incumbent banks are different. The digital banks are competing on much lower costs, potentially 8x cheaper and 3x times better in advocacy and customer experience, which is going to be lethal in the long term to the incumbents whose business models are not made to withstand such an onslaught. Digital banking channels are no match for these digital banks, as it requires the entire bank's effort to bring to bear the improvements in costs and customer experience, and certainly not just from a channel perspective. The digital banks that are profitable or have deep pockets will necessitate a vigorous response from the incumbents, who will need to **launch digital banks of their own**, to first defend against the onslaught, and second, to start changing the incumbent bank to be able to morph its business model to compete with these digital competitors.

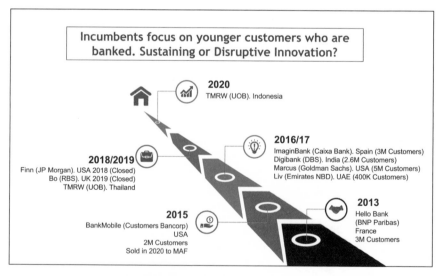

Figure 16 – Sample of digital banks launched by incumbents

Most of the digital banks launched by incumbent banks focus on younger customers who are already banked. Figure 16 shows some of the digital banks launched by incumbent banks in recent years. These moves could be seen as more defensive, to buy insurance for an uncertain future. In this chapter, we delineate two different approaches in the industry. One approach is the battle between digital banking and digital banks (described in the prior chapter), and the other is the digital bank attack from the bottom of the industry, first focusing on the unbanked, and then once successful, penetrating more and more segments – the underbanked, mass market and then mass affluent.

An interesting lens to view these two approaches is through the **disruptive innovation theory**, made famous by the late Clayton Christensen in his book, *The Innovator's Dilemma*, first published in 1997. In a 2015 article in the *Harvard Business Review*, Christensen defined disruption as "a process whereby a smaller company with fewer resources is able to successfully challenge established incumbent businesses". Disruptive innovators start by attacking incumbents in segments that they have no interest to defend, as they are focused on serving their best, most demanding and profitable customers.

The history of the steel industry provides a salient example. Leveraging disruptive technologies like the electric arc furnace that initially could only smelt scrap iron to make rebar[31] steel (as opposed to the traditional integrated steel mills which made steel from iron ore that could produce sheet steel), the mini-mills gradually improved their technology and since the late 1980s have been able to produce sheet steel as well. Initially the incumbents were only too pleased to forgo their low-end products, like rebars, but as the technology improved, the incumbents found themselves continuously ceding their lowest-performing products to the disruptive attackers, eventually finding themselves cornered and surrendering entirely.

Today, the mini steel mills dominate steel manufacturing in the US. Will this same phenomenon play out in digital banks that are currently serving the unbanked and underbanked? In contrast with this approach, other challenger digital banks like Monzo, Starling, Kakao Bank, as well as digital banks from incumbents shown in Figure 16, are focusing mostly on customers who are already banked, but usually younger segments that are more likely to do all their banking on their mobile phones. How will incumbent banks react to these two different approaches?

Let's start by examining the characteristics of **disruptive innovation vs sustaining innovation**. Disruptive innovators get started in markets largely ignored by incumbents or markets the incumbent is prepared to forgo, e.g., low-end or new market footholds. Examples include the case of rebar steel above (low-end), or the small personal photocopier market which was non-existent before Canon

---

31. Rebar (short for reinforcing bar), known when massed as reinforcing steel or reinforcement steel, is a steel bar or mesh of steel wires used as a tension device in reinforced concrete and reinforced masonry structures to strengthen and aid the concrete under tension.

introduced the PC-10 and PC-20, which it claims to be the world's first personal copying machines with replaceable cartridges, introduced in 1982. Before that, the industry was dominated by large photocopiers made by Xerox and its competitors such as Ricoh, which served large corporations.

If we apply this lens to banking, then Webank, MYbank, and to some extent Nubank would qualify as disruptive innovators. Webank was established in 2014, and from the beginning it focused on unbanked individuals and SMEs. Using the formula of low cost through modern cloud technology, artificial intelligence to solve service issues cheaper and faster, and alternative data to provide new credit scoring approaches, Webank and MYbank were able to create a business model predicated on high-volume, low-ticket transactions that incumbent legacy banks deemed not viable because the cost to serve these customers would outweigh the returns. In fact, Webank only incurs US$0.50 cost per account annually versus a cost of 6 to 30 times that for incumbent banks, and yet customers applying for credit usually receive their results in under 5 seconds and successful applicants can draw down funds in 1 minute, with a 2019 non-performing loan ratio of just 1.24% (Liu & L'Hostis, 2019).

Webank serves 200M individual clients and 1.3M SME clients, employing little more than 2,000 employees, with just over half of them in technology, and the average revenue per client for 2019 was only US$10 (Marous, 2020). At MYbank, it's the same story. Launched in 2015, it strictly serves SMEs; as of the end of 2019, it had served more than 20M SMEs in China. Average loans outstanding were US$4,300 in 2019, and similar to Webank, their collateral-free loans take 3 seconds to apply for, 1 second to approve, and involve zero human intervention. China's digital banks now have approximately 5% of the country's US$700B unsecured consumer loans. Nubank operates in Brazil where four banks have traditionally controlled more than 80% of the deposits, and where 1 out of every 4 Brazilians is unbanked, but 80% of them have a mobile phone. According to Nubank company data, 20% of their customers have never previously had a credit card.

Closer to home, one out of every two individuals in Southeast Asia's population over 18 years of age remains unbanked, whilst an estimated 24% or 98M are underbanked, as shown in Figure 17. This represents a **huge opportunity for a disruptive innovator** to serve these unbanked and underbanked customers who are largely neglected by the incumbent banks. If this was the only fact to consider, then it might not be as interesting, but when you add the fact that there is a digital payments transformation happening in parallel, then it becomes pivotal. Data from Bain's Indonesia SME Merchant Survey shows that the likelihood of accepting digital payments amongst SMEs will increase from 15% to 46% by 2022 (Bain & Co, Google, and Temasek, 2019). The Covid-19 pandemic is likely to boost this number even higher.

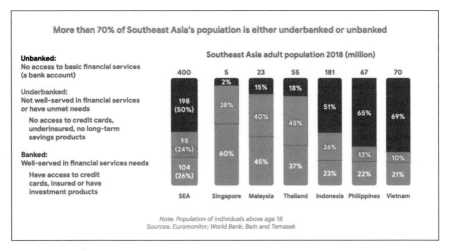

Figure 17 – Unbanked, Underbanked and Banked in Southeast Asia
(Source: The future of Southeast Asia's digital financial services report
by Bain, Google and Temasek)

One of the issues serving the unbanked has always been that since they are not part of the banking system in that their income is mostly in cash, how do they fund their accounts? The **rise of digital payments** and the **interconnection between wallets and banks** will greatly facilitate this, as it has in China. As reported in *The Straits Times*, "According to the (Chinese) central bank, 66.5 per cent of people in rural areas were already using digital payments by 2017" (Morris, 2019). This means that an unbanked customer may already be accepting payments to his digital wallet, and if the wallets are then connected to a digital bank account, and if that digital bank's cost structure is low enough, all the unbanked will be bankable. This also creates a rationale for the wallet players in countries with large unbanked and under-banked to acquire or partner with digital banks. Indonesian ride-hailing giant Gojek is doing just that, paying US$160M to increase its stake in Bank Jago to 22.16% (Y. Lee & Ho, 2020).

The disruptive innovation takes time to move from the low-end, but with each improvement of its core technology, it starts to move up the food chain, squeezing the industry incumbents. For the steel industry, the battle of the mini-mills and inte-grated steel mills took many years, starting with the first Nucor mini-mill in 1969, which only produced 200K tons per annum. By 1975, this became 30+ mini-mills, and today, the mini-mills together ship more tonnage than the integrated mills. Same story with disk-drives. Between 1975 and 1990, successive generations of disk drive technologies – 14-inch, 8-inch, 5.25-inch, 3.5-inch and 2.5-inch disks – faced the same disruption, and each time **the newcomers disrupted the markets of their**

predecessors only to be themselves disrupted. Christensen found this pattern time and time again, in automobiles (where the Japanese upstarts Toyota, Honda and Nissan challenged the Big Three automobile makers, General Motors, Ford and Chrysler), and in small off-road motorcycles (with Japanese disruptive innovators like Yamaha, Kawasaki and Honda). Christensen is often quoted as saying, "The leaders get killed from below" (Laambert, 2014).

Are there industries where the theory of disruptive innovation doesn't apply? Michael Raynor, a student of Christensen's who co-authored *The Innovator's Solution* with his mentor, found that in **industries without a technological core** such as hotels, entrants entering the low-end stay in the low-end, like Holiday Inn. Another example is McDonald's, which has not moved upmarket. These industries don't have a significant technological core – a system inside the product that "can define its performance and can be extended upmarket to do better things".

Banking, though, clearly has a technological core, and that technological core, with the aid of greater modularity, scalability and redundancy afforded by APIs, better banking application software and the cloud, plus the use of data for credit underwriting and insight generation, is going to over time **allow digital bank entrants entering at the low-end to migrate upwards**. Therefore, my conclusion, supported by the theory of disruptive innovation, is that in countries with large segments of unbanked and underbanked (e.g., China, Brazil, Indonesia, Philippines, Vietnam, etc.), incumbent banks have to take the disruptors very seriously if they don't want to find themselves eventually squeezed out altogether.

What about the digital banks that are targeting existing banked customers? To answer this, we have to examine the concept of **sustaining innovations**. Unlike disruptive innovations, which are initially seen as inferior to an incumbent's existing customers (and hence these customers are likely to reject the innovation initially until the technology gets much better), a sustaining innovation is targeted at those existing customers. The sustaining innovation makes good products better, and thus threatens to steal customers from the incumbent. An example is Uber. Uber isn't a disruptive innovator, because it's not appealing to people who don't take taxis. Rather it's providing a better taxi ride, and so it's a sustaining innovation. So far, incumbent banks have responded by attempting to modernise their technology stack or by adding micro-services layers that allow for faster and more flexible application development, and some banks are launching digital banks of their own, as shown in Figure 16. But is this sufficient?

The current response can hardly be described as vigorous. Could it be because the challenger banks are acquiring banked customers who are less core to incumbent banks' current profitability – i.e., younger customers, who are mobile-first, and are borderline profitable unless they utilise their unsecured facilities – and thus **the attack is in reality a disruptive innovation**, and largely being ignored? This is interesting, as it would likely lead incumbent banks to underestimate the long-term impact of the digital banks. Just as many of the non-banking cases in Christensen's book took the approach of ignoring the disruptive innovator and serving their best customers, are incumbent banks likely to do the same? History isn't on the side of the incumbents. Kodak, despite having invented the digital camera, eventually succumbed to the digital camera (more of this story in Chapter 4.7 "Fostering an innovative culture"), while Blockbuster succumbed to streaming giant Netflix.

A final observation is that the truly disruptive digital banks that are attacking from the bottom **may not need as big an advantage in NPS®** compared to the incumbents. They are not serving customers who are currently banked, and thus don't need to be significantly better in overall experience, whereas the sustaining innovation digital banks need to, as they are taking customers away from incumbents. What the disruptors need to do is attain a sufficient ease-of-use score, be very proficient in using alternative data to do instant credit assessment and lower their marginal cost significantly using the approaches we discussed in this chapter. So, the approach differs slightly depending on whether you are a disruptive innovator or a sustaining innovator.

Few companies have faced a disruptive innovator and lived to tell their story. As Joshua Gans wrote in the *Harvard Business Review*, "In many cases, disrupted incumbents find themselves **unable to transfer the new technologies into their mainstream operations** because doing so requires them to fundamentally change the way they manufacture and distribute their products. In essence, the basic architecture of the product – how it is put together – changes along with customer expectations and preferences, creating "supply side" disruption" (Gans, 2016). This could very well play out in many incumbent banks around the world.

Who are these rare companies that have overcome disruption, and what did they do to buck the odds? Two firms come to mind, and both are Japanese, Canon and Fujifilm.

Canon, together with many other companies like Konica, Leica, Contax, Agfa, Olympus, made film cameras. But unlike the rest, Canon not only navigated the shift from analog to digital photography, they also increased their market share, whereas the rest have either exited the business (Agfa in 2001, Konica in 2006, Olympus in 2020) or like Leica, have become niche players (Leica moved upmarket to make $5,000 cameras). According to IDC, in 2004 Canon sold 12.6M digital cameras with a market share of 17%. Today it sells almost one out of every two digital cameras, with a market share greater than Sony, Nikon and Fuji combined (Nikkei, 2020). According to Chris Sandstrom, who has studied Canon's rise, Canon entered the digital camera market early, but did not make any significant investments until upstart Casio launched their QV10 digital camera in 1995 with an LCD display, 0.25 megapixels (far inferior to 35mm film cameras at 87 megapixels), and powered by four AA-sized batteries (Sandstrom, 2009). This jolted Canon into action, as it was a clear sign of things to come. They formed a Digital Imaging Business Centre, **separating it from the rest of the company** to give it freedom and prevent starvation of resources from the incumbent film camera business.

Fujifilm, like Kodak, had the bulk of its sales come from photographic film and chemicals. "What Fujifilm did was go one step further than simply shift to digital photography from analog. Instead, it leveraged its chemical expertise to pioneer new business fields" (Fujii, 2016). Some of those fields include X-rays, endoscopes, a 70% share in tac film (a crucial component in LCD displays), and cosmetics. Yes, you read it right, cosmetics. Fujifilm found that its core competence in developing capabilities to prevent colour photos from fading could be applied to human skin, and this became the foundation for their skincare products. This quote in *The Economist* sums it up; "Kodak acted like a stereotypical change-resistant Japanese firm, while Fujifilm acted like a flexible American one" (Schumpeter, 2012).

The equivalent of the launch of the Casio QV10 of banking has arrived, so CEOs and board members of incumbent banks reading this book should be concerned. History is not on the side of the incumbents, as we have seen time and time again. My observation is that there is a misplaced focus on technology to solve the disruptive innovation threat, when the threat is really a **business model threat driven by lower cost and better experience that is enabled by technology, process and design skills**. And the technology done within a legacy bank is not going to produce the quantum difference in cost required. It's time for boards to hit the reset button.

Key takeaways

- Digital banking channels are no match for digital banks, as it requires the entire bank's effort to bring to bear the improvements in costs and customer experience, and certainly not just from a channel perspective.

- Disruptive innovators start by attacking incumbents in segments that they have no interest to defend, as they are focused on serving their best, most demanding and profitable customers.

- Webank, MYbank, and to some extent Nubank would qualify as disruptive innovators in banking.

- One out of every two individuals in Southeast Asia's population over 18 years of age remains unbanked, whilst an estimated 24% or 98M are underbanked, representing a huge opportunity for a disruptive innovator.

- The rise of digital payments and the interconnection between wallets and banks will greatly facilitate the ability for the unbanked to fund their accounts, as it has in China.

- The theory of disruptive innovation supports the view that in countries with large segments of unbanked and underbanked, incumbent banks have to take the disruptors very seriously if they don't want to find themselves eventually squeezed out altogether.

- There is a possibility that challenger banks who are acquiring younger banked customers who are less core to incumbent banks' current profitability have disguised this attack as disruptive innovation rather than a sustaining innovation.

- Truly disruptive digital banks that are attacking from the bottom may not need as big an advantage in NPS® compared to the incumbents as they are not serving customers who are currently banked.

- Canon, one of the few survivors of the film camera wars to survive and gain share in the digital camera market, formed a Digital Imaging Business Centre, separating it from the rest of the company to give it freedom and prevent starvation of resources from the incumbent film camera business.

- There is a misplaced focus on technology to solve the disruptive innovation threat, when the threat is really a business model threat driven by lower cost and better experience that is enabled by technology, process and design skills.

- It is time for bank boards to hit the reset button. The equivalent of the launch of the Casio QV10 (the first commercial digital camera that was a clear sign of things to come) of banking has arrived.

Challenges facing legacy incumbent banks

Existing banks will find it much easier to design and develop their digital banking offerings than to build a digital bank. The difference, as discussed extensively in Chapter 2.2, is the obsession with and focus on customer experience. Most incumbent banks will find it hard to compete against a digital bank that is simpler, leaner and totally focused on providing a better customer experience. Yes, the digital banks will need to play the long game, but with enough cash and solid execution, they will become a long-term threat to current incumbents who are not as obsessed with customer experience. So what prevents legacy banks from improving their customer experience and driving down their costs? That's the focus of this chapter.

In this book, I use Net Promoter Score or NPS® as the indicator of advocacy, the outcome of having great customer experience. It's not the only way to measure customer experience and engagement; using a different metric doesn't change anything you read in this book. I would also like to clarify that I believe in a balanced scorecard approach, and therefore, it's not just NPS® that's important, but also marginal profitability, the ability to make a profit over your annual fixed cost and eventually pay back the initial invested sum when the business scales. It goes back to the fundamental tenet and belief that if you are attracting customers and building your digital bank by offering a much better digital transactional banking experience, then **your NPS® (or whatever other measure you are using) has to be significantly higher than the incumbent competition**. Otherwise, there is no threat, and no sustainable differentiation.

Few incumbent banks score high in NPS®. While it's difficult to give a cut-off at which NPS® can be considered good, as it varies by industry and country, a 2018 study of US Net Promoter Score Benchmarks puts **the average for financial services at +35**, as shown in Figure 18 (Nice, 2018). But the average can be misleading, as evident in Figure 19, from GlobalData's 2018 retail banking survey in the UK (GlobalData Financial Services, 2019). The average NPS® of the 11 UK banks featured shown is +24, pulled up by the scores of the two leaders, who are far ahead of the rest. Without the two leaders, the average NPS® falls to +17.

Is this large gap unique to the UK market? Well, from a Bain report from 2018, it appears that in most markets in the Americas, Asia-Pacific, Europe, Middle East and Africa, there is a large gap between loyalty leaders and laggards (du Toit et al.,

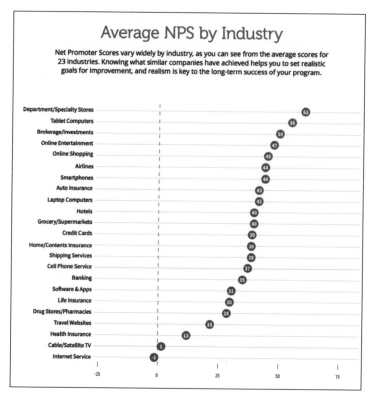

Figure 18 – Satmetrix NICE 2018 average NPS® by industry report
(Source: Satmetrix)

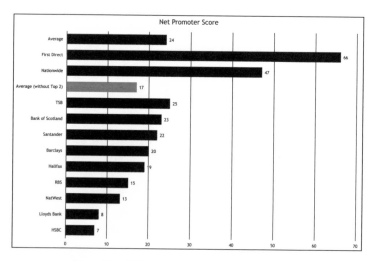

Figure 19 – 2018 current account NPS® in the UK
(Data: Globaldata, 2018)

2018). Bain's research shows that the leaders' NPS® can lead the rest of the banks by between 20 and 80 points. And while the sample is not statistically significant enough to make a definitive conclusion on this point, **direct banks**[32] **have higher NPS® than traditional banks**. In Canada, Tangerine bank is a clear NPS® leader. In the US, it's USAA, in Australia ING Direct, in South Korea Kakao Bank, in France and Spain again ING Direct, and in the UK First Direct. The same report also shows evidence that loyalty leaders have faster net interest income growth than laggards. Figure 20 indicates that Kakao Bank has a very significant lead in NPS® over other South Korean banks, and what's more, there isn't a clear leader amongst the incumbent banks to challenge it. Whilst there are currently more traditional banks that are loyalty leaders vs direct banks in Asia-Pacific, the equivalent charts for the Americas and Europe indicate that a significantly larger proportion of direct banks have taken the lead.

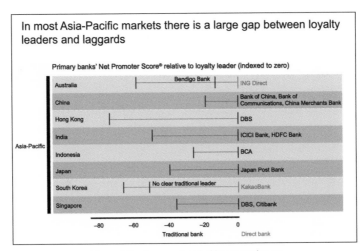

Figure 20 – Legacy banks' biggest threat
(Source: Bain)

So why is it so hard to do well? I offer a few key reasons centred around the focus on growth and profits-first; a structure that is aligned to products, not customers; and a lack of attention to detail and business processes at the top of the organisation.

Most banks do proclaim in their annual reports that customers are important, but look at their scorecards and you'll find that **most banks place revenue generation, profit and risk mitigation first**, before customer experience. Most are also still organised around products, e.g., deposits, credit cards and personal loans,

---

32. Bain's term for a bank that does not have bank branches

home loans, investments, insurance, etc. Their KPIs usually don't put a measure on experience or advocacy, their organisational structure is product-led, and their mantra is to sell more products. When you couple that with a disdain for discussing business processes in detail – processes that directly impact customers – you create an organisation that isn't materially vested in or focused on the customer. The kind of obsession with detail needed to do well in an experience business is rare. Which is why there are so few examples of companies that have an NPS® of +60 and above.

Those of you with an iPhone, turn on your Apple flashlight in the Control Centre. The light turns on as it should, but how many of you noticed that the on/off button on the flashlight icon also turns on and off? You can clearly see it from the icons here. How's that for detail? Who is setting the tone for detail at the top at your organisation? **This is what it takes to produce a high NPS® company**.

Too few banks today will sweat the details to excel at the experience business. A great example is shown below on the left.[33] Many banks send out their SMS OTP without bothering to put the OTP at the top of the message. This means that every time you need to enter the OTP, you have to go to your SMS messages, memorise the number, get back to the app, and enter the number. The best put their SMS OTP before the warning, so that you can view it within the app. And the very best are even better. As shown on the right below, all you have to do is tap on "From Messages 149990" to fill in the OTP. What separates the left and the right examples? **Well, it's all about detail and design.**

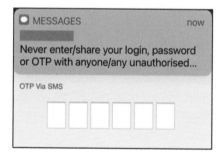

---

33. I've intentionally masked the name of the bank but if you work there and you are reading this, you should do something to fix it. It's not just one bank – quite a few have this issue. And the example on the right is not from a bank.

The major impact of the internet has been to put the power in the hands of the customer, so you can't divorce any digitisation effort from the need to be the customer and think like a customer. Most organisations, however, remain resolutely organisation-centric rather than customer-centric. In fact, they find it downright "alien and counter-intuitive to be customer-centric" (McGovern, 2013). They don't believe that the obsession with customer experience will lead to stronger profit growth, because in the short term, it may not, until you have worked out how to perfect your processes and focus on the minutiae needed to perfect the experience.

Furthermore, it's true that if your NPS® is high but your revenue-generation model is wrong (e.g., you focused on gathering deposits but not enough on lending), higher NPS® alone may not lead to higher profits. In other words, it's a necessary criterion but not a sufficient one. When you take all these factors together, it is the exception for any bank to be equally obsessed with customers and profits.

The Singapore banks' NPS® scores in Figure 20 show a pattern that could be a **remake of Kakao Bank's success in South Korea**. The incumbent banks' NPS® scores are in the teens and below the US average for financial services at +35. So, to make an impact, the challenger banks would have to come in at an NPS® of around +40 and above. This would place the challenger in a position similar to Kakao Bank. That means there will need to be an obsession with getting all the finer issues in banking in Singapore identified and fixed – both the things that are visible in the app and everything else that's not visible. Can one of the two newly awarded digital full bank licence-holders (Grab-Singtel and Sea) and a current incumbent intending to set up a separate digital bank JV (SCB-NTUC) do it? I believe the answer is yes, but it requires them to adopt this approach wholeheartedly from the very start and see it through to the end.

So, if you are an incumbent legacy bank CEO, what's the takeaway? First, the risk is too high and the probability of success too low to try and change the mothership. This assumption is likely to be true. If you exclude that, then what are the options?

A **joint venture (JV)** with a firm that can inject a different way of doing things is possible, but that company will operate at arm's length, and thus, bringing back the new approaches and embedding them into the mothership will be more difficult. And that's not even considering the differences of opinion and goals that typically afflict a JV.

The other alternative is to start **a disruptive unit within the mothership** and have a transformational senior leader take on the responsibility of change from within. This leader must work directly for the CEO and be a senior member of the top management committee. Over time, the new ways of working that are customer-centric, non-hierarchical, mission-based, involving new cloud-based infrastructures, data-driven solutions and algorithms that can provide great engagement and service at low cost, start to take hold and spread as the leader proves that the new model can indeed thrive. Existing business would gradually be transferred over to the new disruptive unit, creating a path of internal revitalisation and renewal.

I see very few alternatives to this latter approach, yet not many banks have started or have created the conditions needed for such a unit to succeed. Acquiring a digital bank might be another option, but the success rates here are again likely to be low, given the inevitable culture clash between the new entity and the mothership if merged; and if they remain separate, the issues will be similar to a JV. If a suitable internal leader can be found, I believe this model is well worth the additional costs, as the disruption will happen. It's no longer a matter of if, only a matter of when, and whether there is still time to do something about it.

Key takeaways

- If you are attracting customers and building your digital bank by offering a much better digital transactional banking experience, then your NPS® (or whatever other measure you are using) has to be significantly higher than the incumbent competition.

- A 2018 study of US Net Promoter Score Benchmarks puts the average for financial services at +35.

- Bain's research shows that the leaders' Net Promoter Score can lead the rest of the banks by between 20 to 80 points, and that direct banks (Bain's term for banks without branches) have higher NPS® than traditional banks.

- Kakao Bank has a very significant lead in NPS® over other South Korean banks, and what's more, there isn't a clear leader amongst the incumbent banks to challenge it.

- An eye for detail is what it takes to produce a high NPS® bank.

- Most organisations remain resolutely organisation-centric rather than customer-centric. In fact, they find it downright "alien and counter-intuitive to be customer-centric".

- Singapore banks' NPS® scores show a pattern that could be a remake of Kakao Bank's success in South Korea.

- The risk is too high and the probability of success too low to try and change the mothership.

- A joint venture can inject a different way of doing things, but bringing back the new approaches and embedding them in the mothership will be more difficult.

- Another alternative is to start a disruptive unit within the mothership and have a transformational senior leader take on the responsibility of change from within.

- If a suitable internal leader can be found, I believe this model is well worth the additional costs.

- It's no longer a matter of if, only a matter of when, and whether there is still time to do something about it.

Experience starts with engagement

Many banks and bankers are stating the obvious when they say banking needs to become more invisible so that customers can spend less time banking, and more time on the benefits banking brings. I agree that consumer banks need to continue to remove friction from banking by not asking customers what the bank already knows about them, and by customising the user experience to their behaviour and situation. For example, not asking which account you want to pay from when you only have one account you can debit from (as TMRW has done). However, without finding a way to increase frequency of engagement, such actions will only further commoditise banking, leading to further erosion of profits as banking becomes more and more of a utility.

The key, therefore, is engagement through the form of many **digital micro-conversations** that can help customers by nudging them towards better financial habits and serving their needs to a level not yet achieved by conventional banking.

In essence, banks really only perform three functions: (1) Have conversations with customers; (2) collect information required to fulfil customer transactions and ensure regulations are complied with; and (3) change digits due to transactions or new data. The third point has largely been computerised at the backend for all banks since Bank of America introduced ERMA in 1955. As for the second point, many banks have introduced ways to digitise data collection and input without the need for manual intervention, while more progressive banks have begun to eliminate the need to ask customers for information they already have about them. Hence, the battleground between banks will certainly shift to the first point: mastery of digital conversations with customers.

The new **holy grail of banking will be digital engagement**, as described in Figure 10. Digital banks of the future will be able to have tens, and the most successful ones, hundreds or thousands of conversations annually. They will assign an engagement index to every customer to measure how engaged they are (Warden, 2019a). They will understand that generating more data through transactions will fuel their insights engine so that they can generate more conversations to deeply engage with their customers. Engaged customers will buy more products from these banks and transact more, thus fuelling a virtuous cycle that will lead to

sustainable profits in the long run. While this has been on the horizon for some time, I believe that all the necessary components have finally arrived to put together the data-driven digital bank of tomorrow. **The digitisation of conversations represents a fundamental inflection point for every bank.**

Banking today is personalised only for the high-net-worth customer through the likes of private banking. The relationship manager provides the personalisation, shielding the complexity of the bank from the client. This is costly since the processes are not necessarily automated, with smaller standalone private banks having cost-to-income ratios in the 90th percentile. If the three banking functions outlined above can now be digitised, the digital bank of tomorrow will enjoy **low cost-to-serve**. Coupled with the falling prices of smartphones to under US$50, more and more young professionals in countries all over the world can be served by a digital bank. These customers represent a large profit pool for tomorrow. It will drive more financial inclusion than ever before, thus allowing digital banks to rapidly scale whilst maintaining the ability to deliver a banking experience that is very different from the banking of yesterday.

Engagement should be measured on two core metrics. The first is the basic definition of who is an active customer. It is common in digital banking to define "active" as a channel metric, i.e., if you login to view your account on your digital banking channel, then you are considered to be active. To me, this isn't sufficient for a digital bank. Building off Chapter 2.2, this is a good point to illustrate the difference. The "active" measures for a digital bank need to be **based on transactions first, and not just activity.** Therefore, a stricter measure for activity should be adopted. Only if a TMRW customer transacted four or more times within a month did we consider that customer genuinely active (Warden, 2020).

This is a very important factor to note, as banking isn't even comparable to a freemium game where you try and don't have to buy, but you are so addicted you end up paying for the premium items like more powerful weapons, no time limit, no advertisements, etc. ("Making 'Freemium' Work", 2014). Banking is **"try for free"**, and banks don't charge you most of the time until you take up a loan product or forget to pay your credit card bill. Many deposit products, due to competition and the entry of new digital banks, no longer have fall-below charges or have very low fall-below balance thresholds.

The second metric is how engaged these active customers are. And you obviously can't engage customers who simply signed up for the "try me" offer and then became dormant. TMRW's engagement can be tracked and measured based on frequency of usage and actions taken by the customer as a result of the Smart Insights in the TMRW app (Warden, 2019a). See Figure 23 for an example of Smart Insights. These insights are generated from transactional data fed into Personetics.

Why is engagement important? I believe that given time, all the leading banks, both traditional and new, will be able to provide an extremely good transactional banking user experience. Working on engagement therefore becomes the way for progressive digital banks to compete over and above this. It answers the question of how banks can be invisible and visible at the same time.

What are the areas where a bank can choose to be visible in engaging their customers? Banks have traditionally been providing advice in larger-ticket financial transactions like home loan affordability, insurance and investments. And even then, such advice tends to be given to high-net-worth or high-net-revenue clients and clients who are managed through relationship management. **Transactional advice, on the other hand, isn't really provided by anyone, and definitely not to the mass market or even mass affluent segments**. Transactional advice revolves around the ins and outs of your account(s). Even though it's easy to do, most banks today still don't tell you how much your cash balance or investment balance has increased or decreased last month vs the month before.

A third area is personal financial management (PFM), in its new form as PFM 2.0, which focuses on **minimum upfront work and high real-time actionability**. TMRW by UOB pioneered introducing real-time expense tracking, where you can easily set an amount for a category of spend, and every time you spend in that category, TMRW will let you know how you are doing against your target. This proved to be a feature that most of the beta-users who road-tested it found beneficial and easy to use.[34] I don't think the industry is at the stage where any bank can prove that such engagement is as effective as a gain benefit[35] like a usage coupon or a usage promotion. But it offers one way to compete in an industry clearly headed for greater margin compression that doesn't involve continuously providing more and more benefits to customers. Such benefits are also very easy for competitors to copy and hence tend to reduce profits for the industry as a whole.

One additional method of engagement is a **breakthrough in the manner in which user interfaces (UI) can be designed**. In TMRW, we removed as many first-level menus as we could (Warden, 2019b). This was possible as the segment we started with, young professionals, have simple products. Since there is only one transactional account that can be used to pay bills, there wasn't a need to specify which account to pay from, hence reducing one step of the journey. When customers have multiple transactional accounts, this is no longer so straightforward, but I believe there is a significant breakthrough that is possible in user interface design where menus can be tailored to specific segments.

The current approach to UI, used by almost everyone today, usually involves many tedious steps. First, information needs to be gathered about where the

---

34. Real-time expense tracking has since been launched in Thailand (Efma, 2021).

35. Gain benefits don't solve any real customer problems. They simply provide them with more financial benefits.

experience is poor or broken. This could be feedback from customers, focus groups, analysing complaints going to the service centre, etc. Then a group of designers, product owners and customer experience staff will sift through the feedback and ideate a new user interface experience. Several options are usually created and then tested with customers to see which one generates the greatest appeal.

Software to log a user's interface experience already exists – Glassbox[36] and Tealeaf[37] are two such vendors. However, currently they are used mainly to trouble-shoot customer problems and understand where in the code the customer could have experienced a problem. I see a future where such data is used to **segment customers by the different ways they prefer to navigate and adjust the user interface to suit their navigation preferences**.

For example, a user may have problems finding a less-used setting, like checking the upper limit of their transfer amount. This would normally be housed within the settings function of an app. Analysis of the user navigation data would reveal the customer's struggle to find this feature, and at the next login, the user could be allocated a specific shortcut at the highest menu level, to access this function the next time it is required. Another example is where some users might want to see their balance before and after a payment is made. This could be surmised from their navigation patterns and data, and again specific provisions can be made to **show only these users this information**.

The options within a selection list are also an area of future differentiation. Currently the options are static. If you want to use a particular account for certain payees, you always have to scroll down to that payee. Again, navigation data allows us to detect this and present the option as the first in the list. This could be made even more intelligent by changing the order based on the time of the month and which account is being debited. These data-based interface design capabilities offer banks who are already at the forefront of frictionless user interface design a way out of the current plateau and onto a new S-curve of user interface development that can engage the customer by being **proactive about anticipating their needs**. No bank is the leader in this arena today. I believe it to be an arena where progressive banks can dominate and distance themselves from the competition.

Through all this, data is the main ingredient that any company will need to leverage in order to engage their customers. It's no different for banks. With this realisation, a flywheel business model (Collins, 2020) that was dubbed ATGIE, an acronym for Acquire, Transact, Generate data and Insights, and Engage, was created. ATGIE outlines the different steps in the engagement-focused business model and will be discussed in detail in Chapter 3.5.

---

36. Glassbox is an Israeli software company. It sells session-replay analytics software and services.
37. Tealeaf is an analytics solution for web and mobile applications owned by Acoustic.

Key takeaways

- Actions to remove friction in the user experience will only further commoditise banking, leading to further erosion of profits as banking becomes more and more of a utility.

- The key is engagement through many digital micro-conversations that can help customers by nudging them towards better financial habits and serving their needs to a level not yet achieved by conventional banking.

- Generating more data through transactions can fuel the insights engines of progressive banks so that they can generate more conversations to deeply engage with their customers.

- Engaged customers will buy more products from these banks and transact more, thus fuelling a virtuous cycle that leads to sustainable profits in the long run.

- Banks have traditionally been providing advice in larger-ticket financial transactions like home loan affordability, insurance and investments.

- Transactional advice isn't really provided by anyone, and definitely not to the mass market or even mass affluent segments. Transactional advice revolves around the ins and outs of your account(s).

- Most banks today still don't tell you how much your cash balance or investment balance has changed vs the month before.

- PFM 2.0 will focus on minimum upfront work and high real-time actionability.

- One additional method of engagement is a breakthrough in the manner in which user interfaces are designed.

- In the future, by analysing customer logs to understand where the user is having problems in navigation, digital banks can segment customers by the different ways they prefer to navigate and adjust the user interface accordingly.

What should legacy banks do?

When I speak to legacy bank executives, the inevitable question that is asked at the end of the conversation is "What should we do?" Or a remark such as "The board needs to debate how it would like to respond." The decision is not obvious to them because they perceive that the threat is not immediate, and that the majority of digital banks are not making a profit. As I spoke to more and more incumbent banks, this question kept coming up.

An industry transformation is clearly in the works. Throughout Chapter 2, I have introduced several important clues as to the changes that lie ahead. The first is the change in the way banks compete, **from 6Ps to only 1P: Process**. I offer evidence that this change will be of a large magnitude because process is now done in the bottom one-third of incumbent players. Without strong abilities in process and attention to detail, banks will not be able to compete and create the frictionless and intuitive experience in onboarding, approval of credit, transactional banking and service required as a basis to compete. These capabilities power the "invisible" part of banking, which is going to get dramatically better amongst the leaders, leaving the incumbents who don't catch up behind.

The second shift is in the **use of data** to engage customers. Data-centric digital banks will leverage this capability to serve customers better, have conversations with them, and help them manage their personal finances better, in real time. Data will also be pivotal to extending credit to many retail and SME customers in Southeast Asia who are denied credit today because the data doesn't exist to risk-rank customers and discern who is able to repay and who isn't. As there is a steep learning curve required to do this well, banks that don't start to experiment with supplementing their data with external sources to provide ever richer interactions with customers are likely to fall behind. These capabilities power the "visible" part of banking and will become the battleground of the future.

Thirdly, I introduce evidence of a long-term shift in banking from a vertically integrated construct to one that is **horizontally configured**, similar to the shift that happened in computing, but lacking the degree of standardisation that allowed the new horizontal players in computing to overtake the incumbents in a period spanning 10 years. If standards were to accelerate, both in open banking as well as in methods and procedures that allow horizontal players to effectively perform banking functions such as customer due diligence with the same scrutiny as banks but at lower costs aided by new technologies, then this shift is likely to accelerate.

Fourth, I offer evidence that new digital banks leveraging customer intimacy and cloud technologies are achieving **NPS® scores that are 3x higher and costs that are 8x lower** than incumbents. And I believe this to be just the starting point, which means the gaps will get larger and not smaller. These capabilities allow the challenger banks to serve segments that legacy banks have traditionally shunned, like the underbanked rural retail and micro and small SME segments in many countries of Southeast Asia.

Fifth, the **culture** and ways of working of incumbent banks are very likely to resist and prevent the necessary changes required to be sufficiently customer-centric to compete with smaller and more nimble competitors entering the banking scene today. We examined the complex reasons why seemingly simple things aren't easy to change if they revolve around organisational and cultural changes.

We also examined the profitability of current challenger and neo-banks and found them wanting, with the exception of a few who have good genes imparted by their parents and thus had the ability through association to quickly scale at low costs. Webank, MYbank and Kakao Bank leveraged their DNA well and have grown profitable quickly, but their market shares are still tiny, and so there are a lot more lunches for them to eat in the future. If you remove these outliers (which also include Tinkoff), **the majority of the remaining digital banks are not profitable yet**. This majority can be classified into two groups. In one category are those who have built the capabilities to lend from inception and are focused on the high-quality acquisition of customers and the aggressive lowering of cost of acquisition and cost of operations and service. These banks like Starling are likely to reach profitability sooner than the other category of banks, namely those who have gone for large acquisition numbers and are not obsessed with profitability. We examine this in greater detail in Chapter 4.3 "The path to profit".

Next, we framed the disruption within banking by leveraging the powerful lens of **disruption theory**. In industries with a technological core like banking, incumbents have succumbed to disruptive attacks from new entrants that first served their least-valued and lowest-margin customers and products. Over time, as the technological core gets better, the incumbents find themselves ceding more and more, until there is nothing left to give. Few companies attacked by disruptive innovators have lived to thrive another day.

I think the evidence presented is too strong for anyone not to conclude that the winds of change are here, and it is a question of when, not if, these changes will cause large shifts in the market shares and viability of existing legacy banks. But the question still remains, what should incumbent banks do?

Figure 21 attempts to answer this question. On the vertical axis is the current operating cost per customer; "lower" and "higher" mean lower or higher than competitors in the industry. On the horizontal axis is the current NPS®, serving as

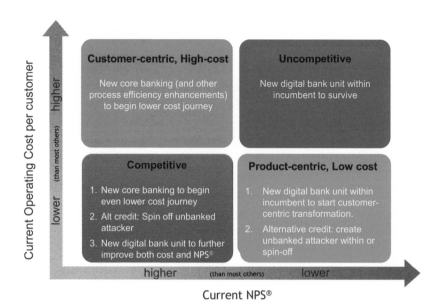

Figure 21 – What should legacy banks do?

a proxy for the current quality of customer experience. This matrix splits current legacy banks into four quadrants: competitive (low operating cost per customer, high current NPS®); uncompetitive (high operating cost per customer, low current NPS®); customer-centric but high cost; and product-centric but low cost. Incumbent banks who are not sure what to do should first determine independently where they are in this matrix.

Banks that are **competitive** have the widest set of options. They can choose to lower their costs further by focusing on a fourth-generation core banking platform and start the journey to radically simplify their products, services and processes. They have the additional option of being able to spin-off a separate unit that will gain the alternative credit capabilities (alone or in partnership) to attack the bottom-of-the-pyramid opportunity in the unbanked or underbanked (which would include young professionals and young professional families that should receive better service and experience but are currently treated as mass market customers). This unit is best set up separately to gain access to the data and ecosystems needed to rapidly grow the unbanked and underbanked. Or they can set up a new digital bank unit within the incumbent to further their improvements in both cost and NPS®. This is done within the incumbent to facilitate the easy transfer of knowledge and experience.

Banks that are **uncompetitive** currently have few choices. They should form a new digital bank unit within the incumbent reporting to the CEO, and gradually move more and more units across to the new unit, until the child becomes the parent in the future. These banks don't have any other options as they are uncompetitive currently.

Banks that are **customer-centric but whose costs are too high** have the option of designing a new core banking platform, together with process optimisation across the entire bank to improve efficiencies and gradually transferring more and more existing products over to the new platform, after rationalisation (it would not make sense to do so without rationalising and simplifying the legacy product structures). With a higher cost structure and customer-centric focus, these banks have a DNA that is different from that required to defend or launch a disruptive attack from the bottom until they move into the competitive quadrant.

Finally, the incumbents that are **product-centric but low-cost** can chose to go customer-centric, shift to the left, and leverage a new internal digital bank unit to make this transformation happen. Or, given their low-cost structure and product expertise, they have the DNA to launch a disruptive innovation to serve the unbanked if they acquire the alternative credit capabilities and ecosystem partnerships. This attack needs less customer-centricity as compared to stealing a customer from a bank with high NPS® and can be set up within the incumbent or spun-off.

Key takeaways

- An industry transformation is clearly in the works, fuelled by:

    - change in the way banks compete, from 6Ps to only 1P: Process.

    - use of data to engage customers.

    - long-term shift in banking from a vertically integrated construct to one that is horizontally configured.

    - new digital banks leveraging customer intimacy and cloud technologies who are achieving NPS® scores that are 3x higher and costs that are 8x lower than incumbents.

    - the culture of incumbent banks being very likely to resist and prevent the changes required to be sufficiently customer-centric to compete.

- If you remove the outliers (Webank, MYbank, Kakao Bank, Tinkoff), the majority of digital banks are not profitable yet.

- In industries with a technological core like banking, incumbents have succumbed to disruptive attacks from new entrants that first served their least-valued and lowest-margin customers and products.

- Few companies attacked by disruptive innovators have lived to thrive another day.

- The evidence presented is too strong for anyone not to conclude that the winds of change are here, and it is a question of when, not if.

- Banks that are competitive have the widest set of options.

- Banks that are uncompetitive currently should form a new digital bank unit within the incumbent reporting to the CEO.

- Banks that are customer-centric, but whose costs are too high, have the option of creating a new core banking platform. This enables them to port more and more existing products over after rationalisation.

- Incumbents that are product-centric but low-cost can chose to go customer-centric by building a new internal digital bank with such a charter. By acquiring capabilities in alternative credit underwriting and ecosystem partnerships, such banks can also choose to serve the unbanked. This needs less customer-centricity compared to stealing customers from a bank with high NPS® and can be set up within the incumbent or spun-off.

CHAPTER 3

First, get the basics right

This chapter serves to correct common myths. These myths aren't just in the minds of people outside financial services. They are often also **believed by experienced bankers**. What's required to build a digital bank is an obsession with customer experience, the need to identify the required changes in the business model, and the ability to design great processes and automate them so that they are faster, more modular, more scalable, and seldom fail. To do this requires breadth, and few banks have ensured that their staff are sufficiently broad-based to operate in this new dynamic. Therefore, even before we can begin to talk about how to build a digital bank, we must get the basics of digital transformation right. With the exception of Chapters 3.4 and 3.8, which are banking-specific, the content in Chapter 3 is applicable to companies in any industry undergoing such challenges.

We first look at the role of technology in Chapter 3.1 "Is building a digital bank just about technology?". Consumer banking isn't a deep tech space. Most of what you do in banking tech isn't patentable. Banks generally aren't in a position to manufacture or productise their software; they are integrators of software solutions. Just like a builder is an integrator of building solutions. If you were commissioned to build the best and most liveable building in town, you wouldn't appoint the builder first. So, saying that digital is all about tech, or that building a digital bank is all about getting the right tech person, is obviously wrong. You do need a good tech person, but this person won't be able to excel without a great designer of products, services and a new bank business model.

You also need a superb process team – otherwise, if the process is broken, there is nothing tech can do. Thus, the role of the design head, the process head and the tech head are all equally important. Too much emphasis has been placed on just the tech head. As expounded in Chapter 4.1 "Designing it right", the responsibility for setting up the concept-to-code software factory is not the tech head's alone. It must be the **joint responsibility of the design head, process head and tech head**. This is where, as head of the digital transformation or CEO, you need to step in and get these functions to work together. Once the software factory is created and running smoothly, your tech head can put his focus on lowering the cost of tech ownership, maintenance and upgrades – which is where the real costs lie – and to build a solution that is highly modular, scalable and able to have high uptime.

The role of design is equally misunderstood. Yes, in designing a building, you will need the interior designers and you will need to match the interior colour scheme with the furniture and finishes. But the role of the architect in design is almost paramount. This role is about designing the bank business model, and the products and services that come with it. So, design is more than just design thinking. It's about the **entire design and architecture of the bank**, using the new techniques found in Chapter 4.1 and Chapter 5 "The allDigitalfuture Playbook™". This is a skill that combines business management, strategy and design. My recommendation is that if the top executive is not well-versed in all these areas, then a committee of the lead accountable executive, chief design officer, chief process officer and chief technology officer should be formed to oversee it. You must get this right before you start to build. It is pivotal to your success.

Is building a digital bank just about technology?

If you were commissioned to build a new building that would be the talk of the town, you would not appoint the builder first. You would start by looking for the right architect – one who can design both a great exterior as well as an extremely habitable interior. The architect would base his design on your client's preferences, tastes, use of space, colour preferences, etc.

In the same way, building a digital bank is firstly about design – finding the right designers who can build a bank that delivers a superior experience, supported by processes that are fast and with few or no errors, and at very low cost. **The architect is the equivalent of your head of design; the civil engineer is your head of process; and the builder is your head of technology.** In terms of importance, I would put design and process first, followed closely by technology. Yet, today, technology always tends to get the most attention.

If you think about tech in banking in its simplest terms, it is a largely an engine for keeping track of the ins and outs of your accounts and their impact on your balances, with no room for error, and with the strictest rules for privacy. Banks are users of software; they are rarely producers of software. If they were, that software would likely have a captive customer of only one. Hence, most banks except the largest global banks have traditionally used software vendors to provide solutions. These solutions are now also called B2B Fintech, and the software is increasingly not being purchased but rented and run on a Software as a Service (SaaS) model.

As a dominant software player has never emerged in banking, banks' backend systems tend to be a **spaghetti of software solutions**, each potentially from a different best-of-breed vendor, meaning that there could be a different solution for transactional accounts, credit cards, personal loans, mortgage loans, wealth management, insurance, credit management, CRM[38], customer identification, customer due diligence, financial management, etc. The integration, management, obsolescence, maintenance and enhancement of these systems – as many as 50 to 100 systems – is a **major cost and speed issue** in most major banks.

In addition, as traditional transactional products get commoditised, what has driven differentiation in banking has been concentrated on giving the customer

---

more "gains" or benefits, rather than resolving pain points, as many of the obvious pain points have been addressed. Traditional banks have also targeted more specific segments, like women, business travellers, young professionals, the silver generation (those over 50 years of age), etc. As they targeted more specific segments and introduced more benefits, banks kept an eye on profitability by putting in more exclusions and conditions. Often the big headline rate would only be applicable if all conditions were met. This approach has resulted in a massive increase in products and customisation.

This has a **domino effect on the complexity of the backend system**, and in turn on the difficulty of upgrading the software to the latest version, as all prior enhancements may need to be redeveloped and tested for them to work. Testing also becomes an issue as the logic embedded in the backend systems becomes increasingly complex. Older core banking platforms don't segregate code by layering, so the code is monolithic, requiring complete re-testing every time a change is made. When you put these factors together with an omni-channel servicing approach, the complexity quickly multiplies. All this is typically run in-house within the bank, with a high dependence on external software providers. Add in a bent towards risk mitigation, and you can see why the costs are escalating and the work queue is getting longer.

Apart from not being saddled with this legacy, the new-born banks will also have a distinct advantage in their ability to **leverage the cloud**. I believe that in the next 5 years, not only will the cloud become a reliable platform to host bank backend solutions, but the leading core banking software providers will also adopt industry standard APIs[39] that will make core banking connectivity to customer-facing systems not just easier, but swappable. This will bring about lower costs of implementation, scalability, redundancy, security, etc., thus reducing capital expenditure on IT and creating a smaller annual fixed cost IT footprint. The incumbents won't be able to match this if they are not setting up similar pilots and programmes within their own banks.

In addition, the shift to **experience-based competition** should also reduce the need for digital banks to go down the route that leads to an explosion of products which plagues the legacy banks. This together with the superior configurability of newer and more advanced core banking solutions will mean less coding, which translates to easier enhancement and testing.

So, there are many areas where technology can play a role in the development of digital banks. However, for this technology capability to be deployed successfully, **great design and great process abilities are paramount**. If you don't have these

---

39. Application Programming Interface defines the kinds of calls or requests that can be made, how to make them, the data formats that should be used, the conventions to follow, etc. Through information hiding, APIs enable modular programming, allowing users to use the interface independently of the implementation.

two abilities, no tech can save you, no matter which tech wizards you hire. Just like the best builder won't be able to compensate for a less capable architect and civil engineer.

What about the development of the end-user application? My learning from building TMRW is that if you spend the time to set up your **software factory** (see Figure 73), the development will be much smoother, and you will make fewer mistakes. More than just a team of programmers, what you need is a clear strategy that drives how you design the navigation and content so that the user experience is extremely friendly and easy-to-use. Paying close attention to how you implement the processes that encourage the production of efficient yet maintainable code and leverage a common library of routines based on your overall design system, will also be pivotal to success.

When you combine a well-designed bank with the latest core banking technology (Chapter 3.8) and make the right design choices, you should achieve a cost advantage that significantly reduces your marginal cost, as your total operating costs become more efficient, even if you are a legacy bank. Figure 22 showcases this advantage and indicates **a cost base that is 60–70% lower**.

While this is a higher figure than the US$25 shown in Figure 13 for digital banks, it is nevertheless a significant reduction for incumbent mid-tier banks. This will allow such mid-tier banks to establish initial beachheads where the competition is not keen to penetrate because of their higher cost structures, e.g., young professionals, young professional families, the under-served and even the unbanked.

Technology can help you realise the full potential of a digital bank with a modern core platform and a customer experience that is world-class. It just must be done in tandem with design and process and not on its own. Technology is obviously important; it's just not *more* important than design and process. Good technology can also lead to better design and a better ability to evolve the initial design when changes happen. So, better technology can also influence design, just as design will naturally influence the technology choice. Thus, having business designers that know technology and technology designers that know business is one of the factors that differentiate the transformation programmes that succeed from those that don't.

Lastly, technology has a big impact on the operating cost per customer. One way to go about reshaping your cost structure is to set up a digital bank within the incumbent, and to learn by doing. This mitigates the risk of porting the entire bank to a new cloud solution. These learnings can then be gradually transferred to the mothership, as was the case with TMRW.

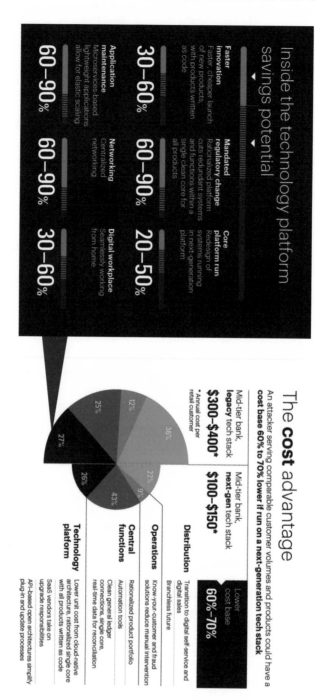

Figure 22 – Cost advantage of next-gen banks vs legacy banks
(Source: Bain)

Key takeaways

- The architect is the equivalent of your head of design; the civil engineer your head of process; and the builder your head of technology.

- Banks are users of software; they are rarely producers of software. If they were, that software would likely have a captive customer of only one.

- As a dominant software player never emerged in banking, banks' backend systems tend to be a spaghetti of software solutions, each potentially from a different best-of-breed vendor.

- The integration, management, obsolescence, maintenance and enhancement of these systems – as many as 50 to 100 systems – is a major cost and speed issue in most major banks.

- Product complexity has a domino effect on the complexity of the backend system, and in turn on the difficulty of upgrading the software to the latest version.

- Apart from not being saddled with this legacy, the new-born banks will also have a distinct advantage in their ability to leverage the cloud.

- In the next 5 years, the cloud will become a reliable platform to host backend solutions, and bank core banking software and providers will also adopt industry standard APIs that will make core banking connectivity to customer-facing systems easier.

- Experience-based competition should also reduce the need for digital banks to go down the route that leads to an explosion of products.

- However, for this technology capability to be deployed successfully, great design and great process skills are paramount.

- If you spend the time to set up your software factory properly, the development will be much smoother, and you will make fewer mistakes.

- The cost advantage of next-gen vs legacy bank showcases a cost base that is 60–70% lower, enabling initial beachheads where the incumbents are not keen to penetrate because of higher costs.

What's the role of design in an experience business?

It's hard to be customer-centric. Most people pay lip-service to it because it's much easier to say that you are customer-centric than to really be customer-centric. Design – or more specifically, a part of design called design thinking – is instrumental in cultivating a human-centred or customer-centric approach to problem-solving and ideation. This is important because in the technology, there is inherently too much focus on the idea or the solution and thus you always run the risk that nobody wants to pay for the solution you are offering. Human-centred design is an approach that avoids those costly mistakes.

Design can also be seen as part of a larger "software factory" (more accurately "software integration factory" as banks more often integrate solutions rather than create software from scratch). Here, design is part of a triumvirate of design approach, journey and data mapping, and Agile and waterfall software development (see Figure 73). These three components, properly put together, can be a **powerful software production/integration engine** for the new digital banks.

Design is vital in an experience business because most experience businesses don't rely on a large technological breakthrough as their key differentiator. Instead, they rely on great attention to detail to fix any number of small issues that create friction in the user experience, where none of the issues are serious enough to warrant an immediate change of provider. Consider the case of the bicycle for contrast. When the first "safety bicycle" was invented in 1885, it didn't include brakes – something we consider an essential feature of a standard bicycle today (Andrews, 2018). But because the functional benefit of the new invention was so great, the minimum viable proposition (MVP) approach applied.

However, as the degree of functional benefit reduces, **the focus changes from innovation to experience.** This isn't to say that there isn't any innovation involved. It's simply that the innovations each have smaller impact and must be taken together for the overall experience to be much better than before, and in doing so have a large impact on the customer.

Most banks are not organised for design. Many end up with a solution looking for a problem (more on this in Chapter 3.3). To avoid this, you need to know what are the problems faced by the customer when doing what he needs to do, often called the **jobs to be done** (Christensen et al., 2016). The first step is to be very clear about the segment being served, as different segments have different jobs to be done. If you ignore these differences and assume that all segments are alike, this will affect the take-up later on. The next step is to understand the problems in detail. Here, the greatest hindrance tends to be financial objectives, as the more oriented you are towards meeting the objectives, the more likely you are to be product-centric rather than customer-centric. In the end, you must come up with some insight that is new, that gives you some perspective that you didn't know before.

As an example, as we were Singaporeans building the TMRW digital bank in Thailand, we were less familiar with the problems faced by the Thai young professionals (YP) and young professional families (YPF). This was a blessing in disguise, as it **forced us to understand the customer better** than if we started a digital bank in Singapore. More than two dozen YPs and YPFs were selected per country for ethnographic research to start us off, and my team visited them wherever they were comfortable talking to us, which varied from the rented 1-bedroom apartment of a PC gamer in central Bangkok to the old Sampoerna office of a YP in Jakarta. One respondent was so comfortable with such visits he would show off his guitar-playing skills and collection of anime figurines. These **in-depth immersions** into the lives of these customers helped us understand how we could create something truly customer-centric.

YP and YPF customers often go to great lengths to bypass troublesome banking fees, such as opening bank accounts in three local banks to avoid interbank transfer fees or withdrawing from one bank's ATM and depositing the same amount in another bank's cash deposit machine just next door to achieve the same. The concept of savings is very different for millennial customers. Often, the act of saving, not the actual amount saved, is enough to make them believe they are in control of their finances. The insights gathered led to the creation of a **savings game** targeted at YP and YPF customers – "The City of TMRW" – as well as a rethink of transaction fees in TMRW.

These nuances, in addition to what we already knew about millennials (internet-savvy, mobile-first, chat-oriented), served as the input for the design of the banking product for TMRW. It also provided a framework for rethinking how TMRW could make banking simpler, more engaging and more transparent for this target segment. The role of the design function was to ensure that the TMRW team remained customer- and not product-focused.

Once the segment, jobs to be done and problems encountered are clear, the team should draft the initial **customer value proposition (CVP)**. The CVP states the new value you will bring about so that your customers will experience a proposition different from and superior to anything that exists today. Once this is on paper, the initiative then enters its next phase, where there is an iterative process between understanding how well the competition has already solved the problems identified, and synchronising this with the size and importance of the problems to the customer and the ability to centre the value proposition around the solution to these problems. All of this is packaged in a way that their elimination creates a superior experience for the customer.

The role of design is also pivotal in the user interface. This is often misunderstood as a screen generation exercise, with a team of people discussing their likes and dislikes about the various screen prototypes. Rather, it is a sophisticated process of designing the strategic navigation and user experience of the app to ensure a high degree of friction-removal. The lesson I learnt building TMRW is that **strategic navigation design must be done first**.

In hindsight, this developed as a result of a goal I had: **to develop an app with no menus**. Just like how too many buttons get in the way of using any consumer electronics device, menus are points of friction in a user interface. The insight here was that menus are really a company's way to force you to navigate the way they want you to, rather than the way you actually want to. The strategic navigational design thus started with having as few first-order level menus as possible. Realistically, a completely menu-less interface would be near-impossible to achieve, but this ideal served as a guiding light for the overall design (Figure 23), differentiating it from other banking apps.

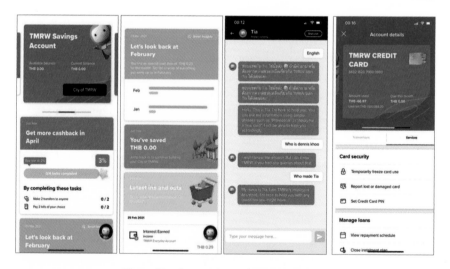

Figure 23 – Screenshots of TMRW Thailand

After this step, it is essential to begin the work of formulating the design system. This consists of setting up a **centralised library** of all the major navigation functions that you plan to incorporate in the strategic navigation design. Avoid having each designer and programmer write their own navigation function, which results in a chaotic situation where a global change cannot be effected later to correct an error in any function. You don't want to learn this the hard way and have to replace each navigation function one by one later on in the development process. Similar to my building analogy, after the building is up, it's very hard to move the plumbing around.

The big advice here is, **if the design isn't good enough to produce the experience breakthrough you need, don't do a public launch**. I would recommend you launch to a small group of customers first and stay in beta to keep improving your experience until your NPS® hits the target you have set. In designing TMRW, we spent close to 10 months getting the big-picture design right, and then many more months finessing the details. If we learnt one thing that can most impact you, it's this: there's no Minimum Viable Product (MVP) in building a digital bank unless the standards of digital banking in your country are low to non-existent. Replace the letters MVP with NPS and focus on launching with a minimum NPS® instead.

Key takeaways

- Design is vital in an experience business because most experience businesses don't rely on a large technological breakthrough as their key differentiator.

- These businesses rely on great attention to detail to fix any number of small issues that create friction in the user experience, where none of the issues are serious enough to warrant an immediate change of provider.

- The first step in your design journey is to be very clear about the segment being served, as different segments have different jobs to be done.

- There must be some insight that is new, that gives you some perspective that you didn't know before.

- The role of the design function was to ensure that the TMRW team remained customer- and not product-focused.

- Designing the user interface is a sophisticated process of designing the strategic navigation and user experience of the app to ensure a high degree of friction-removal.

- Menus are really a company's way to force you to navigate the way they want you to, rather than the way you actually want to.

- If the design isn't good enough to produce the experience breakthrough you need, don't launch.

Start with the solution or the problem?

This short chapter is all about the need to "fall in love with the problem and not the solution". Some senior executives in your company probably attended a briefing and came back saying, "We have to implement AI." That's a classic case of solution before problem. Many failures in digital transformation stem from not truly understanding the customer problem and starting with the solution instead of the problem.

Technology companies tend to operate this way because they are invention-oriented. They take a new invention, perfect it and then try and find a use case that is so large and compelling that it will justify the rationale to invest in the invention in the first place. When the transistor was first invented, no one realised it would eventually be the invention that would create the microprocessor. In fact, one of the first commercial applications was the transistor radio. This approach works in fields where pivoting to find the killer use case is a battle of survival of the fittest and thus many tech start-ups don't make it. It doesn't work well at all when it is used in a regular business whose purpose is not invention but usage of the invention to solve everyday business problems.

There are two general ways to transform a business. You can **start with an idea**, make the idea work and then see what problem it solves. For instance, 3M sticky notes were a glue invention gone wrong until the researchers applied their solution to a problem where very sticky glue was a problem rather than a solution. The other way is to **start with the problem** at hand, e.g., how to re-use a note on a piece of paper through its ability to stay sticky enough to hold up the note but not so sticky that it causes damage to the surface it's pasted on.

Each method has its own approach, and constraints. Starting with problems facilitates an understanding of the customer in his own environment and what might help to solve the problems they encounter in the jobs they have to do in their life or work. But it also potentially introduces constraints and bias as a result of understanding the issues in detail. Starting with ideas, on the other hand, can free you from these constraints but you may not be clear if it really solves the critical problems the customers have.

Criteria	Start with the Problem	Start with the Solution
Starts With	With an issue, e.g. why don't people invest more?	With an idea, e.g. let's make everyone invest online
Characteristic	It's a real problem perhaps with no solution yet	It's potentially new solution perhaps with no problem yet
Unknown	Do enough people have this problem?	Do enough people need this solution?
Limitation	Could lead to over empathising with the customer, and getting boxed in or incremental improvement	Could lead to exponential breakthrough but also the risk that the solution doesn't solve a problem anyone will pay for

Figure 24 – Start with the problem vs start with the solution

Figure 24 illustrates the difference between the two approaches. The two are not necessarily mutually exclusive, and can be used in combination. For example, you could start by understanding the problem, then use the solution approach to derive a better solution to the problem.

In industries that need a lot of depth, science and maths to derive a solution, it's harder for people without these insights and expertise to partake in the solution. That's not the case in consumer banking and other retail businesses, where almost everyone is a customer, and everyone experiences problems, which they think everyone else might have. The key is not with the idea, as it takes many ideas to get just one working innovation. It's whether a large enough number of people feel that the idea when launched creates sufficient value to a problem that makes it worthwhile to pay for it, or switch provider.

Given that the raw science of the banking industry doesn't move especially fast compared to industries where scientific advancements are throwing out many new solutions (e.g., in miniaturisation and Moore's Law, which allows more and more electronics to be packed in a smaller and smaller form factor, or in biotechnology, where rapid understanding of the genome is unlocking genetic secrets to address all manner of diseases), there is even more reason why one should **start with the problem, and ascertain that the problem is big enough to be worthy of the customer paying or switching**. The rationale for this is that if the raw science isn't moving very fast, then the probability that the technological progress will deliver a breakthrough solution of 5x or more is low. Thus, the focus on problems and gathering enough problems to make the experience great is likely to have a higher probability of occurrence.

Key takeaways

- You can start with an idea, make the idea work and then see what problem it solves.

- Or start with the problem at hand and figure out how to solve it.

- Technology companies take a new invention, perfect it and then try and find a use case that is so large and compelling that it will justify the rationale to invest in the invention in the first place.

- This approach doesn't work well at all when used in a regular business whose purpose is not invention but solving everyday business problems in the most effective and efficient way.

- Starting with problems facilitates an understanding of the customer in his own environment.

- But it also potentially introduces constraints and bias as a result of understanding the issues in detail.

- Starting with ideas, on the other hand, can free you from these constraints, but you may not be clear if it really solves the critical problems the customers have.

- In industries that need a lot of depth, science and maths to derive a solution, it's harder for people without these insights and expertise to partake in the solution.

- The key is whether a large enough number of people feel that the idea when launched creates sufficient value to a problem that makes it worthwhile to pay for it, or switch provider.

SME vs consumer banking as beachhead segments?

This is an interesting question. If you eliminate serving larger companies due to the capital requirements and risk of a single borrower bringing down a bank when it is still small and not as well-capitalised, the real decision in setting up a digital bank is between serving small firms or consumers. While we would need to go country-specific to understand the obstacles in serving these segments, I would generalise that **business banking for small firms still has a lot of room for pain removal** whereas consumer banking has less room. The profit dynamics of serving small firms would also be better as the loan quantum tends to be larger. The downside, of course, is that bad debt would also tend to be higher.

The large proportion of retail customers are salaried rather than self-employed, and thus unless an economic shock that drives significant unemployment uptick happens (e.g., Covid-19 and unemployment in the travel, hospitality and retail sectors), banks have already built into their debt servicing ratios a higher interest rate as a buffer to more realistically factor an individual's ability to repay at higher levels of interest. Small firms, however, may have higher variability and fluctuation in their income generation ability, introducing greater uncertainty in their ability to repay. To mitigate against this, banks generally ask to see their bank balances over a 6-month period to ascertain cash-at-hand and use this as a **proxy to compute the debt servicing**. However, vital data missing in this calculation is what other loans the SME has taken, a service generally provided by business credit bureaus.

The SME credit bureau landscape is generally underdeveloped in Southeast Asia. A report by the Asian Development Bank Institute found that "in the bank-dominated financial systems in Asia, SMEs have difficulty accessing cheap finance" (Yoshino & Taghizadeh-Hesary, 2018). Two examples of a nationwide SME credit bureau, in Japan and Thailand, were highlighted, but the report concluded that "other parts of Asia lack such systems to accumulate and analyse credit risk data and to measure each SME's credit risk accurately". Hence, most banks are still assessing credit based on bank statements and collateral, and **SMEs who can't show such assets are not receiving the working capital loans** that are vital to their survival and growth. According to a Bain & Company report, SMEs remain a largely underbanked segment in most markets. Approximately 80% of surveyed SMEs say they need to borrow but lack access to affordable credit (Bain & Co, Google, and Temasek, 2019).

It doesn't look like the SME credit bureau situation will get significantly better any time soon, and thus some of the most progressive banks are turning their attention to **accounting systems** to obtain the crucial data needed to underwrite an SME customer. An example is Mettle by NatWest, which announced in 2020 that it was giving all its customers free access to FreeAgent's cloud-based accounting software (Hinchliffe, 2020). UK digital banks like Starling, Tide and Mettle all support connectivity to SaaS-based accounting software Xero and FreeAgent. Starling and Mettle also support QuickBooks, while Tide supports Sage. Native connectivity between accounting systems and digital business banking will become a standard in a couple of years.

What's key is the use of the accounting information for underwriting. Balance in the bank, which is the most common evaluation method today, isn't a good predictor of an SME's ability to repay the working capital loan. It's what I would call third-order data, in the sense that the predictability gets better as you move from third-order (bank balance) to second-order (monthly profit) to first-order (accounts receivable AR vs accounts payable AP). These second- and first-order data are found in the accounting systems of most companies.

One of the concerns about using accounting data for underwriting is the ability to **discern legitimate entries from fraudulent ones**. I had the opportunity to speak to a senior executive in a UK bank who was heavily involved in the design and development of a digital SME bank serving micro and small SMEs. His view was that they have not encountered major issues with fictitious entries. The jury is probably still out on this topic, and to avoid moral hazard problems, routines that can ascertain the authenticity of the transactions via comparisons against time, day and person making the entry, etc., can and should be implemented.

Right now, there are more banks using SaaS accounting software connectivity for lead generation than credit underwriting. That's the next stage for any progressive digital SME bank. This will represent a significant breakthrough in the ability to extend lending to businesses that don't generate the cash flow to show sufficient bank balances, but it also represents a significant breakthrough for the industry at large, as banks will now be able to **dynamically flex their working capital limits based on AR and AP movements**. Frequent adjustment of limits isn't something that happens today, and the ability to do it automatically based on a firm's business velocity will allow savings in capital (as capital needs to be put against undrawn limits), and also create a means to reduce limits as business slows, so that funds set aside for working capital cannot be used for other purposes, which is the case now as the loop isn't closed. In fact, this development isn't limited to SMEs. It's applicable to all businesses, and my prediction is that such a development will happen and transform the way banks lend to businesses globally.

SME digital banks can also help small businesses become **more efficient in**

their operations. Operational efficiency is an issue with small firms, whereas it is generally a non-issue with retail customers. One contribution to operational inefficiency is the delay between the outlay of expenses to order or build the product or solution required and the time they receive the payment from their customer. Late invoicing, late payments, long credit terms all contribute to lengthening this timing mismatch, and the gap needs to be funded with working capital loans. Integrating the digital banks' payments capabilities with the accounting system can eliminate the need for double entries in both the accounting and digital bank platforms. In addition, reconciliation can be much reduced, by automatically assigning all invoices a unique sub-account number, so that the system can tell who has paid and who hasn't, without reconciliation. Late payers can also be automatically sent collection notices and reminders. Other capabilities include sending invoices where payers have the ability to click on the invoice to pay. These are all opportunities for SME digital banks to remove pain points for small businesses.

A final reason to build a digital bank to serve the micro, small and medium SMEs (MSMEs) is that in many countries where the consumer digital banking is already of a relatively high standard, the **SME digital banking often lags behind significantly**. Banks have tended to prioritise consumer and corporate banking for their digital transformation initiatives. After the substantial investments in these segments, what's left is usually a lack of further appetite to invest in MSME digital banking. Almost all of the territory we have explored so far is similarly applicable, e.g., the same opportunity to attack from the bottom using disruptive innovation, the focus on creating a data-enabled digital bank to help MSMEs with their business financial management, significantly improving the banking experience, lowering operating costs so that you can target the MSME, etc.

So, in conclusion, let's answer the question we started with at the beginning of this chapter – if you had to pick between SME and consumer, what would you pick? I would choose SME in a smaller market like Singapore, where the consumer banking pool size is limited and well-penetrated. This doesn't mean that a consumer digital bank can't make a significant impact on experience, advocacy and data-driven engagement – it just means it's hard to be profitable in a small market. In a larger market, I would say, why choose? If you had the resources, do both. But if in that larger market, consumer banking already has a lot of entrenched digital bank competitors, then launching an SME bank might prove to be more viable.

Key takeaways

- Business banking for small firms still has a lot of room for pain removal whereas consumer banking has less room.

- The profit dynamics of serving small firms would be better as the loan quantum tends to be larger, but the bad debt would also be higher.

- A 2018 Asian Development Bank Institute report concluded that Asia lacks systems to accumulate and analyse credit risk data and to measure each SME's credit risk accurately.

- Most banks are still assessing credit based on bank statements and collateral, and SMEs who can't show such assets are not receiving the working capital loans that are vital to their survival and growth.

- A Bain & Company report concluded that SMEs remain a largely underbanked segment in most markets. Approximately 80% of surveyed SMEs say they need to borrow but lack access to affordable credit.

- Progressive banks are turning their attention to accounting systems to obtain the crucial data needed to underwrite an SME customer.

- One of the concerns about using accounting data for underwriting is the ability to discern legitimate entries from fraudulent ones.

- Integration with SaaS accounting software provides progressive digital SME banks with a significant breakthrough in the ability to extend lending to businesses that don't generate the cash flow to show sufficient balances in their bank accounts.

- It would also power the ability to dynamically flex working capital limits based on AR and AP movements, a significant breakthrough for the banking industry at large.

- SME digital banks can help small businesses to become more efficient in their operations.

- Integrating digital banks' payments capabilities with SaaS accounting systems can eliminate the need for double entries in both the accounting and digital bank platforms.

- Reconciliation can be much reduced, by automatically assigning all invoices a unique sub-account number.

Data and its role in a digital bank

With the commoditisation of banking products and services, and now, the neutralisation of access to banking as a competitive differentiator, the battleground will shift to **data and the use of data for engagement**. I see no other credible alternative for competitive differentiation in consumer banking in a digital world. Banks that do not invest in this capability for the future will have to depend on scale and efficiency to compete and aim to be the lowest-cost provider. However, consumer banking is not a global business: local regulations and customer norms create differences in offering that will become a drag on economies of scale. In recent times, large international banks have begun to close consumer banking operations in countries where they do not have the scale to compete.

Banks have always had a treasure trove of data, but they've also had difficulty putting the data to use to benefit customers. This can be attributed to disaggregated transaction systems, lack of a single data store, poor timeliness of data (which makes useful actions difficult), and the lack of an obsession with using the data to simplify customers' lives.

These reasons will no longer cut it. To survive, banks will need to be able to **assemble the digital solutions for harnessing data to benefit their customers** – and do it very well. Data will need to be readily available, some in real time, and fed 24/7 into machine learning algorithms that will search for patterns and generate relevant insights. Examples of insights include missing payments, overspending, credit card spend analysis, unusual amounts, new merchants, net cash growth or decline month to month. Such insights will lead to better engagement with customers.

There are few businesses as digital as a digital bank – or banking, for that matter. As banks are intermediaries in payments and funding, they are not directly involved in the actual production of goods and services but only aid in the exchange of goods and services. Whether in the form of facilitation of payments, taking of deposits, or the subsequent lending of those deposits to borrowers, these exchanges all come down to bookkeeping or ledger entries – pure digits. These digits were originally stored on paper, and then in the age of computing, stored as digits in disk drives, and now more and more, in the cloud.

Put another way, you could say that **banks are nothing but data**. This data has traditionally been used to help the bank run its business better, e.g., by using it to optimise the deposit balances versus the amount of loans. Or it has been used to help target customers to take up more products in cross-selling activities. Or it may be used by the regulator to monitor the health of the bank.

That is the past. In TMRW, we envisaged a future where more data led to more insights, which would exponentially increase the capability to engage customers. Chapter 2.5 established the critical role that engagement will play in the battle for customer experience. The key ingredient enabling this is data, i.e., data-driven engagement. To propel this change, a **data flywheel** (Collins 2020) that became known as ATGIE, which stands for Acquire, Transact, Generate data, Insights, and Engage customers (Figure 25), was created. Let's look at each component in turn.

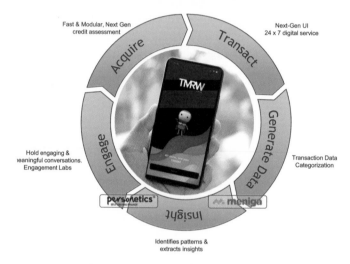

Figure 25 – TMRW's ATGIE flywheel model
(Source: UOB Website, December 2020)

Acquire. Traditionally, customers have to wait in long queues and file lots of paperwork at physical banks to open an account – a major pain point for busy customers. For TMRW, we used biometric identification, such as thumbprint and facial recognition, re-engineered the processes and reduced the number of fields, etc., so users can sign up for a product at their convenience (Lam and Koh, 2020; Fintech Singapore, 2019). In Indonesia, the process can be done completely online. In Thailand, because a straight-through process to onboard a customer was not available when TMRW was launched, biometric kiosks installed at convenient locations allow customers to scan a valid ID, put in their thumbprint, and open an account. A migration to Thailand's new online national identification scheme is taking place now. This will make the whole process as seamless and frictionless as possible.

Additionally, in Indonesia, TMRW "taps Avatec's AI-driven credit assessment engine, using alternative data and machine learning to assess the credit-worthiness of customers during the onboarding phase" (Ho 2020). This will enable TMRW to assess with greater certainty the credit quality of potential customers.

Transact. Around 90% of digital bank transactions are made up of fund transfers, bill payments, and viewing account transactions and balances. All of these are possible with the TMRW app, but the experience is made especially convenient with a user interface so simple that it doesn't need a dropdown menu.

Through the use of chatbots, TMRW is also reinventing the customer service experience. Not only does it make the whole process faster, simpler, and more easily accessible, it also remembers previous chats, so customers don't have to repeat their queries. A frequent complaint with traditional call centres is that customers often have to repeat their queries every time they get transferred to a different line. But TMRW's chatbot makes it possible to create an electronic trail of all previous chats, which the chat agent has access to, so repeating your request can finally be a thing of the past (Tech Wire Asia, 2019).

Generate data. TMRW stores its customers' data, from basic customer information to daily transactional data. This serves as the foundation for understanding the customer and anticipating their needs. Not all banks have a central data store to keep the necessary information – or at least, not all banks have invested in the infrastructure to maintain such an operation. Constructing a central data store is essential for this business model. Fintech solutions such as Meniga help to clean and categorise all this data to make it more useful.

Insights. Through the data generated, TMRW leverages predictive analytics that can understand and anticipate customer needs. Every action and transaction completed by a customer creates data points, and these data points are used to improve customer experience. UOB partnered with Personetics to obtain insights from transactional data. There was a choice to leverage geolocation to engage customers or to leverage the bank's own transactional data. I chose the latter to start, as that's something banks have in abundance, but don't leverage.

Engage. This is the core of the ATGIE business model. It's where TMRW personalises and enhances the banking experience by instigating small conversations with customers, anticipating their needs, and offering helpful solutions. These micro-conversations can nudge customers in the right direction and help them reach their goals, whether that means saving or spending better.

This is the unique differentiation that TMRW is piloting. Once mature, it holds the possibility of enabling TMRW to lower acquisition costs and increase future profitability. By engaging customers, TMRW creates more transactions, which generates more data and allows the bank to serve customers even better. If customers are served well and delighted, they become advocates who recommend the bank to their friends and family. This in turn grows the customer base and drives more transactions and customers in the long term.

To accelerate the discovery of the best ways to engage customers, engagement labs should be part of your arsenal. This lab brings together practitioners from across functional units and disciplines – analytics, data, decision science, behavioural science, communications, marketing – and uses an engagement index to help determine the impact of different engagement initiatives (Warden, 2019a).

The ATGIE flywheel is the approach that banks of the future will need to take. No longer can a bank afford to keep transaction data merely as a record. Or to dump masses of unlabelled data in a "data lake" and hope that something useful emerges. Data must be elevated to the **same level of importance as capital** in a bank.

Towards this end, data must be handled with rigour and integrity. The design considerations for data storage and retrieval should specify that the data must be fully described at source, and that the creator of the application requiring the new piece of data is the party responsible for ensuring this, within the guidelines and confines of the process drawn up by the Chief Data Officer (CDO). Additionally, this needs to be reinforced by the top management through a data committee or council. Getting data management right, coupled with a culture and mindset of using the data to drive customer engagement and experience, will be critical to the success of digital banks.

Key takeaways

- The battleground will shift to data and the use of data for engagement, as no other credible alternative for competitive differentiation exists for banking in a digital world. It's also true in many industries outside banking.

- Banks that do not invest in this capability for the future will have to depend on scale and efficiency to compete and aim to be the lowest-cost provider.

- In banking, local regulations and customer norms create differences in offering that will become a drag on economies of scale.

- To survive, banks will need to be able to assemble the digital solutions for harnessing data to benefit their customers – and do it very well.

- By engaging customers, TMRW creates more transactions, which generates more data and allows the bank to serve customers even better.

- If customers are served well and delighted, they become advocates who recommend the bank to their friends and family.

- This in turn grows the customer base and drives more transactions and sales in the long term.

- To accelerate the discovery of the best ways to engage customers, engagement labs should be part of your arsenal.

- The ATGIE flywheel is the approach that banks of the future will need to take.

- Data must be elevated to the same level of importance as capital in a bank.

Alternative credit scoring and its role

Whether you select the young professional segment as the best bet for your entry as a foreign bank, or if you are a local bank with the option to target the entire mass market segment, **unsecured lending is going to be key to profit generation**. This is also true for micro and small SMEs. And thus, the degree to which you can lend and keep your bad debt under control is going to be paramount to your path to profit. At TMRW, we were aware from the outset that while we needed to raise deposits to create the liabilities to lend against, the real profit would be made through unsecured lending.

This assumption was confirmed in the course of TMRW's journey, as the transaction account and credit card bundle commanded a larger revenue compared to the standalone transaction account. And when we visited Kakao Bank, unsecured personal loans, which were taken up by just 10% of the customer base, seemed to be able to generate enough revenue to make the entire bank profitable. The original thinking had been to start building this capability after the bank in Thailand was up and running. However, in the middle of 2017, a visit to New Hope Bank in Sichuan, China, revealed that they were able to offer instant loans through an **automated credit risk assessment system**. Upon my return, I discussed with UOB's Chief Risk Officer and UOB's Head of retail credit and decided to accelerate the ability to underwrite unsecured loans using non-traditional data.

The best indicators of a customer's ability to repay a loan are their total debt obligations, whether they are growing or slowing, their past history of repayments, and their ability to service their debts based on their income. That's why proof of income and a declaration of all debts are what traditional lenders rely on. A credit bureau fulfils the second obligation, while the first obligation is still being fulfilled by documentary evidence – payslip, letter from employer, etc. The problem with relying on this is that it can be easily forged. Where the bureau has incomplete information about the borrower or the borrower has never borrowed from an institution that submits information to the credit bureau, **data from alternative sources like Telcos or even social media** have proven to be effective in risk-ranking applicants according to their ability to repay (Wei et al., 2014).

Without these new sources of data for credit scoring, the application of machine learning algorithms is unlikely to improve the risk-ranking output, especially when it comes to segments that have non-existent bureau records or thin credit files. This will be important given the **untapped opportunity for micro-lending** in the emerging countries in ASEAN where one out of every two working adults is unbanked.

At the same time, the awareness of the importance of alternative data, the growing emphasis on data protection, and unorthodox methods of scraping data from mobile phones, etc., may have the effect of limiting availability of such data or increase the cost of legitimately obtaining such sources of information with consent.

Once access to plentiful alternative data is established, **algorithms need to be improved** from traditional logistic regression and decision tree approaches and

Name	Type	Description	Advantages	Disadvantages
Linear Regression		The best-fit line through all data points	Easy to understand You can clearly see what the biggest drivers of the model are	Sometimes too simple to capture complex relationships between variables Tendency for the model to overfit
Logistic Regression		The adoption of linear regression to problems of classification	Easy to understand	Sometimes too simple to capture complex relationships between variables Tendency for the model to overfit
Decision Tree		A graph that uses the branching method to match all possible outcomes of a decision	Easy to understand and implement	Not often used on its own for prediction because it's often too simple and not powerful enough for complex data
Random Forest		Takes the average of many decision trees. Each tree is weaker than the full decision tree, but combining them we get better overall performance.	A sort of "wisdom of the crowd" Tends to result in very high-quality results Fast to train	Can be slow to output predictions relative to other algorithms Not easy to understand predictions
Gradient Boosting		Uses even weaker decision trees that increasingly focus on "hard examples"	High-performing	A small change in the future set or training set can create radical changes in the model Not easy to understand predictions
Neural Networks		Mimics the behaviour of the brain. NNs are interconnected neurons that pass messages to each other. Deep learning uses several layers of NNs to put one after the other.	Can handle extremely complex tasks. No other algorithm comes close in image recognition.	Very, very slow to train, because they have so many layers Requires a lot of power Almost impossible to understand predictions

Figure 26 – Algorithms commonly used in credit scoring
(Source: medium.com)

supplemented with neural network algorithms or deep learning techniques (which are essentially neutral networks of more than three layers, including the inputs and outputs). Deep learning is in turn a subset of machine learning, which has added capabilities to cluster and classify inputs through pattern detection. Such techniques together with rich alternative data, as well as traditional applicant and bureau data (if any), have the potential to better risk-rank borrowers, resulting in fewer false positives (should not lend but passed through undetected) and false negatives (should lend but rejected).

Figure 26 illustrates some of the algorithms commonly used in credit scoring. Each technique has its advantages and disadvantages.

Fraud is another key consideration in lending. Syndicates often attack weaknesses in the lending process, for instance by using stolen identities to apply for loans. Alternative data from Telcos, or from data contained within the applicant's mobile, could help to ascertain if the applicant really works at the company address or lives at the home address provided.

Other issues revolve around the **sharing of data** – for example, while data used in model development can be stripped of markers that may be used to uniquely identify the customer, the issue of whether the customer consented for his data to be shared with third-parties may not be so clear-cut.

For owners of **large ecosystems**, e.g., e-commerce ecosystems, offering loans for goods purchased is synergistic in that it increases sales on the e-commerce platform. Many of the large ecosystem players are also thinking of how they can monetise their trove of alternative data built from the transactions of their consumers and merchants.

In 2018, UOB partnered with China-based technology platform Pintec Technology Holdings Limited (PINTEC) in a joint venture to launch Avatec.ai. This is a joint-venture company that helps banks and other financial institutions **assess the credit quality of potential customers based on alternative data, e.g. Telco data, e-commerce data, location data, etc.**, including those who are new to credit. This is important when you consider that credit card penetration in Southeast Asia, with the exception of Singapore and Malaysia, languishes in single-digit percentages.

As can be seen, alternative data is key to improving a bank's ability to lend unsecured and keep its **non-performing loans (NPL) below 1.5%**. MYbank and Webank reported NPLs in 2017 of just 1.23% and 0.64%, respectively (CBNEditor, 2019). It shows the power of alternative data in lending.

Key takeaways

- Whether for the micro and small SME segment, the mass market segment or the young professional segment, unsecured lending is going to be key to profit generation.

- The best indicators of a customer's ability to repay are their total debt obligations, whether debt is growing or slowing, past history of repayments, and their ability to service their debts based on their income.

- If the credit bureau has incomplete or no information about the borrower, data from alternative sources like Telcos or even social media have proven to be effective.

- This is key given the untapped opportunity for micro-lending in the emerging countries in ASEAN, where one out of every two working adults is unbanked.

- Once plentiful alternative data is available, algorithms need to be improved from traditional logistic regression and decision tree approaches and supplemented with neural network algorithms or deep learning techniques.

- Alternative data from Telcos, or from data contained within the applicant's mobile, could help to ascertain if the applicant really works at the company address or lives at the home address provided, reducing fraud risk.

- MYbank and Webank reported NPLs in 2017 of just 1.23% and 0.64%, respectively. It shows the power of alternative data in lending.

Designing a seamless onboarding experience

The trials of onboarding customers of different cultures and countries were one of the biggest challenges in TMRW. One of TMRW's key features is the ability for customers to sign up for an account without having to step into a physical bank. This involves **balancing customer convenience with proper security**.

On the security front, traditional banks typically employ CDD[40] or KYC[41] authentication processes. KYC prevents the bank from being used by criminal elements for money laundering or terrorist financing activities. Software and systems are in place to perform automated checks, and verifications are done with a host of internal and external databases. Banks also double down on training their branch staff to identify potential fraudsters and pick up signs that might indicate that the information given by a new customer is false, or that the person is not who they say they are. Needless to say, **performing KYC remotely** via a mobile device or over the internet is invariably more challenging.

The KYC process consists of three key areas in which banks need customers to provide evidence:

1. **Who you are:** e.g., customers must show proof that their face matches their ID card photo.

2. **What you have:** e.g., customers must make sure that their fingerprint matches the fingerprint stored in the ID card chip.

3. **What you know:** e.g., customers must give the right answer when asked a security question.

Giving a less than satisfactory answer to any of the above questions is usually a red flag and will require an exception-handling process to verify the identity of the customer. A big dependency of good KYC is having a **source of truth** to verify data against. This typically comes in the form of a national database or platform where

---

40. Customer Due Diligence
41. Know Your Customer

entities can verify national ID numbers and/or passport numbers. In Indonesia, we were able to apply for access to such a database to perform the required verification (WE Online, 2021). In Thailand, we were able to confirm the details entered with those found on the chip encoded into the Thai identity card and if the Thai identity card presented was valid.

However, there are times when even this golden source of truth is not entirely accurate. Thailand is a nation of people who are mainly Buddhists, many of them staunchly religious. As part of their beliefs, changing their names is thought to bring luck and fortune. Some do so several times within a year. If citizens do not inform the relevant authorities of their name changes fast enough, the records in the national database become outdated.

As part of the account opening process, customers' names in both their Thai and Romanised versions were collected. It was later discovered, however, that while Thais have a Romanised version of their name, they don't often use it, and it is not uncommon for them to have different Romanised spellings of their own name. Therefore, when customers entered their names during the onboarding process, and the information didn't match the data from the national database, these applications were rejected. This was a learning for us, and subsequently the English name was removed as a mandatory check.

The customer onboarding user journey model in Thailand saw **multiple iterations**. We went through countless workshops with stakeholders from various departments and areas of expertise, from product teams to compliance experts and systems owners. The physicality of these workshops allowed us to thrash out differences in opinions and generate ideas quickly. No stone was left unturned. We acted as antagonists and questioned why each field was collected, its purpose and whether it was absolutely necessary for a digital bank like TMRW. The respective teams had to explain and defend their rationale if they wanted to include an information field that others felt was not instrumental to the account opening process. Through the workshops, we were able to reduce the length of a bundled-product application by 50% down to 22 fields, thereby trimming the time taken to complete it to within 10 minutes on a mobile device.

One of TMRW's key executives tasked with the TMRW onboarding experience recalls: "Due to language and cultural differences, online discussions with the various stakeholders, including the legal and compliance teams, were not the most effective. As a result, we had to redevelop a particular component four times. That's four sprints to build what was a small feature and caused a two-month delay." It was much better to meet and discuss things face-to-face. In the era of the Covid-19 pandemic, there is no choice but to do this over video, but the time taken and frustration will be there and need to be managed well.

"I also learned that Thai words can be very long, and the Thai language doesn't have the concept of punctuation. Because of the limited display space on a mobile screen, some Thai words got broken into two lines at the wrong places. In some instances, the legality of the words being broken at different parts actually had different meanings. We only managed to get them resolved when we went up to meet the country teams face-to-face. We did high-fidelity mock-ups for them, screen by screen, line by line. We went through with the country teams and finally got the sign-off. But, two weeks later, it was changed again. It wasn't easy, but it was a very good learning point for us. With those learnings, we did things differently for Indonesia.

"TMRW has a regional vision and, thus, had the many complexities of a regional onboarding platform that came along with it. In order to standardise and speed up development time, we often asked ourselves what are must-haves and what are nice-to-haves. We have to make sure what we develop are in line with local regulations and policies, while balancing the need to have consistent, innovative and superior customer journeys. The struggle is real."

Key takeaways

- The trials of onboarding customers of different cultures and countries were one of the biggest challenges encountered.

- The design of the process to perform KYC remotely via a mobile device or over the internet is invariably more challenging than doing it face-to-face.

- A big dependency of good KYC is having a "source of truth" to verify data against. This typically comes in the form of a national database or platform.

- There were many iterations of the onboarding user journey to ensure that no stone was left unturned in the ambition to produce a great experience.

Core banking and its evolution

Core banking systems – which are basically ledgers containing credits and debits of the transactions into and out of customers' accounts – have evolved significantly over the past decade. I believe that today, we have just reached the stage where a new digital bank could **run everything on the cloud** without having to own its own infrastructure, and yet achieve uptime, modularity and scalability better than existing banks who own their own infrastructure. This is what IDC calls **"Fourth Generation" core banking**, as illustrated by Figure 27. Fourth-generation core banking is the most truly digital, and the most able to meet a design-first approach. While you can perform some limited amount of core transformation with any generation, only fourth-generation provides a fully digital bank that can be changed easily with little technical debt moving forward.

I spoke to Yves Roesti, who is CEO of the Synpulse Group[42], a company that has implemented a fourth-generation core banking solution in Asia. He recommends that "when evaluating these new next-generation core banking solutions, one needs to pay attention to vendors whose products are based on legacy third-generation architectures but claim to be fourth-generation or pseudo cloud-native[43]". Many of these third-generation core banking providers are urgently re-architecting their solution while trying not to lose market share. If you choose such a provider, you **might compromise important fourth-generation features, such as true cloud-native architecture, hyper-scale computing**[44] **and fully decoupled architectures**[45].

While it is possible to achieve high NPS® with great design, great experience and great processes supporting the experience, it is **not possible to achieve very low costs by clinging to existing core banking solutions**, even the third-generation solutions from the 1990s. IDC estimates that the average age of core banking of the top 150 banks in Asia-Pacific is 20+ years. Approximately 65% are using second-generation and 30% using third-generation solutions. It will be simply

---

42. www.synpulse.com

43. Cloud-native is an approach to building and running applications that exploits the advantages of the cloud computing delivery model (Patrizio, 2018).

44. In computing, hyperscale is the ability of an architecture to scale appropriately as increased demand is added to the system. This typically involves the ability to seamlessly provision and add compute, memory, networking, and storage resources to a given node or set of nodes that make up a larger computing, distributed computing, or grid computing environment.

45. Decoupled architecture is a framework for complex work that allows components to remain completely autonomous and unaware of each other.

Fourth generation core banking is the future

Fourth generation core banking has recently evolved to help banks keep pace with the speed and scale required to drive digital transformation.

Core feature	First generation	Second generation	Third generation	Fourth generation
Released	Late 1970s	Mid-1980s	Late 1990s	Mid-2010s
Life expectancy/replacement	Forever – no expected replacement	Once a generation (20-30 years) replacement	Annual or semi-annual updates until EOL	Ongoing with continuous updates
Software architecture	Monolithic	Towers upon foundation harness/frame	Towers upon abstracted layers with fixed APIs	Reusable microservices repository/API gateways
Software development	Heavy coding with much duplication	Heavy coding using some reusable calls, subroutines	Partial process and product definition as data with moderate code	Complex process automation and product definition as data with low code
Platform archetype	Mainframe	Mainframe with thin client	Mainframe with thick client	Cloud native running infrastructure as code
User availability	9 am - 5 pm on business days	Almost 24-hour, almost 7 days, scheduled downtime	24x7x365; some transaction latency next business day	Anytime with immediate transaction fulfilment
User access	Branch only	+ ATM/EFTPOS	+ Internet/kiosks	+ Mobile apps/third-party & aggregator apps
User interface	Text green screen	Colored text with graphic output	Windows, graphical user interface (GUI) and HTML	Device agnostic native apps
Data	Sequential, siloed	Indexed, siloed	Relational, cross-silos	Sharable and intelligent
Development culture	Proprietary, non-reusable code	Standardised code aligned to architecture model	Data-driven with process orchestration	Engineering supplemented by machine learning
Transaction processing	Overnight batch	Event or time period schedule batches	Real-time posting with overnight downstreaming	Real-time posting with real-time downstreaming
Scalability	Fixed, unplanned	Fixed, planned	Vertical	Elastic
Embedded legacy IT costs	Massive, unsustainable competitively	Significant and continues to grow	Significant, and limits agility	None, and future technical debt minimal
Resilience/Recovery	Reasonable, but downtime of manual recovery and potential data loss	High, but with downtime of automated data recovery	Self healing with infrequent outages	Highly predictive self healing with zero downtime
Migration options	Big bang, extended downtime	Phased with complex migration scenarios	Optimised big bang in 2-4 day weekend with fail-back option	Continuous deployment with no downtime

Unique benefits of fourth generation

- Provides true digital transformation
- Continuous change without disruption
- Automatically scales with business volumes
- Easy integration to internal and external systems
- Leverages newest technology cost and performance curves, controllable by bank
- Real-time downstreaming on transaction level basis
- Future-proofs investment in new technology
- Six-sigma resilience
- Change is traceable, auditable, and system-managed

IDC

Figure 27 – First to fourth generation of core banking
(Source: IDC Infobrief 2020. IDC Financial Insights, co-authored with Thought Machine)

impossible for them to migrate their existing core banking at one go due to the extensive customisation that has been introduced into the system. But at the same time, continuing to build on the existing legacy platform will just make the situation worse.

It is therefore inevitable that banks will need to implement the new fourth-generation core banking **alongside the existing legacy core** for some time. All ground-up initiatives should be built using the new core banking solution, and over time, more and more existing applications moved over to the new core.

One development that will facilitate the upgrading of core banking systems is the emergence of a set of industry standards. The Banking Industry Architecture Network (BIAN) is a collaborative not-for-profit ecosystem formed of leading banks, technology providers, consultants and academics from all over the globe. BIAN is defining **the financial services industry's first set of open banking APIs** and has delivered the first wave of these APIs. BIAN is truly industry-led and therefore gaining more universal acceptance, especially with multiple core vendors signing on. If momentum continues, and more banks ask their core banking systems providers to adopt this standard set of API definitions, then it will become much easier for them to replace an ageing core banking system.

Another important development is the support for segregating individual, country and global code, yet providing interoperability using a set of tools and standards. This will remove one of the current bugbears in the industry: so many banks have modified their core banking system to such an extent that it has become their own software, unique in every way but name. This makes it very difficult to upgrade. Increasingly, we will be seeing **greater segregation of client-specific modifications** (e.g., new products that are not in the catalogue), **country-specific modifications** (e.g., to connect to a country's unique payment system) and **core or global code** (i.e., what everyone receives out of the box).

Interestingly, Yves mentions that this is where "choosing a true fourth-generation provider... can have its own set of maturity challenges: the aforementioned segregation, commonly referred to as the Triple C model (Core/Country/Client code), is not always implemented efficiently with the newer generation of core banking providers. This can make maintenance expensive."

Along with this, there are a few other architectural points one needs to pay careful attention to. Many banks are planning to launch their platform in more than one country. This requires a whole set of design principles towards the so-called MESI principle (Multiple Entity Single Instance). The MESI principle indicates that the software is capable of running multiple logical tenants (read: business units) on one single physical server – provided the data residency laws of each involved jurisdiction allow for that. This not only has implications for the code and object model congruence and efficiency across units but also impacts the regional operating model. With operational scalability and high efficiency in mind, such multi-tenancy features are very important considerations in the roadmap for regional digital banks.

When you combine these modularity capabilities with those afforded by the cloud like redundancy and scalability (e.g., having more computing power on payday or peak statementing days), and with computing, memory and hard disk power on tap, the cost of implementing the entire backend of the banking technology infrastructure is significantly lowered. The issue of not having a single major software provider may still exist for time to come or may always persist. But with better interface specifications in the form of APIs, interoperability will hopefully improve and result in the reduction of the need to integrate the solutions in a way that is peculiar to each bank.

All signs point to the **commoditisation of the backend**. The arena of competition has already shifted to where the customer interfaces with the bank. This is where the battle for the biggest improvements in customer experience that will cause customers to switch banks over time is being fought. If the battle is now less about headline rates with lots of exceptions built in, and more about product bundling (like at TMRW, where if the transactional account is active, there is additional cashback on the credit card), then there is an opportunity to ensure that everything you need can be configured and does not need any programming. This will allow you to keep the core banking system from excessive customisation and free you to focus on the customer interface layer. If your most complex product bundle can be achieved through configuration, then you minimise the amount of code that is written, improving your ability to maintain and upgrade the system down the road. This must be a requirement for all digital banks, and while the vendors may not be able to deliver this fully yet, there is a very high likelihood that they can in the near future.

So, in building a new digital bank today, a key decision to be made is **choosing a core banking software** that will both be reliable and give you a path to the future I have described above. I believe this transition will happen in the next 5 to 10 years. Traditional banks will increasingly feel the brunt of higher technology costs without the corresponding impact that the much-smaller digital banks will have for the same dollar of spend. This is one of the reasons why incumbent banks should operate a separate digital bank, ideally sharing the capital base requirement, like what Standard Chartered Bank intends to do with its collaboration with NTUC Enterprise in Singapore ("StanChart, NTUC Enterprise plan digital-only bank in Singapore", *The Straits Times*, 2020). This will allow them to start plotting a path towards a **totally cloud-based solution** for their core banking needs.

Key takeaways

- Today, a new digital bank could run everything on the cloud without having to own its own infrastructure, and yet achieve uptime, modularity and scalability better than existing banks who own their own infrastructure.

- This is what IDC calls "Fourth Generation" core banking.

- Third generation core-banking providers are urgently trying to re-architect their solution.

- By choosing such a provider, you might compromise important fourth-generation features, such as true cloud-native architecture, hyper-scale computing and fully decoupled architectures.

- It is not possible to achieve very low costs by clinging to existing core banking solutions.

- The emergence of industry standards like BIAN (Banking Industry Architecture Network) will make it easier to replace an ageing core banking solution if more providers adopt the standard.

- The ability to segregate individual, country and global code, yet providing interoperability using a set of tools and standards is critical to lowering the cost of ownership for core banking solutions globally.

- Current fourth-generation core banking may not be as efficient in implementing such segregation and this can make the maintenance expensive.

- Regional digital banks require the MESI principle (Multiple Entity Single Instance) in their core banking design to be lean.

- All signs point to commoditisation of the backend. The arena of competition has already shifted to where the customer interfaces with the bank.

- The key decision to be made is choosing a core banking software that will both be reliable and give you a path to the future

- Incumbent banks should operate a separate digital bank that will allow them to start plotting a path towards a totally cloud-based solution for their core banking needs.

What do we do with product?

This chapter was written last, as I initially didn't think it was necessary. My thoughts were to tell the story without entering into a discussion around products. The rationale stems from the point that while revenue generation still comes from the sale of banking products and you do need competitive products to attract customers, building a digital bank is not first and foremost about products.

This is a major reset in thinking, especially for those who have been successful in banking. In consumer banking, the product management roles are the prized roles. It's where I picked up all the essential knowledge, experience and skills to manage large portfolios. Most successful heads of consumer banking have done a product management role in their rise to the top. So, it was an almost 180-degree shift to start TMRW by saying: "It's not about the product. Yes, we need a competitive product and we need to manage the product profit and loss and the product portfolio well, but product cannot be on centre stage in a digital bank, because the customer already occupies that position."

Looking at the final manuscript without this chapter, however, I felt that the story just wasn't complete without explaining the paradigm shift in thinking, so I decided to add this chapter to let the product tell its story.

First, let's talk about the overall approach. As always, the starting point was the customer. We ensured that we understood their needs thoroughly. As mentioned in Chapter 1, we were cognisant that ASEAN has different markets with very different cultures and customers, and we wanted to see through the lens of TMRW's YP and YPF customers: who they were, their aspirations, behaviours, habits, unmet needs, etc. In total, we spoke to 3,000 customers (Finews.asia, 2009), and we built both the banking product and the digital product around the needs of these YP and YPF customers.

We learnt that customers often opened savings accounts with foreign banks to make it harder for them to make withdrawals, so that they would be less likely to spend the money in the account. We therefore constructed a **sweep program** to move money from a customer's transactional account to a savings account that they could not pay or transfer from.

A 2017 research revealed that millennials "respond better to prompts that are fun and do not make them feel guilty" when it comes to managing their personal finances (Design Council Singapore, 2019). Leveraging this knowledge, the sweep was accompanied by a **savings game**, the City of TMRW, as shown in Figure 28.

The interest rate on the savings account was higher than that of the transactional account, and to prevent customers from transferring all their spare cash over, a counter was introduced that specified the next time another sweep could be made. Each time the account holder put more money in, the virtual city grew. Starting from a little village, it could potentially develop into a small city. The Thai YP and YPF customers found the City of TMRW novel and refreshing, and we received a lot of accolades for it.

Figure 28 – TMRW savings game

In addition, many customers were worried about **overspending on their credit cards**, so the ability to lower the credit limit and set an online spend limit, overseas usage limit or cash withdrawal limit were included in the final feature set. This also helped to mitigate online fraud, one of the frequent concerns customers cited, as you could set your limit to zero after a purchase.

Customers also asked to be able to **tailor the cashback** on their TMRW credit cards, which we included in the enhanced rewards that became available if customers made a minimum number of transactions every month on their transactional account. The intention from the outset was to have customers own a bundle from the first relationship rather than cross-sell them later. Many incumbent banks sell standalone products and then try and cross-sell customers the next product later. This is expensive and also reduces your share of wallet. To make this successful, we needed to ensure that this was a true proposition that encouraged customers to use both products in the bundle. The TMRW bundle design was such that if you used your transactional account, you would get a higher cashback and be able to choose the cashback categories that enjoyed this higher cashback.

Next, as mentioned earlier, the mantra was **not to cross-sell to engage but to engage in order to cross-sell**. I wanted to avoid statistical cross-sell beyond the first decile of correlation.[46] Yes, it does bring you more income but it is intrusive and destroys your goodwill in the long term. It also makes little sense when the base is small, and the base would start small and grow with quality, as we didn't want to grow large fast and waste money with inactive accounts on the journey to get big. The start-ups have this option because they are funded by venture funding, whose yardstick is the number of eyeballs the start-up has, never mind whether the eyeballs are open or closed permanently, as they are prepared for the wastage. This mantra of using cross-sell cautiously is hard to convince the banking community of.

How could you even reach digital bank customers to cross-sell? After all, they don't go to the branch network anymore. How far should you go to bombard the insights feed with cross-sell and damage the long-term possibility of positioning yourself as a bank that's different. Cross-sell has become a necessary evil. To get 5% of respondents, you consistently irritate 95% of your customers. Customers are consistently asking banks not to call them and bombard them with offers they are not interested in. I insisted on not falling into the trap of doing so whilst I was in charge, but I knew it's hard to keep this promise within any incumbent bank. Much easier with a challenger bank who is out to change banking. That will always be an advantage the challenger has over the incumbent.

Over the mid and long term, TMRW would need to improve its ability to mine transactional data and collect even more data through conversations. The prize is a paradigm-shift to a needs-based approach that recommends targeted solutions to the customers that really need them, rather than bombard 1,000 customers to secure the 50 that eventually take up the cross-sell offer. The ability to **collect data through conversations** was something I felt excited about. In my entire career in banking, I had wanted to do this, but was never able to secure the platform to do it. Now that we had it, the path to a new paradigm was in sight. To those incumbents who come after me, do continue to try, for I think it is a breakthrough worth fighting for, even if everyone else looks at you strangely.

---

46. The 10% of customers that show the highest propensity to take up a cross-sell offer.

Another key difference between a digital bank and digital banking is that in a digital bank, the product is one piece – an important piece no doubt – but still **one piece of the entire experience**. Together with the right intuitive and frictionless user interface, great service every time (without the customer having to repeat himself or herself), and leveraging data to anticipate the customer's needs and fulfil them before he or she even knows it, all the pieces of the experience puzzle come together, so that customers will actively transact, love the experience and advocate the bank. Digital banking, however, exists mostly to serve the product and provide a channel for it.

One conundrum for the digital bank is that the leaders with strong product backgrounds are likely to want to pursue a product-led approach. In reality, due to the commoditisation of products and the sheer proliferation of different products in the market for every conceivable sub-segment in the banked population, the product-led approach is in reality mostly about giving more rewards and benefits to specific customers. I didn't see the sense of doing that when such **a great job is already being done by the incumbents in the form of price-based competition**. So whilst you need banking product expertise in your key team, unless you have a contrarian in your midst, your designer for the digital bank has to be someone convinced that getting service and experience right is more important than designing the most attractive product. There is no mistaking that the products must be competitive, but that doesn't mean it needs to be the most attractive. Having **simpler products that are more evergreen also means less demands on customising the core banking system**. And we all know how big a problem this has become in existing incumbent banks.

Now, let's talk about the **trade-offs that had to be made**. Here, a few key design considerations were obvious from the start. One of the most important was not having a lot of products. This is the problem incumbent banks have, and it's the result of micro-segmentation as they try to win customers away from competitors in mature markets by providing them with products that are tailored for them. This comes at the expense of having very complex product line-ups and complexity in the core systems. TMRW had the ideal starting point to start simple. YP and YPF customers only needed three transactional products – a current account, a savings account and a credit card – and this would fulfil the needs of the majority of the target segment's everyday banking needs.

Incentives. They are an unending topic of discussion, and a sure sign of the true nature of competition in consumer banking today. I wanted to position TMRW in third place in the race to be the most attractive in the interest rate and sign-up objectives, but could accept being the runner-up if the rationale was sound. My rationale was simple: After spending all the investment to build a bank whose experience would be "wow", **how could we pay to incentivise customers to apply at**

the same level as others whose experience isn't on par with TMRW? You will find that this needs so much convincing, because there will be so much disbelief within those steeped in the existing banking paradigm. Therefore, if you are the top executive chartered with building the new bank, you must **secure the ability to have the ultimate say on this matter from the start**. And nonetheless, it would be common sense to not give incentives just to open an account, but to ensure that there is a requirement to do a minimum number of transactions before any incentives are awarded.

I tried to find a gap in the market between the size of deposits and the interest rate being paid. In one country, a gap did exist and we capitalised on it to establish a unique positioning. In the other country, there wasn't a gap, so we simply priced appropriately. Whatever the case, I was adamant that we would not be the price leader. It's OK to be #2 or #3. The key is to provide just enough incentive to incentivise signups and not more. Don't leave any money on the table if you can. Conjoint analysis of the various incentive offers can help you to optimise cost vs attractiveness. I've found it to be very effective fact-based decisioning.

As a foreign bank, TMRW targeted YP and YPF customers with higher lifetime values (LTV). That way, the overall eventual return on investment would be better. These customers will eventually have a foreign bank relationship anyway, so why not start one earlier? The ceiling for cost of acquisition would also be higher, given their higher lifetime value, giving us more leeway to attract a higher profit pool segment. The marketing and brand affinity development would also be tuned to target the YP and YPF, in alignment with the chosen segment.

A lot of context and understanding from years in product management and thus comprehension of the linkages and the limitations went into these considerations and trade-offs. So the irony is that **only someone with the requisite banking experience would fully understand the context to make these trade-offs**. It emphasised the unique nature of building a digital bank, its new thinking, but yet, you needed to know the way things work in banking to do so. And that's because the streams of revenue and profit remain largely the same. You just can't run the business the way it used to be, yet to find a new way to run the business, it surely helps to know how it used to be.

Unsecured lending is vital to early revenue growth and profits. That's because lending products generate the majority of the revenue, especially in a low interest rate regime. Credit cards help but building a portfolio that can generate sufficient revenue takes time. The revenue generation ability of unsecured personal loans is speedier, because the balances are usually larger, and there is usually no interest-free period. Low-cost transactional account deposits help to improve your margins, but the impact is in the long term as this takes time to build up. If you had to prioritise because you can't do both, then I would **recommend launching**

personal loans first, and transactional accounts bundled with credit cards shortly thereafter. This would be my key product learning, having done it the other way around. Doing it this way shortens the time to ramp up income, as the loan product is ready from day one. The timing gap can't be too large because personal loan participation amongst the population is narrower, and thus new digital banks will still need a large credit card base to ignite their personal loan portfolio growth through bundling and targeted cross-selling. Personal loans on a standalone basis won't be able to achieve significant volume without the broadband products like transactional accounts and credit cards.

Challenger banks, on the other hand, may have difficulty raising sufficient deposits to fund their loan book, but if the credit underwriting algorithm is improved by supplementing it with alternative data, and there is appreciable loan volume with non-performing loans well under 3%, then depending on the competitiveness of loan pricing in the countries concerned, you **may have room to give away more margin to attract more deposits** to fund your loan book. Incumbents setting up a digital challenger bank within the same licence scheme should be able to tap on the deposits from the mother bank initially, providing more room for the digital bank to grow their low-cost deposits in the mid and long term.

It is an imperative to improve your credit scorecard by reducing false positives and false negatives. If you target customers that desire a mobile-only experience, they are likely to be younger, and hence unsecured credit is likely to be a major driver of profitability. You can't make substantial profit from unsecured credit if your credit underwriting algorithms either let in too many customers, some of suspect ability to repay, or by letting in only the very best credit profiles who never borrow at all. The investment in avatec.ai was directed at exactly doing this in Indonesia.

Indonesia also does not require proof of income for personal loan applications, making it possible for banks to offer instant loans at checkout or within an e-commerce experience. The P2P players like Kredivo already offer pay-later loans, but most banks haven't, as the onboarding requirements are much higher. Offering such services would help achieve a higher loan book, acquire more customers and also hopefully at a lower cost of acquisition. A new name has been recently coined to describe this – embedded finance[47], and it's so new, you don't see many mentions of it till 2020 onwards.

Eventually, some YPs and YPFs will need to buy a home and need a mortgage. The YPFs would have insurance needs to cover the breadwinner's inability to work. However, mortgage and insurance won't be of appreciable size until an accurate way of detecting the window of opportunity where the need is present is perfected. No

---

47. In 2019, Matt Harris coined the term "embedded Fintech" to describe how software-driven companies will embed financial services into their applications, from sending and receiving payments to enabling lending, insurance, and banking services (Shevlin, 2021).

bank has a high probability algorithm to solve this use case yet, and as mentioned in Chapter 2.1, property agents still provide a large percentage of referrals for home loans. This underscores and highlights the **challenges digital banks have with banking products that are time-bound in certain windows of need**, like mortgages and insurance, or to be able to convince the generally larger risk-adverse majority to invest more over time. The former needs a data-driven approach that can accurately detect such a window of opportunity, and the latter still needs a human to convince the risk-adverse, at least for now.

Another question often asked is whether you need a separate digital products team and banking products team, and the answer is yes. In a consumer bank, the P&L and portfolio expertise are still found within the banking products teams. The digital products team's exposure and experience is in designing and building the new features and functionality in digital banking. It's hard to find someone who has expertise in both.

TMRW transactional products leverage UOB's core banking platform (L'Hostis, 2019). I felt that the core platforms could always be upgraded later and didn't want to deal with that at the start. All the energy was targeted at systems that touched and interfaced with the customer directly, e.g., insights, fund transfers and ease of use. It will become increasingly difficult for future incumbent digital banks to follow suit. As the number of challenger banks grows, being cost-competitive will become as important as having great customer experience.

The TMRW product was created regionally, with countries making the least number of changes to cater to country regulatory requirements and inherent country differences that are unavoidable. A good example is the fund transfer process. In Singapore and many other ASEAN countries, you specify the "To" account then the "From" account. But in Thailand, the norm is the other way around. You can't change what's a country norm, so that was a change we agreed to.

In the end, however, TMRW didn't ask the "From" account as we only had one transactional account, so we built in the intelligence to recognise this. For most other changes, the country digital heads had to justify robustly why it was needed. Especially so in products, where everyone is so vested and convinced that their country is unique. Once you start to do that, it's a slippery slope towards having completely different apps for different countries, which raises the cost of maintenance and management significantly.

Key takeaways

- A competitive product is important, but product cannot be the main draw or consideration in a digital bank.

- The overall product approach begins with the customer by understanding their needs thoroughly. Our research connected us to 3,000 customers, and we built both the banking product and the digital product around the needs of these YP and YPF customers.

- It is vital that as many customers as possible own a bundle from the first relationship rather cross-selling them later. That's expensive and also reduces your share of wallet.

- To facilitate this, the TMRW bundle design was such that if you used your transactional account, you would get a higher cashback and be able to choose the cashback categories that enjoyed this higher cashback.

- The mantra was not to cross-sell to engage but to engage in order to cross-sell. Avoid statistical cross-sell beyond the first decile of correlation. Yes, it does bring you more income, but it is intrusive and destroys your goodwill in the long term.

- If digital banks improve their ability to mine transactional data and collect even more data through conversations, the prize is a paradigm shift to a needs-based approach that recommends solutions to the customers that really need them.

- In a digital bank, the product is one piece of the entire experience, but digital banking exists mostly to serve the product.

- There is no mistaking that the product must be competitive, but that doesn't mean it needs to be the most attractive. You don't have to be the price leader.

- Simpler products that are more evergreen also mean less demands on customising the core banking system, and thus not replicating problems the incumbents already have.

- After building a digital bank whose experience is wow, it wouldn't make sense to pay incentives to customers to apply at the same level as others whose experience isn't on par.

- Launch personal loans first and transactional accounts bundled with credit cards shortly thereafter.

- Digital banks are still challenged with products that are time-bound in certain windows of need, like mortgages and insurance, or convincing the risk-adverse majority to invest more over time.

CHAPTER 4

Building a digital bank

We are now ready to dive into how to design and build a superior digital bank. Chapter 4.1 "Designing it right" covers the fundamentals you need to get right to ensure that your new digital bank is designed correctly from the start. Just like in the design and construction of any building, where changing the electrical wiring, plumbing, lighting, etc., after everything has been finished is very difficult and costly, in building a digital bank there are some things where you have only this **one chance to get the design right**.

Designing it right is a key lever to achieve the target cost/income ratios that digital banks need in order to be cost-effective so that they can target segments that are unprofitable or marginally profitable for current incumbents. These design considerations also cover cost methodology, enterprise-wide and functional design considerations, data, construction of transparent risk registers, etc. We discuss how digital banks can set up their control functions as both service centres and advisory centres.

New ways of working must be taught and inculcated in the digital bank. We cover some of the key methodologies like design thinking, Lean Six Sigma and Agile. When these three methodologies are put together, they form the basic building blocks for a software factory. The design, setup and smooth running of a **"concept-to-code" software factory** is critical to the success of your digital transformation initiative. Spend the time to understand these new ways of working as they will save you a lot of time later. It will be near impossible for you to design and build a high-NPS® bank without this.

We walk through a 3-phase process to design a digital bank. Phase 1 involves the design of the customer value proposition (CVP). In designing your CVP, finding the right customer insights are crucial. Many ambitious projects fail due to the lack of insights that can drive the creation of new experiences. If your insights don't match your ambition, you either have to lower your ambition, which might damage your CVP, or find more insights by spending more time with customers.

Phase 2 is about journey development and getting the customer journey mapping and design right, together with mapping the required data inputs and outputs. This is a new adaptation from existing practices that can reduce the error rates resulting from mapping data only in the software development phase.

The last phase involves the use of Agile software development approaches to manufacture the software code required to power your customer experience.

Designing it right

Not many people have the opportunity to build a bank from zero. My experience in TMRW came close, in that although we didn't change the core banking systems, we built almost everything else from scratch. Building a digital bank from scratch is more than just defining and building the product offering. It's an opportunity to **build a bank for great efficiency**. This is crucial, as the digital bank would be unable to compete effectively without a low variable and annual fixed cost.

Well-designed business processes tuned both to efficiency and effectiveness will allow for lower operating costs, which are pivotal to your bank's ability to target under-served customers whom the incumbent banks may not be prepared to serve.

From my experience, there are several areas a new digital bank can focus on, from the start, to get the design of the business process right, so that when operationalised, the bank will be extremely efficient. How do you accommodate frequent changes in onboarding? How do you ensure you don't end up over-customising your backend so that you become the sole owner? How do you ensure that data is fully defined at the point of creation? How do you ensure total transparency of the risk register? How do you ensure that there is a well-defined internal library of routines for the user interface design and coding? How do you radically improve the efficiency of the relationship-managed segment? These are just a few examples of areas that could be designed to be a lot more efficient than they are today.

To be truly efficient, my guide would be that a digital bank's **cost/income ratio should eventually hit 30%**, compared to 50–60% for a typical large local bank.

If the new digital entity is not cost-effective, it will be unable to go for clients that the incumbents are not interested in because they are considered too small. This is the primary path of attack for new digital banks – starting with the under-served before moving up quickly. As Sun Tzu's Art of War puts it, better to attack the enemy where it is weakly defended than where it is well defended. (The only exception to this is when the whole market is under-served, like how China was when Alipay and WeChat Pay were emergent. There was no way to pay for goods online; it had to be created.) So, it is essential that the new entrant be very cost-efficient so that it is **able to go for segments that are deemed unprofitable or only marginally profitable for the incumbents**.

The first order of the day is to **get the cost methodology right**. What are the elements of cost that are variable and will increase as customer activity increases? If, for example, the software-as-a-service (SaaS) commercial agreement for core banking varies by transactions, and the more active a customer is, the more costs he will attract, then this will be classified as part of variable cost per customer. Operations, sales, servicing, acquisition, transaction-based fees, are all part of the variable cost base. Next, you look at the fixed cost base, and the attribution and allocation by product and by customer segment. This will ensure that the foundational formulation of the cost components is done correctly. Ideally, get as close to **activity-based costing** as practical, where the activity of internal staff and technology costs – which are the main cost components in a digital bank – can be properly allocated to the right cost drivers. For example, technology costs might be classified into the backend costs, middleware or API costs, and front-end costs. Front-end costs might be further allocated to onboarding costs, transaction and payments, user interface, engagement, etc.

The next step is to **gather the design considerations** for the new digital bank at the bank-wide enterprise level and at the major functional units – risk management, data, technology, operations, product, etc. Let's take data as an example. There should be no piece of data anywhere in the bank that cannot be connected back to a relevant entity, e.g., department, customer, client company, etc. This is an issue in existing banks. One of the ways to prevent this is to ensure that all data are fully described at creation. This would include the metadata (data about the data), e.g., name of the data field, field descriptor, purpose, computation, common index key, etc. The process for managing this would be owned by someone at the functional unit level, perhaps the Chief Data Officer. Data is equal to capital as a differentiator in a digital bank, so accord it the same attention.

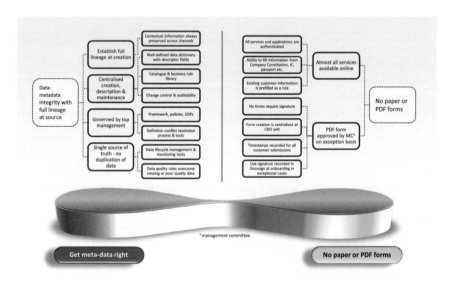

Figure 29 – Design challenges in digital banks

Figure 29 illustrates two of the many **design challenges** a digital bank needs to resolve to operate efficiently. What seem to be simple objectives at the first level – getting data/metadata right and eliminating paper – branch out into more considerations one level down, and by the third level, things get very messy.

This is an example of the sheer level of detail it takes to get the design right in a digital bank. That's because digital banks fall into the category of start-up ventures that call for **simple strategy, brilliant execution**, as opposed to those where you have **brilliant strategy, simple execution**. If you are the inventor of the bicycle, then you fall more into the second category. If not, then you fall into the first category, where no single differentiator is big enough to cause the shift. Digital banks focused on consumers and SMEs definitely fall into this category.

The control processes in a bank often act as friction to speed, as they ensure the required time is spent on checking that the proper controls are in place. This in turn helps to ensure compliance to regulations, policies and guidelines that are needed for the safe functioning of the financial system. In order to make these control processes work more efficiently, a **risk register** and the required details of the checks required to ascertain the integrity of the control measures must be made transparent and available to everyone in the initiative.

Risk registers represent the key risks that a regulated entity like a bank should seek to address and mitigate. These could be regulatory requirements, operational risk requirements, adherence to key internal policies and controls, etc. Most leading banks already adopt a standardised method to evaluate the probability and impact of these risks. If a risk is assessed to be medium or above, it would generally not be allowed to proceed without mitigation to low or low-medium levels.

However, the process by which risks are assessed and mitigated is not always very transparent. It may sometimes feel like the organisation is simply saying no to taking any risks, with vague criteria and explanations that are not well understood, and without offering solutions to assist. It doesn't have to be that way. I believe that all the key control functions in a digital bank – like compliance, credit, operational risk, IT security, fraud – must not only serve a risk control function, but also an **advisory function** on how to mitigate such risks. If the risk registers are clearly spelled out and made available online as checklists for staff to consult and use, then whether a risk is sufficiently mitigated becomes a very transparent process. Therefore, the risk control function's ability to proactively help with advice on mitigation should not pose a systemic risk.

A well-defined risk assessment and mitigation process would encompass training everyone in the bank to assess risk and forming workgroups with active control function participation to concur with the assessment of the risk, and the design of mitigants. In this regard, **control functions must be managed as service centres** – much like service centres for customers, except this is for internal staff.

Timeliness of responses from the control functions, signing off on the risk assessment when there is concurrence, agreeing with the level of reduction brought about by the mitigant, are all activities that the control function needs to be able to perform as a service centre. This is hard to accomplish as natural filtering and selection of candidates for such control functions may not align with these characteristics, and there is a general perception of disconnect between the words "control" and "service" in risk mitigation functions. Naturally, the control function is also chartered with control reviews, to ensure that the required controls and mitigants deployed are robust and adequately control for the risks identified.

Designing a digital bank involves using design thinking to ensure that you are extremely customer-focused and understand the customers' jobs to be done and the issues they face getting them done. Instead of specifying all the requirements at the start, work is simultaneously being specified, reviewed from the standpoint of multiple stakeholders, and refined. The output is tested, put into beta or production, or further refined to pass all required checks for quality before being put into production. This, in essence, is what Agile is all about. Taken together, design, customer journey development and Agile software development form the basic elements of the software factory of any digital transformation. I call this the **"concept to code"** process. Figure 30 shows how the "concept to code" factory is made up of these three distinct but interrelated phases.

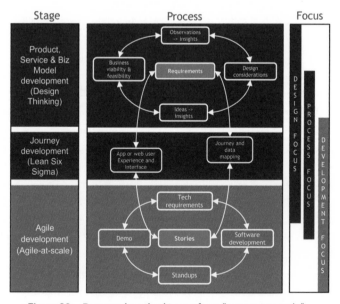

Figure 30 – Proposed method to get from "concept to code"

Phase 1

The first phase of the software factory consists of the design of the value proposition, or more specifically, the product, service and business model design. As you are building a bank, you are building more than the products and service propositions; you are also building the business model of the digital bank, e.g., to achieve very low variable costs, solving service issues at the point of origin, etc.

There are four interrelated actions in this phase: Business viability and design considerations are fed by observations and ideas that you can translate to insights about how the product or service helps the customer or how the business model improvement helps the bank (Dalton, 2016).

Most people think that this phase is exclusively customer-oriented, but in fact it also needs to be business-oriented so that you create value that customers are willing to pay for, at a cost that can generate a profit. **Business viability** is about alignment to the bank's business objectives, the revenue and profit, the cost structure, the timeframe and horizon, the long-term strategy. This needs to be aligned with the customer value proposition, which is derived from observations about the jobs the customers want to do and the difficulties they have doing them, plus new ideas about how they can be done better.

In both the observations and ideas boxes, the **translation into insights is crucial**. This is an often-misunderstood part of the method. The best definition of an insight that I have come across is this: "An insight is a penetrating observation about consumer behaviour that can be applied to unlock growth" (Drake, 2012). Insights allow you to uncover problems that customers have in performing their jobs and to eliminate these pain points. Let me illustrate with an example: If you observe customers using their phones, you'll see that when typing in a small form factor like a mobile phone, they sometimes hit the wrong key. Observing if there is a pattern to the keys the customer gets wrong might allow you to make adjustments to improve the typing accuracy. For instance, this pattern might be caused by the spacebar being too short, which if you use an iPhone, happens with the keyboard that pops up when you are entering the "To" field in an email.

Figure 31 – Normal spacebar vs shortened spacebar

The observation is that the "Customer inputs wrongly", and the idea might be "Make certain keys bigger depending on what errors the user makes". But in actual fact, the idea is off-track, once you have the insight. This becomes obvious when I put the keyboards side-by-side, as shown in Figure 31. The insight is that "The spacebar is too short because the "@" sign and "." sign have appeared", and thus it might be better to remove the emoji key (since email addresses don't need this) or remove the spacebar as email addresses don't usually have spaces.

Here's another example. I've observed that some customers prefer voice input more so than other customers. Chinese-speaking customers, for example, tend to use it more than English-speaking customers. The insight here is that Chinese does not have an alphabet but uses a logographic writing system. Thus, it is much harder to input the Chinese language with a keyboard than it is for English. The insight gives us an understanding of what is driving the observed behaviour, and hence allows us to take the correct path towards a breakthrough innovation.

The output of Phase 1, **design considerations**, captures the key design elements of your offering after balancing solutions to customer problems by considering the key drivers or insights in mind, and business viability and feasibility. For example, based on the example above, one of the design elements to be considered might be to default Chinese-speaking customers to voice interface rather than text interface.

The first phase of the factory process culminates in the documentation of the product, service and business model requirements. Note that the four action boxes – business viability, observations, ideas and design considerations – can affect each other, e.g., if an idea is found to be too difficult to translate into a profitable innovation, the idea should be dropped, and you will need to have more observations or ideas that generate insights to progress.

Phase 2

Traditionally, the second phase – **journey development** – has been combined with Phase 1, with a product owner in charge of both phases. In my experience, this isn't optimal, as it's hard in Asia to find a senior product owner who is able to span both phases (but if you do find such a person, there's nothing to stop you from giving this person the autonomy to do so). Hence, in the factory process I'm introducing in this book, I have made journey development a phase on its own.

One reason it's hard to find someone conversant with both phases is that **the skills required are different**. In Phase 1, the skills have to do with human-centred design or design thinking, i.e., asking fundamental questions about customers and their behaviour to uncover the insights needed for experience and/or innovation breakthroughs. This is coupled with knowledge of how profit is made. In Phase 2, the skills are firstly about designing the process of fulfilment, identifying the right inputs and outputs (mostly data points that are needed, and processing of those inputs for onboarding or transacting), and reducing friction; and secondly about designing a user interface that embodies both the experience and process envisaged. The former skills are more aligned with methodologies like Lean and Six Sigma (Antony, 2016), whereas the latter are user interface and experience design skills.

So, in my concept-to-code methodology, it is the Phase 2 team that has primacy for interpreting the product, service and business model requirements generated in Phase 1, and translating them into stories that allow the software development team to produce code aligned to these requirements with as few mistakes as possible. This usually involves **mapping the journey, identifying the correct data inputs and any outputs needed for decision making, asking for information in the right order, and ensuring that instructions and output shown to the customer are clear**. Once the journey maps are sufficiently well-defined, user interface design can begin in parallel, but close synchronisation between the two streams of work needs to be maintained throughout.

Finally, my methodology departs from the traditional process in calling for **data mapping to be done in Phase 2** and not Phase 3. An example will illustrate why: In designing TMRW for Indonesia, an error caught my attention. After all the robust discussion and refinement that we put into the onboarding process, I discovered that we only detected an error in the address field after the build had completed. You should not have this problem if you're starting from scratch with a new core banking system. But we weren't. The field length in the onboarding screen was longer than that in the backend systems, and thus the address was truncated. Why did this happen? Because data mapping was not done at Phase 2 but only in the coding stage. If it had been, we would have caught the problem in the design phase. A final recommendation is to embed experienced user interface software engineers into the UX/UI design team. This will shorten the discovery time of design complexities that are better dealt with in the design phase than in the software development phase.

Phase 3

The output of Phase 1 feeds the stories that are the input for Phase 3. If Phase 1 is about customers and business (making use of design thinking), and Phase 2 is about internal processes and user interface optimisation (calling upon Lean processes), Phase 3 is about software development – specifically **Agile software development**.

As the digital leader for any initiative or transformation, it is critical that you understand the foundations of design thinking, Lean and Agile. A great resource to help you do this is *Understanding Design Thinking, Lean, and Agile* by Jonny Schneider (Schneider, 2017). Figure 32 is found in chapter 1 of the book and is the best articulation of the difference between the three approaches I have come across to date.

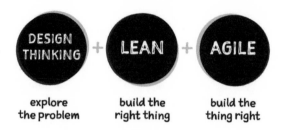

Figure 32 – Understanding Design Thinking, Lean, and Agile
by Jonny Schneider

It's beyond the scope of this book to explore this fascinating area in greater detail, but I think it would be useful to quote Jonny's definitions of the three approaches:

"At a distance, **Design Thinking** is a mindset for exploring complex problems or finding opportunities in a world full of uncertainty. It's a search for meaning, usually focusing on human needs and experience. Using intuitive and abductive reasoning, Design Thinking explores and questions what is, and then imagines what could be with innovative and inventive future solutions."

"The **Lean** mindset is a management philosophy that embraces scientific thinking to explore how right our beliefs and assumptions are while improving a system. Lean practitioners use the deliberate practice of testing their hypotheses through action, observing what actually happens, and making adjustments based on the differences observed. It's how organisations set their course, learn by doing, and decide what to do next on their journey to achieve outcomes."

"The heart of **Agile** is building great software solutions that adapt gracefully to changing needs. Agile begins with a problem – not a requirement – and delivers an elegant solution. The Agile mindset acknowledges that the right solution today might not be the right solution tomorrow. It's rapid, iterative, easily adapted, and focused on quality through continuous improvement."

For me, the power of design thinking lies in its foundation in human-centric design, and understanding what customers need to do their jobs well. This is especially important in industries and organisations that are product-centric because they can't help themselves but start with the product and their business objective first. Lean has manufacturing origins, and to me the power is the focus on less hand-offs and finding the most efficient way to do something. When you combine this with design thinking, you not only get a faster and cheaper process, but also one that the customer can easily appreciate and understand.

With Agile, you **break the development into modules** instead of developing the entire code at one go, which was how software was traditionally developed, where all the code would be developed, then tested, then debugged in one release, and the next release would repeat this whole process in a "waterfall" fashion, with a few releases in a year. The power of the Agile method lies in its ability to make adjustments along the way, something very useful in contexts that are uncertain and where you are continuously refining and adjusting to customer feedback, competitor reactions and industry changes. This fits the hyper-competitive situation in today's business environment much better than monolithic development and has the additional advantage of being able to support many frequent smaller releases in a year, reducing risks and achieving better time to market.

Instead of a purely serial process, some parts of requirements and coding, testing, are done in parallel in Agile development. In the words of TMRW's Chief Technology Officer Juan Jose Cebrian: "What was game-changing was believing that we could deliver working software in small increments with multiple teams working in parallel. This allowed us to deliver end-to-end working software packages from front to back, shortening timelines and increasing our delivery capacity. That was a turning point, because we were coming from a more waterfall kind of approach."

And instead of each team looking at things sequentially, **teams are multidisciplinary**, comprising people from business, IT, operations, service, compliance, etc. These multidisciplinary teams work together across all three phases. They make decisions as a cross-functional unit to deliver the required outcomes. In this approach, more latitude is given to the teams to take an experimental approach, where you don't need to falsely claim that you know everything about what needs to be built. To balance this flexibility, however, more focus must be put on the process so that the increased flexibility is balanced by increased robustness. This ensures that Agile doesn't become an excuse for putting off problems in the belief that you can always fix them later.

Key takeaways

- Building a digital bank from scratch is more than just defining and building the product offering. It's an opportunity to build a bank for great efficiency.

- To be truly efficient, my guide would be that a digital bank's cost/income ratio should eventually hit 30%, compared to 50–60% for a typical large local bank.

- New digital banks need to be very cost-efficient so that they are able to go for segments that are deemed unprofitable or marginally profitable for the incumbents.

- The first order of the day is to get the cost methodology right.

- Get as close to activity-based costing as practical, where the activity of internal staff and technology costs are properly allocated to the right cost drivers.

- The next step is to gather the design considerations for the new digital bank at the bank-wide enterprise level and at the major functional units.

- There should be no piece of data anywhere in the bank that cannot be connected back to a relevant entity, e.g., department, customer, client company, etc.

- The digital bank will need to tackle many design challenges to operate efficiently.

- Design challenges like getting data/metadata right and eliminating paper get very difficult and messy by the third level of detail.

- Another example of a design challenge is the construction of a transparent risk register that is always updated.

- Control functions must be managed as service centres – much like service centres for customers, except this is for internal staff.

- Design, customer journey development and Agile software development form the basic elements of the software factory of any digital transformation.

- The first phase of the software factory consists of the design of the product, service and business model. Here, the translation of observations and ideas to reveal the insights is crucial.

- The output of Phase 1 – design considerations – captures the key design elements of your offering after balancing solutions to customer problems by considering the key drivers or insights, and business viability and feasibility.

- Phase 2 – journey development – is a phase on its own, and involves mapping the journey, and mapping and identifying the correct data inputs and outputs.

- Design Thinking is a mindset for exploring complex problems or finding opportunities in a world full of uncertainty. It's a search for meaning, usually focusing on human needs and experience.

- Lean practitioners use the deliberate practice of testing their hypotheses through action, observing what actually happens, and making adjustments based on the differences observed.

- The heart of Agile is building great software solutions that adapt gracefully to changing needs. Agile begins with a problem – not a requirement – and delivers an elegant solution.

- With Agile, you break the development into modules instead of developing the entire code at one go.

- The power of the Agile method lies in its ability to make adjustments along the way, something very useful in contexts that are uncertain and where you are continuously refining and adjusting to customer feedback, competitor reactions and industry changes.

- Agile teams are multidisciplinary, comprising people from business, IT, operations, service, compliance, etc. They make decisions as a cross-functional unit to deliver the required outcomes.

- More latitude is given to the teams to take an experimental approach, where you don't need to falsely claim that you know everything about what needs to be built.

- With Agile, more focus must be put on the process so that the increased flexibility is balanced by increased robustness.

Selecting and understanding your segment

	2015	2016	2017	2018	YoY % ch. Abs	Def. move %
India	18%	18%	16%	24%	7%	8%
China	8%	6%	21%	14%	-7%	2%
Brazil	7%	9%	7%	11%	4%	3%
USA	8%	9%	18%	10%	-8%	4%
Mexico		10%	8%	10%	2%	2%
Indonesia		7%	9%	8%	0%	2%
Turkey		6%	5%	8%	3%	3%
UK	5%	6%	6%	8%	2%	3%
Global	6%	6%	8%	8%	0%	2%
Denmark				7%	n.a.	3%
France	5%	8%	8%	7%	-1%	2%
Australia	3%	5%	10%	6%	-3%	2%
Russia	7%	4%	6%	6%	1%	2%
South Africa	6%	5%	6%	6%	0%	2%
Sweden	4%	4%		5%	n.a.	1%
Singapore	4%	4%	4%	5%	1%	0%
Spain	7%	5%	4%	5%	1%	1%
Norway				5%		2%
Germany			7%	5%	-2%	1%
Hong Kong			6%	5%	-2%	0%
Switzerland			5%	3%	-2%	0%

Source: UBS Evidence Lab; Note: Our global survey doesn't take in all countries every year. Blanks denote no country survey in that period.

Figure 33 – Propensity to switch banks[48]

The segment you choose to go after will impact the time and path to profit, in a way that is hard to change later. Targeting **younger, more digitally savvy customers** naturally means that you can more easily acquire them with a good customer-centric digital experience. However, their revenue potential is lower at this stage of their lives, and revenue generation will come predominantly from unsecured credit, where loss rates will be higher unless additional information can be obtained to increase approval rates and reduce incidents of fraud, and with good containment of bad debt. Targeting segments with **higher income-generation potential** like the mass affluent poses its own issues as these customers are generally more well-served

---

48. Source: Singapore Banks - UBS Evidence Lab inside: Will virtual banks be a disruptor? © UBS. All rights reserved. Reproduced with permission. May not be forwarded or otherwise distributed.

and have more complex needs and are hence likely to be less attracted to a standalone digital-only proposition.

To select your target segment, it helps to understand the segment's propensity to switch providers. Figure 33 shows the result of a UBS online survey across 21 countries involving 25,849 participants in 2018. As you can see, **the propensity to switch banks is not high**. This is a double-edged sword in that it probably costs a lot to get someone to switch, but once they've switched, it is equally expensive for anyone to pull them away.

The UK offers a good example of primary account "stickiness". In 2013, a current account switching service was introduced by BACS (the organisation responsible for automated payments in the UK) which offers a 7-day switching procedure (Choose, 2019). The service is free, and it moves all incoming and outgoing payments from the old current account to the new one. Despite the ease that the service offers – one of the easiest in the world – switching has been low. Estimates vary between 7% and 11% of the customer base yearly, and if you take out secondary accounts, the estimate could be as low as 3–5% (Skinner, 2021). In fact, the situation doesn't seem to have changed very much from before the regulation was introduced (Insley, 2010).

All this leads many bankers to interpret the chart in Figure 33 as "We are safe". I would argue that what it really is saying is, "Danger lies ahead!" Because switching has already happened when digital banks get their experience right. For example, since its inception, Kakao Bank has successfully attracted 12m customers away from traditional South Korean banks, with an NPS® that leads the industry with no close challengers. Once a customer has switched over, they may no longer view the incumbent bank as their main bank, ever. Danger indeed lies ahead for incumbents, especially in countries like Singapore, where the average NPS® is low, and where a high-NPS® entrant could make the switch happen, and incumbents will subsequently find it hard to bring the relationship back when the NPS® is at a higher level, as the gap would have narrowed.

A 2019 Accenture global study (Gera et al., 2019) identified a segment that is **least loyal** to their existing banking provider. This segment is dominated by younger consumers aged 18–34 who are more open to risk and more tech-savvy (87% say their smartphone is their principal device for transacting online), and nearly half of them belong to a high-income bracket. Their main reason for switching was **better-value products and services**, but two-thirds also said that **corporate social responsibility (CSR)** would influence their choice of a new provider (which deserves further exploration as a part of the overall CVP, as social responsibility ranks higher amongst millennials globally).

So, in summary, what we know is that while most people don't want to switch their primary bank accounts, **younger customers (e.g., millennials or young**

professionals) are more likely to do so. Research done by FICO, as well as experience, indicates that this is mostly due to their desire to avoid paying ATM and low-balance fees, and because their mono-channel (mobile-only) needs make the switch easier.

In TMRW, we homed in on the **young professional** segment, as it had the best of both worlds – younger, digital-savvy customers who are under-served who desire a mono-channel mobile-only experience, but also whose income levels would rise the most over the next 10 years due to their education levels and better job opportunities. This does require patience and a long-term view, otherwise the initial investments will not yield the corresponding results over time.

Key takeaways

- The segment you choose to go after will impact the time and path to profit, in a way that is hard to change later.

- Targeting younger, more digitally savvy customers means that you can acquire them with a good customer-centric digital experience but at the expense of lower revenue potential in the earlier years.

- Targeting segments with higher income-generation potential like the mass affluent poses issues as these customers are well-served, and digital-only propositions without large incentives may not be sufficient.

- A UBS survey across 21 countries involving 25,849 participants in 2018 found that the propensity to switch banks is not high.

- It costs a lot to get someone to switch, but once they've switched, it is equally expensive for anyone to pull them away.

- Switching has already happened when digital banks get their experience right, e.g., Kakao Bank.

- Younger consumers aged 18–34 who are more open to risk and more tech-savvy are most likely to switch and nearly half of them belong to a high-income bracket.

- So, while most people may not want to switch their primary bank accounts, younger customers (e.g., millennials or young professionals) are more likely to do so.

4.3

The path to profit

Of the approximately 200 digital banks of all forms, both start-ups and within incumbent banks, I found only four that were profitable in 2019: Kakao Bank, Webank, MYbank and Tinkoff Bank. My analysis was not exhaustive so I'm sure there may be a few more profitable banks, but most other research corroborates the finding that just a handful are profitable (Choi et al., 2021; Weng, 2020). My research showed that the first three had a huge benefit in the form of low cost of acquisition and activation due to their association with their parent companies (KakaoTalk, Alibaba and WeChat, respectively), who had lots of potential customers and data that the banks could leverage.

When I asked Kakao Bank during a visit in February 2020 what factors were most responsible for their success, they named two: their unique shareholding, and their timing, citing that when they launched in 2016, there wasn't a truly credible Korean mobile banking app. In their first month of operation, they signed up 1M customers. As of March 2020, they boast 12M users (23% of the population of South Korea), of whom 10M are active (Crisanto, 2020). Kakao Bank is now reportedly worth an estimated 20 trillion won (US$18B), putting it neck-and-neck with the country's largest banking group, KB Financial, valued at 22 trillion won.

From its inception, Kakao leveraged the immense popularity and trust factor of its parent KakaoTalk, the mobile messaging app used by over 90% of Koreans, and thus they were able to attract a wide spectrum of customers (Kim & Park, 2020). Featuring Kakao Friends characters on the bank's app and debit cards helped immensely in attracting customers in the early stage. Whilst Kakao has stated that it targets 30- to 50-year-olds as they are more profitable, as of June 2019, Maeil Business News Korea reported that "32.1% of Kakao Bank customers were in their 20s, 31.2% in their 30s, and 21.0% in their 40s. When looking at Korea's entire population, this means 46.4% of all 20s and 42.8% of all 30s are using Kakao Bank" (Goh & Paul Raj, 2019; S. Lee & Kim, 2019).

In my view, **most digital banks will not have Kakao Bank's good fortune**. They will not get profitable so fast, as the incumbent banks in their countries have digital banking that performs reasonably well, and there isn't a platform like KakaoTalk to help rapidly accelerate customer capture.

Instead, for most digital banks, the key to profitability starts with understanding marginal and fixed cost accounting. Businesses lose money if their marginal profitability is negative. The easiest way to think about this is to do the maths on the next customer you acquire. If that customer's current annual revenue is less than his cost to acquire and his annual servicing costs, then the marginal profitability of the business is negative. This means that **as the business expands and acquires more customers, it incurs more and more losses**. In a traditional bank, new product profitability is mixed with the profitability of the bank's existing cash cows, so one rarely has to think about marginal profitability the way a start-up has to go about it.

Definitely, there will be a temptation to think about large revenue generation potential early. This would be a mistake. All routes to a successful digital bank will require **obtaining positive marginal contribution first**. This also means keeping your acquisition costs and servicing costs low and containing your annual fixed costs within the ability of your customer base to recoup. Even Webank and Kakao Bank would have passed through this stage first – only in their case they managed to reach this point much sooner. In the case of Kakao Bank, they did it within 18 months of launch (Kim & Park, 2020; Sendingan, 2019).

If there are patient investors who are willing to trade short-term profit of a smaller business for long-term market capture to build a bigger business, then the company's appetite to sustain a negative marginal contribution could allow it to take these losses in its stride. This patience would also depend on the possibility and probability of share capture. If the population is large and there are a lot of unbanked customers, and scale would lower the cost to acquire and serve and spread the annual fixed cost to be incurred over a bigger base of customers, then there may be light at the end of the tunnel for sustaining losses in the hope of building a bigger business. More often, the patience isn't there, and in that case the cost incurred needs to be commensurate with the revenue generation ability.

There is a distinct connection between the path to profit and the revenue generating potential of the chosen segment. If the team has decided to develop the younger, more digitally savvy segment, then there is a need to contend with their lower revenue generating potential. Therefore, from the outset, **the focus will be on costs** – in particular the cost of acquiring an active customer and the annual cost of servicing this customer.

The first decision is to select **how long you are prepared to allow the digital bank to sustain negative marginal profitability**. The higher the focus on share capture, presumably due to a large pool of unbanked customers, or an anticipated upswing of revenue in later years due to a focus on young professionals, the bigger must the appetite be to sustain a negative contribution. You can't have your cake and eat it too. Tell your board that from the beginning.

There must be a focus on **active customers**. In my experience, it is better to have a smaller base of highly active customers than a large base with a very small proportion of active customers. The numbers speak for themselves: If you have 2M customers with an active rate of only 10%, then you really have only 200K active customers, and it's the same as having 500K customers at a 40% active rate. But from a cost standpoint, things may be very different. If 80% of your 2M customers are eligible for the $25 reward you dangled to attract them to apply, then you might have spent $40M to acquire 200K customers at $200 per active customer. But in the case of 500K total customers at the same 80% eligibility, the spend is only $10M, or $50 per customer.

If the segment's immediate revenue generating potential is small, and if there isn't a large appetite to sustain many years of losses for the eventual prize at the end of the rainbow (a situation that will be faced by almost all incumbent banks), then the key is **not to pay a lot for acquiring active customers**. This goes back to concentrating the spend on the initial build to ensure that the experience is very good and sells itself, rather than saving on the spend and not being able to achieve the level of advocacy needed to generate sufficient active customers at lower cost. Therefore, the minimum viable proposition is really the features and experience required to ensure that the advocacy measure, e.g., net promoter score (NPS®), is high enough so that the cost of acquisition falls to the required price point to produce a positive marginal profit in the target year.

So, my recommendation to banks setting up is that they should not set a launch target date or a customer target first; rather, the first and most critical KPI is the customer experience differential between the existing competitors and the service you are about to launch. For example, the 2019 NPS® scores for the top 7 retail banks in Singapore don't exceed the legal age for buying cigarettes, and so to make an impact, I would recommend setting an NPS® target of double that. This means you should **only launch your new retail bank if you can hit an NPS® of +40**.

If you were to launch with an NPS® that was, let's say, +20, you would have to **spend more to attract the customer to switch over and stay active**. Bankers operating in Singapore would also know that among the ASEAN countries, customers in Singapore are best at extracting maximum benefits from various banking products. When I was head of consumer banking, I recall that Singaporean customers often knew the terms and conditions as well as – or even better than – the bank's product managers. So, the tactic of incentivising them till your NPS® becomes much better might cost you more or not even work in Singapore.

In the case of TMRW, we launched in Thailand in August 2019. Over the following 6 months, we worked very hard to improve the NPS® many-fold to +33 (Khoo, 2020). We verified the inverse relationship between NPS® and the cost to acquire an active customer.

Acquiring customers just using Google or Facebook is an expensive exercise. One study showed that in 2018, for every A$100 spent by Australian advertisers, A$49 went to Google and A$24 to Facebook (Chua, 2021). Paying for click-through without customers signing up is thus very wasteful and expensive. I would recommend all digital banks to design their solution such that you are only paying for active customers from day one. Certainly, a **CPA (cost per acquisition) model** is more expensive than CPC (cost per click), but it makes more sense as you end up with active customers.

Eventually we improved the system so that we could distinguish between customers that only signed up for a deposit account and those who signed up for a bundle of deposit account and credit card. Since the latter generated more income, we were prepared to pay more to acquire them.

In hindsight, I would strongly recommend that from the very start, you should only pay for signed-up customers. Your system should also allow you to know **which partner the customer was acquired through**, so that you can activate agreements where you acquire directly from the partner, bypassing the middlemen like Google and Facebook. You can pay the acquired customers in the currency of that partner (e.g., vouchers issued by that partner). These steps will help you reduce the cost of acquisition as much as possible from the start.

Once you achieve positive marginal contribution, first remember to celebrate! It's the first sign of success. After this significant milestone, the subsequent strategy will depend on the potential size of the segment you have chosen and what customer share you desire. In a larger market, where the larger customer numbers can make up for low individual ticket sizes, the design needs to defray the higher cost required to launch a more superior experience at a higher level of NPS® needed to acquire more customers. To ramp up the level of acquisition and continue to have positive marginal contribution, **the NPS® must thus move even higher over time**.

This simple set of maths gives you the perspective. If you make $5 annual revenue per customer, and your cost of acquisition was $10, spread over 5 years your annual cost of acquisition would be $2. Let's say you add $1 for annual servicing costs, then you would make an annual marginal contribution of $5 - $2 - $1 = $2 per customer. That would amount to a $10M total contribution if you had 5M customers. Thus, your annual fixed cost needs to be less than $10M if you want to break even on a total cost basis, and this assumes you could acquire 5M customers. So, the more customers, the higher the annual fixed cost you can afford. Likely at the point where your marginal contribution is zero, the total customer base is much smaller than 4M, say 1M–2M customers. So, you need to scale further, but without increasing your cost of acquisition further, as this might cause you to regress to negative marginal contribution. Thus, your NPS® must increase. My recommendation would be to improve it by **1.5 times of your NPS® at launch**. If, however, your annual fixed cost is $8M, then your annual fixed cost would be covered by the marginal contribution of 4M customers acquired.

In a digital bank, the annual fixed costs would comprise mostly people and technology costs. If your annual fixed cost footprint is much larger than $10M in the example above, then you would not be able to turn total profit positive even if your marginal contribution is positive, assuming it would be too much of a challenge to target more than 5M customers. This is where **designing for operating efficiency** comes in. If from the very start, the processes are designed to be mostly automated and straight-through, this would result in a lower people count and thus a lower headcount cost. In doing so, you will be trading lower labour cost for higher technology costs, but you also need to ensure that annual technology costs are not well beyond your ability to recoup by prioritising the features that have the maximum impact on advocacy.

In a market with better demographics and a steeper increase of customers' disposable income as they age, a case can be made that sustaining more losses gives you a bigger business in the end. If $20M is the ongoing annual fixed costs required to ensure that your NPS® keeps heading upwards so that you can lower your acquisition costs, then going from 5M to 10M customers at a marginal profit of $2 mentioned previously would neutralise the $20M annual fixed cost base required. It will take you time to reach a 10M base, and before you cross that line, you will not be able to recover your annual fixed costs fully, and hence you will be making a loss in the fixed cost lens but a profit in the variable cost lens. This is a good place to be if you are going for more aggressive growth. Note that at this stage, we aren't even talking about recovering the initial investment put into starting up the bank. Thus, you can see why starting a new digital bank is a long-term strategy. It is a business where you put in a lot of costs initially[49], in the hope of building an annuity stream of income for many years to come.

If, on the other hand, the market is small, like in Singapore, then you may not be able to afford a $20M cost base, as you don't have 10M customers to spread your fixed costs over, even if you capture 100% of the market. Going global may not totally solve this issue as banking doesn't lend itself as well to the software industry to global reach, as previously mentioned. In this scenario, **a design that allows you to create and launch a bank at a low initial investment and at the same time achieve the NPS® breakthrough lift required is essential**. Once that initial experience difference is established, then more care and prudence are needed to improve or initiate only what has a good payback in terms of cost vs additional NPS® lift. This can be to either maintain the current acquisition momentum against competitive moves or to accelerate it.

Once the base is big enough, that's when you can start to mine it for additional revenue, leveraging the data gathered from the initial base of customers to encourage appropriate engagement that can facilitate cross-selling of additional

---

49. Traditional banks would build internal infrastructure and hence this cost would be a combination of fixed costs depreciated over a certain number of years, but for the digital bank running on the cloud, these costs could all be mostly annual operating costs.

products. Too much focus on short-term customer generation may result in bringing in customers who are not active and serve just to prop up acquisition numbers without corresponding increase in revenue, or too much risk in lending may result in higher bad debt later. The maximum revenue potential of the customer in the short term was already set when you selected your target segment. What is now in your control is how the costs are spent and what is the right amount to pay to acquire active customers.

To sum up, the path to profit requires you to **manage three measures simultaneously and holistically**:

1. The absolute number of active customers
2. The advocacy measure, e.g., net promoter score (NPS®)
3. The cost to acquire and serve

The absolute number of active customers needs to continuously move up. The NPS® must start higher than the competitor banks you aim to take customers from (assuming you are starting with bankable customers rather than the unbanked) and continue to move up from that point. How fast it needs to move up is a function of your ambition to grow the number of active customers. The faster you want to accelerate this, the faster the NPS® needs to ramp up. And this is tied to the cost to acquire, as the cost to acquire will start to rise as you ramp up the number of customers acquired if there isn't a corresponding increase in NPS®. The cost to serve is less directly associated with the number of customers acquired, but you still have to find ways to lower the cost to serve over time so that the total marginal cost (cost to acquire and cost to serve) will fall below the revenue per customer at a target date in the future.

Key takeaways

- Kakao Bank, Webank, MYbank had a huge benefit in the form of low cost of acquisition and activation due to their association with their parent companies (KakaoTalk, Alibaba and WeChat, respectively), who had lots of potential customers and data that the banks could leverage.

- Kakao Bank is now reportedly worth almost as much as the largest banking group in South Korea, KB Financial.

- Most digital banks will not have Kakao Bank's good fortune and will not get profitable as fast.

- For most digital banks, the key to profitability starts with understanding marginal and fixed cost accounting.

- Businesses lose money if their marginal contribution is negative, meaning that as the business expands and acquires more customers, it incurs more and more losses.

- All routes to a successful digital bank will require obtaining positive marginal contribution first.

- Patient investors who are willing to trade short-term profit of a smaller business for long-term market capture to build a bigger business may need to sustain a negative marginal contribution for a longer period.

- If the team has decided to develop the younger, more digitally savvy segment, then there is a need to contend with their lower revenue generating potential.

- Therefore, from the outset, the focus will be on costs – in particular the cost of acquiring an active customer and the annual cost of servicing this customer.

- The higher the focus on share capture, the bigger must the appetite be to sustain a negative contribution.

- If the segment's immediate revenue generating potential is small, and there isn't a large appetite to sustain many years of losses, then the key is not to pay a lot for acquiring active customers.

- Concentrate the spend on the initial build to ensure that the experience is very good and sells itself, and not save on the spend and not achieve the level of advocacy needed to generate sufficient active customers at lower cost.

- My recommendation is to launch at two times the average NPS® of your industry, in your country.

- Acquiring customers just using Google or Facebook is an expensive exercise.

- From the very start, you should only pay for signed-up customers, preferably active customers.

- Once you achieve positive marginal contribution, first remember to celebrate! It's the first sign of success.

- To ramp up the level of acquisition to negate the annual fixed costs and continue to have positive marginal contribution, the NPS® must be at least 1.5 times of your NPS® at launch.

- In a digital bank, the annual fixed costs comprise mostly people and technology costs.

- From the start, processes have to be designed to be mostly automated and straight-through. This would result in lower headcount cost, but you also need to focus on not incurring unnecessary annual technology costs.

- In a market with better demographics and a steeper increase of customers' disposable income as they age, a case can be made that sustaining more losses gives you a bigger business in the end.

- Making a loss in the fixed cost lens but a profit in the variable cost lens is an acceptable strategy to improve the NPS® during the path-to-profit to end up with a bigger business, naturally with correspondingly higher risk.

- In a small market, a design that allows you to create and launch a bank at a low initial investment and at the same time achieve the NPS® breakthrough lift required is essential.

- This means improving or initiating only what has a good payback in terms of cost vs additional NPS® lift.

- Too much focus on short-term customer generation may result in bringing in customers who are not active.

- Too much risk in lending may result in higher bad debt later.

- The path to profit requires you to manage three measures simultaneously and holistically: the absolute number of active customers, the advocacy measure, e.g., net promoter score (NPS®), and the cost to acquire and serve.

The role of service in a digital bank

If you look at the typical calls coming into a banking call centre, up to 70% of them are related to the status of an application or transaction, a waiver, a query that has yet to be answered, etc. However, digital bank customers have very different service requirements from traditional bank customers. They do not call the contact centre or visit a branch for transactional enquiries. They do so digitally, through the bank app.

Thus, in designing service for a digital bank, the assumption would be that no customer would call up asking for balances, as they could login and view it themselves. The service focus should be on "non-green" flows, which are processes that are not fully automated, status-of-transaction enquiries which are not available on the digital bank app, or requests for waivers of fees and charges that can't be handled automatically.

One reason not to offer high interest rates is that it will also attract older and wealthier customers, who may not want to be served through only the mobile channel and they may call the contact centre frequently, increasing your cost of servicing substantially.

The ability to offer an intuitive combination of automated servicing (e.g., a chatbot) and human assistance (through chat or voice) will define the new standards of customer experience in a digital bank. With the usage of social messaging platforms growing exponentially, we foresee the Gen Y and Z customers of tomorrow **using chat for nearly all of their servicing interactions with banks**.

The focus for TMRW was on self-help, and thus we tried to make almost everything available in a self-help format, to provide fast and consistently good service at lower cost.

TMRW's digital app service design focused on providing customers with the quickest and most efficient way to resolve an enquiry, depending on its nature and perceived urgency. For instance, TMRW's chatbot, Tia (TMRW Intelligent Assistant), is powered by Personetics and can function as a smart assistant to find the right answers through digital conversations, or it can also serve responses through an intelligent search if the customer prefers. When interacting with TMRW's contact centre, customers can simultaneously chat online so that they can be guided through the resolution process.

Banking servicing issues are unique in that the majority involve **non-clarity of information**, not so much troubleshooting banking functionality that doesn't work. This suggests that chatbots – which will be seeing significant advancement in Natural Language Processing (NLP) capabilities in the next 3 to 5 years – will be able to take over most of the regular servicing conversations handled by contact centres today.

In the near future, customers will not be able to tell if they are talking to a bot or a human. The chatbot will be able to detect frustration and move the customer from bot to human assistance. Customer interactions with chatbots are expected to provide rich insights into conversation patterns and behaviours which banks can use to sharpen interactions and identify the most appropriate opportunity to introduce a relevant product or service without being intrusive or pushy. Contact centres will become **relationship centres** that monitor the customer relationship and interject for instant service recovery or to create exceptional delight.

I also foresee advances in user interface design that will largely eliminate the need for customer interactions with bank servicing agents regarding product, service or promotional information. In fact, availability of all possible servicing functions to **aid easy self-help** will be the service norm, leading to users having their issues resolved via self-help pop-ups at the point a service outage occurs within the digital bank app. The litmus test for digital banks in demonstrating customer service as a key differentiator will be their ability to manage the seamlessness of resolving service issues surfaced on social media across its servicing platforms, from chatbot to contact centre.

As banks become experience companies, great service becomes an imperative to get right. The most advanced thinking in service is to design it so that **the problem gets resolved immediately where it happened**. This means detecting the problem when it happens and solving it there, rather than having the customer call after the fact. When a customer has a longer delay than usual entering information, or when his navigation pattern indicates he can't find something, in-app self-help software can be triggered to provide assistance. Some examples of such software solutions are WalkMe[50] and inSided[51].

Traditionally, banks have implemented chatbots as a **standalone channel** (e.g., standalone capability on their website) or as a **complementary capability to an existing channel** (e.g., call deflection capability on their contact centre interactive voice response). The inherent flaw of such implementation is that it creates multiple

---

50. WalkMe is an American multinational software-as-a-service (SaaS) company with headquarters in San Francisco, California. Its Digital Adoption Platform (DAP) was recognised in Everest Group's PEAK Matrix Assessment of DAP vendors as the leading DAP product.

51. inSided is a customer self-service solution that scales support, and powers customer success for high-growth companies, based in Amsterdam, Netherlands.

disparate channels for customers, which results in users needing to repeat their query all over again whenever they switch between channels.

In TMRW, we eliminated this problem by **making the chatbot Tia the central orchestration point for customer service delivery** (Digital Banker, 2020). On receiving a customer's input, Tia can bring in an assortment of capabilities – such as multilingual response management, human support through chat and voice, deep-linked screens for ease of usage interactions, in-app web page FAQ support, sentiment determination for response moderation and intelligent routing logic – to deliver a seamless experience (Figure 34).

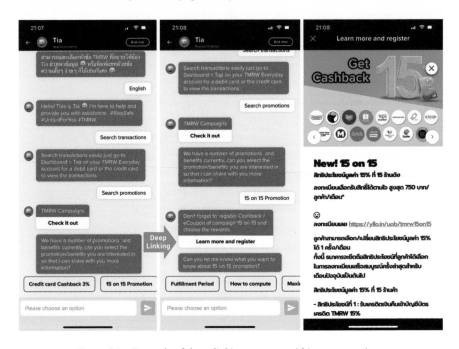

Figure 34 – Example of deep-linking screens within conversations

There are **three service capabilities** available: customers can chat with a chatbot, chat with a live customer service agent, or speak to a live customer service agent using a data call via the TMRW app. TMRW's customer service centre was designed this way so that customers with common and easily answerable questions can get immediate service from a chatbot. But in the event that the chatbot cannot fully address their query or issue, a live customer agent will be able to take over the conversation. Customers also have the option to skip the chatbot and speak to a live agent directly if the problem is severe, as in the case of a lost card or a fraudulent transaction.

We knew that Tia would not be able to answer all queries, especially in the beginning, since AI-powered chatbots need time to learn from past conversations. So, if a customer asked a query a few times and didn't get an answer, he or she would be automatically transferred to a live agent. A feedback loop based on how the agent eventually solved the problem allowed us to train Tia until it got better at understanding common issues, technical terms, and even nuances in language. But the right investments have to be made in the beginning so that future operations and processes become easier, more streamlined and cost-efficient.

In time, we discovered that the Thai language was exceptionally difficult for a chatbot to comprehend; we had to work with Personetics, who was the chatbot solution provider, to revamp the NLP routine to improve its performance.

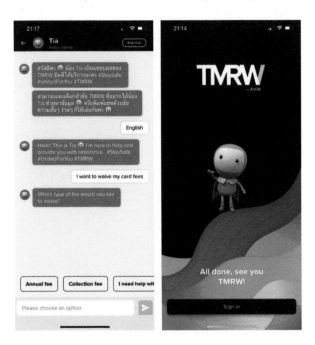

Figure 35 – Tia's dual language capabilities (Tia is depicted on the right)

TMRW's digital customer service model boasts **many firsts in the Thai and ASEAN banking industry**. It is the first digital service model that uses chatbots to orchestrate the delivery of various forms of customer service without ever having to exit the TMRW app. It is also the first full Thai-language NLP-capable chatbot, with Tia achieving a high comprehension accuracy rate. Tia handles over 95% of its interactions in Thai. At the same time, it is also the first chatbot with dual-language response capability, allowing customers to switch seamlessly between Thai and English, as shown in Figure 35. In answering customer queries in an accurate and efficient way, Tia helps improve user confidence in AI-led conversation capabilities.

To emphasise the importance of service, every month I would personally chair the **service reviews**, where we would look at the top drivers of live chats and also the hotline[52]. We also reviewed the cost-to-serve projection versus actual, to drive the cost-to-serve down. There would also be cost attribution based on volume of calls and cost attribution based on the Centres of Excellence (COEs) or units within TMRW. This allowed us to accurately pinpoint the root cause of these calls.

NPS® for servicing was also tracked monthly, and I drove month-on-month improvements by continually pushing for better **first call resolution (FCR)**. FCR for the hotline was in the top two deciles, and in March 2020, live chat FCR actually exceeded hotline FCR for the first time. The chatbot FCR was still markedly lower – detractor analysis revealed that most of the negative experiences revolved around the chatbot's understanding of the customer's query – but we worked hard to hone it and make it better and better over time. Before launch, the team spent 8 months training Tia with 25,000 Thai words sentences and phrases. After launch, the upgrading continued with over 10,000 phrases monthly, with a total lexicon of words and phrases that now exceeds 100,000.

I am certain that continuous focus on making small and steady progress in enabling Tia to handle more and more customer queries with consistently high quality will pay off. This will allow TMRW to deliver a very high service experience at very low servicing costs. The latest update from UOB lists the chatbot FCR at over 80% and the chatbot NPS® at +45.[53] We know this is possible as the Webank equivalent of Tia can handle 98% of customer queries (Huang, 2018).

---

52. It was never intended for a hotline to be established, but there were inherent errors in the comparison of the fingerprint scan and the fingerprint image stored on the chip, which required it. Being the first to introduce this means of onboarding meant that it wasn't completely straight-through like Indonesia, and thus more prone to customer usage issues. A hotline was set up to manage these issues.

53. April 2021 update from UOB at a virtual Goldman Sachs conference. The chatbot FCR before passing to a human agent was >80% and the chatbot NPS had improved to +45 in January 2021.

Key takeaways

- Digital bank customers do not call the contact centre or visit a branch for transactional enquiries. They do so digitally, through the bank app.

- Service in a digital bank is for status-of-transaction enquiries that are not available on the app and any other transactions or requests that can't be handled automatically.

- With the usage of social messaging platforms growing exponentially, I foresee the Gen Y and Z customers of tomorrow using chat for nearly all of their servicing interactions with banks.

- Banking servicing issues are unique in that the majority involve non-clarity of information, not so much troubleshooting banking functionality that doesn't work.

- Customer interactions with chatbots are expected to provide rich insights into conversation patterns and behaviours which banks can use to sharpen future interactions.

- The most advanced thinking in service is to resolve the problem immediately where it happened by detecting the problem when it happens and solving it there, rather than having the customer call after the fact.

- Traditional chatbots are standalone or complementary to an existing channel; the inherent flaw is that it results in users needing to repeat their query all over again when they switch between channels.

- In TMRW, we eliminated this problem by making our chatbot Tia the central point for customer service delivery.

- Tia can bring in an assortment of capabilities (such as multilingual response management, human support through chat and voice, deep-linked screens for ease of usage interactions, in-app web page FAQ support, sentiment determination for response moderation and intelligent routing logic) to deliver a seamless experience.

- Initially Tia was configured to escalate to a human agent faster, as it would take time to learn and get better.

- Over time, as Tia learns and develops a higher comprehension accuracy rate, and also a higher resolution rate, the number of human agents should decline on a per customer basis.

- We know this is possible as the Webank equivalent of Tia can handle 98% of customer queries (Huang, 2018).

How to differentiate?

The question most asked of me was: "How is TMRW different?" The fact that this question arose so frequently shows just how commoditised the industry is and reveals the lack of deep tech changes in financial services that can drive rapid change.

My experience tells me that the arena of differentiation is moving towards **business process improvement**. In the omni-channel era, differentiation lay in people, place, product, promotion and process. Where process wasn't strong, people could still make up for it. But within the next 10 years or sooner, the majority of customers will be banking via a digital channel for their transactional needs. In this stage, people, place and product will mostly fall by the wayside, **making process the most important element in the experience**. People will still be needed, but more and more they will be involved in the design and not the delivery of the experience.

However, process isn't a top management agenda in most banks today. It should be taken as seriously as risk, revenue, profit, capital, etc., but it isn't. Without world-class business process capabilities, traditional banks will not be able to significantly improve their customer experience. And if the only P left in the digital world is process, how are these banks going to compete? Company DNA is hard to change. Process is a complex topic that needs massive attention to detail. It doesn't appear to be strategic at first, until you make experience your top priority.

So, the answer to the question "How is TMRW different?" is found in **putting customers first, and designing, implementing and sustaining an experience that is so simple, intuitive and frictionless so that the customer-centric proposition will be a reality**. This alone, if achieved, serves as its own differentiator, as it is very hard for anyone to copy, requiring a cultural change and an attention to detail that is very hard to spark. I believe traditional bankers still can't get away from the people, product, place, price and promotion orientation. It's not to say that you can't make some differentiating features or have promotional offers. **The question is whether these are the heroes or the supporting cast**. TMRW had features that solved some of the problems young professionals experience, e.g., allowing them to change their ATM cash withdrawal, online spend and credit card limits, to better control their spending, introducing a savings game and a savings account that made it harder to spend the money within the account, ability to set a spend budget and get alerts real-time as you spend, etc.

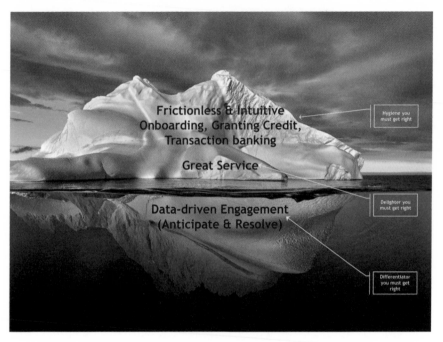

Figure 36 – How to differentiate?

If you buy into the thinking that focusing on customers and process is paramount, you might still be asking: "So where does this focus lead to?" Figure 36 shows the key differentiation for any digital bank. Having studied this space extensively, I don't see many other alternatives.

1. **Being frictionless** and having very intuitive transactional banking is the ante to play in the race to be the best digital bank. This is very basic but also very hard to do. It requires understanding intimately the small problems customers face, and then addressing them with great process and attention to detail, to create a brilliant experience. In addition, before you can transact, you need to onboard the customer, and you need to be able to decide if you can grant credit. In countries where the credit bureau is not able to risk-rank customers reliably, being able to use alternative data to improve your risk-ranking becomes pivotal (see Chapter 3.6).

2. The next differentiator is **great service as a delighter**. From information about products to instructions, fee waivers, promotion mechanisms, etc., you need to minimise anything that can lead to a service call, and if you can't, then you need to resolve it wherever possible at the point where the outage happens

and minimise service contacts after the fact. Again, being customer-centric and having great processes and attention to detail are important capabilities for delivering great service.

3. The final differentiator is **data-driven digital engagement**, using transactional, location and other data to anticipate your customers' needs and resolve potential problems before they occur. For example, if a customer has a regular payment, but his balance has dipped below the required amount, the bank actually knows this is going to happen before it does. This means the bank can open a conversation with the customer on topics ranging from anticipating a payment failure to tracking their expenditure in real time.

In UOB's case, another key differentiator was the **TMRW brand** itself. The first question we had to ask was whether we should go to market with the UOB brand or create a new separate brand. UOB had never taken this approach before, so it was something new for everyone. The decision had to go all the way to UOB's Group CEO, Wee Ee Cheong. We presented him with the idea of setting up a separate brand and doing things differently, and a few weeks later, we got the green light from him to go ahead. He added: "If we don't try, we won't learn."

The brand was the brainchild of Wendy Ong, Head of marketing for TMRW. It was designed from the ground up as a brand that would appeal to young professionals in Thailand. The theme of the TMRW brand launch for Thailand was **"Different Generations, Different Solutions"** – essentially a message to the millennials in Thailand that they didn't have to choose the same bank as their parents. We observed that children often opened their first bank account with their parents' bank, and so, in the absence of intervention, that's where TMRW's millennial customers might have begun their first bank relationship. We designed a campaign to send the message that they were now free to choose, and we were offering just that alternative: a bank that was designed from the ground up, just for them.

This campaign resonated with a lot of Thai millennials. One video depicted a young professional taking notes on her mobile phone, which her senior colleagues mistook as a sign that she was not paying attention. Another depicted a mother chastising her son for his earrings and hairdo on his first day at work and telling him not to leave the office before his boss. These were situations that the YP and YPF customers could easily picture themselves in. To view some of these videos, visit the Facebook page of TMRW Thailand, go to the "Videos" tab and scroll to the bottom.

Figure 37 shows the success of TMRW's brand activities, where we achieved results like 32M views of the TMRW theme song, performed by the top three local artists in Thailand – a first for any bank in ASEAN. Customers found TMRW's brand

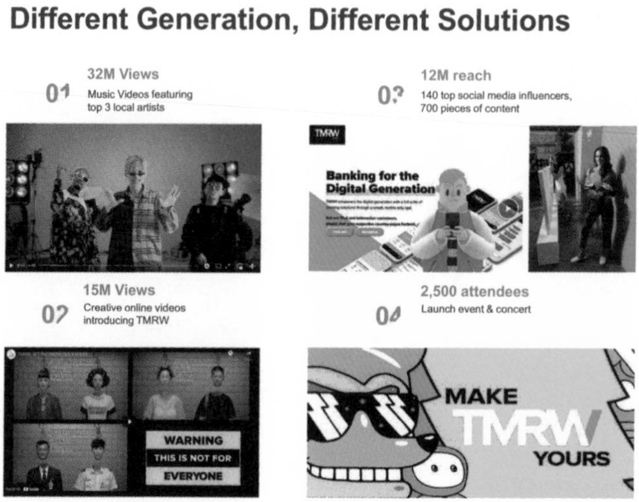

Different Generation, Different Solutions

Figure 37 – Launching a new TMRW brand
(Source: UOB Website, 15 May 2019)

impression very appealing. These YP and YPF users felt that it wasn't an app for their parents, but an app tailored just for them. They also commented on the beautiful UI design and TMRW's bright brand colours, which were unlike any other bank's. Millennial customers in Thailand loved the City of TMRW savings game, where you grow a virtual city through your savings, which made them want to save more. Engagement and insights also surfaced as a differentiator, as customers credited TMRW for reminding them when their expenditure was going up. The most encouraging results for me came from **advocates who had switched banks**, some moving substantial funds and transactions from leading Thai banks to TMRW.

By early 2020, TMRW's NPS® rose to be among the top three in Thai banks, at +33 (Khoo, 2020a). And when we took the best of Thailand and delivered it in the TMRW Indonesia app, it achieved an NPS® of +60 in 2020.[54]

---

54. +60 was the NPS for TMRW Indonesia as of October 20. The December 20 measurement was +51, above the nearest local leader at +45. Source: UOB Website.

Key takeaways

- TMRW's differentiation is putting customers first, and designing, implementing and sustaining an experience that is so simple, intuitive and frictionless that the customer-centric proposition will be a reality.

- Three areas of focus present themselves as key differentiators for digital banks:

  - Being frictionless and having very intuitive transactional banking is very basic but also very hard to do. It requires understanding intimately the small problems customers face, and then addressing them with great process and attention to detail, to create a brilliant experience.

  - Great service as a delighter. From information about products to instructions, fee waivers, promotion mechanisms, etc., you need to minimise anything that can lead to a service call. If you can't, then you need to resolve it wherever possible at the point where the outage happens.

  - The final differentiator is using transactional, location and other data to anticipate your customers' needs and resolve potential problems before they occur.

- "Different Generations, Different Solutions" was a differentiator in that it sent the message to millennials that they didn't have to choose the same bank as their parents. They now had an alternative: a bank that was designed from the ground up for them.

- Customers found TMRW's brand impression very appealing. YP and YPF customers felt that it wasn't an app for their parents, but an app tailored just for them.

- The City of TMRW savings game, where you grow a virtual city through your savings, made customers want to save more.

- Engagement and insights also surfaced as a differentiator, by reminding customers when their expenditure was going up.

- By early 2020, TMRW's NPS® rose to be among the top three in Thai banks, at +33.

- When the best of Thailand was implemented in the TMRW Indonesia app, it achieved an NPS® of +60 in 2020.

Learning as a differentiator

The speed of imitation has probably never been higher. So, it's no longer about being ahead, it's also very much about staying ahead. This brings us to the topic about how customer-centric differentiation can be enhanced continuously through **constant learning**. If you are going to make learning a big item on your agenda, you need to experiment, and you need to get comfortable with the fact that not everything you try is going to work, otherwise the learning wouldn't be rich. The need to learn from customers gets harder after you launch.

In a way, it's better to receive a complaint from a customer than for the customer not to complain but simply give up using your app, as you don't receive the feedback you need to improve your system. One of the learning opportunities for us at TMRW was studying the complaints and feedback from the service centre. The monthly reviews involved the chat, call-centre and operations staff – as they are the people closest to the customer, who may not get enough face-time with management – and often yielded much valuable information about which service issues to fix first.

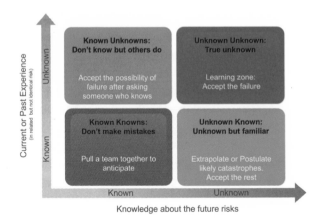

Figure 38 – How to properly accept failure

The environmental setup for learning is also important. Often people tend to start deploying without the required thinking. A list of known areas that can go wrong because they have gone wrong before (**known knowns**) and a list of areas which are new to the team but not new to people outside the team (**known unknowns**), if incorporated as part of the thinking process, can quickly weed out obvious mistakes (Figure 38). What's left after this is usually learning, i.e., the unknowns. A learning organisation must continue to explore and gain knowledge, which helps it stay one step ahead of the competition.

Learning is not just confined to knowledge. There is also learning that involves process improvements. This is especially important in Agile development, which otherwise has the danger of disintegrating into an **excuse to "fix it later"**, resulting in a high error or defect rate. One of the improvements made to the Agile process in TMRW was the introduction of root-cause analysis and defect attribution. This allowed a virtuous cycle of continuous improvements to gradually bring down the defect rate. Defect attribution must be done with the aim to improve and not blame. This is much easier if you follow the known knowns and known unknowns approach described above.

I wanted TMRW to have a steep learning curve, as any factor of competition with low learning means it can easily be copied. So, we dug deeper and realised that engagement would be the key differentiation. It had a large learning component and was the driving factor towards creating a bank that is more than just a utility. To increase and concentrate TMRW's ability to learn, we created an **engagement lab** with a multidisciplinary team consisting of communications, analytics, content, and behavioural science specialists. The term "lab" was adopted to represent the learning journey we needed to take to make the engagement strategy successful (Chiew, 2018).

The other ingredient of continual learning is data. Through the data stored in TMRW's systems, we were able to pay close attention to customer sentiment, gauge performance, and identify the key areas where we could improve. More importantly, we could keep track of how customer behaviour shifted over time and adapt to these changes. Through the use of data and the engagement labs, we were able to test theories and **dispel certain myths about customer behaviour** that we never would have considered.

For example, conventional wisdom has it that the more incentives you offer to perform a task, the more likely people will perform it. To test this, we conducted an experiment where we offered one group of customers a higher incentive and another a lower incentive to perform the same task. Surprisingly, the group that was offered the lower incentive had twice the take-up. It was only after talking to customers that we realised why: they felt that offers with higher incentive amounts must have some kind of hidden catch. Even if we told them that this wasn't the case, they were conditioned to assume that anything that's too good to be true usually is.

Another myth is that a digital bank that caters to a young audience will flourish if it uses a playful tone for content. Some of the most playful pieces of content ranked lower than "Your credit card bill is due" among all of TMRW's insights[55]. Through experimentation and testing, we discovered that customers only found insight cards that carried some context matching their own individual behaviour engaging; content without context was meaningless to them, and possibly even off-putting. We tried again on Valentine's Day by **contextualising the content** to cater to different profiles. This campaign ended up being one of the most well-received since the bank's launch. The experiment taught us that conventional wisdom cannot explain real human behaviour, and banks cannot operate on intelligent assumptions alone. This is where the data, testing and learning come in.

---

55. Refer to Figure 24 to check out the insights. They are marked with the words "Smart Insights".

Key takeaways

- Today, it's no longer simply about being ahead, it's also very much about staying ahead.

- One of the key factors to staying ahead is continuous learning.

- If learning is a big item on your agenda, you need to experiment, and you need to get comfortable with the fact that not everything you try is going to work, otherwise the learning wouldn't be rich.

- The monthly learning reviews should involve your frontline staff – as they are the people closest to the customer, who may not get enough face-time with senior management – and often yield much valuable information about which service issues to fix first.

- The environmental setup for learning is also important. Often, people start deploying without the required thinking.

- Learning how to properly accept the right type of failure, and not just any failure, is essential for controlling the number of preventable errors while accepting that some unpreventable errors are part of the learning process.

- A learning organisation must continue to explore and gain knowledge, which helps it stay one step ahead of the competition.

- Learning is not just confined to knowledge. There is also learning that involves process improvements by introducing root-cause analysis and defect attribution.

- Engagement has a large learning component and is the driving factor towards creating a bank that is more than just a utility.

- To increase and concentrate your ability to improve engagement, create an engagement lab with a multidisciplinary team consisting of marketing, communications, analytics, content, and behavioural science specialists.

Fostering an innovative culture

Whilst designing and building a digital bank isn't the type of big innovation break-through that can produce 5x improvement, or what we might call "Big I", there is still the fostering of an innovative culture, or "Small I", that is crucial to success. This is about creating a work environment where there is sufficient challenge, as well as support, so that staff regardless of rank can contribute and there is sufficient robustness in debate and discussion. These small innovations could manifest in the way decisions are made, or in small shifts in thinking that could lead to a very different design downstream. We explore some of these manifestations and how they are inculcated in this chapter.

Innovation can only take place when there is an organisational culture where members feel safe to challenge ideas and decisions. Without sufficient challenge, the best thinking doesn't happen. What you end up with instead is mediocre results. Creating such a culture is much harder than it sounds, however, because staff will always feel it is risky to challenge the thinking of their boss. Hierarchies are a major obstacle to the free exchange of opinions.

To overcome this at TMRW, I encouraged everyone to always ask "Why?" and made it a rule that if the most junior person in the room asked "Why?", it was the responsibility of the most senior staff present to answer the question; if he didn't have the answer, he would find out if the question revealed an important line of inquiry that could lead to a positive outcome. This simple rule broke down the hierarchy barrier. The healthy debates that ensued allowed us to properly flesh out the issues at hand and come up with more rigorous ideas.

One particularly thorny one was whether we should support all existing products that UOB already had. Whilst this may appear to be a very mundane issue, it was one of the most critical design decisions as it affected every single feature that would be rolled out. There were many views for and against. Not doing it meant much greater simplicity in the design, but not doing it also meant that if you had products that were UOB and TMRW, a customer couldn't see all of them which was problematic. Unsecured loan lines were granted at a customer level, and hence there was an obligation to show them in totality. This debate went on for quite some time as it was a major design decision that was hard to reverse once decided. Making quick decisions where the impact was small and making calculated and well-debated decisions where the stakes are high is a crucial balance that the innovator has to strike.

Another of the trade-offs was which brand direction to take. There were two different campaign directions, let's call them path A and path B. Path A was refreshing and clearly differentiated in its use of colour and icons, and somewhat of a breakthrough and innovation in the stuffy world of banking user interfaces. Path B, however, took this to the extreme. It was edgy, loud and in your face. Both were innovative.

Even if I had a strong view on something, I felt it was always important to listen to the evidence or opinions against. The more senior you are, the more important the decisions and hence the probability that the damage is big if the decisions go south, is always present. This quality helps to make for more balanced decisions, especially when the stakes are high. I recall that Wendy, my head of marketing wanted to take path B, and whilst I had many good reasons to prefer path A (sufficiently differentiated but not to the extent that it could alienate), I nevertheless wanted to be sure that the decision was right, as again, this is a major decision that is hard to reverse once made.

So, I asked Wendy to develop both paths, and after listening hard to the case for path B, I finally decided to take path A. And I explained the reasons why as clearly as I could. Some present at the debate felt that the extra work was not warranted, but this is an example of the environment needed to foster creativity and innovation: you are always listening for reasons why you might be wrong in a major decision.

For those that found themselves on the opposite side of the debate, it was never personal. The idea is to have **"strong opinions that are weakly held"** – a framework developed by Stanford University professor Paul Saffo (Ranadive, 2017). This is a useful framework for innovative work that's pushing the boundaries, where there may be no established literature to help you decide. If you have a better perspective and argument, then that carries the day, **not your seniority in the hierarchy**. The patience to listen to another viewpoint not with the intention to rebut but to really understand is critical for this to work well.

Another technique for sparking innovation is adding **constraints**. "Constraints aren't the boundaries of creativity, but the foundation of it" – this quote by Brandon Rodriguez says it all (Rodriguez, 2017). Sometimes, setting **conflicting constraints** can ramp up the innovation process even more. An example of this in TMRW was setting ourselves the goal to engineer the app so that we could achieve simplicity and ease of use – but with the added constraint that we had to do it without using any first-level menus. This at first seemed like a crazy thought. But conflicting constraints have led to breakthroughs before in other industries. "When designing what became the Lexus line, Ichiro Suzuki, Toyota's chief engineer, stipulated that the new car needed to be faster, lighter, and more fuel efficient than existing luxury sedans.

The order was full of contradictions" (Murray & Johnson, 2021). Although we didn't manage to accomplish the removal of all the first-level menus (Under the profile tab in TMRW you can find the few we couldn't remove), it nonetheless resulted in an interface and navigation that is distinctly different in its ease of use and navigation. In fact, the TMRW user interface design is one of the first things you notice about it, from the strategic navigation incorporating vertical scrolling for insights and horizontal scrolling for banking products, to the significant reduction in complexity due to the lack of first-level menus.

Without setting constraints, innovation may be hard to achieve – especially so when you are trying to drive a total experience that is seamless, frictionless and intuitive. If, on the other hand, you are dealing with an innovation of a big breakthrough nature, then it may be possible to let most of the creative solution to a known difficult problem filter up from the ground. However, at TMRW we were mostly dealing with stringing together a range of solutions for pet peeves and regular complaints, e.g., unclear explanations and instructions, repeated service requests that remained unresolved and hence required repeating, poorly designed navigation, inability to perform functions online like changing PIN, etc. These necessarily had to be co-ordinated so that one change didn't make something else worse off and affect the whole experience.

The culture that digital banks of the future must have can best be described as non-hierarchical, with a high degree of involvement and candour, a lack of bureaucracy, low ego but high mission orientation, a clear sense of mission and purpose, where rank is less important than substance. If you build this within an existing complex entity's structure, it will in most cases fail. This is why when people ask me whether the digital bank should be a standalone unit, separate from the main business, my answer is always an unequivocal yes. And once it has taken off, don't try to then merge it with the main business – it will destroy the culture and with it the people you attracted who wanted to work in such a culture. Instead, ensure that whatever innovations are born of this culture are shared with the mothership, which was TMRW's philosophy.

Key takeaways

- Whilst designing and building a digital bank isn't the type of big innovation breakthrough that can produce 5x improvement, there is still the fostering of an innovative culture, which is crucial to success.

- Innovation can only take place when there is an organisational culture where members feel safe to challenge ideas and decisions.

- If the most junior person in the room asks "Why?", it should be the responsibility of the most senior staff present to answer the question.

- Healthy debates allow you to properly flesh out the issues at hand and come up with more rigorous ideas.

- Making quick decisions where the impact is small and making calculated and well-debated decisions where the stakes are high is a crucial balance that the innovator has to strike.

- The more senior you are, the more important the decisions, and hence the probability that the damage is big if the decisions go south is always there.

- To create an environment needed to foster creativity and innovation, you are always listening intently for reasons why you might be wrong in a major decision yet sticking to your guns if you don't hear one.

- A framework developed by Stanford University professor Paul Saffo where strong opinions that are "weakly held" is a useful framework for innovative work that's pushing the boundaries, where there may be no established literature to help you decide.

- If somone has a better perspective and argument, then that carries the day, not their seniority in the hierarchy.

- The patience to listen to another viewpoint not with the intention to rebut but to really understand is critical for this to work well.

- Another technique for sparking innovation is adding constraints. "Constraints aren't the boundaries of creativity, but the foundation of it."

- If, on the other hand, you are dealing with an innovation of a big breakthrough nature, then it may be possible to let most of the creative solution to a known difficult problem filter up from the ground.

- Where you are mostly dealing with stringing together a range of solutions for pet peeves and regular complaints, they must be co-ordinated so that one change doesn't make something else worse off and affect the whole experience.

- The unique culture that digital banks of the future must have can best be described as non-hierarchical, with a high degree of involvement and candour, a lack of bureaucracy, low ego but high mission orientation, a clear sense of mission and purpose, where rank is less important than substance.

Talent: What to look for in key hires?

The ability to acquire the right talent is one of the key success factors in any digital bank setup. As designing and building a digital bank is a relatively new area where most candidates don't have direct prior experience, how can you go about identifying the right candidates?

For the key positions, I would recommend a **three-stage process**, as shown in Figure 39. This was the approach I used as CEO-designate of a consortium bidding for one of three digital wholesale bank (DWB) licences in Singapore. We were not ultimately successful in the bid, but we did manage to attract highly talented individuals who had world-class credentials. Out of 11 CEO one-down reports, we managed to field 10 candidates. Each had to go through this three-stage process.

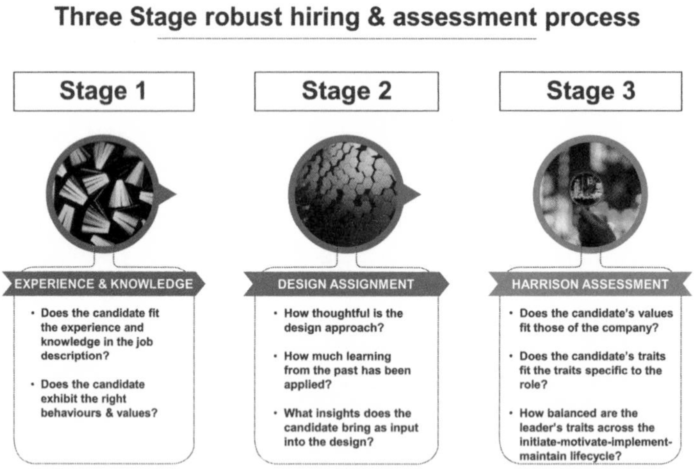

Three Stage robust hiring & assessment process

Stage 1	Stage 2	Stage 3
EXPERIENCE & KNOWLEDGE	DESIGN ASSIGNMENT	HARRISON ASSESSMENT
• Does the candidate fit the experience and knowledge in the job description? • Does the candidate exhibit the right behaviours & values?	• How thoughtful is the design approach? • How much learning from the past has been applied? • What insights does the candidate bring as input into the design?	• Does the candidate's values fit those of the company? • Does the candidate's traits fit the traits specific to the role? • How balanced are the leader's traits across the initiate-motivate-implement-maintain lifecycle?

Figure 39 – Recommended assessment and hiring process

Stage 1: The first stage is similar to a traditional interview. It's the first meeting with the candidate. You are looking for overall fit. The questions centre around motivation, an understanding of the candidate's experience and how it fits the job description. No interviews should be conducted without a well-written job description, which includes the key traits and qualities required for the role. Focus on what the candidate learnt from their previous roles. Delve into how the candidate managed failures and mistakes. Understand what inspires the candidate – what makes him or her want to turn up at work early. As we were planning to create a new digital bank, we spent time ensuring that the candidate really understood the mission, vision, culture and values that we wanted the new company to have. A list of vision and values, brought to life by an inspiring pitch, goes a long way to interest even the most sceptical of candidates.

Stage 2: Candidates who made it to the next round were asked to do a design assignment. Building a digital bank, as described in this book, is all about design. It calls for great attention to all the details that go into the design, both the exterior bits which are grand, bold and motivational, as well as the mundane, in-the-trenches work where the team will spend the better part of their time. So, understanding what factors the candidate would consider in the design, what issues they might face, how would they mitigate them, what key processes they deem critical, etc., is vital in the selection process.

Stage 3: Candidates that passed the design process were then given an assessment to complete. I had been certified in Harrison Assessments at the end of 2019 and found it to provide excellent predictive talent analytics that can reveal the hidden behaviours of candidates in a way that few other instruments can (and I have been through quite a number). The assessment takes about 20 minutes to do online and consists of sorting a series of statements according to the candidate's preferences. We then produced a few reports: a report on the candidate's fit to the company's values, a job suitability assessment, and something Harrison calls "paradox graphs", which look at 12 pairs of traits that seem contradictory but are actually complementary and synergistic (see Figure 91).

To understand the Harrison paradox graphs, a great example I like to call on is how we assessed a candidate's organisational ability. As a start-up bank, we were looking for candidates who were both organised and flexible. Now being both organised and flexible might seem to be a paradox, but in reality, you can be both organised – which is the tendency to establish and maintain order in a situation – and flexible, which is the ability to adapt easily to change. **A start-up is an unusually chaotic form of organisation because you are bringing together a bunch of people who likely have not worked together before, in a situation where no processes or systems of working exist, and everything has to be built from scratch**. So, if the candidates are not organised, they will compound the situation and make it even more chaotic. If they are highly organised but not flexible, they will tend to be rather rigid. This is a problem because in a start-up everyone is learning at the same time and you must be prepared to change your mind – hopefully not very often, but it's going to happen. Candidates who are not flexible won't be able to handle this well.

The paradox graphs feature 12 different paradox areas, classified into 4 areas:

1. **Initiating**: This is the conceptual phase of an initiative, dealing with issues like how could we do it, what are the obstacles, how would we mitigate the risks, etc. Here, opinions, decision approach, dealing with strategic risks are critical.

2. **Motivating**: This is about getting people onboard with the idea or concept. Here, balancing self-esteem and self-improvement, balancing self-motivation and stress management, and balancing enforcing vs warmth and empathy when driving others, becomes crucial.

3. **Implementing**: This is about getting it done. Here, managing directness and tactfulness when communicating, how we approach trying new things and overcoming obstacles, and how we approach self-responsibility and collaboration, can make the difference between success and failure.

4. **Maintaining**: This is about keeping things going. Here, balancing helping others vs asserting your needs, how you deal with adaptability and creating structure or organisation, and finally how you approach opportunities while mindful of difficulties, are key.

In each of these paradox areas, candidates who **score well in both traits**, like the example of organised and flexible, are more balanced and more versatile – qualities that are critical for designing from scratch in a start-up environment. Leaders who exhibit these complementary and synergistic traits that appear at first contradictory are more balanced and more versatile – qualities that determine how considered a leader is and thus how well he can put these considerations to work in the design and execution.

Only candidates that passed all three stages were selected. The result was a robust assessment and recruitment process that allowed us to home in on the key talent we needed.

Key takeaways

- Adopt a 3-stage process: a regular interview to match experience, knowledge, cultural and behavioural fit; a design assignment to understand the candidate's thought process; and a Harrison Assessment to delve deep into the candidate's behaviours and traits that cannot be verified by asking.

- No interviews should be conducted without a well-written job description, which includes the key traits and qualities required for the role.

- Stage 1 questions look for the overall fit. The questions centre around motivation, an understanding of the candidate's experience and how it fits the job description. Focus on what the candidate learnt, and how he or she went about their previous roles. Delve into how the candidate managed failures and mistakes. Understand what inspires the candidate – what makes him or her want to turn up at work early.

- Spend time ensuring that the candidate really understands the mission, vision, culture and values that you want the new company to have.

- A list of vision and values, brought to life by an inspiring pitch, goes a long way to interest even the most sceptical of candidates.

- Stage 2: Since building a digital bank is so much about design, it calls for great attention to details – both the exterior bits which are grand, bold and motivational, as well as the mundane, in-the-trenches work where the team will spend the better part of their time. Understanding what factors the candidate would consider in the design, what issues might be faced, how they could be mitigated, what key processes they deem critical, etc., is vital in the selection process.

- Stage 3: The Harrison Assessments provided excellent predictive talent analytics that can reveal the hidden behaviours of candidates in a way that few other instruments can.

- Harrison Assessment's "paradox graphs", which look at 12 pairs of traits that seem contradictory but are actually complementary and synergistic, are a good indicator of a leader's balance.

- Leaders who exhibit these complementary and synergistic traits are more balanced and versatile – qualities that determine how considered a leader is and thus how well they can put these considerations to work in the design and execution.

4.9

Ecosystem (its misuse) and partnerships

Not everything is an "ecosystem". This is probably one of the most frequently abused words today. The term was originally used in biology to mean "the complex of a community of organisms and its environment functioning as an ecological unit" (Ecosystem | Definition of Ecosystem by Merriam-Webster). In business today, it has come to be used to describe a dynamic group of largely independent economic players who create products or services that together constitute a coherent solution (Pidun et al., 2019).

There are two types of ecosystems: solution ecosystems and transactional ecosystems, as explained by the BCG Henderson Institute (Figure 40).

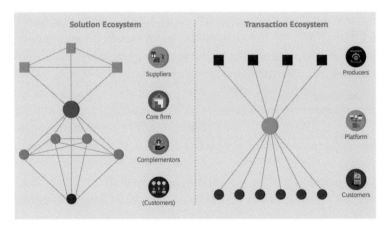

Figure 40 – Solution vs transaction ecosystem[56]

In financial services, an example of a **solution ecosystem** would be debt origination and securitisation. The suppliers are banks that originate the mortgages. Examples of the core firm would be entities like the US Federal National Mortgage Association, more commonly known as Fannie Mae, and the Federal Home Loan Mortgage Corporation, known as Freddie Mac. They buy the mortgages from banks

56. Source: BCG Henderson Institute. Ulrich Pidun, Martin Reeves, Maximilian Schuessler. Do You Need a Business Ecosystem? September 2019.

and securitise the mortgage for sale in the bond market as mortgage-backed securities (MBS). Customers who buy the MBS could be retail or institutional investors. An example of a complementor would be the ratings agencies that rate the MBS issuance. Solution ecosystems make sense when you want to buy a solution rather than develop it yourself, and/or where regulations don't allow you to partake in an adjacent or complementary business that your customers are likely to need. A familiar example of the former is partnerships between insurance and banks. The insurance company provides the insurance solutions, so they are the suppliers. The core firm is the bank, while the complementors could be property agents recommending home loan term-reducing insurance.

Software is another good example. The core firms are **B2B Fintechs** selling Software-as-a-Service (SaaS). Banks have been customers of software vendors for a long time. What's changed is that more and more, software isn't bought, it's rented. The complementors could be system integrators that customise the software to fit the bank's specifications. The suppliers to the Fintech could be other software companies producing modules that the Fintech doesn't specialise in, like a credit card processing module to complement a core banking SaaS provider.

Does the solution ecosystem apply to **B2C Fintechs**? In this case, the core firm would be the bank offering, say, robo-advisory services to their wealth management clients, with the B2C robo-advisory Fintechs as the suppliers. In some jurisdictions, like Australia and the UK, retail banking and wealth management are two separate businesses that must be segregated in order to ensure that there are no opportunities for banking staff to cross-sell complex investment products to the man-in-the-street retail customer. In such a scenario, partnering with someone already in the business makes a lot of sense. B2C Fintechs in the wealth management space could complement banks who are not licensed to perform wealth management services. Other than such opportunities, it's difficult to foresee that there will be widespread collaboration between banks and B2C Fintech. The reason for this is that if you agree that banking is now purely an experience business, as product, place, even people will over time be marginalised, then it is unlikely that any bank would want to introduce a third-party player when they could participate directly and design the experience with the customer.

So, there will be a place for providers of robo-advisory software, whether selling licences for the bank to use internally or renting software as a service. However, it is unlikely that there will be large-scale partnerships with B2C robo-advisory who want to own the customer experience. The exceptions will be where the bank is renting its licence and infrastructure to a start-up operating in a market the bank finds hard to go into themselves. Such models already exist in Europe with banks like Solaris providing such services to anyone who wants to run a banking service. But in this case, it's clear that the bank isn't responsible for the end-user experience; it's in the infrastructure business and provides APIs to build a front-end experience for anyone who wants to build a bank. I think there will continue to be many B2B Fintech in future, but the future of B2C Fintech that can't make it on their own and need bank partnerships would in my view be in serious doubt.

Usually when someone refers to an ecosystem in the Fintech space, it is more likely they are referring to a **transaction ecosystem**, or what's more commonly called a platform. The platform serves as an intermediary between the producer and the customer, using information technology to help match buyers and sellers. For example, Grab and Gojek match customers who need a ride to those who have the vehicles to provide the ride; or Shopee and Lazada, who match sellers to buyers, and buyers to sellers. Such transaction ecosystems that have a large number of buyers and sellers have network effects, i.e., more sellers attract more buyers, and more buyers in turn attract more sellers.

Such platforms are in a position to present to their large client base of online customers additional products or services that they need. Therefore, these platforms lend themselves to distribution, especially distribution of digital services, as their customers are all mobile-savvy. Leveraging these ecosystems in ASEAN **to gain scale would be an essential capability to grow faster at a lower cost**. Banks are a platform in themselves. The producers are the customers that have cash to deposit; the customers are those who need to borrow.

However, how do we distinguish between joining an ecosystem, and simply advertising on a site with a large number of customers? This is an important distinction. We found that the latter was a more prevalent form as the role of a bank as an extender of credit would seem to be the key reason for joining an ecosystem, but not **many of these ecosystems that currently exist match lenders to banks or banks to lenders in ASEAN**. Most of these platforms today match borrowers to individuals who have money to lend, or non-bank lenders. One obstacle is that bank onboarding is much more robust and onerous, making it harder to offer instant "buy now, pay later" loans at checkout.

A general rule is that lower-frequency sites don't make good acquisition targets for higher-frequency providers looking to grow their base. For example, the frequent flyers of an airline would not need to go through a bank app to reach their airline, and the customers that very infrequently go to an airline site to book a flight wouldn't remember to use a bank's site as their entry point. When you check-in to your flight, it would make sense to book a ride on Grab from the airline's app, as most people don't drive to the airport. This is an exception to the rule, where lower-frequency app (airline) creates a link to a high-frequency app (ride-hailing) because from a customer journey perspective it makes sense. Embedding an airline into a bank, however, doesn't. Banks don't really produce end-goods or services. They are intermediaries. **So, ecosystem partnerships should not just be a new**

term for partnering with anyone with an app in the hope of becoming a super-app yourself.

Ultimately, partnership stories are all about tenacity and patience more than anything else. A key learning from this experience is that the success and longevity of a partnership stems from jointly arriving at a **win-win arrangement**, without any of the partners having to bend backwards to achieve an outcome. Focus on large, established consumer players looking to expand their product offerings to include financial services, such as Telcos, retail conglomerates, and the like. In addition, large consumer technology platforms that are looking to embed financial services within their existing services, like Grab and Gojek, are also synergistic as they have similar goals and ambitions that resonate with digital banks. These companies want to better monetise their data, provide a seamless online-offline experience for customers, and focus on customer engagement instead of just cross-selling. It was also important that potential partners' ecosystems and target audiences aligned with those of TMRW.

Eventually, we were able to close a regional collaboration partnership with Grab with a target to acquire TMRW customers across Southeast Asia. We also closed partnerships with Shopee Thailand, and Au Bon Pain, to name a few. One quick win that worked well was partnering with a large e-commerce player like Shopee and offering the Shopee vouchers instead of cash as sign-up incentives. Whilst this seems easy, the onboarding module had to be designed to identify the originating partner and reward the customer with the correct incentives.

This proved to be a good way to acquire active users for TMRW. One guideline to set is how much less it must cost to acquire through a partner vs acquiring direct. You don't have to pay the partners as you are buying vouchers from them to give successful applicants, and those applicants would spend more as a result. TMRW has partnered such large platform ecosystem partners to acquire customers in both Thailand and Indonesia, and the quality of customers acquired from these partners has been good.

It is also generally cheaper than just using Google or Facebook to target customers, as you simply reward these customer sign-ups with vouchers from the ecosystem partners. It's a win-win for all parties. Traditionally consumer banks take many years to scale because of the time it takes to open branches, acquire customers, and deepen relationships over their lifetime. Digital banks, on the other hand, are untethered by these constraints as there are no physical branches or staff required to acquire new customers. Instead, digital banks need to look to **existing ecosystems with a large base of digital customers** to broaden their own customer base and turbocharge their growth.

Part of my responsibility as Head of TMRW Digital Group was to design and map out the partnerships and ecosystems required to support and accelerate TMRW's growth, as opposed to just growing organically. We understood from the very beginning that scaling would be a major issue, on par with path-to-profit, and success meant doing both very well. Figure 41 shows **three different paths to scaling**.

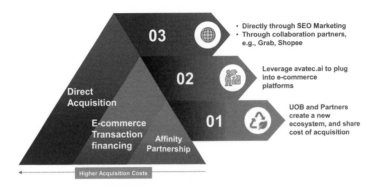

Figure 41 – TMRW partnership model
(Source: UOB Website, 15 May 2019)

1. The highest cost model we believed to be **direct** – acquiring customers directly or through collaboration partners like Grab, Shopee, etc.

2. In Thailand, all personal loans required banks to sight proof of income before disbursement, and hence the next lowest cost model – **through e-commerce transaction financing** – could only be piloted in Indonesia leveraging the avatec.ai joint venture. This involved a partnership with Chinese software Fintech Pintec to create an alternate credit-scoring capability, which we could leverage to partner with the big e-commerce ecosystems (The Straits Times, 2018; Khoo, 2019b). The e-commerce companies would benefit from more sales if we could provide instant e-commerce loans, and we would acquire more customers at a lower cost of acquisition if this happened.

3. The lowest cost but perhaps the most involved method we termed **affinity partnerships**, where UOB would partner to create a new ecosystem, and share the cost of acquisition with the partner. Only one affinity partnership emerged during my tenure, and this was with the Vietnam Investment Group, to jointly set up a digital loyalty programme for companies in Vietnam that could be a springboard for TMRW in Vietnam (Sia, 2019).

From quite early on in the design, well before we started coding the software for TMRW, we already had a partnership team scouting for potential partners. You can imagine how hard this was considering we had nothing but ideas and enthusiasm then. Michael Koh was the partnership head at that stage, and it was really only him and me. One of Michael's gifts is his positivity and energy. These came to very good use as we were rejected many times.

Here's Michael recounting his early experience: "The biggest hurdle that I had was getting people to take us seriously. It doesn't help that in the initial phase when we were looking for partners, we went to the biggest companies while we had not launched yet. We went to the biggest players because the motto was **'Go big or go home'**. So, the first hurdle was getting people to take us seriously because when we had these conversations, we didn't go there with the UOB halo. We went as TMRW. It was a new brand. However, the partners were thinking, a traditional established bank like UOB, more than 80 years − how can I be assured that you are truly serious to push the frontier in the new experience for the digital customer?

"To convince partners, we had to demonstrate that we were tenacious. Even before we launched, we actively pursued partners with much bigger customer bases to propel our growth at launch. We seldom took no for an answer and would go out of our way to convince potential partners of the benefits of partnering with a bank that would put customer-centricity first. It was a great testimony of the attitude of the team and our hunger to make things happen."

Key takeaways

- There are two types of ecosystems: solution ecosystems and transactional ecosystems.

- In financial services, an example of a solution ecosystem would be debt origination and securitisation.

- There will continue to be many B2B Fintechs in future, but the future of B2C Fintechs that can't make it on their own and need bank partnerships would be in serious doubt.

- When someone refers to an ecosystem in the Fintech space, it is more likely that they are referring to a transaction ecosystem, or what's more commonly called a platform.

- Platforms serve as intermediaries between the producer and the customer, using IT to help match buyers and sellers.

- Such platforms are in a position to present to their large client base of online customers additional products or services that they need. These platforms lend themselves to distribution of digital services, as their customers are all mobile-savvy.

- Leveraging such transaction ecosystems in ASEAN to gain scale would be an essential capability to grow faster at a lower cost.

- A general rule we uncovered is that lower-frequency sites don't make good acquisition targets for higher-frequency providers looking to grow their base.

- One guideline to set is how much less it must cost to acquire through a partner vs acquiring direct.

- Working directly with transaction ecosystems is cheaper than using Google or Facebook for marketing as you simply reward these customer sign-ups with vouchers purchased from the ecosystem partners.

- The highest-cost model we believed to be direct acquisition of customers, even if it's through a partnership with a transaction ecosystem player.

- Instant e-commerce transaction financing, where allowed by regulations, could lead to lower acquisition costs due to the convenience of the embedded financing feature.

- The lowest-cost but perhaps most-involved method is affinity partnerships, where a digital bank partners with a suitable partner with retail businesses to create a new ecosystem and share the cost of acquisition with the partner.

Biggest obstacles you will face

We'll look at this topic from the perspective of three types of banks. First, for an incumbent bank, the biggest obstacle you'll face is that internally **someone or the bureaucracy will oppose it due to lack of belief**. Building a digital bank is long-term, and thus, if one takes a shorter-term view, together with the uncertainty of outcome, it could be viewed as a poor allocation of resources that could be directed at other priorities. In my view, such ventures will fail if there isn't a strong and committed believer at the very top of the organisation to protect it from other parts of the organisation that oppose it. There is no way to prove conclusively that it's going to work, so belief is crucial for success.

The next biggest obstacle is surprisingly, why actually do it at all? The threat is not immediate, so why not wait and see? After all, it will suck up a lot of resources and capital, and we won't see the light at the end of the tunnel for many years. The strongest rationale for an incumbent bank to act now is the conviction that if this new model does work, it won't be possible to respond to it in 10 years' time.

This is the essence of the Kodak story – an evergreen portrayal of a company's fear of change and reinvention. Kodak was born out of George Eastman's invention of the negative in 1884. By 1963, Kodak dominated photography globally, selling no fewer than 50M Kodak Instamatic cameras between 1963 and 1970. In 1978, Kodak filed the **first patent for a digital camera** using a CCD (charge-coupled device) sensor (Figure 42). This camera used a cassette tape and took 23 seconds to record an image in black and white.

When shown the new invention, Kodak executives were not impressed. It was clunky and slow, took poor-resolution pictures, and most of all, they wanted to know about the prints: "Where are the prints?" They couldn't understand why

Figure 42 – The first digital camera
(Source: George Eastman Museum)

anyone would want a camera that couldn't print – a process that generated most of Kodak's profits. So, Kodak squandered the opportunity to reinvent itself as a digital imaging company. It took two decades for the era of the digital camera and digital photography to finally arrive. In all that time, Kodak had the technology and resources to develop and lead the digital photography business, but by the time they got their act together, it was too late, and Kodak filed for bankruptcy in 2012.

Similarly for incumbent banks, they have the resources and capability to build a digital bank, but the threat isn't immediate. And just like Kodak, many of the executives in incumbent banks are asking the equivalent of the question: "Where are the prints?" What they should be asking themselves instead is, when the threat becomes imminent, can they still respond? Hence the best positioning for an incumbent is to assess how much it can afford to invest as an insurance against not being able to respond to a future where customer experience is all that matters.

This is summed up perfectly by Scott Anthony from Innosight, co-author of *Dual Transformation: How to Reposition Today's Business While Creating the Future*: "The right lessons from Kodak are subtle. Companies often see the disruptive forces affecting their industry. They frequently divert sufficient resources to participate in emerging markets. **Their failure is usually an inability to truly embrace the new business models the disruptive change opens up**. Kodak created a digital camera, invested in the technology, and even understood that photos would be shared online. Where they failed was in realising that online photo sharing was the new business, not just a way to expand the printing business" (Anthony, 2016).

The biggest obstacle to success in most incumbent banks will be the bank's culture and ways of working. The likelihood is very high that the culture is a mismatch for one of risk-taking, innovation and execution in an entrepreneurial way. If this is not resolved, very little else matters.

For the second type of bank – a **neo-bank without its own licence to run a bank** – you need to borrow those licences from a bank that has. Your customers will be customers of both the neo-bank and the bank of record, which holds the licence. In the eyes of the regulator, the bank of record is the regulated entity and will be the party the regulator holds responsible for any lapses. The poster child for this model is Solaris Bank, which has a full German banking licence that allows it to operate in the European Union and deliver to any neo-bank a completely digital Bank-as-a-Service (BaaS) platform. There aren't that many licensed banks that are renting their licences out, still fewer offering it as a BaaS model where they provide the platform and processes to power the offering to an interested neo-bank. One distinct advantage of this model is the ability to scale up across multiple countries if the enabling bank has the licence to operate in several countries.

Chime is a neo-bank in the US that has 12M customers. It has received US$1.5B from investors and is currently valued at US$14.5B. Chime doesn't have a banking licence; instead, it partners with two FDIC-insured banks, Bancorp and Stride. It positions itself as a technology company. Chime targets Americans who earn between US$30,000 and US$75,000 a year. It offers free checking accounts. The price-to-earnings ratio of North American software companies was 42.7 vs 10.56 for major banks. So being positioned as a software company allows Chime to command a higher valuation compared to a bank. But is Chime really a technology company or is it more of a platform? Chime could be positioned as a platform that matches deposits to borrowers if it can partner with multiple enabling banks. Whether this is viable or not remains to be seen.

However, the long-term viability is complicated by the relationship between the neo-bank and the enabling bank with the licence, in that if the neo-bank is successful, what are the possible **exit strategies**? A trade sale to potential competitors of the enabling bank would likely be blocked by the enabling bank, leaving either an initial public offering on a stock exchange to remain an independent company or a sale to the enabling bank (higher probability) as the two likely options. The valuation for the neo-bank can be negatively affected by factors such as lower profit margin due to the profit-sharing arrangement with the enabling bank, and the total reliance on the enabling bank's multi-country licences. Generally, it would be very difficult to substitute the enabling bank because there are limited banks in the world with substantive multi-country licences.

If the enabling bank partners are not global but specific to a country, then perhaps it would be easier to swap banks if you are unhappy with the current enabling banks. But having a different bank per country also introduces greater complexity interfacing to different banks. So, the strategy for this approach needs to take the portability of the enabling bank into account. Given that the exit valuation could be lower, there could be significant dilution in ownership if the investment required to build and run the neo-bank is too large. Hence this necessitates a review of how the neo-bank can be more cost-efficient. For example, can the enabling bank offer significant parts of its processing capabilities through APIs to lower operating costs? Can the neo-bank leverage the enabling bank's compliance processes and technology platform? This essentially is what Solaris offers – a new solution ecosystem in banking, similar to franchise models in the fast-food industry.

Finally, let's consider **challenger banks with a licence from the regulator**. Banking, especially consumer and SME banking, isn't a global business, so unless the country opportunity is large, **how can it scale affordably**? Interestingly, all four profitable digital banks in Figure 15 hail from countries with significant populations, e.g., Tinkoff is in Russia (pop. 144.4M), Webank and MYbank are in China (pop. 1,398M) and Kakao Bank is in South Korea (pop. 51.7M). Challenger banks starting in smaller countries like Singapore and Hong Kong may need to expand internationally very quickly to achieve sufficient scale. This entails setting up subsidiaries in every country of operation and introduces further complexity into the business model. Regulations are different in every country, adding to the difficulty of expansion. In recent times, all three international banks, Citibank, HSBC and Standard Chartered, have exited countries where they failed to achieve sufficient scale.

Capital is also an issue, and as most regulators require captive capital in-country for any consumer bank that is sizeable, challenger banks will require significantly more capital as they expand internationally. The requirement for a challenger bank to set up a bank in each country looks to be capital-intensive. As it stands, we already know that each challenger bank in each country is a long-term play, as these challenger banks are unlikely to be profitable in a short time. In totality, it would appear that **becoming a regional challenger digital bank is going to be both costly and complex**. Even if the bank were able to be extremely efficient in standardising to a standard global platform, it would still need to cater to local payment systems and local regulatory requirements.

Key takeaways

- For an incumbent bank, the biggest obstacle you'll face is that the bureaucracy will oppose it.

- There must be a strong and committed believer at the very top of the incumbent bank to protect it from other parts of the organisation that want to kill it.

- There is no way to prove conclusively that it's going to work, so belief is crucial for success.

- The next obstacle is "Why do it at all?" The threat is not immediate, so why not wait and see? After all, it will suck up a lot of resources and capital, and there won't be light at the end of the tunnel for many years.

- Just like Kodak, many of the executives in incumbent banks are asking the equivalent of the question: "Where are the prints?"

- The strongest rationale for an incumbent bank to act now is the conviction that if this new model does work, it won't be possible to respond to it in 10 years' time.

- Companies often see the disruptive forces affecting their industry. They frequently divert sufficient resources to participate in emerging markets.

- Their failure is usually an inability to truly embrace the new business models the disruptive change opens up.

- For the neo-bank without a licence, there aren't that many licensed banks that are renting their licences out, still fewer offering it as a BaaS model to power the offering to the neo-bank.

- Long-term viability is complicated by the relationship between the neo-bank and the enabling bank with the licence, in that if the neo-bank is successful, what are the possible exit strategies?

- For the challenger bank, banking isn't a global business, so unless the country opportunity is large, how can it scale affordably?

- Challenger banks starting in smaller countries like Singapore and Hong Kong may need to expand internationally very quickly to achieve sufficient scale.

- This entails setting up subsidiaries in every country of operation and introduces further complexity and cost into the business model.

- Becoming a regional challenger digital bank is both costly and complex.

The allDigitalfuture Playbook™: A step-by-step guide for any digital transformation

When we set out to design and build TMRW, there wasn't any structured approach for us to follow. While there are many toolkits available in the market (e.g., business model canvas, customer value proposition canvas, customer empathy maps, a myriad of traditional strategy tools, etc.), they are disparate and, without an overall holistic and structured approach, often appear haphazard and reactive. Even if you hire management consultants to help you, they don't utilise any specific structured approach. The available methods tend to be overly simplistic and unable to handle the complexity you will likely encounter in anything apart from the most trivial digital transformations.

A playbook from which we could take reference, see the path ahead and adapt to TMRW's specific situation would have made the journey clearer and easier. A playbook that could delineate the key dimensions we would need to consider, how the dimensions interact with one another, and thus surface the trade-offs that we would need to make. Such a playbook would also have established a common language and approach to guide us through the difficult and confusing early days.

Having spearheaded the creation of TMRW and developed a model digital wholesale bank[57], I have created a playbook to help other companies as they embark on their digital transformation journeys. This work has become **The allDigitalfuture Playbook™ (TaP)**. It represents what I think every digital leader will need at the start of their transformation. Although it is built on my experiences in banking, I have created TaP to allow it to operate in any industry, not just in financial services.

Why do you need a playbook? The answer is simple. While spending on digital transformation has skyrocketed globally, research shows that few digital transformations achieve their desired results (Bendor-Samuel, 2019; Wade, 2018; Solis, 2020; Rogers, 2016; Kitani, 2019; Sutcliff, Narsalay, and Sen, 2019; McKinsey & Company, 2016; Boutetière, Montagner, and Reich, 2018; Deakin, LaBerge, and

---

57. As part of a bid for one of Singapore's digital bank licences.

O'Beirne, 2019). According to IDC, worldwide spending on digital transformation technologies (hardware, software, and services) is expected to be more than $2.1T in 2021. Yet, of the S$1.3T that was spent in 2018, it is estimated that $900B went to waste (Tabrizi et al., 2019).

A 2019 survey of 1,000 C-level executives by Celonis[58] supports the call for a more holistic approach, as it was found that almost one in two don't know where to start, with 4 out of 10 confirming that their transformation has been a waste of time. "It's a matter of leaping before they look", with "70% intending to invest in AI, machine learning and automation and yet only 32% intend to invest more in getting better visibility of their processes" (McKendrick, 2019).

To avoid this fate, we need to understand **why the majority of digital transformations fail**. Thomas Davenport and George Westerman, writing in the *Harvard Business Review*, had this to say: "Digital is not just a thing that you can buy and plug into the organisation. It is multi-faceted and diffuse and doesn't just involve technology. Digital transformation is an ongoing process of changing the way you do business. It requires foundational investments in skills, projects, infrastructure, and, often, in cleaning up IT systems. It requires mixing people, machines, and business processes, with all of the messiness that entails. It also requires continuous monitoring and intervention, from the top, to ensure that both digital leaders and non-digital leaders are making good decisions about their transformation efforts" (Davenport & Westerman, 2018).

Many transformations fail, therefore, because the organisations vastly underestimate the complexity of the many dimensions, elements and considerations involved. In particular, it is the **circular interactions** between these multiple factors that give rise to severe complexity.

Figure 43 illustrates the interactive nature of the challenge at the heart of any complex issue or system. For example, developing a strong customer value proposition naturally provides more differentiation, but that usually means potentially a bigger gap between the core competences you have and those you need to develop. This in turn increases both the risk of execution failure and the cost of the transformation as the capability gap is large. But yet if the differentiation isn't strong enough due to a weaker proposition, it may result in an inability to scale, affecting the revenue and profit in turn. Exposing and managing circular interactions is one of the unique approaches found in TaP that can help improve the success of your digital

---

58. Celonis is the New York- and Munich-based leader in business transformation software, turning process insights into action with the process mining technology it pioneered. Celonis commissioned research to explore how businesses were managing their transformation strategies and what the obstacles were to success. A survey of 1,009 business analysts and 1,002 C-level executives in companies with over 500 employees in the UK, US, Germany and the Netherlands was conducted by Opinion Matters in January 2019.

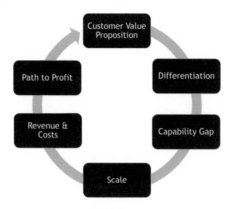

Figure 43 – Circular interactions cause severe complexity

initiative. By exposing these interactions, TaP makes it easier for you to identify the trade-offs required.

In order to manage these complex interactions, you have to look at your initiative from a **systems approach**, which means looking at dimensions like customers, business, capabilities, people and leadership – the four TaP dimensions – and how within each dimension, elements such as target segment, insights, differentiation, profit, scaling new methodologies, leadership, etc., interact with each other.

In highly competitive and commoditised industries like banking, because there are **few big singular breakthroughs left, you need the patience and attention to detail to sweat over the finer points** and be very fussy about the eventual experience for both customers and staff of the new bank. Banking tech has very little that can actually be considered proprietary intellectual property. It's not the deep tech that you find in LCD displays, where the drive for better resolution cannibalises older models, e.g., 1K TVs giving way to 4K and now 8K resolution in a matter of a few years, or in mobile phones, where having the technology to shrink the size and weight whilst increasing the battery life is paramount.

Innovation is still needed to build a digital bank, regardless of whether you are an incumbent bank looking to buy insurance against an uncertain future, a neo-bank looking to expand regionally quickly, or a digital challenger bank looking to build the new model bank for the digital era, but it's a different form of innovation vs deep tech. The innovation, in my view, is mostly about breaking out of the existing paradigm of the industry, designing and implementing a new business model and creating a different way of thinking and working. Many digital transformation initiatives in other industries probably fall into this category as well.

Our starting point is a better understanding of innovation within the context described in the prior paragraph. Borrowing from the concept first made popular by IDEO, and now almost universally adopted by the majority of design practition-ers, I define innovation as "a novel proposition that is desirable, feasible and viable" (Fenn & Hobbs, 2017; Jeffries, 2011; Osterwalder, 2017). **The world has plenty of ideas but few innovations, because unlike ideas, innovations must meet the desirable, viable and feasible criteria**. "Novel" indicates that an innovation must be something new; no matter how small, there must be a new twist in the way something is done, e.g., disposable one-time-use superglue would count as a packaging innovation, whilst the invention of superglue itself would qualify as a product performance breakthrough.

"Desirable" establishes that it is only an innovation if customers want to pay for it, and this is linked to viability, because if no one pays for it, then eventually the idea cannot be turned into an innovation that can sustain itself. Even stuff that's free isn't really free. A good example is Google search. Google search was free from the start for the individual customer so that Google could quickly ramp up the number of customers using it, and once there were enough customers using it, Google could monetise search by charging advertisers and companies for lead generation. Freemium games work the same way. They attract players with free games who get addicted and are then enticed to buy the additional power-up or weapon to progress faster in the game.

So, in the context we are addressing, the customer must want it and must be willing to pay for it. The amount the customer is willing to pay for it is an indication of how desirable it is, but also how viable it is, given that there must be enough customers who are willing to pay that price for the whole proposition to make suf-ficient profit. This leads to the second criteria: **it must be viable in that it must be profitable at some stage and able to sustain itself**. And finally, the innovation must have **a high likelihood of being brought to life, i.e., feasible**. In order to achieve this, a clear idea of the capabilities, people and leadership required are essential. All this sounds simple enough, but it quickly gets very complex as we move one level down and look at how to tick the boxes on all three criteria, and bring the innovation to life.

The four dimensions of TaP, as illustrated in Figure 44, are: Customers, Business, Capabilities, and People & Leadership.

1. The **Customer** dimension examines the rationale behind the selection of the target customer segment and the gaps as dictated by their behaviour, habits, pain points, unmet needs and expectations. An analysis of the size and attractiveness of the segment and other target segment options should also be completed to fully ascertain both the profit pool and desirability of the proposition. The output of the customer dimension is the **customer value proposition**.

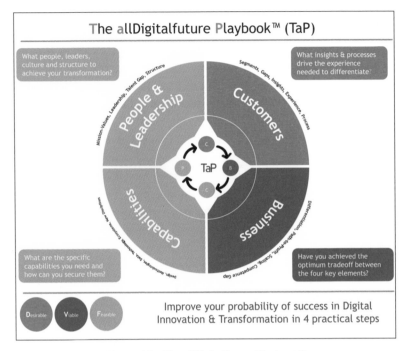

Figure 44 – The allDigitalfuture Playbook™

2. The **Business** dimension examines four important elements that determine the viability of the proposition, namely, path to profit, differentiation, scaling and gaps with the current core competence of the business. The output of the business dimension is the **business model**.

3. The **Capabilities** dimension looks at the enablers required to deliver and bring the proposition to life. Here the focus is on the design of the proposition, consideration for new disciplines, e.g., in analytics, instrumentation, or specialised manufacturing, ecosystems that can help the business produce the proposition or scale up the adoption. Technology to digitalise the proposition, the use of data and the introduction of new methodologies like design thinking, Lean thinking, Agile delivery, etc., would complete the elements needed to make the proposition feasible. The output of the capabilities dimension are the **business enablers** you need to succeed.

4. The **People & Leadership** dimension is the last but arguably the most important dimension, as in the end, it is the people and the leaders that bring the initiative or proposition to life. The output from this dimension are the **people enablers** you need to design, build and deploy the transformation.

In the following chapters, we will delve into each of these dimensions in turn. Just remember that everything is interconnected. There is sometimes a tendency in digital transformations, when faced with all these interconnected interactions, to believe that there must be a simple way out. Yes, there is a role for simplicity, especially in the offering, the messaging and the design and use of the product or service. But there are also **severe shortcomings in thinking that everything is simple**, because it is not. Trying to initiate, design, build and run a digital transformation initiative within an incumbent business of scale is a complex problem, period.

Figure 45 shows how the four TaP dimensions and elements drill down further, providing a means to navigate the crucial considerations and interconnections. This is an excellent way to view the entire TaP approach, with all the dimensions, elements and considerations in play. Download a pdf from https://allDigitalfuture. com/downloads, print it out and put it up in a spot where you can refer to it often.

In addition, what makes TaP truly groundbreaking is how it integrates traditional business strategy practice with human-centred design, continuous improvement, comfort with ambiguity, design considerations and methodologies like design thinking, Lean Six Sigma, Agile. There is no other business playbook out there that offers such an integrated approach that can significantly increase the success rate of your digital transformation or innovation initiative.

As I reflect on what factors most contributed to TMRW's ability to produce a world-class digital bank platform in TMRW, this one stands out most. I concentrated my time and attention on connecting the dots and ensuring that before we acted on one dot, we fully understood its impact on all other dots. I found this very challenging without a map of possible dots but nonetheless essential to success. But there is no better way to raise the odds. If there were, we would have taken that path. In Figure 45, you have a map, and by following it closely, you have given yourself a higher probability of success.

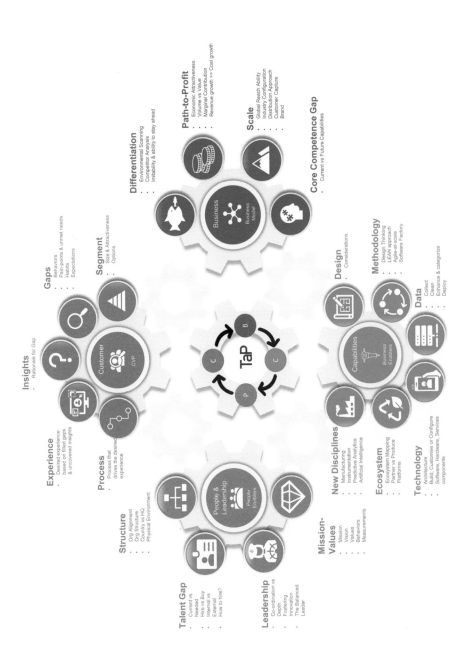

Figure 45 – Dimensions, elements and considerations

Customer dimension

Let's start with the first dimension, Customers. The Information Age, powered and enabled by the World Wide Web, has placed unprecedented power in the hands of consumers. The ordinary consumer is now able to gather all the knowledge he needs to understand and analyse almost any topic he desires – at his fingertips and even on the go (Perkins & Fenech, 2014; Umit Kucuk & Krishnamurthy, 2007).

It is thus apt that **desirability** is the starting point of my playbook. Desirability leads us to first connect with and understand who we want to serve, and to identify what gaps exist. This allows you to exploit these gaps to serve your customers better, so that they will desire your proposition and offerings over your competition.

The more successful a company is, the more they tend to think they know what the customer wants, but in actual fact, **as companies get larger and more successful, they tend to become more organisation-centric and less-customer centric** (Innovation, 2018; McGovern, 2013; Morgan, 2019; Williams, 2019). My advice is to never start with the capabilities first – a simple rule but a hard one to follow. If you go to any conference, the discussions are usually around the solution and what it can do. Executives attend these events and come back excited about Artificial Intelligence (AI) or predictive analytics or design thinking, but without a clear understanding of their segment of interest or the patience to understand and frame the problems their customers are having. Without understanding what customers are willing to pay for, these are just solutions looking for a problem. I have always felt it's better to have a question you don't have an answer to than to have a solution without knowing what the problem is.

5.1.1
Segment and gaps

Segments

As shown in Figure 46, the very first step is selecting your target segment. A quantitative analysis will tell you the size of the segment, their wallet size and the share you could potentially capture. It's a good idea to have a few target segments as options, so you can select the most suitable amongst them. Segment selection, gap analysis and insight generation are iterative. Thus, you might not quickly find a segment opportunity big enough, with obvious unmet needs that customers are willing to pay for, that can bridge you to your target share of wallet, for what's desirable to be viable. This has obvious linkages with the viability of the business model, which is the second dimension in our playbook.

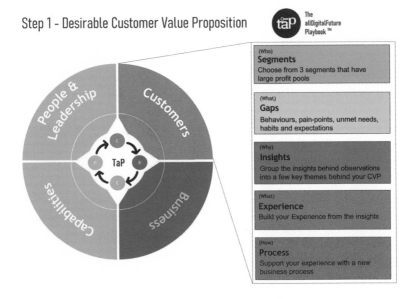

Figure 46 – Designed for customers

The young professional and young professional family or millennial professional was the segment of choice for TMRW. As the goal was to create a truly mobile digital bank, we needed to tap into an audience that was **already highly connected and mobile-first**. We also wanted to start with simple products so that we could grow along with these customers as their product needs changed and grew. Millennials have simple banking needs and expect everything to be seamless and on-tap due to their experience with mobile phones. Having a product that they desire would entice them to eventually switch main banks, making them the easiest segment to acquire and eventually turn into main bank customers.

The alternative was to target the affluent, but the affluent are well-served, and because they are older, we would need to design TMRW as an omni-channel offering, which is an expensive proposition. Since the traditional offering was already targeted at this segment, focusing on the millennial professional would allow us to design and build a lower-cost model that was mobile-only. The general mass market was ruled out as a first target as the path to profit would be even harder given their smaller disposable income, and multiple studies have indicated that the propensity to bank digitally is related to education and income (Sulaiman, Jaafar, and Mohezar, 2007; Fall, Orozco, and Akim, 2020; Magotra, Sharma, and Sharma, 2015).

We saw the potential of capturing the millennial audience early on. We believed that the future of consumer banking lies in serving millennials. Already, millennials (as well as the subsequent younger generations) make up more than half of the world's population. By 2025, they will account for 75% of the global workforce, bringing in a whole new set of demands and expectations, and shaping the digital economy. This is evident in ASEAN, which has a very young population and the third-largest concentration of millennials globally. **Millennial professionals have generally been treated as mass-market consumers by traditional banks and are under-served in relation to their potential**. The reason for this is that most millennials lack high disposable incomes.

Another reason is that millennials' priorities and aspirations are starkly different from those of their predecessors. Having children, buying homes, and other traditional "success markers" are trumped by other priorities, such as travelling the world or making a positive impact on society. It's not that the traditional success markers aren't important. Millennials still have these aspirations, but they tend to make financial life decisions on a different timeline compared with baby boomers. Also, the millennial generation is the one that has challenged traditional banking the most over the years. They have a low perception of banks due to the latter's inability to be simple and very transparent. And their highly mobile and tech-enabled nature has pushed banks to make all their services fully digital.

There are downsides to serving this segment. Their current income level is not high, and this makes the ability to recoup the large upfront investments needed to build a millennial bank hard. We estimated the ASEAN millennial banking revenue pool to be worth S$10B, but much of this potential is likely to be happen later, when their incomes rise. In spite of this, it became imperative that we tap into this market not for their current investment potential, as they currently have less spending power, but because they are likely to be **early adopters of the mobile-only digital bank, are under-served, have greater affinity for a millennial branded experience, and finally, will have much higher lifetime value (LTV) in time to come**. As this segment ages, their incomes will rise exponentially, and thus could potentially provide huge returns in the future. If you are able to capture this audience early on and engage them sufficiently to turn them into loyal advocates of your business, you will be able to foster more transactions from them in the future and reap the benefits. But it is obvious that a lot of patience is needed, as the costs come first, and the revenues are backended.

Similarly, you will need to undergo the same selection process to determine what is the right target segment for your transformation or innovation.

Gaps

Sometimes, you just don't realise the issues your customers face until you speak to them up close. And many senior executives also do not experience their products the way customers do, as they are placed on VIP lists that get special treatment. Let me give a simple example. Before the ubiquity of videoconferencing during the Covid-19 pandemic, many companies used teleconferencing. The teleconference details in your calendar were a real pain. First there's the conference phone number, then the meeting identifier is some long string of digits and so is the password. The only way to enter it properly is to copy it down. This problem has been in existence for a long time but likely has not been big enough of a pain for customers to report. There should be some way to trigger the whole string of digits into the conference facility rather than copying it down so you can see it whilst entering the digits.

As a provider of teleconferencing services, you might therefore not be aware of this pain point unless you speak to a customer and ask him how he uses your product or service. In fact, there is a solution that allows you to auto-dial by entering, for example, 18005555555,,123456789# into your calendar, where 123456789 is the access code for the conference call. So, as part of the onboarding process to any conference service, this should be a standard instruction or briefing. How many of you are aware of this?

To understand such gaps, one has to interact with the customer. A variety of avenues exist to do this. Having conversations directly with customers and observing how they use and interact with your products and services (or your competitor's) would be the best. It's time-consuming, but it is truly enlightening. Instead of asking customers "How would you...", which might elicit a theoretical answer, this form of research allows you to ask, "Show me how you...", which is more observational in nature. The latest thinking in customer research encourages you to embed yourself in the environment of your target customer – what's called **ethnographic research** – rather than relying solely on standard focus group research (Baxter et al., 2013).

In fact, many experts recommend using both methods in combination (Davey, 2013; Agar and MacDonald, 1995; Baxter, Koners, and Szwejczewski, 2013). Baxter et al. concluded that "ethnographic research is rated as the most effective method for identifying customer needs and it can also help to identify hidden needs, i.e., customer needs which are previously unmet and unarticulated. This makes ethnography particularly well suited to answering the broad questions that can lead to radical innovation." Agar and MacDonald concluded that "focus groups can show a research some new territory, but it can't tell you much about what it is you have just seen", i.e., ability to explain customer behaviour.

After agreeing on TMRW's segment of focus, we delved into the nuances of these customers through ethnographic research. This involved speaking to them – and in a way becoming them – to understand them well. This was followed by many lengthy discussions on what the segment truly needed. We began with the two markets we wanted to tap first: Thailand and Indonesia (Figure 47). These two markets stood out for their high banking penetration potential (or low current penetration), high retail banking pool sizes (which will get even larger as they have big populations that have large unbanked segments with high mobile penetration), and supportive banking regulations. Thailand, for example, initiated the national digital ID (NDID) project that allows individuals to confirm their identities online as part of their ambitious Thailand 4.0 initiative. Indonesian regulations allow digital banks to onboard customers using videoconferencing. Entering these markets would be a good proof of concept for the TMRW digital bank launch.

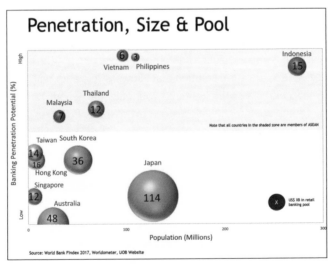

Figure 47 – Most attractive ASEAN markets for digital bank

In building TMRW, we interviewed 3,000 customers to understand their needs in detail (Finews.asia, 2019). This portion of the work cannot be skipped regardless of how long you have been in the business. At the very least, talking to customers when they are using your solution or your competitor's solution to understand the issues faced must be completed. **Qualitative research is exploratory**, and helps you observe and understand your customer's underlying motives, beliefs, behaviours, pain points, unmet needs, habits and expectations. These are essential information to document your gaps in understanding of your customers' needs and wants. Qualitative exploration can consist of in-depth interviews, ethnographic research, focus groups, content analysis (where you analyse words and images from a variety of content related to your target segment) and diary-keeping (where your target segment updates a diary of thoughts and actions related to the subject matter of interest to you). In my view, one of the biggest mistakes you can make is rushing or skipping this step.

Once you have sufficient qualitative input to uncover key insights that can help you design your desired experience, you may have to use **participatory design research**[59] to involve the customer in the design of the solution. This helps you to identify what's most important to them, and why they are important. When high-fidelity prototypes are ready, eye-tracking analysis is commonly used to test the friendliness and usability of your digital solutions, such as your app. Here, your target customers put on a camera, which shows where their eyes focus on when they are looking at your UI, for example. An aggregated eye-tracking map that is very dispersed means that each customer is looking at something different on the UI, and thus may be confused by the content or instructions.

Once the proposition is clear, **quantitative research should be used to gain statistical confidence** that sufficient numbers of customers are willing to pay for the new experience you are going to bring about, so that you can meet your business goals.

---

59. An approach to design that invites all stakeholders (e.g. customers, employees, partners, citizens, consumers) into the design process as a means of better understanding, meeting, and sometimes pre-empting their needs. Source: UX Magazine

Insights, experience and process

Insights

The big prize in the consumer dimension that you are after isn't the gap itself, but the insight that drives the gap.

Figure 48 shows the key differences between observations, insights, unmet needs, ideas, experience design and customer journeys. You can see that if the insight is not known, the idea is merely a suggestion, with no understanding what is driving the behaviour. So, in both observations to understand the problem and in applying ideas to solve the problem (that is, if the problem is clear in the first place, see Chapter 3.3), the key is to discover the insight, as it is the insight that allows us to take the correct path towards a breakthrough innovation. My experience has been that there are **too many people chasing for breakthroughs without looking for new insights**.

No	Observations ("what I observed")	Insights ("why I observed it")	Unmet Needs ("what customer wants but doesn't get")	Ideas/Possible Solutions	Experience design & test	Customer Journey Mapping Process
1	Removes pretty bank notes as a way to save.	Finds this a fun and easy way to make small savings	No easy means to save	Design a game to help customers save that is fun and easy	A. Map out the low fidelity prototype to test the game with customers to see how it feels. B. Is it too simple? C. Or too complex?	A. Map out the detailed step by step customer journey. B. How does the actions in the game result in changes to the savings balance?
2	Doesn't want to apply for more credit cards	Fear of overspending with too many cards	No easy way to prevent overspending	Allow customers to set limits for online spend, cash withdrawal and to lower their card limits	A. Test out the changes to the limits in a wireframe prototype to see if it's easy to understand and use.	Map out the detailed step-by-step customer journey and figure out all the inputs and outputs needed for the frontend to backend host interfaces
3	Finds his bank's menu design confusing	Menu's force users to navigate in a standard way	No easy way to get task done	Design a banking app that has very few first level menus, e.g. don't need to ask from which account if there is only one transaction account	B. Is it clear or confusing. C. Iterate till it's good and clear	Ensure that the final instructions, data inputs and outputs are in the right sequence, and that the UI design is stored as standard libraries in the design system
4	A. Younger customers are very worried about overspending. B. Some have been burnt as a result of not being able to pay their debts	A. There is a cultural aspect to this as there is peer pressure to look good and be seen to have the latest. B. Many customers are prone to impulse buy and don't have the discipline to stop or budget	No easy real-time method to avoid overspending. All existing methods report at month's end.	Allow customers to set a budget for a category and whenever a spend occurs in that category, alert the customer as to how he is faring against the budget	When the alert comes, what is the customers reaction to how he is doing against his budget? Does this make the customer more careful and less impulsive about the next purchase?	A. Map the entire journey the customer takes before the alert and after the spend alert. B. How and where will the real-time data about the customer's spend be obtained and what is the longest permissible delay? C. If the payment is made but the transaction not transmitted by the merchant till later, what problems will it pose?
5	Customers speaking to their phones instead of typing	Some languages are hard to type as they are not easy to represent as alphabets	No easy way to communicate without a two-way call	Make this a standard feature for all phones and default to voice.	What kind of customer would prefer voice versus text?	A. Map the onboarding journey and figure out where a decision needs to be made if the default mode is voice or text. B. Should we default all logographic and non-alphabetical languages to voice?

Figure 48 – CVP creation checklist

Breakthroughs no matter how small, but especially so in highly competitive industries, require you to have the mechanisms in place to spot the insights that allow you to uncover the underlying reasons customers behave the way they do. This is often linked to unseen problems customers have in performing their jobs. This will allow you to focus on new pain points rather than putting too much emphasis on giving your customers additional benefits and hence dilute your profitability without actually solving any of their problems. This approach is not only wasteful but is also highly imitable by your competitors.

However, deriving a good insight is an art rather than a science. You know it when you see it, when everything comes together, and the magic happens. Here are three examples of valuable insights that meet all the criteria of a good insight:

1. **Peloton (exercise bikes):** When the brand first launched, it offered 45-minute classes, because that was standard in the industry. But by carefully gathering customer feedback through many channels, including a very active Facebook group, Peloton decided to offer shorter rides that run at 20 or 30 minutes (Segran, 2017). The reason was that when you travel to the gym, it takes time to get there and back, and so it makes sense to have a longer session. However, Peloton connects high-bandwidth large screens to their bikes where you can have classes live or on-demand at home. So, this didn't apply to them, and cutting the time made sense for both Peloton and their customers. Shorter rides are also beneficial from a mental perspective when you are just starting a fitness routine.

2. **Three (Telco):** Customers used 71 times the amount of data they would have used had they been charged as normal – most of which was used to post holiday snaps on social media, rather than waiting to use free WiFi at the hotel or other locations. The increased volume could allow a decent profit even at reduced roaming charges (Michon, 2021). This insight was the genesis of Three's #HolidaySpam campaign in 2015.

3. **TMRW (bank):** Customers don't want information for the sake of information; they want to act. Hence, all budgeting should be real-time as you spend, rather than a report at the end of the month, when you have already spent everything and can't act. Real-time tracking and budgeting became one of the key proof points of proactivity that differentiated TMRW.

How do you know you have a good insight?

Figure 49 illustrates the five key ingredients of a good insight. First, a good insight should explain an observation about a behaviour that most people may not have

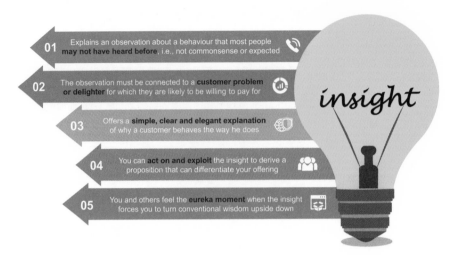

Figure 49 – How will you know if you have a great insight?

heard before, i.e., not common-sense or expected. Secondly, the observation must be connected to a customer problem or delighter which they are likely to be willing to pay for. The insight should offer a simple, clear and elegant explanation for why a customer behaves the way he does, and you should be able to act on and exploit the insight to derive a proposition that can differentiate your offering. Finally, you and others around you should feel the "eureka moment" when the insight forces you to turn conventional wisdom upside down.

As shown in Figure 48, observations and insights are the output of the customer research. The key difference is that **observations are "what I observed" and insights are "why the customer is behaving this way"**. Knowing "why" is vital in that it allows you to understand the real motivations driving customer behaviour, rather than just the symptoms you observe. Most times the insights are not immediately obvious but come later when you are reviewing the transcripts, notes and video recordings of the customer interactions.

Framing what the problem really is is a vital step in this process. If you get the problem or "unmet need" wrong, then you will be working on the wrong thing for the rest of the initiative! For example, in Figure 48, item 4, the observation from customer research is that customers have a fear of overspending. However, the cause of the overspending is usually not examined in detail. In this example, the driver is peer pressure to keep up with friends. Without the insight that they often have peer pressure to own the latest gadgets or accessories, the assumption might be that the interest rate is too high. This would lead to the design of a lower-rate product solution. But with the insight, the more appropriate solution might be a real-time expense tracker that makes you reconsider the pressure to keep up, instead of a

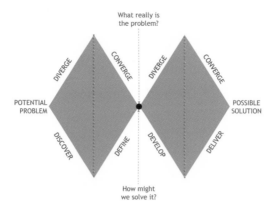

Figure 50 – Double-Diamond method

more affordable loan. Similarly, item 5's observation that some customers like to speak instead of type might lead to the idea that it should be done for all users, if the insight that it is mostly users whose languages are logographic who find it harder to type was not uncovered.

A good way to begin to formulate the ideas or potential solutions is to use the **double-diamond method** shown in Figure 50. The double-diamond forces the user to start from a potential problem, and repeatedly diverge and subsequently converge to discover the root cause. **Diverge** is the answer to the question "What else might the problem or solution be?" **Converge** is the answer to the question "Which of the options (problem or solution) might be most appropriate answer, and why?"

So, in diverge, you don't knock out any options, but keep trying to expand the repository of possible answers you have. This often reveals the true nature of the problem. If asking why this problem occurs leads to the discovery of yet another unseen problem, then you may have uncovered the root cause, which helps to frame the real problem at hand.

In converge, you start to identify which answers are a better fit for the problem at hand. Most people spend little time thinking through the problem, and in my experience, they end up solving the wrong problem. This is actually worse than the right problem with the wrong solution because you can then pivot to the right solution. But when you have the wrong problem to begin with, no amount of pivoting the solution is going to help you. The double-diamond method is a good way to be more certain that you have indeed identified the right problem.

There is also a perennial temptation to suggest the current "trendy" technology or solution, like AI or gamification, without thinking through clearly what is the actual problem the customer is facing. For example, someone might suggest traditional personal financial management (PFM) as a solution to item 4 in the table. From the insights, however, you note that the cause of the overspending is mostly attributed to impulse buying. Traditional PFM is typically presented to the customer at the end of the month, but impulse control needs to happen during the month, when the actual purchase happens and before the bank statement comes in.

Desired experience

Once you have sufficient insights, you are ready to design the desired experience for your target segment. This incorporates all the observations you have gathered in your gap analysis, with clear indications as to the insights you have discovered. Start by identifying possible solutions, which is depicted in the second diamond of the double-diamond method.

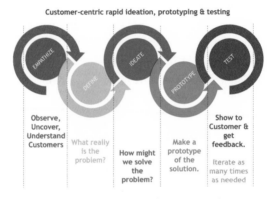

Figure 51 – Design Thinking approach

Once the possible solutions are identified, you can now adopt a human-centred or design thinking approach to **build a prototype and then refine it in an iterative manner**. This method is shown in Figure 51. The first prototype may be a low-fidelity prototype using pen and paper or just simple wireframes that can be quickly done with tools like Figma, Adobe XD, etc. (Myre, 2018; Newnham, 2020). If you are not sure what a wireframe is, here's a quote: "A wireframe is a visual mock-up that outlines the basic structure of your website, app, or landing page" (Myre, 2018). Traditionally, a wireframe is fairly simplistic. Basic shapes and elements are used to block out where each piece of content and UI element will go. And the power of the wireframe lies in that simplicity: Elements can be rearranged quickly and easily for iteration and approval before moving on to a higher-fidelity prototype. The prototype is tested in an iterative fashion, improving the solution with each iteration, as the customer's feedback is evaluated, and improvements are made to the solution to make it more effective. Doing so now avoids costly mistakes later when the functionality is already built, only to find that customers don't really appreciate it.

At this stage of the development of the customer value proposition (CVP), you should begin to have a sense of **how differentiated the CVP could be**. The more differentiated the CVP, the more difficult it is for current competitors to replicate or new entrants to imitate. However, the more differentiated it is, the more existing capabilities need to be enhanced; and if the new core competences required differ substantially from current competences, then the executional risks will be larger, and the feasibility of the innovation might be affected. So, as you can see again, the TaP approach exposes the complexity that originates from the interaction between the dimensions and elements, and highlights the need to balance them so that you maximise desirability, viability and feasibility simultaneously.

Creating and testing higher and higher-fidelity prototypes dramatically reduces the chances of failure of your innovation. It is remarkable that more organisations don't leverage this means of de-risking. If you don't think even high-profile and successful companies have expensive duds in their innovation track record, look no further. Figure 52 illustrates some of the biggest failures in innovation in recent history.

	Innovation	Company	Year of Launch	Units sold	Amount spent	Desirable	Details	Feasible	Details	Viable	Details
1	Edsel	Ford	1957	116000	$250M	X	gas guzzler	✓	colorful	✓	if sold enough
2	Post-it Notes	3M	1977	50B per year	not disclosed	X then ✓	not strong	X then ✓	didn't work	X then ✓	when used for restickables
3	QuickTake Camera	Apple	1994	not disclosed	not disclosed	X	no viewfinder	X	awkward, ahead of time	✓	if sold enough
4	Iridium	Motorola	1997	not disclosed	$5B	X	bulky, costly	X then ✓	but took too long	X	no demand
5	Segway	Segway	2001	140000	$100M	X	looks cool but accidents happened	✓	performs	X	too high end
6	Fire Phone	Amazon	2014	35000	$170M	?	no apps	X	buggy	X	no demand
7	Galaxy Fold	Samsung	2019	recalled	$130M	✓	looks cool	X	screen problems	✓	if sold enough

Figure 52 – A sample of the biggest failures in innovation

Don't be frustrated if it takes many iterations to come up with something that is desirable. If it's difficult to do, then others will also find it difficult, and you will have less competition. Rushing through – or worse, reverse-engineering what you already have in mind – is a bad start. If the customer doesn't desire it, and you spend a lot of money to create it, then it's an absolute waste of resources. Remember that for every hit product or service innovation you name, many others were unsuccessful. The rigorous application of The allDigitalfuture Playbook™ will improve your chances of bringing your innovation to fruition. For more information on the experience and process elements, refer back to Chapter 4.1, where I talk about examples from the building of TMRW.

At the end of the customer dimension, you should have a very clear understanding of your chosen segment, the gaps you observe from their behaviours, pain points, unmet needs, habits and expectations. From these observations, you need to extract the insights or the fundamental reasons why customers behave this way or have such needs. Using insights to inform strategy isn't new, although we think it is because of the recent adoption of design thinking in creating digital businesses.

My favourite management article about strategy, which in my view remains the seminal work on applying strategy to business, is a 1997 article entitled "What's wrong with strategy?" (Andrew & Marcus, 1997). I make this a recommended read for all my students when teaching strategy. The main difficulty in crafting and implementing strategy is that **objectives, tactics and strategy have a sequencing problem**. Do you first set an ambitious goal – what some may remember as a BHAG (Big Hairy Audacious Goal) from Jim Collins' book, *Built to Last* (Collins, 1994)? Then set the strategy to achieve that goal and then the tactics? What Andrew and Marcus highlight is a problem I have encountered time and time again in developing a winning strategy:

"The strategy to develop new products faster and more effectively than the competitors is only viable if the manager can envision the tactics for its implementation. If the manager knows where to recruit additional staff, see parts of the product development process that can be streamlined and have ideas about how to involve customers and suppliers more fully in product development, then the strategy is viable. If not, the strategy may not be realistic. Tactics need to be worked out before the strategy can be determined and the strategy needs to be clear in order to define the objectives."

A similar conundrum exists with strategy and objectives. If the leader sets a BHAG, "then realism enters into the discussion". In other words, "how would the management team know if the objective is realistic, unless they can generate a strategy for reaching the objective"? Therefore, the authors recommend that "the solution to such impasse is to understand the fundamental building block of good strategy: insight into how to create more value than competitors can". Such insights into value creation can be found through a deep understanding of suppliers', customers' and employees' behaviours, needs, pain points, habits and expectations.

In addition, separating strategy from tactics is also generally not a good idea. This is because most of the insights required to generate good strategy are often found in the heads of staff responsible for operating the business, because it is they who know the suppliers', customers' and employees' behaviours, needs, pain points, habits and expectations. And so often when leaders set strategy amongst the leadership team without involving such staff members, they get it all wrong! Andrew and Marcus raise another interesting point: "Tactics are not only about implementing today's strategy but also about discovering tomorrow's strategy. Tomorrow's insights arise from today's operating experiences. Unless implementation is also viewed as being part of strategy development, tomorrow's strategy is likely to be short on insights."

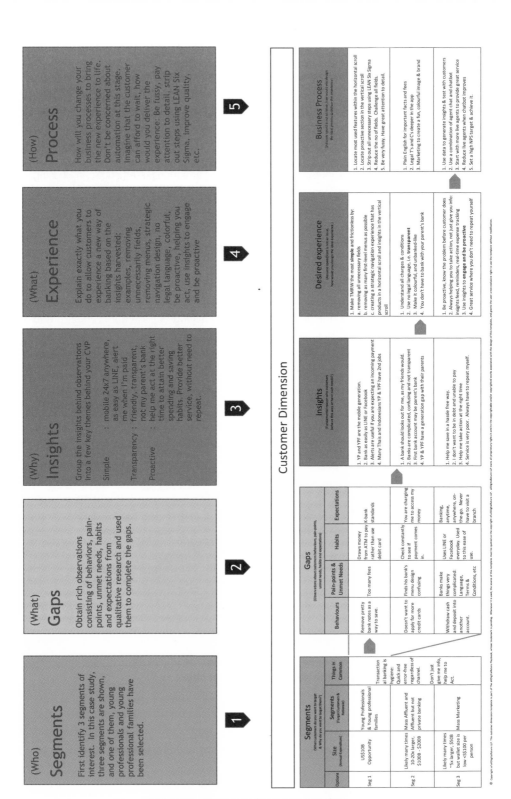

Figure 53 – Customer dimension template

The customer dimension focuses on discovering the key insights from your customers, illustrated in Figure 53 with an example from the TMRW digital bank's customer dimension. The customers could be (1) internal customers, i.e., your own employees; (2) external customers, i.e., the clients who pay the bills; or (3) partners and suppliers – because the techniques are the same. Once the insights are obtained, the desired experience can be designed, and then tested and refined using the double-diamond and design thinking techniques. Finally, you need to ensure that you have in place the right business process to deliver the experience.

Business process

To ensure that the new customer journeys[60] and customer experience are properly designed and documented, a cross-functional team of designers, product managers, process mapping experts, staff with knowledge of the data required and technical staff who will translate the stories into code should work on the customer journey together, to map the journey and the data required to fulfil that journey.

In parallel, there is the internal business process mapping which details how the processing is done, especially when it is not a flow that is "all green", meaning that it is not 100% digital because exception-handling of some form is required. Lean Six Sigma techniques should be used here to design processes with low friction, low hand-offs and low error rates. These methodologies that can help you design the best journeys and processes are described later in the capabilities dimension, under the methodology element (Chapter 5.3.2).

When designing the business process at this stage, assume that speed and cost are not constraints. How would you go about designing the ideal process to deliver the experience? You do not require any technology at this stage. You must be able to do this with pen and paper because if you can't, then technology can't help you anyway, as technology's role is simply to make the process run much faster. Business process is introduced here and not later, so that if you find that some experiences require significant capabilities that are non-trivial or require collection of large amounts of data over time, or capabilities that take time to build up, then a trade-off to lower the desired experience to fit current feasibility can be evaluated. **If this is only done much later, the feedback loop will be too long, introducing too much back-and-forth in the design of the proposition.**

Figure 53 introduces a flow, from your segment of choice, to uncovering customers' gaps – comprising their behaviours, pain points, unmet needs, habits and expectations – and then extracting the insights, leading to the design of the desired experience and required business process. **The key to doing this well is to focus on**

---

60. The customer journey is the path the customer takes which allows him to experience what you have created.

the flow. This flow makes it easier to see how the different elements in the customer dimension are interrelated, and how by focusing on aligning them, you can derive a stronger proposition for your customers. This customer dimension flow is a new creation I derived from my experience building TMRW.

The magic in deriving a differentiated CVP lies in how you translate the right insights into the right experience. For example, the insight that YPs and YPFs want to bank as easily as using Line or Facebook may be viewed as obvious. However, the experience of having very few first-level menus to make navigation very simple is directly connected to this insight. When combined with removing all unnecessary fields and introducing a strategic navigation experience with horizontal and vertical scrolling, suddenly the experience becomes very different. Getting to the best flow is currently more art than science. You are likely going to have to iterate many times before you discover something that is highly differentiated. Most people don't do this step well. No matter how well you think you know the customer, don't skip this step!

If the insights are "Why YPs and YPFs behave the way they do", the desired experience is "What you are going to do to address this and why", then the business process answers the question "How you are going to make it happen". So, the complete flow now looks like:

Insight: Bank as easily as LINE or Facebook

Experience: Remove as many first-level menus as possible

Process: Locate most-used features within the horizontal scroll
                 (shown below)

Using this new customer dimension flow technique, you are more likely to be able to derive many small breakthroughs in your customer experience similar to the example above.

At this stage of TaP, you should have a proposed experience as well as a business process that can help deliver on it. But how will you know if it's sufficiently differentiated for you to win customers and scale, yet not so heavily differentiated that the costs will significantly outweigh the revenues? Figure 54 showcases this dilemma, which may require several loops before you resolve it and reach a position where the **differentiation, path-to-profit, scaling ability and core competence gaps are all optimal**.

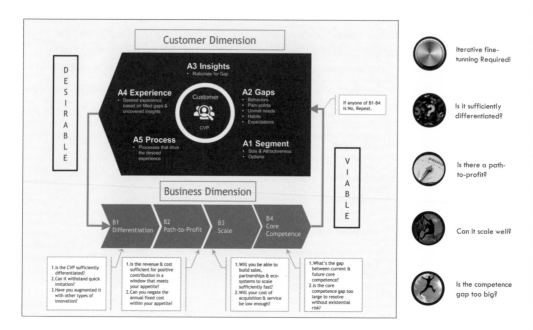

Figure 54 – Customer and business dimension interaction

You may have to navigate this loop by iteratively using the customer dimension flow tool to refine your insights, experience and business process, but also stack the customer dimension output against the business dimension considerations by answering the questions shown in Figure 54. If any of the answers to these questions is no, then you will have to iterate again until they become a yes. Resolving circular interactions is part of what's different in TaP. This is the first of the three circular interactions that we will examine. The other two circular interactions can be found later in Figure 64 (customers, business and capabilities) and Figure 83 (customers, business, capabilities, people & leadership).

Let's now explore the business dimension in greater detail.

Key takeaways

- The more successful a company is, the more they tend to think they know what the customer wants, but in actual fact, as companies get larger and more successful, they tend to become more organisation centric and less customer centric.

- Never start with the capabilities first, a simple rule but a hard one to follow. Without understanding what customers are willing to pay for, these are just solutions looking for a problem.

- It's better to have a question you don't have an answer to than to have a solution without knowing what the problem is.

- Segment selection, gap analysis and insight generation are iterative. Thus, you might not quickly find a segment opportunity big enough, with obvious unmet needs that customers are willing to pay for, that can bridge you to your target share of wallet.

- To understand such gaps, you have to interact with the customer. A variety of avenues exist to do this. Having conversations directly with customers and observing how they use and interact with your products and services (or your competitor's) would be the best. It's time-consuming, but it is truly enlightening.

- Qualitative research can uncover key insights that help you design a desired experience that is truly differentiated.

- Participatory design research should involve the customer in the design of the solution. This helps you to identify what's most important to them, and why they are important.

- Once the proposition is clear, quantitative research should be used to gain statistical confidence that enough customers are willing to pay for the new experience you will bring about, so that you can meet your business goals.

- The big prize in the consumer dimension that you are after isn't the gap itself, but the insight that drives the gap.

- Insights are often linked to unseen problems customers have in performing their jobs.

- A great insight has five characteristics – something you may not have heard before, connected to a customer problem or delighter, offers a simple, clear and elegant explanation, which you can act on and exploit, and it generates a eureka moment.

- Observations are "what I observed" and insights are "why the customer is behaving this way".

- Most times, the insights are not immediately obvious, but come later when you are reviewing the transcripts, notes and video recordings of the customer interactions.

- Framing what the real problem is is a vital step of this process, as if you get the problem or "unmet need" wrong, then you will be working on the wrong thing for the rest of the initiative.

- A good way to begin to formulate the ideas or potential solutions is to use the double-diamond method.

- Once the possible solution is identified, you can now adopt a human-centred or design thinking approach to build a prototype and then refine it in an iterative manner.

- The TaP approach exposes the complexity that originates from the interaction between the dimensions and elements, and the need to balance them so that you maximise the desirability, viability and feasibility criteria simultaneously.

- Creating and testing higher and higher-fidelity prototypes drastically reduces the chances of failure of your innovation.

- Don't be frustrated if it takes many iterations to come up with something that is desirable. If it's difficult to do, then others will also find it difficult, and you will have less competition.

- Designing the business process to support the experience based on the insights you discovered can be done on pen and paper because if you can't, then technology can't help you anyway, as technology's role is simply to make the process run much faster.

- The Customer Dimension Template showcases a flow from your segment of choice, to uncovering their gaps comprising their behaviours, pain points, unmet needs, habits and expectations, and then extracting the insights, leading to the design of the desired experience and required business process.

- Using this new customer dimension flow technique, you are more likely to be able to derive many big or small breakthroughs in your customer experience.

- A cross-functional team of designers, product managers, process mapping experts, staff with knowledge of the data required, technical staff, etc., should work on the customer journey together.

- You may have to navigate the customer and business dimension loop by iteratively using the customer dimension flow tool to refine your insights, experience and business process, but also stack the customer dimension output against the important business considerations by answering key challenge questions involving the four elements of the business dimension.

- If any of the answers to these questions is no, then you will have to iterate again until they become a yes.

Business dimension

The interactions between dimensions – whether the customer, business, capabilities or people & leadership dimensions, as shown in Figure 55 – are the source of complexity. This is a sequencing issue similar to what Andrew and Marcus discovered for objectives, strategy and tactics, just that in TaP, they are represented as customer, business, capabilities, and people & leadership (Andrew & Marcus, 1997). For example, your segment choice and value proposition will affect your revenue and cost dynamics significantly.

In building TMRW, we went back and forth fine-tuning these interactions for almost 10 months in 2017 to **achieve both the desirability and viability criteria**. I recall the team being frustrated that we kept going back and forth, and the consultants wanted to start testing something, and start prototyping, and gamification was mentioned many times as something we should try. This was something I was against. If we had done that, the result may have been very different. I think many organisations feel the same tensions and conflicts at this stage of their transformation. My advice to the leader is to hold firm and continue to fine-tune until you achieve the right balance that can check both the desirability and viability boxes.

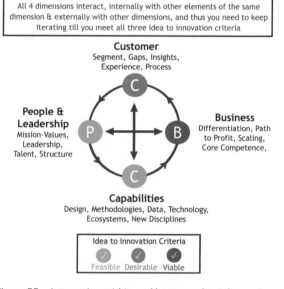

Figure 55 – Interaction within and between the 4 dimensions

Jamorn, who was one of the first product owners in the pioneer team, recalled: "The main thing that we got right was to really question the status quo. That was the key. I was quite worried early on that we would **fall into the trap of just doing another banking app – the same thing but with nicer skins on top of it.** So we spent a lot of time in the ideation and design phase for TMRW, throwing around a ton of ideas. Which led to a lot of frustration since at one point I felt that we were going in too many directions. We were diverging a lot and it was very hard to be focused on delivering a targeted end-to-end experience. However, without sufficient divergence, we may not have discovered what's needed to impress, i.e., the key differentiators. It's tough to balance and find the optimal point but doing so is crucial to success."

The power of The allDigitalfuture Playbook™ lies in its ability to expose all the dimensions, elements and considerations and how they interact with each other. This gives you a map for how to navigate them. My belief is that this is the key to greater probability of success for digital transformation and innovation initiatives. Most initiatives fail because the interactions and ensuing complexity simply overwhelm the programme.

At the end of the business model dimension, we arrive at the gap between your firm's current core competence and the future core competence needed to deliver the differentiation imbued by the Customer Value Proposition (output of the customer dimension). But before we can do that, there are 3 hurdles to cross:

1. Is the CVP sufficiently differentiated and resistant to imitation?
2. Can the offering achieve the required path-to-profit on a per customer basis?
3. Can you scale the offering fast enough deliver the absolute revenue and profits needed?

The degree to which competitors can imitate the proposition affects the sustainability of the differentiation. If the differentiation will be quickly narrowed by the competition, then the path to profit will be longer and the scaling harder. The degree of imitability will also have a connection with the capability dimension and the degree of difficulty in acquiring the needed capabilities to make the innovation feasible, i.e., the more differentiated, the bigger the gap between current and needed core competence, the bigger the executional risk. Path-to-profit focuses on producing a positive marginal contribution and negating the annual fixed cost per customer thereafter. Finally, you need enough customers that are profitable on a per customer level to deliver the absolute revenue and profits needed. When the offering does so, it would have met both desirability and viability criteria.

5.2.1
Differentiation

Figure 56 shows the four elements that make up the business dimension: differentiation, path to profit, scale and core competence gap. A company's ability to compete is based on how it differentiates its proposition to its customers. Innovation usually results in some degree of differentiation, but is it enough to attract customers away from competitors' offerings? Or if it's a brand-new offering, is the value created sufficiently differentiated to generate enough demand so you can scale? If the innovation is sufficiently differentiated, there is a higher probability that the proposition would attract enough customers to make the business viable, provided the costs required to produce the offering can be contained.

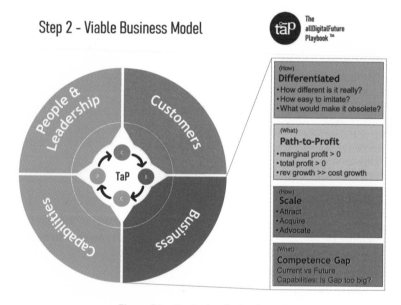

Figure 56 – Designing for business

Differentiation through innovation can take different forms. A good way to categorise these innovation themes is the **Ten Types of Innovation**, a methodology by Doblin, which was acquired by Deloitte (Figure 57).

Most people focus only on product innovation, or "the offering", as the Doblin methodology puts it. **By combining product, experience and configuration types of innovations, you can make your innovation more difficult to copy.** It is

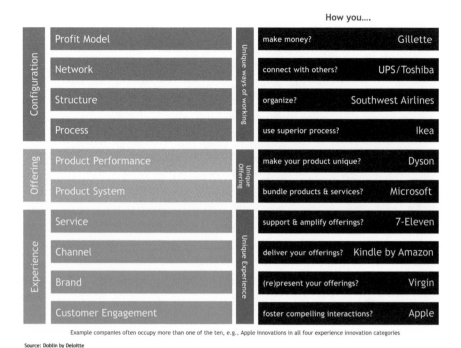

How you....

Configuration — Unique ways of working	Profit Model	make money?	Gillette
	Network	connect with others?	UPS/Toshiba
	Structure	organize?	Southwest Airlines
	Process	use superior process?	Ikea
Offering — Unique Offering	Product Performance	make your product unique?	Dyson
	Product System	bundle products & services?	Microsoft
Experience — Unique Experience	Service	support & amplify offerings?	7-Eleven
	Channel	deliver your offerings?	Kindle by Amazon
	Brand	(re)present your offerings?	Virgin
	Customer Engagement	foster compelling interactions?	Apple

Example companies often occupy more than one of the ten, e.g., Apple innovations in all four experience innovation categories

Source: Doblin by Deloitte

Figure 57 – Ten types of innovation by Doblin

increasingly difficult to compete just on product performance or product system (where you bundle products and services together). The reason for this is that globalisation and the internet have narrowed the time taken to manufacture, copy and learn, and thus the ability to imitate has improved significantly. Consequently, it has never been more important to expand your offering innovation to include experience or configuration innovations as illustrated in Figure 57 (Keeley et al., 2017). Many companies are therefore incorporating experience into their differentiation, intentionally using "services as the stage, and goods as props, to engage individual customers in a way that creates a memorable event" – or what's better known as the experience economy (Newman, 2015; Pine & Gilmore, 1998; Pine II & Gilmore, 2011). This doesn't mean that every proposition must focus on the experience, but it caters to the possibility that if you can, it could be a more sustained differentiation.

Without a doubt, figuring out TMRW's differentiation was one of the biggest challenges. Whilst low-cost mobile devices and mobile subscription plans have brought a bank within reach of almost every potential customer, and regulations were looking even more likely to support authentication without a face-to-face meeting, this didn't resolve the issue of differentiation. We cast the net wide to look for an answer, speaking to challenger banks and Fintech companies. Challenger banks like Monzo, N26, Nubank, and even first-generation mobile banks like mBank were studied, as well as big-tech companies worldwide. We found that mBank was successful in the internet-banking era by having service and experience as key differentiators. So, we knew that the basic transactional capability of TMRW had to be excellent, and we would not be able to launch a digital bank with a low Net Promoter Score (NPS®). This could give us the entry point to compete, but how could we sustain this as more competitors entered? In the course of all this, we found one common theme: the use of data. Google uses data to improve its search capabilities. Uber, Gojek, and Grab use data to perform surge pricing. I also visited a bank in Suzhou that uses alternative data to underwrite credit for customers.

Banks have a lot of data about their customers, and that data increases every time a customer transacts. Banks know when customers pay, who they pay, and how their payments change – for example, if merchants raise or lower subscription charges. With all this information, banks have the opportunity to create better customer experience by anticipating their customers' needs and helping them fulfil that need before they even know they have it. This became the genesis of **Anticipate, Converse and Serve** (Khoo, 2019). The aim was to become the most proactive digital bank, to be able to anticipate our customers' needs using the data we had about them, to be able to have conversations about their personal financial situation and get them to act on it.

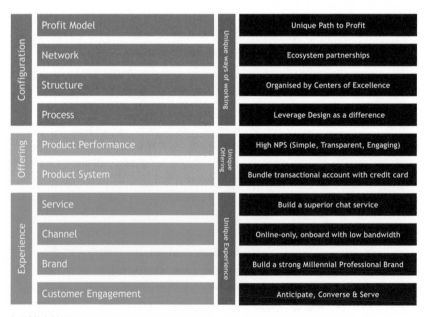

Source: Doblin by Deloitte

Figure 58 – Ten types of innovation in TMRW

One of the influential insights I recall early in the design phase was work done by CEB (formerly known as the Corporate Executive Board and acquired by Gartner in 2017) that shows that **banks are better at providing information (e.g., statements) than they are at making things actionable for their customers (e.g., helping you save or track expenses or just showing you your monthly balance increases or decreases)**. We therefore tried to ensure that whatever we did was actionable. One of these was expense tracking, where giving the customer real-time updates on his expenditure, versus a set budget when he does a transaction in the category being tracked, was viewed as critical to the feedback loop for the customer. Contrast this with getting the data at the end of the month, when the expenditure is already made, and actionability is low.

So, if we compare the differentiation in TMRW using Figure 58, we actually **embedded many innovations across the spectrum of the 10 different types of innovation**. Besides the product offering, which comprises product performance centred around a simple, engaging and transparent banking service, and a product

system that bundled a credit card and transactional account[61] together, TMRW also extended innovation into the configuration and experience types of innovation. In service, TMRW was the first in ASEAN to build a conversational chatbot, called Tia[62], to provide servicing for clients.

In channel innovation, TMRW was the first digital bank in Thailand and one of the first in Indonesia to allow onboarding without having to go to a branch. In Thailand, the TMRW onboarding kiosks (shown in Figure 59) spread out across Bangkok made this possible, although it wasn't ideal as the customer still needed to visit the kiosk to complete the onboarding. Eventually, the kiosks would be replaced by a national identity verification system. Indonesia allowed for a straight-through onboarding using video-conferencing identification. Both countries granted access to a national database that afforded online verification of customers.

Finally, scanning the environment is important, as this can help to **mitigate investments in**

Figure 59 – TMRW kiosk at BTS station in Bangkok

---

61. Current account or savings account that is a transacting account in nature

62. Tia: TMRW's intelligent assistant

technologies or trends that don't have longevity. An example is the investments made into NFC payments by Telcos and banks when the solution was not mature and required provisioning of the secure element embedded in the mobile phone. Eventually, this gave way to another technology, NFC with host card emulation, that eliminated the provisioning. The specific differentiation you would like to build is evaluated against the trends in your industry or market, how it matches against competitor offerings, how easy it is to quickly imitate, and thus the ability of your innovation to stay ahead.

Sometimes it is better to wait till the technology is more mature, but at other times it might make sense to move before the ultimate enabling technology is available. This was the case when TMRW was being launched in Thailand. We decided to launch using biometric kiosks available at convenient locations throughout Bangkok rather than wait for a straight-through method. Customers could simply scan a valid ID and their fingerprints and open up an account. This made the whole process as seamless and frictionless as possible and a first in Bangkok. Because the segment we served were frequent users of the BTS transit system, placing kiosks through the BTS network meant customers didn't have to make a special trip to complete the final step – authentication – to open a TMRW account. It could be done when they were travelling to and from their homes. The kiosks were later upgraded to include facial recognition first before trying fingerprint due to a lower inherent error rate in facial versus fingerprint recognition in Thailand.

Path to profit

Path to profit starts with confirming the economic attractiveness of the target segment and pricing. The attractiveness of the segment is re-evaluated in the business dimension to provide another opportunity to ensure that the segment selected in the first step of the customer dimension is sound. This is so pivotal that a second opportunity is provided here to again validate the attractiveness and the penetration, size and revenue pool. Your addressable market, i.e., the portion and size of the market that needs what you have to offer and is prepared to pay for it (and not the entire market) is identified so that this size multiplied by price can give you an indication of gross revenue. The size of the revenue pool is related to your pricing approach and whether it's a value vs volume strategy, as shown in Figure 60. Use Figure 60 to help determine your pricing approach.

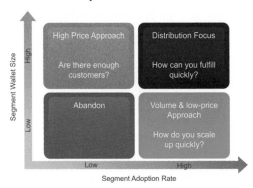

Figure 60 – Size vs adoption matrix

There is a big distinction between size and effort. **Having a big addressable market doesn't mean the effort to reach and acquire them is feasible**. Effort is a function of multiple factors. For example, is the need obvious and thus the customer generates demand organically? Or is the need subtle or hidden, and thus convincing the customer to take up the solution is needed? The latter can take up substantial time and effort and thus slow down the process of scaling significantly. At this stage, an educated estimate is required to provide input to the path-to-profit calculations and assess the feasibility of the business model to generate a profit. Specific partners and intermediaries can be identified later when ecosystem is covered in the capabilities dimension.

Stage 1: Marginal contribution > 0

Figure 61 illustrates a path to profitability that has been adapted from my learnings and generalised to be applicable in any industry. For TMRW, the target was to be marginally profit positive within five years (Asian Banking and Finance, 2020). **In the first phase, the aim should be to get the cost of acquisition (COA) down to a level where the revenue could negate COA and service or operating cost per customer, within a period commensurate with your loss appetite, for example 2–3 years.**[63] If your company doesn't practice amortisation for COA, it will be treated as a one-time operational expense in the year of acquisition.

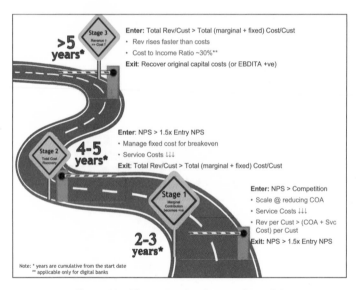

Figure 61 – Three-stage path-to-profit model

When building TMRW, I was adamant that we **focus on active customers**, as I was aware that raising low-cost deposits could only materialise if customers were active. In most businesses, there may be a higher tolerance of inactive customers, due to the need to show traction in acquisition. In TMRW, there would only be transactional accounts and credit cards at the start, so acquiring active customers was the main focus.

---

63. The number of years provided in this example and the years shown in the figure are cumulative, i.e., the 4–5 years in Stage 2 in Figure 61 includes the 2–3 years in Stage 1.

If you target a higher-volume segment, you are likely trading lower revenue per customer for a larger pool of customers and thus taking a longer path towards profitability because the average revenue per customer is low (for banks in developing countries in ASEAN, approximately S$100–S$200 revenue is derived for a YP and YPF customer with a lending relationship).

The cost of acquisition can be high during the initial launch, as lower-cost customer acquisition methods like leveraging partners or referral models have not kicked in. Digital banks that quickly became profitable like Webank and Kakao were able to lower their COA by attracting customers from their parents (WeChat and KakaoTalk), and also leverage data to accelerate their ability to lend and yet keep their non-performing loans low. In TMRW, we didn't have those advantages and so we spent the better part of the second half of 2019 enhancing TMRW by leveraging key feedback from TMRW's Thailand customers. This raised the NPS® to +33 by early 2020. As of 7 December 2020, TMRW has an NPS® of +45 for Thailand and +60 for Indonesia.[64] These are outstanding accomplishments in both countries.

The cost of acquiring an active customer dropped significantly as we expanded from just acquiring customers directly to acquiring customers with partners as well. In Indonesia, with a higher NPS® at launch and applying all the learnings from Thailand, the COA dropped at a much faster pace, **making the target of getting to marginal contribution positive more likely**. This experience clearly demonstrated that there is an inverse correlation between the NPS® gap with your key competitors and the cost of acquisition. Most professionals are not used to the marginal cost concept (Gallo, 2017). Most of them didn't start the firm from scratch, and thus they don't worry about marginal costs. In many larger firms, the loss from one emerging product line is just simply absorbed by other mature product lines.

But in a start-up or new initiative, this is very crucial. The start-up will keep losing money if the acquisition cost and servicing cost at a per customer level is higher than the revenue. And the ability to generate revenue is inextricably linked to the target segment chosen and isn't easily changed after you have designed and launched an entity or initiative targeted at that segment. If you are a bank targeting young professionals, they may not have a lot more wallet-share to give you right now, and in such a volume business model scenario, cutting the cost of acquisition and the cost of servicing rapidly is key to attaining the exit of Stage 1 in Figure 61.

Many experienced professionals in your industry may not appreciate this. You may be told that all that matters is revenue, don't worry about profit initially. Revenue is a good measure in a mature business, but in a business that is starting up, breaking the revenue and profit measures into the three stages as depicted in this chapter

---

64. April 2021 update from UOB at a virtual Goldman Sachs conference. The chatbot FCR before passing to a human agent was >80% and the chatbot NPS had improved to +45 in January 2021.

is more appropriate and suited to the nature of a start-up. It is vital that you secure agreement from your key stakeholders early on these appropriate measures. There are many excellent and well-written articles that expand on the whole concept of marginal contribution that you can read (Gallo, 2017; Kwatinetz, 2018).

The most common rule of thumb on the topic of lifetime value (LTV) vs COA **pegs COA at no more than 1/3 of the LTV of the customer**, so bear this in mind when you are setting your COA. If you don't amortise your COA, you will make a bigger loss in the first year as your revenue is likely to be insufficient to cover your COA. If you do amortise it, **it's probably better to be conservative and use an LTV of 5–8 years**. This will make it a lot easier to be marginal contribution positive but will obviously delay Stage 2 recovery of annual fixed costs. **LTV and low attrition are key to the eventual profit equation, as there is little point onboarding customers with low active rates, as they are likely to become dormant and thus their LTV is zero**. This again reinforces the active customer mantra. For a digital bank, once you acquire a customer, a big enough percentage must like it enough to transfer some of their money and start using it as their secondary transactional account. Over time, some of these customers will migrate to using your digital bank as their main transactional bank if the experience continues to be brilliant. This applies equally to any retail business that needs to scale in volume.

The other component of marginal cost besides the COA is the annual cost to serve (COS) a customer, comprising all the servicing and operating costs a customer incurs in a year. **To lower your COS, your initiative must factor this in at the design phase**. This has already been discussed in previous chapters. The advantage of digitalising your business must be a large reduction in manual servicing, which then lowers the COS. Solving servicing issues at the point of occurrence with intelligent self-help, and not introducing the problems in the first place (e.g., having promotions that cause more servicing issues because the design does not adequately factor in customer comprehension of the programme mechanisms), will all work towards a lower annual COS per customer. You will recall that for the digital banks, their operating cost per customer was 8x less than a traditional bank. For a traditional bank, unless you set up a digital bank as a separate entity, it may be very difficult to achieve this level of operating leverage due to the inherent legacy costs.

The final factor is revenue per customer. This can be derived from the gross revenue that was assessed in the economic attractiveness consideration earlier. If your deposit and loan balances are already trending towards the portfolio average in a 24-to-36-month timeframe, then as a general rule, you are already capturing your fair share of the revenue pool. Rapidly accelerating your loan book is not advisable as it could lead to moral hazard issues where you attract customers with a higher likelihood of not repaying their loans, resulting in high bad debt later. What you should focus on from the beginning is how you are going to increase your credit underwriting pass-through rates by leveraging alternative data like Telco data, transaction data and other data sources not normally used today, to determine who you can lend to and get repaid. This should probably be done in parallel with building your digital bank, so that you can start lending small amounts to determine the efficacy of your new credit model as early as possible. Note that almost all the digital banks in Figure 15 that are profitable have a big lending business with low NPL rates.

One interesting aspect to note is that as you exit Stage 1, having achieved positive marginal contribution, you will also need to improve your NPS® further. My recommendation would be to improve it by 1.5x between the entry and exit of Stage 1. The rationale for this is that once you attain positive marginal contribution, you will need to scale customers further. This happens in Stage 2, but **as you scale customers further, you may have to increase the incentives for sign-up, and hence COA, if your NPS® doesn't go up further**. Obviously, there are situations where the additional uplift in NPS® required will be minimal, e.g., where you attain positive marginal contribution quickly, and the number of customers being acquired daily has not plateaued. This is likely only if your NPS® at launch is much higher than the industry, and thus will depend on the existing competitive level of the mobile banking experience (equally relevant in whichever industry you are in), which will likely vary between countries. As an example, in the case of TMRW, we found that when we assimilated the learnings in TMRW Thailand and applied them to the launch of TMRW Indonesia, the NPS® was much higher at launch, as we had designed TMRW to try to equal the experience of the top banks in Thailand, which had highly developed digital and mobile experiences.

Stage 2: Marginal contribution = Annual fixed cost per customer

In Stage 2, the marginal contribution becomes positive and thus, **every additional customer acquired, no matter how small the contribution, goes towards recovery of the annual fixed cost**. By this point, some of the portfolio should have reached your average portfolio revenue based on deposit and loan balance growth over time. One of the immediate issues is that if your contribution per customer is small and your annual fixed cost per customer is large, then you will have a problem fully recovering your annual fixed cost. This again emphasises the need to make good decisions about where to invest to keep up the NPS® growth and the investments into predictive analytics that can start to develop an engagement experience in addition to an effective and frictionless transactional experience.

It also means that for smaller countries with smaller demographics and potential customers, you have to cap the upfront outlay and the ongoing annual fixed costs so that they are not so bloated that you can't ever recoup those costs in later years. This will make for good discipline. A common observation in the digital banks that were profitable was that they didn't spend a lot on their initial technology expenditure. **A figure of around US$20M seems to be the optimal going-in number from my research**. If you are an incumbent bank, you are likely to exceed this number as legacy infrastructure is likely to cost much more and hence again **the operating leverage against a properly designed challenger or neo-bank is likely to be much lower**.

In Stage 2, an interesting trade-off presents itself, in that you can invest more heavily in annual fixed costs to bump up the NPS® differential through even better frictionless transactional experience and accelerate your ability to engage customers using predictive analytics. This is what TMRW started to do by leveraging the predictive capabilities of Personetics and the categorisation capabilities of Meniga. Doing so may lengthen the payback period needed to recoup total annual fixed costs, but it **potentially allows you to grow the customer base more aggressively, resulting in more customers to defray the annual fixed cost**. The other alternative is to start recouping fixed costs sooner with a smaller base. **This trade-off decision is directly linked to the investment appetite of your company and its shareholders.** Doing so in Stage 1 will result in more and more losses to the company but doing so in Stage 2 is a calculated risk and trade-off between higher differentiation (and thus more rapid customer capture should the differentiation be successfully executed) and profitability.

Thus, there is a range of exit criteria in stage 2. At the less risky end of the range, a digital start-up with high NPS® gap versus its competition could exit within 48 months having achieved full annual fixed and variable cost recovery, but with potentially a smaller base of customers. Those with higher risk appetites can scale up the annual fixed cost outlay to accelerate the upward trajectory of the NPS® between the start of Stage 1 and the end of Stage 2. In this option, the exit condition may not be a positive profit after accounting for all annual fixed and variable costs, but a target annual fixed cost per customer that is shrinking dramatically, so that at some point in Stage 3, every customer acquired is bringing significant profit contribution to the bottom line.

Stage 3: Efficiency (Revenue growth >> Cost growth)

Finally, in Stage 3, your annual fixed costs would be fairly steady, but stacked against a large number of customers in your base, you would see a declining annual fixed cost per customer curve. This will allow you to increase revenues disproportionately to costs, bringing down the cost-to-income ratio (C/I ratio). For a digital bank, my recommendation is to target a C/I ratio of 30%. It is only at this stage that you focus on generating sufficient profit to pay back the initial capital costs of setting up the new digital bank. For low-ticket but high-volume businesses like a consumer digital bank, you can clearly see that it's a long-term play, and that building a bank with lower variable costs and an annual fixed cost that can be spread over many, many customers is paramount to a business model that can scale well.

The operating efficiency offered by Stage 3 may not materialise if constant additional annual fixed cost increases are required due to poorly directed fixed cost investments, rapidly advancing technology capabilities that necessitate rapid upgrades or competitors catching up quickly, requiring additional investments to differentiate. The interactive loops depicted in Figure 54 attempt to reduce this but may not be able to entirely prevent it.

5.2.3

Scaling

At this stage, you are ready to delve deeper into the approach you should take to scale your customers and volume of business. Scaling looks at the ability of your innovation to have **global reach**, examines your industry configuration to reveal any opportunities for scaling, and then looks at your distribution approach and customer capture ability. Finally, it looks at the role your brand will play in customer capture.

The first consideration is whether your innovation has the ability to reach customers globally with **little customisation** (e.g., support for local language, voltage, local preferences, etc.) and whether there are significant regulatory variations across countries. This gives you an idea of the adaptations needed. For example, can you run a global instance of your software or app, or will you need an instance per country? In banking, you usually need a different instance per country, as every country has its unique payment system, and a local entity is usually required due to local capital requirements. And of course, you need a licence to operate per country or per bloc of countries (as in the European Union). In contrast, a company offering software-as-a-service – for example, a service to apply for domain names, company email and build your company website like GoDaddy[65] – can provide a standard product to a global audience with mostly just language customisations.

The second consideration is whether the target country has a **large enough market** to support your product and your sales or revenue ambition. This is known as the local market and product fit. If you have the luxury of starting in a large market like the United States, China, India, Russia or Indonesia, then a more focused local approach would make more sense initially to build scale. If you are starting in a small market (like Singapore), your next few target markets should be immediately identified and catered to so that you have enough room for growth. Whichever the case, you will need to consider carefully the adaptations needed for your offering so that you are ready when the time comes to expand to another country (Moed, 2019).

An analysis of the industry you are entering or already participating in would also help you to understand the industry configuration and to craft your scaling approach. I recommend **mapping the ecosystem** of your industry, and then looking at the interactions between the various players and the customers you are targeting. Refer to Figure 80 for more information on how to perform the mapping exercise.

---

65. GoDaddy Inc. is an American publicly traded Internet domain registrar and web hosting company headquartered in Scottsdale, Arizona and incorporated in Delaware.

The ecosystem map highlights the participants and intermediaries that you will need to propel your scaling. This should inform you as to what your best distribution approach would be. Is it through direct sales, partnerships and/or marketing? And to what extent is brand building directly to your target audience effective in achieving more sign-ups? Would your channels of sales require both physical and digital, and what kind of co-ordination is required for customers who utilise both modes – or would you just restrict it to a purely digital channel?

Next, we examine the **distribution approach and customer capture**. This has implications on acquisition, which is a big cost for any new start-up business. TMRW was no different. We set out to achieve a high advocacy score, so that we could lower the cost to acquire by having advocates do it for us. Cost of acquisition was high when we started, as we leveraged search engine optimisation[66] (SEO) marketing to start the acquisition. As previously mentioned, we moved rapidly on two fronts. One was to pay for sign-ups instead of pay-per-click, moving much lower in the sales funnel. This resulted in better-quality acquisitions. The other was to use more viral methods like member-get-member and to average down high SEO costs by going direct to e-commerce sites with a large number of online customers.

Having spoken to digital banks like Nubank and Kakao Bank, and indeed from my experience building TMRW, the cost of acquisition needs to fall rapidly – by a factor of more than 10x from the initial COA – to reach a stage where it becomes efficient enough to create a positive marginal contribution. For more information about scaling TMRW through partnerships, please refer to Chapter 4.9.

---

66. Search engine optimisation (SEO) is the process of improving the quality and quantity of website traffic to a website or a web page from search engines.

Core competence

You are now in a position to detail the gap between your current core competence and the competence you need to bring your innovation to life. Using a **gap analysis method**, you can compare your current state and future state, define what the gap is, when you need to fix it, how to fix it, and who will do the fixing. With that as a starting point, you can then detail the competences you will need to build in the capabilities, people and leadership dimensions. A sample output of your core competence gap is depicted in Figure 62.

	Current state	Future state	Gap	Actions to close gap
Gap #1 Design Ability	Design Ability at present is medium at best. Human-centered design ability is missing. Lack ability to do the strategic navigation design to make the complex simple.	Leaders in human-centered design, which is basic entry-point training. Skilled in business innovation design. Establishment of design center of excellence.	1. Training in design thinking 2. Hire staff with prior experience 3. Upgrade the entire organisation 4. Create UX and UI team that can do both tactical and strategic design	To be completed in Capabilities, People and Leadership Dimension
#2 Business Process	Some business process ability is present but the needs to be upgraded. Degree of attention to detail and process efficiency and effectiveness needs to be improved.	Adept in ability to translate experience into required business processes. Strong ability to map business processes to create superior customer experiences.	1. Acquire internal talent familiar with key processes 2. Training in journey and data mapping 3. Recruit experienced outside talent	
#3 Data-based Engagement	Lack the competence to leverage data as a tool for engagement, data lifecycle management, solutions to turn data into insights, etc.	Strong collaboration with internal data office to map the requirements. Expertise across data use case, database design, operational data delivery, etc.	1. Scout for and acquire key data engagement solution providers 2. Beef up internal data design skills 3. Workshop best use cases 4. Create an engagement lab staffed with multifunctional talent	
#4 Digital Service	No one with deep service design and contact center experience.	Create a digital service team with the necessary digital servicing expertise across processes, customer service, service solutions, chatbots, chat agent management.	1. Design upfront a higher agent to customer ratio and reduce as chatbot ability increases. 2. Hire new team with necessary skills and expertise. 3. Scout for required solutions	
#5 Agile Software Development	No one with strong background in building development teams with ability	CTO skilled in digital initiatives within banking, with deep experience in Agile software delivery. External help to put in place required scrum processes.	1. Hire CTO with required ability 2. Hire internal management staff to manage the initiative and contractors 3. Put required scrum process in place	

Figure 62 – Core competence gap

At this stage, you would have considered all the elements in the customer (desirable) and business (viable) dimensions and have a clear articulation of the customer proposition and business model that you want to create. You would also have made the necessary trade-offs between the two to achieve the right balance that you feel has the best probability of success. It is critical that you do not start to decide on the specific capabilities needed till you have achieved this balance between desirability and viability. Figure 63 shows desirable, viable and feasible as three interlocking circles, and pins the biggest innovation failures listed in Figure 52

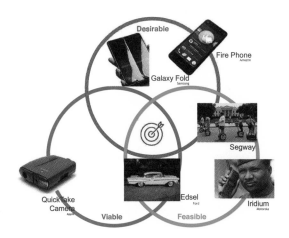

Figure 63 – Desirable, viable and feasible

onto these three circles. Some like Iridium[67] failed after spending US$5B without ensuring that there was sufficient desirability, viability and feasibility. It was eventually feasible, but it took 11 years from the time the concept was mooted, way too long, as by then cellular mobile services had improved significantly. This is the danger of a solution-led approach.

Some like Edsel[68] were both viable and feasible but in the case of Edsel its launch coincided with an economic recession, and buyers wanted a less expensive car that was cheaper to maintain. Others like Post-it notes actually failed on feasibility – Post-it notes don't stick well, but the innovation eventually found its way to the sweet spot by changing the use case to one where the ability to stick, move and re-stick was more important than staying stuck. Apple's QuickTake camera is an example of an innovation that would have been viable if it could be sold at the price of US$750 in 1994 but there was no way to view the image you took until you connected it to a Mac or Windows computer, making it not desirable, mostly because it wasn't feasible to add a viewing capability in a small enough form factor affordably back in 1994. Besides, the resolution was only 640x480 pixels, which was far inferior to 35mm film. In QuickTake's case, feasibility affected desirability and thus made it not viable.

Here we reach the end of the business dimension, and the next stage of the TaP methodology goes into feasibility, i.e., can you actually build, launch and maintain

---

67. Iridium operates the Iridium satellite constellation, a system of 66 active satellites (and 9 spares in space) used for worldwide voice and data communication from handheld satellite phones and other transceiver units.

68. Edsel was a brand of automobile that was marketed by the Ford Motor Company from 1958 to 1960. It was marketed in an effort to give Ford a fourth brand to gain additional market share from Chrysler and General Motors.

the innovation with a high probability of success? In this phase, you identify the enablers you need. These enablers, if they prove to be too rare or difficult to obtain or execute, could imperil the launch, and thus you may have to iterate and go back to the drawing board, to examine the customer–business dimensions for possible optimisation to resolve the trade-off. Figure 64 illustrates this. If you are not iterating enough when using TaP, it is one indicator that your approach may not be sufficiently robust. I have split the feasibility considerations into business enablers (capabilities) and people enablers (people & leadership) to underscore the importance of people talent and leadership in any transformation.

A printed A1-size copy of Figure 64 or Figure 45 can be plastered in the key meeting and discussion rooms as a reminder of the interactions and trade-offs to look out for. This will encourage your staff to account for their interactive impact as standard approach rather than an exception.

Let's now dig into the details of how to secure the capabilities you need to ensure that your transformation or innovation is feasible.

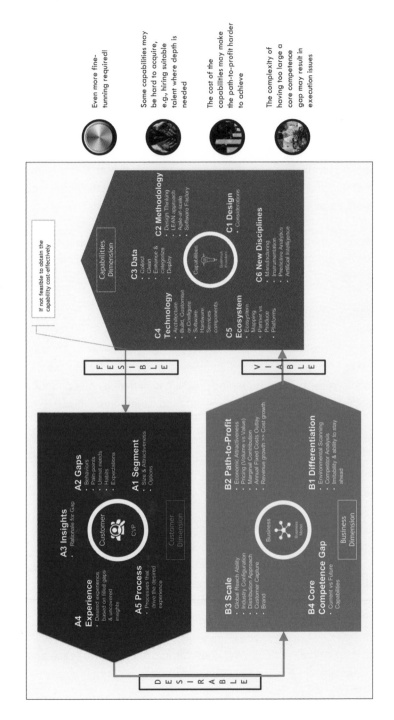

Even more fine-tunning required!

Some capabilities may be hard to acquire, e.g., hiring suitable talent where depth is needed

The cost of the capabilities may make the path-to-profit harder to achieve

The complexity of having too large a core competence gap may result in execution issues

If not feasible to obtain the capability cost-effectively

Capabilities Dimension

C3 Data
· Collect
· Clean
· Enhance & categorize
· Deploy

C2 Methodology
· Design Thinking
· LEAN approach
· Agile-at-scale
· Software Factory

C1 Design
· Considerations

Capabilities
Business Enablers

C4 Technology
· Architecture
· Build, Customise or Configure
· Software
· Hardware
· Services components

C5 Ecosystem
· Ecosystem Mapping
· Partner vs Produce
· Platforms

C6 New Disciplines
· Manufacturing
· Instrumentation
· Predictive Analytics
· Artificial Intelligence

F E S I B L E

V I A B L E

A3 Insights
· Rationale for Gap

A2 Gaps
· Behaviors
· Pain-points
· Unmet needs
· Habits
· Expectations

A1 Segment
· Size & Attractiveness
· Options

Customer
CVP

A4 Experience
· Desired experience based on filled gaps & uncovered insights

A5 Process
· Processes that drive the desired experience

Customer Dimension

B2 Path-to-Profit
· Economic Attractiveness
· Pricing (Volume vs Value)
· Marginal Contribution
· Annual Fixed Costs Outlay
· Revenue growth >> Cost growth

B1 Differentiation
· Environmental Scanning
· Competitor Analysis
· Imitability & ability to stay ahead

Business
Business Model

B3 Scale
· Global Reach Ability
· Industry Configuration
· Distribution Approach
· Customer Capture
· Brand

B4 Core Competence Gap
· Current vs Future Capabilities

Business Dimension

D E S I R A B L E

Figure 64 – Customer, business and capability dimension interaction

Key takeaways

- In optimising between the CVP (output of the customer dimension) and the business model (output of the business dimension), you are likely to go back and forth fine-tuning the interactions between these dimensions to achieve both the desirability and viability criteria.

- This process will be frustrating to you and your team. There will be others pushing to start testing something, and start prototyping, and to gamify. This is something you should avoid. Many organisations feel the same tensions and conflicts at this stage of their transformation.

- My advice to the leader is to hold firm and continue to fine-tune until you achieve the right balance that can check both the desirability and viability boxes.

- A good way to categorise your innovation themes is the Ten Types of Innovation, a methodology by Doblin.

- Most people focus only on product innovation, or the "offering", as the Doblin methodology puts it. By combining product, experience and configuration types of innovations, you can make your innovation more difficult to copy.

- Globalisation and the internet have narrowed the time taken to manufacture, copy and learn, and thus the ability to imitate has improved significantly. Consequently, it has never been more important to expand your offering's innovation to include experience or configuration innovations.

- Scanning the environment is important, as this can help to mitigate investments in technologies or trends that don't have longevity.

- The attractiveness of the segment is re-evaluated in the business dimension to provide another opportunity to ensure that the segment selected in the first step of the customer dimension is sound.

- Having a big addressable market doesn't mean the effort to reach and acquire them is feasible.

- Effort is a function of multiple factors, e.g., is the need obvious and thus the customer generates demand organically or is the need subtle or hidden, and thus convincing the customer to take up the solution is needed. The latter can consume substantial time and effort and thus slow down the process of scaling significantly.

- In the first phase of the path-to-profit, the aim should be to get the cost of acquisition (COA) down to a level where the revenue could negate COA and service or operating cost per customer, within a period commensurate with your loss appetite.

- A start-up will keep losing money if the acquisition cost and servicing cost at a per customer level is higher than the revenue.

- In a volume business model scenario, cutting the cost of acquisition and the cost of servicing rapidly is the key to attaining the exit of Stage 1.

- The most common rule of thumb on the topic of lifetime value (LTV) vs COA pegs COA at no more than 1/3 of the LTV of the customer.

- LTV and low attrition are key to the eventual profit equation, as there is little point onboarding customers with low active rates, as they are likely to become dormant and thus their LTV is zero.

- The other component of marginal cost besides the cost of acquisition (COA) is the annual cost to serve (COS) a customer, comprising all the servicing and operating costs a customer incurs in a year. To lower your COS, your initiative must factor this in at the design phase.

- As you exit Stage 1, you will also need to improve your NPS® further. My recommendation would be to improve it by 1.5x between the entry and exit of Stage 1. The rationale is that once you attain positive marginal contribution, you will want to scale customers further. This happens in Stage 2, but as you scale customers further, you may have to increase the incentives for sign-up, and hence COA, if your NPS® doesn't go up further.

- In Stage 2, the marginal contribution becomes positive and thus, every additional customer acquired, no matter how small the contribution, goes towards recovery of the annual fixed cost.

- In Stage 2, an interesting trade-off presents itself, in that you can invest more heavily in annual fixed costs to bump up the NPS® differential through even better frictionless transactional experience and accelerate your ability to engage customers.

- This means lengthening the payback period needed to recoup total annual fixed costs, but it potentially allows you to grow the customer base more aggressively, resulting in more customers to defray the annual fixed cost.

- In Stage 3, your annual fixed costs would be fairly steady, but stacked against a large number of customers in your base, you would see a declining annual fixed cost per customer curve. This will allow you to increase revenues disproportionately to costs.

- For digital banks like Nubank and Kakao Bank, and indeed from my experience building TMRW, the cost of acquisition needs to fall rapidly – by a factor of more than 10x from the initial COA – to reach a stage where it becomes efficient enough to create a positive marginal contribution.

Capabilities

Without developing new capabilities, your digital innovation or transformation can't be executed. In all likelihood, there will be **a significant gap between your current capabilities and what you need to successfully bring your initiative to life**. So, whilst it is most ill-advised to start with capabilities without fully understating the customer and business dimensions (so that you have on paper something that is desirable and viable before looking at its feasibility), it is just as important to ensure that once you have your first iteration of an innovation that is desirable and viable, to thoroughly evaluate the capabilities needed, and assess whether the risks of bringing it to life are sufficiently mitigated. This provides an opportunity to fine-tune all three criteria so that you pass the hurdle for all three, and thus significantly enhance your probability of success.

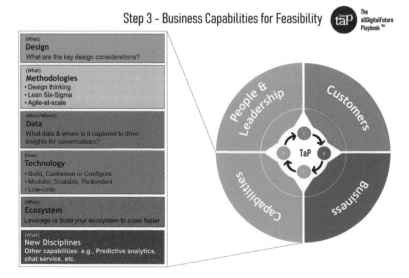

Figure 65 – New capabilities needed

This dimension explores the capabilities needed to make your innovation feasible. At first glance, it would seem that a universal set of capabilities that can apply to a wide variety of industries and accommodate different sizes of company would be quite difficult to achieve. After many revisions and fine-tuning, I arrived at the version you see in Figure 65, which is fairly universal. Of the 6 elements, ecosystems and new disciplines can be tailored to specific industries. Ecosystems will vary based on the industry or sub-industry you are in. New disciplines is the element most custom-ised to the different situations your company faces depending on the market and industry, e.g., new manufacturing facilities or partners may be required, or additional instrumentation, etc.

The rest of the elements – design, methodology, data and technology (infor-mation technology) – are all standard elements of any capability build in a digital transformation. In fact, it is possible that you might want to start the methodology element much earlier, after you have recruited your pioneer team. The first thing I did after TMRW's pioneer team was in place was to conduct a design thinking workshop so that everyone would have the same language and understand the importance of being very customer-centric.

Design was the first element selected for the capabilities dimension, and to me it may be the most important one. We used to think of design as something consumer product companies leverage to differentiate their offerings, and rarely used outside of that realm. But a revolution in the use of design approaches and techniques[69] to create customer-centric experiences for customers everywhere is gaining strong momentum. Design, or business design, "applies design and design thinking to business problems with the objective of bringing innovation to life" (Tanimoto, 2018). Tanimoto explains that business designers have to frame the design process through the lens of the business, so as to solve business problems in a human-centric way that meets both desirability and viability considerations. The Rotman School of Management at the University of Toronto illustrates business design through 3 "gears": empathy and need-finding; prototyping and experimenta-tion; and business strategy.

The confluence of design and business will accelerate. This change is driven by hyper-competition, which is making it harder and harder to differentiate your products from your competition. The traditional sources of differentiation – unique products, unique manufacturing capabilities, distinct and difficult-to-obtain knowl-edge and information, etc. – are no longer sustained sources of competitive advantage. In her 2013 book, *The End of Competitive Advantage: How to Keep Your Strategy Moving as Fast as Your Business*, Rita Gunther McGrath attributes this to the rise of globalisation, the instantaneous flow of information round the clock and round the globe, and the rise of the internet and its ability to reach, tailor and lever-age massive amounts of data that can be used to disrupt all manner of traditional businesses in retail, travel, banking, media, etc. (McGrath, 2013).

This is now driving a change from product competition to competing on total customer experience. In turn, this is requiring a shift towards a deep understanding

---

69. This reference is not to design thinking but more the holistic approach of business design.

of how customers experience the product, how to collect and utilise data to continuously improve that experience, a renewed emphasis on the customer journey and process mapping, and collaboration across departmental units to orchestrate and deliver that total experience. And this data-driven, continuous improvement, deep understanding of how customers experience your product and service end-to-end, which requires cross-functional teams to work together in more Agile structures than ever before is embodied in one word: design. A great piece of work that elaborates on this is *The Business Value of Design*, an 18-page report by McKinsey published in 2018 (Sheppard et al., 2018).

Design

The Cambridge Dictionary defines design as a noun that means "a drawing or set of drawings showing how a building or product is to be made and how it will work and look"; and as a verb to mean "to make or draw plans for something, for example clothes or buildings". This has been the traditional definition of design. The new definition of design in the context of business is an evolving one.

One of the best definitions I have come across is from McKinsey: "Design is not just about making objects pretty. Design is the process of deeply understanding customer/user needs and then creating a product or service – physical, digital, or both – that addresses their unmet needs" (Sheppard et al., 2018). In fact, it's so new, a Google search of "business design" yields mostly literature from around 2018. Sheppard homes in on four capabilities in design; **analytical leadership** ("measure and drive design performance with the same rigour as revenues and costs"), **cross-functional talent** ("make user-centric design everyone's responsibility and not a siloed function"), **user experience** ("break down internal walls between physical,

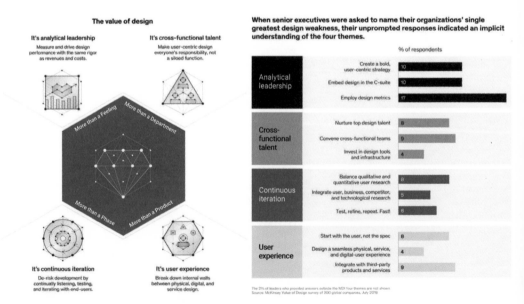

Figure 66 – The Business Value of Design
(Source: McKinsey Quarterly)

digital and service design"), and finally, **continuous iteration** ("de-risk development by continually listening, testing and iterating with end-users"). Figure 66 illustrates this. In designing TMRW, we constantly developed and leveraged these four design capabilities.

An interesting write-up by Tsukasa Tanimoto yields a comparison between business designers and management consultants, as shown in Figure 67 (Tanimoto, 2018).

Figure 67 – Business designer vs management consultant
(Source: medium.com)

I differ from his view that business designers are human-centred while management consultants are profitability-driven. If this were so, the business designer wouldn't be the person driving innovation as innovation requires desirability, viability and feasibility. So, I would create a new term, **business innovation designer**, to be both human-centred and profit-centred, with a bias towards execution and action, embracing ambiguity, and practising continuous refinement to achieve excellence, as depicted in Figure 68.

Business Innovation Designer

- Human & profit-centered
- Innovation as process
- Bias towards executability & action
- Embraces ambiguity
- Strong stakeholder management
- Practices continuous learning & refinement

Figure 68 – Business innovation designer

Another excellent article is the "Ultimate Business Design Guide" by Alen Faljic, founder of d.MBA. There is a natural evolution from the design thinking path or a design background – whether industrial or visual or user experience-oriented in origin – to use design principles in business, as they would be more in touch with the human-centred origins of business design. Many, however, don't have sufficient financial and business experience, whereas the typical modern business leader armed with an MBA doesn't have the human-centred design touch.

This confluence of the design discipline and business discipline has led early adopters like Imperial College Business School in London and Aalto University in Finland to create a Design MBA. The Rotman School of Management was the first to integrate Design Thinking into its MBA programme in 2006 (Which MBA?, 2018). **I foresee a future where such business innovation designers will be in extremely high demand, to lead digital transformation initiatives in companies of all sizes.**

One area that needs more explanation is the output of the design element or the most critical design considerations of your initiative. These design considerations include the business model, not just the product, service or user interface or the overall customer experience. They form a series of **cascading design considerations**, from the top of the organisation to the most junior staff. Figure 69 shows the 6 design considerations that drove the development of TMRW.[70] These are the most important guiding principles and considerations that will guide your innovation to become the breakthrough you want.

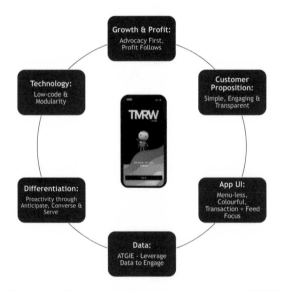

Figure 69 – The top 6 key design considerations in TMRW

---

70. Six isn't a fixed number. It could be anywhere from 5 to 10. If there are too many, then it's not top of mind anymore, and if it's too few, it's likely to be too generic.

The reason why these considerations are found in the capabilities dimension is because they are the key input to the enablers that must be built to support these design considerations, and thus they are a summary of the work done in the customer and business dimensions to date. This will also serve as **a guiding principle to prevent scope creep** that is not required to support the top 6 considerations.

When I created TaP, I refined the design considerations to work as a cascade. Take the TMRW customer proposition, which is to be Simple, Engaging and Transparent. The refinement meant that members of your immediate team will be delegated specific responsibilities and KPIs, for example, to ensure Simple, Engaging and Transparent are robustly implemented. This cascades further down the organisation to ensure that the 6 top design considerations have clear owners and laser-sharp focus. This is an area of improvement I learnt through my TMRW experience. Although we used the concept of design considerations, and prior to any design discussion I would ask the team to summarise their design considerations for the discussion, we did not cascade and name owners to the top 6 in a holistic and rigorous way. If we did, it would have resulted in greater clarity and execution prowess for TMRW. Did TMRW have everything defined as you see in Figure 69 before the build began? No, and you probably won't achieve this in your transformation initiative either. Just make sure that the design considerations get sharper and sharper over time.

These key design considerations become your blueprint for the digital innovation you are driving and form the guiding principles that you must not sacrifice to achieve your innovation breakthrough. Whilst they will morph and change, they provide the compass to guide you through the next stage of TaP, where you bring your transformation to life (i.e., feasibility) by acquiring the capabilities, people and leadership required to execute your design. By cascading these design considerations to your one-downs, you ensure there is alignment and prioritisation around these 6 key considerations. It doesn't have to be 6, but more than 10 is too many and 3 is probably too few. This is a significant new way of working that I highly recommend you incorporate into your initiative, as illustrated in Figure 70. Changes to any of the top design considerations should be made at the highest level in the organisation charged with the initiative or transformation.

A comparison of this and an MVP-approach is important. We found that it was difficult to have an MVP as there was no significant breakthrough we could find that, once achieved, would have convinced users to switch. The business model centred around advocacy first and profit would follow thereafter, and thus requires a transactional experience that is so **simple** (frictionless and intuitive to use), so **engaging** (due to TMRW being proactive in their customer experience) and so **transparent** (no hidden terms and fees that you don't understand).

	Design Consideration #1	Design Consideration #2	Design Consideration #3	Design Consideration #4	Design Consideration #5	Design Consideration #6
CEO or Top Executive	Growth & Profit: Advocacy First, Profit Follows	Customer Proposition: Simple, Transparent, Engaging	App UI: Menu-less, Colourful, Transaction + Feed Focus	Data: ATGIE - Leverage Data to Engage	Differentiation: Proactivity through Anticipate, Converse & Serve	Technology: Low-code & Modularity
Head of Partnerships	Sign up online partners like e-commerce with big online ecosystems	Support	Support	User	Support	Support
Head of Banking Products	Bundle transaction account with unsecured credit	Support	Support	User	Support	Support
Head of Onboarding	Ensure high NPS score for onboarding	Make onboarding simple and transparent to support the proposition	Support	User	Support	Support
Head of Marketing	Design of branding campaign that resonates with target segment		Support	User	Support	Support
Head of Design	Support	Jointly own the creation of the proof points to support the proposition	Creation of strategic navigation & Design system for App UI	User	Support	Devise the approach and solution to achieve Low-code and Modularity
Head of Technology	Support		Support	Support	Jointly own the design and build of infrastructure, processes and service culture to achieve high service NPS	
Head of Service & Operations	Jointly own high NPS score at launch, and continued improvement thereafter		Support	User		Support
Head of Customer Experience			Support	User		Support
Head of Engagement			Support	Jointly own the use of data to drive conversations that showcase anticipatory nature of CVP and towards better and smarter spending and saving habits		Support
Head of Data and Analytics	Support	Support	Support			Support

Figure 70 – Sample design consideration cascade

"Simple" required a transactional banking app that was very different, that was colourful, so easy to use that it had very few first-level menus or "menu-less", and a construct that included a horizontal scroll to get access to more banking products and a vertical scroll to get access to more insights (refer to Figure 6). A new flywheel model was created, "ATGIE" (refer to Chapter 3.5 for more info), that leveraged data to engage customers. Engaged customers buy more products and become advocates; more customers would be acquired, which would in turn generate more data, allowing TMRW to engage even more customers. This would create a differentiation around being proactive through TMRW's ability to anticipate customers' needs, converse with them through insights and Tia, the TMRW chatbot, and serve them very well. Coupled with a focus on low-code and modularity in the technology build, this allowed for a lower annual fixed cost footprint.

Methodology

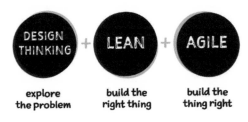

Figure 71 – Design Thinking, Lean and Agile

If you agree that innovation is as much about process as it is about ideas, then methodology must be an essential capability needed to address the new approach to collaboration and processes required to bring the transformation to life. As a basic requirement, the three key methods that must be implemented are **Design Thinking**, **Lean Six Sigma**, and **Agile development**. There may be others that should be added on as appropriate to the situation at hand, e.g., change management, project management, etc. These three methodologies are well covered in Chapter 4.1, but I reproduce the important points here for completeness. If you are a digital leader of a company or initiative, it is critical that you understand these three methods.

A great resource to help you to do this is *Understanding Design Thinking, Lean, and Agile* by Jonny Schneider (Schneider, 2017). Figure 71 is found in chapter 1 of Jonny's book and is the best articulation of the differences between the three approaches or disciplines I have come across.

Jonny provides a definition of **Design Thinking** as follows: "At a distance, Design Thinking is a mindset for exploring complex problems or finding opportunities in a world full of uncertainty. It's a search for meaning, usually focusing on human needs and experience. Using intuitive and abductive[71] reasoning, Design Thinking explores and questions what is, and then imagines what could be with innovative and inventive future solutions."

For me, the power of design thinking comes from its foundations in human-centric design, and understanding what customers need to do their jobs well. This is especially important in industries and organisations that are product-centric because they can't help themselves but start with the product and their business

---

71. Abductive reasoning starts with an observation or set of observations and then seeks to find the simplest and most likely conclusion from the observations.

objective first. The concept of design thinking is an intrinsically human process but is often overlooked because of a preoccupation with profit and gains. We have learned that it is critical in consumer banking because it enables us to reimagine and reinvent the customer journey and improve it in a way that no one else has thought to do before. For example, before the launch in Thailand, we were faced with the issue of authentication. TMRW has no physical branches where face-to-face onboarding would be available, and, at the time, there were no fully digital authentication methods in Thailand. We needed to come up with a way to ensure a frictionless experience while complying with security and CDD regulations.

One idea that came up was to use the post office as a trusted agent to perform authentication as they were already doing activities of this nature. But that would mean customers would have to queue up, and there was the risk that post office staff might be unfamiliar with the authentication process when it was required of them. After much deliberation and design thinking, we came up with the idea of putting up biometric kiosks at strategic locations across Bangkok. Each kiosk would have an identity card reader that would read the customer's fingerprint off the chip on the identity card and compare it with fingerprints taken at the kiosk using a fingerprint reader. The design considerations focused on making the kiosk experience friction-free so a customer could simply approach a kiosk, insert a valid Thai ID, and walk away.

This was just one of the many applications of design thinking in TMRW. Almost every aspect of the digital bank was created through it. To implement the tenets of design thinking across the entire operation, we made new processes and customer-centric KPIs, conducted regular training sessions, and even made changes in terminology like inventing the term "engagement lab" (Gagua, 2020). TMRW was also one of the first banks to implement a design system and design operations, even though this is common practice in other digital organisations (Kaelig, 2016).

The **Lean mindset** is defined by Jonny on page 2 of his book: "The Lean mindset is a management philosophy that embraces scientific thinking to explore how right our beliefs and assumptions are while improving a system. Lean practitioners use the deliberate practice of testing their hypotheses through action, observing what actually happens, and making adjustments based on the differences observed. It's how organisations set their course, learn by doing, and decide what to do next on their journey to achieve outcomes."

Lean has manufacturing origins, and to me the power is the focus on less waste, for example handing off work to another team when it could be done by the same team, with only unit responsibilities preventing the elimination of the hand-off. Lean is about finding the most efficient way to do something, eliminating waste in the process. Lean is about continuous improvement – something important when all your competitors are also improving as you do so. Hence it is a good method for constantly getting rid of inefficiency in your processes, whether internal-facing or external-facing. When you combine this with design thinking, you not only get a faster and cheaper process, but also one that the customer can easily appreciate and understand.

Lean has also been integrated with **Six Sigma**, a data-driven methodology to ensure consistently good output that is 99.99966% defect-free. In summary, Lean Six Sigma combines the best of waste and inefficiency removal in your process with a data-driven approach to reduce variation, ensuring a consistently superior experience by continuously optimising your process for efficiency and ensuring consistently high-quality outcomes. So much time was spent perfecting the process in TMRW. This was probably one of the highest-stress areas, as we sought to review and improve key processes before and after launch, aided by details about the sales funnel and where customers were dropping off or experiencing service issues.

As for **Agile development**, here's Jonny again: "The heart of Agile is building great software solutions that adapt gracefully to changing needs. Agile begins with a problem – not a requirement – and delivers an elegant solution. The Agile mindset acknowledges that the right solution today might not be the right solution tomorrow. It's rapid, iterative, easily adapted, and focused on quality through continuous improvement."

With Agile, you break the development into modules instead of developing the entire monolithic code at one go, which was how software was traditionally developed. The Agile method's power lies in its ability to make adjustments along the way, something very useful in contexts that are uncertain and where you are continuously refining and adjusting to customer feedback, competitor reactions and industry changes.

This fits today's hyper-competitive business environment much better than monolithic development and has the additional advantage of being able to support many frequent smaller releases in a year, reducing risks and achieving better time to market. Agile is also about the way teams work, breaking down the silos and barriers between teams, so that a cross-functional group of business product owners, IT analysts, software developers, customer experience designers, interface designers, etc., work as one team to ensure the right requirements, leading to the right software being developed, tested and released into production.

Scrum is one method of Agile software development, and a great infographic from www.scruminc.com is shown in Figure 72. This incorporates the latest updates made to the Scrum Guide in 2020 (Sutherland and Schneider, 2020).

Putting all three methodologies together yields a powerful production-line concept-to-code software factory, as shown in Figure 73. This is the essence of what you need to build to ensure that you have a world-class facility that is generating the high-quality experience you have promised your customers. For more details on how the software factory works, refer to Chapter 4.1.

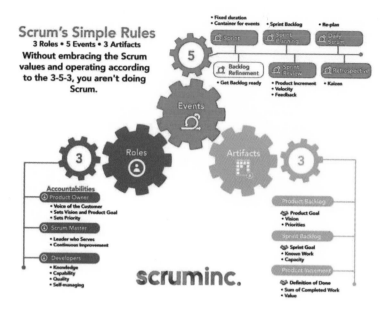

Figure 72 – A pictorial checklist for Scrum
(Source: Scruminc)

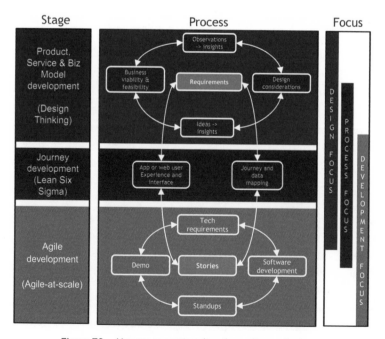

Figure 73 – How to operationalise the software factory

Data

Why is data one of the 6 elements in the capabilities dimension? Hyper-competition enabled by globalisation and the narrowing of the information gap by the internet is pushing companies to differentiate by responding faster to customer needs. This usually entails the use of data to tailor the offering to the customer, e.g., suggesting items the customer may like, filtering out information the customer is not interested in, suggesting new songs the customer would enjoy, using data to make better business decisions about customers, e.g., whether to extend credit, or using data to serve the customer better, e.g., understanding what they are requesting and performing the task without human intervention. **Competitive differentiation is shifting to mass customisation and rapid learning. Both require data.** And because data takes time to collect, only businesses that have been operating for some time have the depth and breadth of data, so it's not something easy to replicate.

In many organisations, data has been used to make decisions about improving the business but rarely about improving the lives of customers. **Data is also usually dispersed throughout an organisation.** Here's a quote that illustrates the

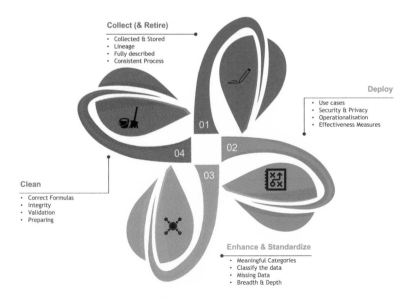

Figure 74 – Four key considerations for leveraging data

complexity from Jamorn, a pioneer member of the TMRW team: "The most challenging task was making use of the massive amount of data we had internally as a bank to create insights for the customer. I thought, how hard can it be? It's transaction data, and we have it. We should be able to just mix it together and create some insights for the customer. But after trying to get that done and finding out how complex, disparate and varied the data was, we realised that it was going to be a much more difficult task."

Almost every company faces this issue, and so the key considerations in the data element are concentrated around how data is collected, how it is cleaned, how it is enhanced and standardised, and finally how it is deployed, as depicted in Figure 74.

Figure 75 explores each of the data considerations in greater detail, providing you a set of questions that your data team should be able to answer satisfactorily to design and build the right data solution and infrastructure to support your data engagement requirements.

Collect (& Retire)		Clean		Enhance & Standardise		Deploy	
Collected & Stored	1. Are current methods of data collection & storage adequate in terms of timeliness, range and depth to serve the business requirement for engagement? 2. How clean is the data source definition & Integrity?	Correct Formulas	1. For data that is derived and calculated from source systems, how do you ensure that the formulas are correct?	Meaningful Categories	1. What are the meaningful categories to group your data (e.g. by merchant classification codes, types of expenditure)? 2. How do you decide amongst these options which categories are most appropriate?	Use cases	1. What data use cases can dramticaly improve your ability to serve customers better and offer them a better experience? 2. How can you validate that it will have a dramatic impact on customers? 3. Do any of the use cases need real-time information? If the data is delayed by 15 mins is there any impact to the use case?
Lineage	1. Can all data be traced back to a common key, company, group of companies, clients, group of clients? 2. How is this implemened so it is consistent?	Integrity	1. What are the Data Quality processes you need in place to ensure integrity of the data? 2. How do you detect and remove any incorrect duplicate data in your company?	Classify the data	1. Is there a consistent process to classify data, e.g. by sensitivity and consumption (public, internal only, confidential, restricted)? 2. What other classifications, e.g. structured vs unstructured data, are relevant?	Security & Privacy	1. How do you ensure that "privacy by design" considerations and applicable privacy laws are strictly adhered to? 2. Review the data security risk management material in the playbook, and ensure you can comply. 3. How is access and usage of sensitive data administered and automated?
Fully described	1. Does the process to define and create the data also fully describe any data field being created? 2. How does this process ensure that this is being carried out consistently and without fail?	Validation	1. Do you have a process that validates the integrity of the data? 2. How does this process ensure the integrity across the organisation?	Missing Data	1. Is there a process to detect missing data? 2. What is the process to obtain such missing data?	Operationalisation	1. How is data processed and consumed by the applications in order to serve, personalise and enhance customer experience? 2. Is the use of real-time data restricted to those use cases that absolutely require it? 3. How and what are the considerations of data sharing inside, ouside the organisation and across borders?
Consistent Process	1. Are there consistent processes across the organisation to ensure that all data created, collected and retired are done according to rigours standards and procedures? 2. Are the processes robust enough to be auditable?	Preparing	1. Is the time your analytics and scientists spend organizing the data for analysis optimal? 2. What are the process and standards in place to ensure data are highly usable in the important business use cases?	Breadth & Depth	1. What is the process to widen the breadth of data, e.g. collecting phsychographic data, preference info, etc to increase the richess? 2. What is the process to deepen the data, e.g. SKU level data rather than just total amount?	Effectiveness Measures	1. How do you measure the effectiveness of the use of data in enhancing service or experience? 2. How do you define a dashboard of key effectiveness measures to understand the impact of leveraging data on your business?

Figure 75 – Designing your data management lifecycle

A big consideration in your design will be **data security**. Breaches in data security can damage your reputation and result in fines or liability for the ensuing losses your customers face. Figure 76 provides some of the basic design principles that you should use to ensure that data security is embedded into your company's core design considerations.

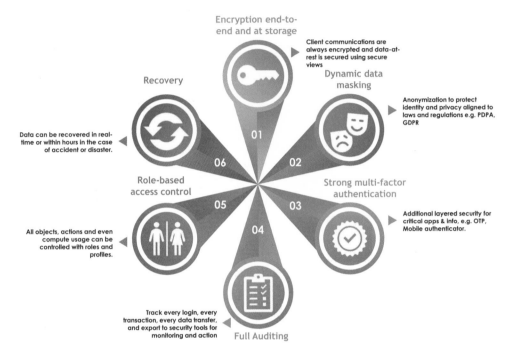

Figure 76 – 6 key design principles to embed data security
into your company's core

Of course, it isn't enough to ensure that you are managing your data management lifecycle well. Many other institutions are already taking this approach. In utilising data to engage customers, there will be a steep learning curve. Some experiments may work, and some may not. This plays to your advantage as any factor of competition with low learning means it can easily be copied. In TMRW, we realised that engagement would be the key differentiation as it had a large learning component and was the driving factor towards creating a bank that is more than just a utility. To increase and concentrate the ability to learn, we created an engagement lab with a multidisciplinary team consisting of communications, analytics, content, and behavioural science specialists. The term "lab" was meant to represent the learning journey we needed to take, to make the engagement strategy successful.

Technology

This section deals with the technology – more specifically, information technology – required to create the software interface and the associated customer engagement and experience you have designed in the customer dimension. This assumes that your core systems already have the ability to expose the core transactional capabilities (e.g., booking a flight, paying a third party, etc.) through APIs.

If, however, this is not the case, then modernising your core capabilities as standard services available through APIs and enhancing the core systems layer with additional capabilities your offering requires (e.g., ability to provide real-time indication that a transaction has taken place) should be done first. The resulting list of API service calls can be viewed as a list of the services that your core transactional systems offer for anyone who would like to build an end-user application leveraging these APIs.

Your digital initiative may also need new disciplines (the 6th element of the capabilities dimension) to power your experience. A discipline goes beyond just the software and hardware. These new disciplines will affect the quality of the experience, i.e., your organisation may need to invest in predictive capabilities comprising manpower, software, algorithms, use cases, training, etc., to be able to leverage data to make predictions that save customers time, e.g., reminding them of payments and pre-filling the details. Or if you are a manufacturer, embedding the required instrumentation in your equipment to send diagnostic and other data back to improve the customer experience may be another new discipline.

Technology will still need to integrate the different capabilities the new disciplines introduce. The distinction is that it breaks technology into the different new disciplines required, and the information technology software and hardware required to integrate the navigation, functionalities and capabilities together into a comprehensive and holistic experience for the end-user. This hopefully makes it easier for the non-tech CEO or executive leading the initiative to compartmentalise the capabilities so that he can better manage the complexity.

The output of technology is software code (and all the required hardware or software-as-a-service) required to orchestrate your customer experience and mirrors your business process defined in the customer dimension. The first priority is to determine where you will **build** (biggest impact on customer), **customise** (mid-level impact on customer) and **configure** (low impact on customer). Figure 77 illustrates an example from banking. The build activity is focused on the **customer experience**

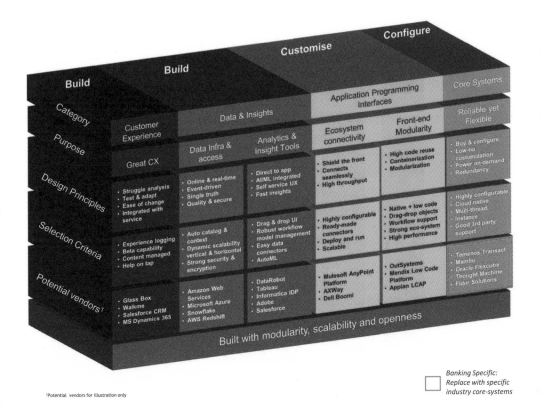

Banking Specific:
Replace with specific
industry core-systems

Figure 77 – Build, customise and configure analysis

category (represented by the app and the associated automated, semi-manual or manual processes), and on the data infrastructure, access and tools to analyse the data and extract insights. These touch the customer directly and hence tailoring them to your specific customer experience and interaction is important for differentiation. The **application programming interface** category is critical for connectivity, modularity and low maintenance, and here the recommendation is to purchase and customise to your specific environment. Finally, in core systems, to be able to configure the most complex product requirement with minimal coding and customisation is key. This determines your prioritisation of technology spend and also the key design principles, selection criteria and hence potential vendors that can deliver on the design principles. You should do a similar analysis as this banking example for your specific industry.

The next step is to determine the **technology architecture**. This topic cannot be explored in detail here and the following serves merely to give the senior transformation executive an overview of the technology architecture. Figure 78 illustrates a

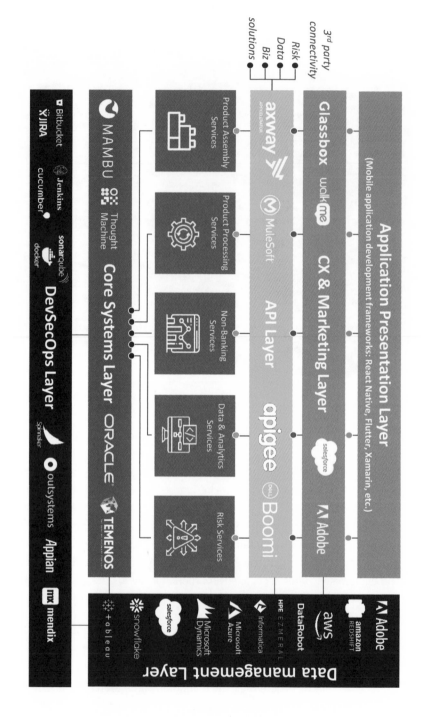

Figure 78 – Sample architecture diagram

typical technology architecture diagram. Let's begin with the layers that are indus-try-agnostic. The **application presentation** layer touches the customer directly through the app. To differentiate the customer's app experience and make full use of the capabilities of mobile devices, apps are built using cross-platform tools that support Android, Android TV, iOS, macOS, tvOS, Web, Windows and UWP. Using open-source mobile application frameworks insulates cross-platform differences, giving users a consistent look and feel while requiring only one-time coding.

React Native from Facebook is one of these commonly used open-source libraries of pre-built components which can help speed up the development pro-cess. Flutter from Google and Xamarin from Microsoft are alternatives. The CX (and Marketing) layer leverages CRM and marketing software for sales, customer information and marketing campaign management. It communicates with the core business transaction systems through the API layer. The **API layer serves to isolate the CX layer from the core systems layer so that changes in the core systems have a reduced impact on the CX layer**. The other key benefit is that it allows the CX and core systems layer to scale separately, and thus interfacing through the API layer enables modularity, lowers maintenance cost and provides the flexibility to support business volume growth. The API layer calls on services provided by the core systems layer.

The API layer also **interfaces with third-party solutions** and allows the CX layer to call upon third-party services. The data management layer manages all the data storage and access requirements of the technology solution, and the DevSecOps layer ensures that a consistent set of practices (e.g., methodology and tools) work together to automate and integrate the processes between software development, automated testing, application delivery, security and IT operations so that software can be built, tested, secured and released faster and more reliably. The final layer, the core systems layer is where the enterprise applications sit. This layer will be specific to industries and sub-industries.

By breaking up capabilities into methodology and technology, we demystify what actually is technology's role in digital innovation and transformation. For most executives, this tends to be a black box. You know what goes in and you know what comes out, but very little in-between. By applying the concept of the software factory depicted in Figure 73, **(information) technology's focus is thus on mod-ularity, scalability and redundancy of the IT solution**. One of the most important architectural decisions that need to be made at the outset is exactly **how much code creation and management you are comfortable with**. The other issue you will have to contend with is the shortage of programming resources globally because the demand is far outstripping supply and will continue to be the case for the foresee-able future. So, on the one hand, there is the drive to personalise and customise so that you can be differentiated; on the other hand, there is the issue of the shortage of resources, the difficulty of managing the code, which in turn impacts future modifications, testing and debugging.

The faster you would like something produced, the more likely the code is not compact, and the understandability of the code will be poor once the original coders are no longer on the project. Therefore, one of the **key trade-offs** at this stage is where can you deploy the software solutions you intend to purchase with low customisation, and where would you expend the energy to write code that you will have to maintain and manage for upgradability in the future. So, it's not just about writing more code. It's always possible to come up with the first version of your software given enough money and dedication. The issue is that **if it's not done properly, you will find the subsequent versions harder and harder to release**.

It may be natural for the senior executive in charge of the digital transformation without direct experience in information technology to think of tech as a project or one-time event for every project. However, **what you build is what you get stuck**

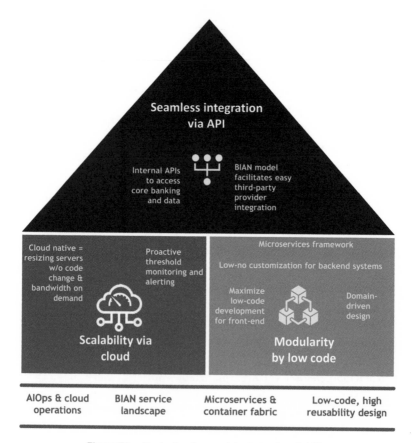

Figure 79 – Designing for modularity and scalability

with unless you are prepared to do expensive revamps very frequently. Thus, the key design considerations that are critical to achieving good total cost of ownership and performance have to do with the degree of modularity, scalability and redundancy, as shown in Figure 79.

Modularity is a software architecture design consideration that looks at how software can be broken up into **independent and interchangeable modules**. Modularity helps to manage software complexity, as software can easily get very complex after a few releases, making it very costly to continue development and testing to produce high-quality software (Delamore, 2020). The use of APIs, which was covered previously, aids modularity as it introduces a method to code once and reuse multiple times. Therefore, the development team no longer needs to code everything from scratch and can focus on building applications that are modular and contain a high level of code reuse, improving efficiency and speed. Scalability explores how software can be written so that it can **perform well under abnormal loads**, e.g., on payday when many customers are logging on to check their balances. Performing well means gradual degradation rather than the entire software coming to a halt. Finally, redundancy allows the software to **continue running when there is a serious outage** by duplicating key parts of the software and hardware.

The next key decision is where you should develop software and where you should buy. We covered at the beginning of the technology element where you should focus on building, on customising or on configuring. Your software team will always want to build something, as they will find their jobs boring if they are simply integrating different software together. The difficulty of originating a software product and then running it like a software company, with a proper roadmap, is non-trivial. There **must be a very strong competitive advantage** for doing it, i.e., no solution is available, and you have gone through a rigorous assessment that you can produce this capability on your own and maintain and develop it. Where it concerns customer experience, it may be permissible to build to plug a short-term gap. Today, most leaders in customer experience develop their own interfaces rather than use standard toolkits that produce similar user interfaces. This may change in the future as the configurability of such toolkits improves to the extent that they can develop high-quality native interfaces with low use of code. In most other areas, first evaluate if you are able to buy and integrate software components to achieve your desired experience and what gap prevents your ideal experience and the cost of ownership before deciding which path is best.

Ecosystem

Ecosystem mapping was used in the scaling element under the business dimension to derive a broad plan for understanding if the scaling required to achieve the forecasted customer base and the revenue was achievable. In the capabilities dimension, the ecosystem element **maps out the entire value chain in detail**, so that we have a very good perspective of the players and how they relate and interact with one another. This can then be used to identify specific partners, platforms, influencers to target to derive a finer-grained partnership plan that will make the scaling feasible.

A good way to understand your industry or sub-industry ecosystem is to plot an ecosystem map. Please refer to Figure 40, which explains the difference between a solution ecosystem and a transaction ecosystem. Figure 80 uses the Apple solution ecosystem as an example. The key players in the Apple ecosystem are depicted – the Apple platform consisting of Apple hardware, Appstore apps, Apple users, retailers of Apple hardware, software developers that write software for the iOS and MacOS operating systems like Autodesk, Adobe, Microsoft Office, etc. Drawing an ecosystem map for your own industry will provide a good view of the key players in the industry or sub-industry where you wish to apply your transformation. The lines represent the flow of goods and services, information or money.

The right-hand side of Figure 40 illustrates a two-sided platform. For a company to be considered a platform, it must have at least two groups of participants, or "sides", that are its customers in some meaningful way, and it must enable a direct interaction between the sides (Hagiu, 2014). Platforms can have more than two sides – for example, alternative credit scoring engines like avatec.ai, Credolab, etc. are 3-sided platforms, with financial institutions (or individuals with money to lend) on one side, e-commerce platforms whose customers would like credit solutions on another side, and information providers who have access to data that can be useful to ascertain if the customers are credit-worthy on a third side. Platforms leverage the ubiquity of the internet and mobile devices to match the needs of the various sides.

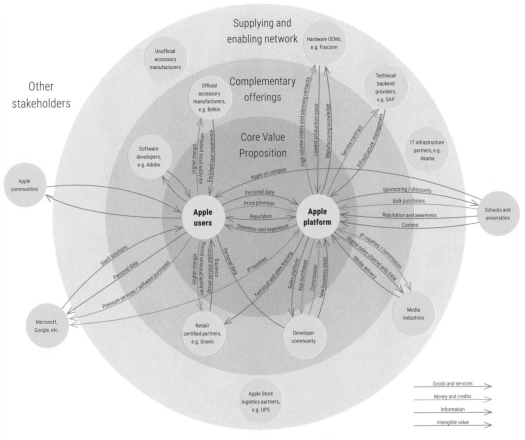

APPLE'S BUSINESS ECOSYSTEM

Figure 80 – Example of an ecosystem mapping exercise
for a solution ecosystem

A good way to understand how potential platforms work is shown in the platform business model canvas in Figure 81[72], which uses Airbnb as an example (Eisape, 2019, 2020). The **platform business model canvas** looks at the relationship between producers (the owners of the properties that are available for rental), the owner of the platform (in this case Airbnb), partners (local service firms that clean and manage the properties on the producers' behalf, and payment partners that help facilitate payments between the consumer, Airbnb and the producers) and consumers (customers who rent the producers' properties when they are on vacation, etc.). The canvas also explores the key platform components, and maps

---

72. Source: platformgeneration.com

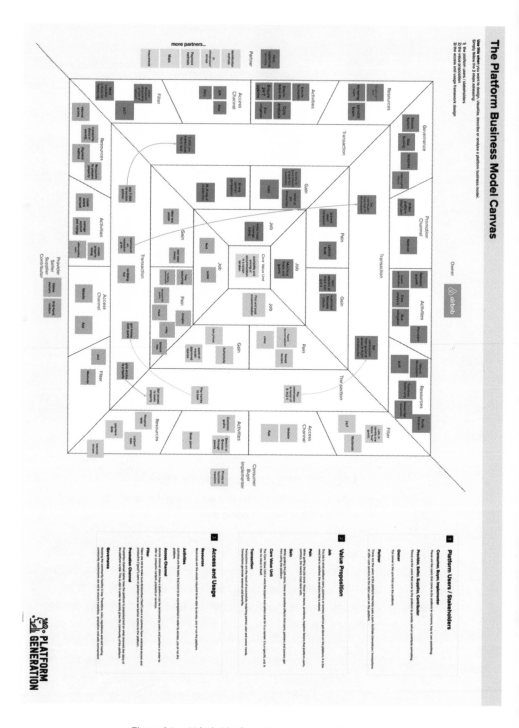

Figure 81 – Airbnb Platform Business Model Canvas

their stakeholder perspectives, value propositions and transaction flows. Using the platform business model canvas, you will be able to examine what it takes for you to be a key participant in a platform or to orchestrate a platform of you own and evaluate your probability of success.

If your digital transformation involves the creation of a platform, a good guide to evaluating its feasibility involves a 6-step process created by the BCG Henderson Institute, shown in Figure 82 (Pidun et al., 2020a)[73]. The authors based their 6 steps on an analysis of more than 100 ecosystems across different industries and geographies.

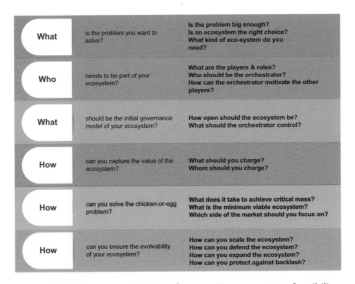

Figure 82 – Six-step evaluation of transaction ecosystem feasibility

Two key highlights of the approach that are worthy of mention are:

1. The problem the ecosystem is trying to solve must be big enough to convince the right participants to join and justify the high upfront cost of building the platform (e.g., "encouraged by the success of B2C marketplaces like eBay and Amazon, many companies tried to transfer this model to the B2B space, building marketplaces for automotive parts, paper, chemicals, and other supplies. However, most failed because they did not realize that the underlying problem of high transaction costs in B2C was not as pronounced in B2B transactions" (Pidun et al., 2020b)).

---

73. Source: BCG Henderson Institute. Ulrich Pidun, Martin Reeves, Maximilian Schuessler. How Do You "Design" A Business Ecosystem? February 2020

2. The business ecosystem must not require taking full control of the experience, as the ecosystem participants are independent economic players. Hence, neither very tight co-ordination such as required in aircraft construction (where every part must fit together within less than 1 mm tolerance) nor solutions that can be sourced in the open market (where conformance of standards allows interoperability), like personal computers and accessories, would qualify as ideal targets for business ecosystems.

Business ecosystems thus make sense when the solution is modular but not too tight and there is a need for co-ordination as adherence to standards is not high enough for full interoperability. The smartphone ecosystem is a good example. The modular components are the phone handset, the phone OS[74], the Telcos providing the connectivity, and the app providers providing content and services. Different smartphone ecosystems have evolved over time: Symbian OS (Nokia, Sony Ericsson, Motorola), Palm OS (Palm), BlackBerry OS (RIM), Windows Mobile, iOS and App Store, Android and Play Store, and these ecosystems are not interoperable.

Ability to evolve the ecosystem is dependent on the demand- and supply-side platform economies of scale. Demand-side economies can accrue from networked effects as more users attract more suppliers, which in turn attracts more users, whereas supply-side economies accrue due to falling fixed or variable costs attributable to low marginal costs (costs nothing to serve an additional customer), increasing returns on data (improves ability to match buyers and sellers) or asset-light models.

---

74. Operating System

New disciplines

The final element in capabilities is a catch-all element, i.e., what other new disciplines do you need to create in your organisation so that you can deliver the digital innovation or transformation? This could be entire new disciplines you need to build in-house or source externally – examples would be predictive analytics, artificial intelligence, manufacturing techniques, instrumentation, etc. In the case of TMRW, we had to build an engagement team and the engagement lab from scratch. This was the new discipline that we didn't have before that we needed to create so that we could be successful using data to digitally engage customers. It required the hiring and training of a cross-functional team consisting of communications, analytics, content, behavioural science, etc.

Bringing it all together

We have covered three of the four dimensions thus far. People & Leadership, the last dimension, is next. We can now look at the interactions of all dimensions and view TaP in totality. As illustrated in Figure 83, the people & leadership dimension envelopes the other three, as people and leadership affect all the rest of the components.

How does the leader create the motivation, impetus for change, the values and expected behaviours to bring about that change? People act according to how they are measured, and so the measurements that indicate if you are successful in your transformation must be aligned with the measures of the team. These form the mission-values element. The mission statement creates the purpose and imbues a sense of pride to be part of such a purposeful mission. The vision statement compels the team to be bold, to reach for what does not seem possible today. The values are the guide on the journey, and if the behaviours that showcase these values are well defined, then there is a good possibility of containing the dark side of human nature (to be overly competitive, egotistical, entitled, to not listen or listen only with the intention to refute, etc.) and elicit the best of what your team has to offer. Measurements round off this first element and ensure that there is a holistic scorecard comprising customer, business and values KPIs, at the entity level, unit level and individual goals.

How the leader balances the trade-off between co-ordination and depth or leverages them both at the same time, or how the leader fosters innovation, and finally how the leader achieves balance between seemingly paradoxical traits to become a

balanced leader, are all critical leadership elements to realise the changes needed to bring the transformation to life.

How do you fill the talent gap, given the capabilities you need to build? That's covered in the Talent Gap element. And finally, the structure and environment form the crucible from which you will orchestrate this change. Let's now look at the people & leadership dimension in greater depth.

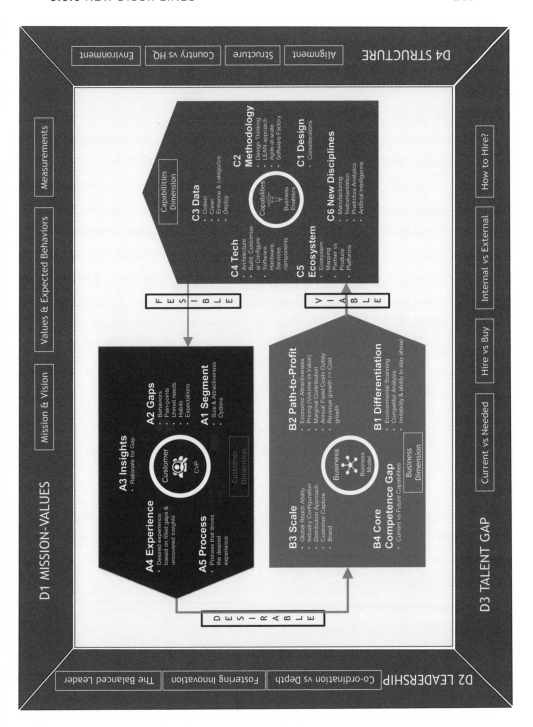

Figure 83 – All Dimension Interactions

Key takeaways

- There should be a significant gap between your current capabilities and what you need to successfully bring your initiative to life.

- The first four elements in the capabilities dimension – design, methodology, data and (information) technology – are standard elements of any capability build in a digital transformation. The last two – ecosystem and new disciplines – are specific to your industry and sub-industry.

- Design is not just about making objects pretty. Design is the process of deeply understanding customer/user needs and then creating a product or service – physical, digital, or both – that addresses their unmet needs.

- The four capabilities in design are: analytical leadership to measure and drive design output and performance; cross-functional talent to make user-centricity everyone's responsibility; user experience to break down the walls between physical (e.g., stores), digital (i.e., online) and service design; and finally, continuous iteration to de-risk development by continually listening, testing and iterating with users.

- The business innovation designer is a new and important role. It requires one to be both human-centred and profit-centred, with a bias towards executability and action, to embrace ambiguity, and to practise continuous refinement to achieve excellence.

- In the near future, business innovation designers will be in extremely high demand, due to the increasing number of digital transformation initiatives in companies of all sizes.

- The output of the design element is the key design considerations of your initiative. There isn't a fixed number of top design considerations. A number between 6 and 10 probably makes sense in practice. These top design considerations cascade downwards from top to bottom.

- The top design considerations document the blueprint you have designed, and become the compass to guide you through the next stage of TaP, where you bring your transformation to life by acquiring the capabilities, people and leadership required to execute your design.

- Methodology is an essential capability needed to address the new approach to collaboration and processes required to bring the transformation to life.

- As a basic requirement, the 3 key methods that must be implemented are Design Thinking, Lean Six Sigma, and Agile development. There may be others that should be added on as appropriate to the situation at hand.

- The power of design thinking comes from its foundations in human-centric design and understanding what customers need to do their jobs well.

- This is especially important in industries and organisations that are product-centric because they can't help themselves but start with the product and their business objective first.

- Lean is about finding the most efficient way to do something, eliminating waste in the process. It's also about continuous improvement, constantly thinking of ways to extract more waste from the process.

- When you combine Lean with design thinking, you not only get a faster and cheaper process, but also one that the customer can easily appreciate and understand.

- Lean Six Sigma combines the best of waste and inefficiency removal in your process with a data-driven approach to reduce variation, ensuring a consistently superior experience by continuously optimising your process for efficiency and ensuring consistently high-quality outcomes.

- The heart of Agile is building great software solutions that adapt gracefully to changing needs. It's rapid, iterative, easily adapted, and focused on quality through continuous improvement.

- Putting all three methodologies together yields a powerful production-line concept-to-code software factory. This is the essence of what you need to build to ensure that you have a world-class facility that is generating the high-quality experience you have promised your customers.

- Competitive differentiation is shifting to mass customisation and rapid learning. Both require data.

- Data takes time to collect, and only businesses that have been operating for some time have the depth and breadth of data.

- In many organisations, data has been used to make decisions about improving the business but rarely about improving the lives of customers.

- Data is also usually dispersed throughout an organisation.

- Data life-cycle management can be broken in 4 distinct stages: Collect (& Retire), Clean, Enhance & Standardise, and finally Deploy.

- The 6 key design principles to embed data security into your core are: Encryption end-to-end and at storage, Dynamic data masking, Strong multi-factor authentication, Full Auditing, Role-based access control, and Recovery.

- Core systems must have the ability to expose the core transactional capabilities (e.g., booking a flight, paying a third party, etc.) as standard services available through APIs or enhancing the core systems layer with additional capabilities required (e.g., ability to provide real-time indication that a transaction has taken place) should be done first.

- The first priority is to determine where you will build (biggest impact on customer), customise (mid-level impact on customer) and configure (low impact on customer).

- The technology architecture consists of several layers; Application presentation layer, Customer experience (CX) and marketing layer, API layer, Core systems layer, DevSecOps layer and Data management layer.

- An API layer serves to isolate the CX layer from the core systems layer so that changes in the core systems have a reduced impact on the CX layer. An API layer also interfaces with third-party solutions and allows the CX layer to call upon third-party services.

- The data management layer manages all the data storage and access requirements of the technology solution.

- The DevSecOps layer ensures that a consistent set of practices (e.g., methodology and tools) work to automate and integrate the processes between software development, automated testing, application delivery, security and IT operations so that software can be built, tested, secured and released faster and more reliably.

- The core systems layer is where the enterprise applications sit. This layer will be specific to industries and sub-industries.

- (Information) Technology's focus is on modularity, scalability and redundancy of the IT solution.

- There is a shortage of programming resources globally because the demand is far outstripping supply, and this will continue to be the case for the foreseeable future.

- A trade-off between the amount of code needed to personalise and customise so that you can be differentiated, versus the issue of the shortage of resources, the difficulty of managing the code, which in turn impacts future modifications, testing and debugging, must be addressed.

- It's always possible to come up with the first version of your software given enough money and dedication. The issue is that if it's not done properly, you will find the subsequent versions harder and harder to release.

- What you build is what you get stuck with unless you are prepared to do expensive revamps very frequently.

- The key design considerations that are critical to achieving good total cost of ownership and performance have to do with the degree of modularity, scalability and redundancy.

- Modularity is a software architecture design consideration that looks at how software can be broken up into independent and interchangeable modules.

- Modularity helps to manage software complexity, as software can easily get very complex after a few releases, making it very costly to continue development and testing to produce high-quality software.

- Scalability explores how software can be written so that it can perform well under abnormal loads, e.g., on payday when many customers are logging on to check their balances. Performing well means gradual degradation rather than the entire software coming to a halt.

- Redundancy allows the software to continue running when there is a serious outage.

- The difficulty of originating a software product and then running it like a software company, with a proper roadmap, is non-trivial.

- There must be a very strong competitive advantage to build your own software, i.e., no solution is available and it is crucial for differentiation, and you have gone through a rigorous assessment that you can produce this capability on your own and maintain and develop it.

- The ecosystem element maps out the entire value chain in detail, so that we have a very good perspective of the players and how they relate and interact with one another.

- This can then be used to identify specific partners, platforms, influencers to target, to derive a finer-grained partnership plan that will make the scaling feasible.

- Drawing an ecosystem map for your own digital transformation will provide a good view of the key players in the industry or sub-industry where you wish to apply your transformation.

- A good way to understand how potential platforms work is the platform business model canvas, which looks at the relationship between producers of value (property owners, car owners, capital owners, etc.), the owner of the platform (Airbnb, Uber, LuFax, etc.), partners (cleaning agencies, restaurants, etc.) and consumers (travellers, riders, borrowers, etc.).

- If your digital transformation involves the creation of a platform, a good guide to evaluating its feasibility involves a 6-step process created by the BCG Henderson Institute.

People & leadership

Some of you will already realise that some aspects of the people & leadership element would already have been in place before you can develop the customer dimension. And that would be true as before you start on the customer–business dimensions, your initial pioneer team should already be in place, and elements of the culture, structure, environment would have been discussed, agreed and put into play. This would undergo change as the organisation and strategy evolve over the course of the design phase. **The people & leadership element is probably both the start and the end of TaP**, and in any case, as mentioned before, as the senior executive in charge, you are constantly evaluating the interconnections and dimensions as you progress and fine-tuning the elements as you go. So, it's not static, but something you constantly check to ensure alignment between the different dimensions and elements.

I have found that attracting the talent you need is a function of **how well you articulate your story and ambition**. In the first stage, when you are designing and building, you obviously need to hire those talented in these areas. Such talented individuals are attracted by your ability to change the world and do something exceptional. Your ability to inspire them to join you on your journey of discovery to deliver something impactful is key to attracting the right talent. Telling prospective hires that we were building the world's most proactive digital bank, and that it was a rare opportunity to build a bank from ground up, allowed us to attract the talent we needed. Later on, when the initiative is up and running, the mix of talent will evolve, as building a business and running it requires different skills.

In starting up something new from scratch, **the nature of initial roles will change, as will the reporting lines** – and sometimes change very quickly. Michael Koh, who was the partnership lead when we launched TMRW, encountered this, and his role morphed quickly as we went from not being able to fill a sheet of paper at first to a full-fledged partnership role within two years, and he had three different bosses in that timeframe.

In spite of these changes, it is important that the qualities of each role, e.g. of a good business development person, need to be determined and detected upfront to ensure success even if the job scope changes later on. Thus, it is mandatory and essential to success to require the hiring manager to write a job description that can be just 1–2 pages long, so that a formal discussion on the roles and responsibilities, the qualities needed, and how he or she would detect these qualities, can take place. Whilst this seems obvious, it is seldom rigorously enforced. Besides hard competences like analytical ability, strategic thinking, relationship skills, behaviours like being collaborative, assertive, risk-taking, etc., are important attributes to look for. For roles that are more nebulous at the start, selecting candidates who are more positive, possess higher adaptability and are more flexible will be important in ensuring the candidates can navigate the changes ahead.

It is the responsibility of the leadership team to create a **culture conducive to innovation and transformation**, and thus the people & leadership dimension starts with creating the right culture by defining the values that will help achieve the mission and vision of the initiative you have started. The mission statement serves to coalesce your team so that there is a clear, compelling and common purpose, whilst the vision statement serves to ignite an ambition that will inspire them to reach for the stars. Your values statement is then the glue that holds everyone together by specifying the right behaviours needed to align to those values and in doing so bring out the best in everyone. Without a clearly crafted set of values and behaviours, you will be unable to form and foster the right culture to bring out the best in those you have worked hard to attract. Highly capable individuals can also be overly competitive and aggressive, and have bigger egos, and thus these behaviours are designed to bring out the best and suppress the worst behaviours.

Chapter 5.4.1 "Mission-Values" ends with a focus on measurement. People's behaviours are influenced by their measurements and key performance indicators. A good rule of thumb is for one-third of the measures to be cross-initiative, e.g., customer NPS®, marginal profit targets, behaviours that align with the values statement, etc. Another one-third can be the individual staff's unit goals, and the last one-third, the staff's own individual goals. This balanced scorecard will support and enhance the ability of your team to work well together, and yet ensure that unit and individual goals still matter significantly.

Chapter 5.4.2 "Leadership" focuses on three considerations. Firstly, how do you organise your team by identifying areas that need breadth, areas that need depth and a few areas that need both? Next, we examine how leaders foster innovation, and finally we explore how you can evaluate leaders on their leadership balance and take steps to increase their balance in areas that are unbalanced. Dr Dan Harrison, founder of Harrison Assessments, has found that "true leadership is a matter of balance" (Harrison, 2018). I use the Harrison Assessment extensively, as I have found that leaders who are unbalanced, i.e., have strong traits that are not balanced by other traits, tend to be very disruptive or overly passive. The balanced leader programme seeks to correct this.

Chapter 5.4.3 "Talent Gap" examines how you can properly assess the talent gap, and how to go about closing it. Where could you buy resources instead of hiring, and if your initiative is within a larger organisation, when would you select internal candidates and which roles are more suitable for internal versus external permanent hires?

Finally, the last chapter looks at the structure and environment of the unit. Alignment is one of the key considerations if you are a start-up transforming the mother organisation from within. Besides alignment, how you structure your unit is also crucial, as is the environment you create for the unit to excel.

5.4.1
Mission-Values

As illustrated in Figure 84, the people & leadership dimension starts with the mission and values of the digital venture orchestrating the transformation.

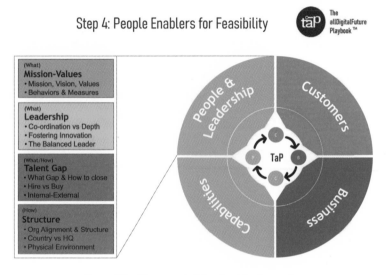

Figure 84 – The people & leadership dimension

People can do amazing things when they are inspired. But how do you inspire them to stretch beyond their job descriptions, and give and do more for their organisation? One way is to **make sure that your company's mission and vision inspire your employees to greater heights**. These statements should be written, reviewed and updated by the CEO of the venture or company on a regular basis, as they embody his or her explanation of what the company does, its goals and what it aspires to be. The culture and values then set the behaviours and values that the company must embrace when it seeks to fulfil its mission and vision.

If, like TMRW, your digital initiative is part of a bigger mothership, you can't have your own mission, vision and values statements. In that situation, you can still define the expected behaviours by defining **principles**, e.g., one of the principles could be "Challenge the status quo", to encourage all members of the team to question why, regardless of how junior they are, and for anyone more senior to encourage them to do so, and to answer or admit that they don't know the answer. This helps break down the hierarchy and encourage participation and challenge throughout the organisation. Some of the other principles you might consider are putting the customer first, owning the outcome and not just the activity, spending money like it is your own, or not encouraging a blame culture. Whatever the principles, this serves as a way to establish a subculture within your transformation that is uniquely different.

A senior HR colleague recalled the culture at TMRW: "TMRW had a unique culture that was quite separate from the core traditional bank of UOB. And how it was different was the mindset, the kind of pace that TMRW was operating in, which in my view, was unprecedented in banking. Dennis commissioned an agency to help us craft the DNA of the TMRW talent. A whole set of behavioural traits was laid out to guide all the leaders in TMRW when conducting interviews. Dennis built a culture where everybody could say anything to anyone, including him. We were very open with each other, challenging hard when needed, yet we never took it personally because it was always done in the spirit of improvement."

That's why this section on mission-values is especially critical. It sets the tone, purpose, ways of working that can make magic happen. My recommended starting point for you is to make your mission purposeful and vision inspiring. The builders you want to hire are most attracted by your purpose in creating this venture or initiative. So, the starting point is crafting your mission, vision, values and the behaviours you expect.

Mission ("Why we exist") statements define why the company exists, i.e., the organisation's purpose and primary objectives. They are intended for both internal and external stakeholders and are usually written in the present tense. Mission statements should be clear and concise, so that recall is high, which makes it impactful when aligning the company's rationale for existence. Mission statements can and should change according to business circumstances and thus need to be reviewed and updated on a periodic basis. Focusing on your mission will attract mission-oriented individuals. When you constantly remind your employees of their mission, you create a sense of purpose that results in higher employee engagement and positive work culture (Ross, 2015; William, 2018). Builders are attracted by purpose first and money after, so it's also a great way to attract the best builders to your organisation.

Vision ("Who we can become") statements on the other hand speak to the company's aspirations, what it hopes to be, and the goals it will achieve along this journey. Above all, they should be ambitious, inspiring and always just beyond reach. They are meant to compel the organisation towards a goal it will never fully obtain, and hence propel it to greatness. For this reason, whilst vision statements can be updated, they do tend to stay more constant than mission statements. Again, the clearer and more concise the vision statement is, the more likely employees will remember it.

Values ("What we stand for") are the core principles that guide and direct the company's employees to behave in a way that embodies those values when they go about their mission. They are often reflective of the leader's own value systems and serve as a way to align the company's behaviour so that a unique way of working develops, i.e., its culture. Value statements are not effective if they are not accompanied by behaviours that exemplify those values. The CEO is also the Chief Culture Officer and must set the tone from the top about the importance of these behaviours in shaping the values of the company.

Figure 85 is an example of mission, vision and values statements from my days bidding for the digital wholesale licence in Singapore. Since this was a separate independent entity, I was able to craft all the statements from scratch. This was one of the first things I did, and many of the candidates I spoke to were attracted by the learning and experience they would gain by building a new bank from scratch, in particular, building a bank using mostly cloud infrastructure and leveraging data from accounting systems to solve operational issues that SMEs face. A larger number, however, were attracted by the values and behaviours we planned to promote. We managed to find 10 candidates whom we concluded salary discussions with and who agreed to join us if we secured the licence. This was out of 11 reports to the CEO – a very high achievement.

So, whether you are a separate company or a unit within a bigger company, find every appropriate means to communicate what your unit or company's purpose, ambition and behaviours are all about. It's not enough to state what your values are. Many companies have lovely values statements, but they don't dictate the behaviours needed to make those values the DNA of the company, defeating the purpose of the values statement in the first place.

Activities to keep everyone inspired

To continuously motivate your team in a multi-year programme, you will need to put together **a set of activities and programmes dedicated to keeping the team inspired**. This was a task I assigned to Gemma Tay, one of the pioneers who was with me from the start. I selected her for the programme management role as I was always very impressed by how organised she was, and her ability to take notes of meetings was legendary. She also complemented me well as she had a way of reading people that I didn't have, and in addition she had been in the bank the longest amongst the pioneer team and would be very adept at interfacing and aligning with the mothership, which was important for success.

In the programme management role, Gemma took care of logistics, programme milestones and timelines, budgets, people, etc. She was an indispensable help to me throughout the TMRW initiative. One of the difficult tasks I assigned to her was how

Sample: The Grow Bank

Mission: The Grow Bank provides sustainable financial services that enable SMEs in Singapore to thrive, so that they can grow into MNCs and help power our economy.

Vision: Our ambition is to be the world's most proactive digital bank. We achieve this through a relentless focus on our customers so that we can anticipate their needs before they do.

Values and behaviours:

1. **Honesty and integrity** – We place honour and integrity above all else. Our word is our bond, and we have the courage to do what's right and rise to a higher standard of conduct. We lead by example, and we will make tough decisions when needed, rather than capitulate to what's easy or convenient.

2. **Accountability** – We are highly responsible. We consider the ramifications of our actions, and we exhibit a high degree of ownership for these actions, never afraid to admit an honest mistake and learn from it.

3. **Competency** – We embrace lifelong learning, and we take it upon ourselves to constantly learn and improve. We are naturally curious, and we are constantly asking why.

4. **Professionalism** – We stay calm and collected under pressure and display exemplary professionalism in its true sense, never taking things personally, even in the most heated debates. The drive is always for the greater good of our customers and our bank, well balanced with what's good for our staff. As leaders, we are last, and we care for our staff before ourselves.

5. **Humility** – No matter how senior we are, we do not exhibit a sense of entitlement. No task is too menial for the most senior employee if it helps our customers or our staff achieve their goals and ambitions. We do not wear our egos on our shoulders. We know that ego is the source of all office politics, and we seek humility instead.

6. **Innovative** – We are constantly looking for ideas that can turn into big or small innovations. We understand that whilst ideas are aplenty, innovations are few, and challenge of the norm and diversity in experience and backgrounds are the sources that fuel innovativeness.

Figure 85 – Sample vision, mission, values and behaviour statements

to motivate the TMRW team. The technology teams had a high ratio of contract to permanent staff. The IT team members were critical as they were the ones that did all the coding, and if they were motivated, the quality of the coding and the speed at which they could troubleshoot a software problem would be much better.

One good example is the organisation of the Deepavali event, shown in Figure 86. I insisted all the key management team turn up. Many members of the IT team celebrated Deepavali. It was also a way to celebrate success. This is still cited every time the TMRW teams get together. We also organised a lot of month-end activities. And we rotated this responsibility across teams. Through these activities we wanted to bring people together. Staff were very enthusiastic, and many took to it with great energy. They saw TMRW as a fun team and could relate to the values, purpose and ambition. These get-togethers were a time to celebrate as well as to get to know everyone better. I also emphasised enjoying the journey, as it was important to me that the team enjoyed and celebrated the small and big accomplishments along the way. I recall that after the Indonesia staff launch in Jakarta, I invited the technology team that made it possible out to celebrate. On the Monday after these events, people greeted each other with fond memories of their time together the week prior, and as a result people got to know each other better.

Figure 86 – Deepavali celebrations in October 2019

Ensuring that staff are onboarded properly is tedious, but I recommend you make it one of your key priorities, as it is the first impression your new hires have of your company, and it makes for a bad impression if not done well. Gemma worked with HR and IT to ensure that staff got their personal computing equipment on the day they arrived. This required processes to be modified to make it happen like clockwork.

Getting to know your junior staff better and getting them involved and giving them a voice should be another priority. Organise sessions to meet all the staff, especially new ones, when you grow bigger and find it difficult to know everyone personally. We paired senior staff who were not in the leadership team (which consisted of senior vice-presidents and above) with junior staff, and asked them to read up on articles that I came across or a topic of interest. These were some of the topics they discussed with the leadership team: "The drumbeat of digital: How winning teams play", "How digital banks increase transactional activity", "The state of the financial services industry 2019: Time to start again", and "What banks can do to keep customers sneaking away". We asked their opinion about these topics and how they thought TMRW fared compared to these case study best practices. In doing so, many told me they were finally given a voice.

Danielle Lee was the development lead for our onboarding stream, probably one of the most complex and prone to changes. She recalls her time with TMRW: "As I look back, in my career of over 20 years, TMRW was one of the best and most successful teams I've worked in. It wasn't about business and technology. It was *one team*. One team under a motivating and inspiring leader. We were a diverse team, with members from so many different companies and vendors. Yet, we left our different badges behind and focused on the vision of becoming the most engaged and best digital bank in ASEAN. Don't digitalise the bank. Motivate your team and treat them well and they will digitalise the bank for you."

Constant engagement

The multi-year journey for your programme can be arduous and stressful for your team. Working too hard for too long can cause burnout. Therefore, constant engagement to motivate and inspire your team, to reiterate the mission, vision, small and big accomplishments along the way and develop new skills needed as the situation entails, is important. As an example, we conducted an MBTI (Myers-Briggs)[75] workshop at Changi Village in August 2018. We could see each other's MBTI types and got to know each other better: for example, how the extroverts overwhelm the introverts with too much conversation; how the introverts seem aloof and cold to the extroverts; how the sensors always need data; how the intuitive can make the jump without, etc. As I was a certified Gallup StrengthsFinder coach, we also spent time understanding each other's innate talents. Someone with lower execution talent could be paired with those with higher execution talent to complement each other. For this Gallup StrengthsFinder workshop, one staff who worked in the programme

---

75. The purpose of the Myers-Briggs Type Indicator® (MBTI®) personality inventory is to make the theory of psychological types described by Carl Jung understandable and useful in people's lives. Source: The Myers & Briggs Foundation

management office compiled a one-page summary (Figure 87) for each member of the TMRW leadership team, so that others could know them better.

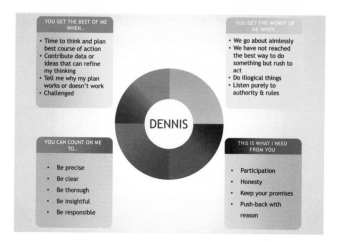

Figure 87 – One-pager to get to know us better

Brown-bag lunchtime talks were arranged so that people could share interesting work they had done; and sometimes we would invite external speakers. I recall one where the Razer Head of Marketing presented. It was interesting to learn about how other companies operated and their thought processes. It kept us from being too insular.

There was a junior staff who had difficulties with his team. I chose to speak to him personally, as I had found him to be knowledgeable, but his attitude sometimes caused issues. This was often cited as an example of how there were little barriers between seniors and juniors. The person concerned was very appreciative that I took the time to speak to him, and Gemma recalls that he was very thankful and in fact apologised for his behaviour to others, and he did make a big change in his demeanour and attitude.

One of the staff who was unhappy with the new seating arrangement complained that it was a pain to split up his team. He was the only one that had team members seated on two different levels. But I stood firm and explained that the rationale was to get to know others better and not just stick to your own team. Customers don't care about departments or teams, and we must break down the silos if we really want to be customer-centric. I requested my leadership team to explain the rationale to all their staff and I requested solidarity on this issue. The team immediately responded in unison to support this.

One of the learning activities that I introduced to the leadership team was to read various books of interest and share relevant chapters in a discussion. Here are some of the books that we discussed and read: *Escaping the Build Trap* (which was a book Jamorn recommended that I read), *What Got You Here Won't Get You There*, *Collective Genius: The Art and Practice*, *User Friendly*, etc. Some people hated it, but others loved it. They only had to read one chapter. Some became very competitive and took it as a challenge to know more than others about their chapter. Some just went to Google to get book summaries. It was funny at times but yet we learnt a lot. It was one way to keep the team abreast of important changes in the market for their personal development.

In 2018, I attended a programme at Columbia University, the Digital Business Leader's Program, or DBLP. The programme lead was David Rogers. We invited David to do a workshop for the entire TMRW team on digital innovation and disruption. He did a talk for the entire bank and trained the TMRW team, and we included colleagues outside the TMRW team who were interested to attend.

Scrum, as previously discussed, is a key process in the Agile way of developing software. We conducted a professional scrum product owner (PSPO) course for all product owners. There were 80 quiz questions. And you must get 85% to pass. Some scored 100%!

Measurements

Measures describe and monitor how the company is doing versus its business objectives over time. These objectives should take into account both short- and long-term measures. The most important performance measures in a company are the key performance indicators, or KPIs. As there are different levels in a company, each level from the CEO down should adapt and cascade the KPIs down the line so that there is strong alignment company-wide.

Often, companies spend a lot of time crafting and refining their strategy but afterwards spend little time discussing the KPIs they should adopt to ensure that the execution of strategy achieves the intended results. A lot of measurements are outcome-based, but should KPIs be more focused on the drivers of those outcomes rather than on the outcomes themselves? After all, focusing on the measures doesn't necessarily make them better, but focusing on the drivers of those outcomes will.

As an example, profit is one of the KPIs we are after, but not what we can focus on in the beginning, as profit is an outcome of revenue, active customers, cost to acquire, and cost to serve. For TMRW, revenue has a low near-term ceiling, and thus active customers, cost to acquire and cost to serve are the key drivers of profitability. Knowing this, I was adamant about focusing on active customers, cost of acquisition and cost to serve at the start. Having a large customer base with very low activity rates is self-defeating. We knew that many new digital banks had fallen into that trap, so we tracked a customer active ratio measure that I was very sensitive to and monitored very closely. It is easy to get the overall acquisition numbers up at the cost of a lower and lower active ratio.

Figure 88 shows the conceptual design of a scorecard for a digital bank, which is also appropriate for experience-focused start-ups. The measures in green are outcomes we would like to achieve, and the measures in blue and brown are the drivers of those outcomes. In red is the downside of driving the outcome measure too hard.

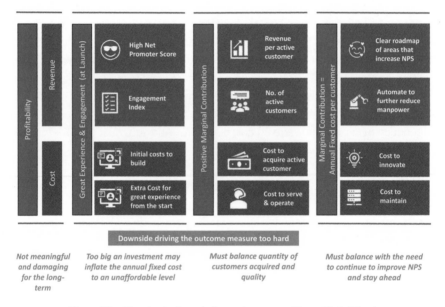

Figure 88 – How to design a balanced scorecard for a Digital Bank

Profit

The first set of measures you see on the extreme left are the traditional measures of profit and loss. If the target segment has low current revenue potential but high future revenue potential, the key to profitability is managing costs extremely well. Therefore, from a **cost measurement perspective**, we focused on minimising three types of costs:

1. The cost to acquire and transact
The cost to acquire and transact is the cost of acquiring new customers and getting them to use or transact with TMRW's products and services. If we can create happy customers through a great transactional experience and superior engagement, we

have a better chance of achieving high advocacy. In turn, advocacy can help acquire more users and reduce the cost of acquisition, thereby helping to create a bank that can scale without losing more and more money.

2. The cost to serve and operate

The cost to serve and operate is the ongoing cost to manage and service a customer. We designed TMRW for low cost to serve by automating and re-engineering many processes so they were as efficient as possible. This included all the functions on the app as well as customer service through chatbots. Any service that customers can do on their own, like changing their ATM PIN, can be done quickly and easily through the app. TMRW performs "straight-through processing" for most transactions, where no human interactions are involved.

We were relentless in identifying service incidents that took up a large amount of service agent time, whether it was a chat or call interaction. Every month, I would personally lead a review of the service performance, and we would go after the top service incidents. We consistently focused on getting the chatbot capability up to take on more service queries, reducing service agents in the process. Eliminating the source of the service incident in the first place, e.g., making the instructions clearer, so that customers would not submit the wrong documents, ensuring that promotional offers did not generate unnecessary queries, etc., was also a key focus.

3. The cost to innovate

The cost to innovate is the cost of continuously upgrading systems and software to keep the NPS® moving upwards and to invest in ongoing innovation, which in the case of TMRW was the cost to keep up with advancements in data-driven digital engagement capabilities. The initial investment mostly went into implementing digital engagement systems and setting up the infrastructure to extract, rationalise, enhance, categorise, and store transactional data for easy retrieval. This data would then be fed into other software to look for patterns and derive insights. When I designed TMRW, I made the decision to roll out a relatively standard banking bundle across countries. This standardisation would keep costs low and avoid a proliferation of country-specific apps that would make future enhancements very expensive.

The use of Fintech solutions helped to reduce the cost to innovate and develop new functionality, and I was insistent that we use Fintech software as far as possible in digital engagement.

Profitability is the **most basic of financial measures, but it is also the worst measure to use** to measure a digital bank's initial success or that of any start-up venture with a high cost outlay to revenue mismatch, as it is not meaningful initially and damaging to long-term success if driven too hard. You will see red for a rather long time, and if you are not prepared for it, then I advise you to think twice about building one. There is an entrenched mindset in incumbent banks to cross-sell and increase revenue quickly. However, how much more revenue can you earn if a customer's current wallet size, the source of current revenues, limits it? Such a mindset can therefore often run counter to building a digital bank to create a new business model based on experience.

Launch with great experience

If you are working for a start-up, the natural tendency is to focus on MVP and launch quickly but this may result in a platform with insufficient starting NPS® at launch, especially in countries where the basics are reasonably good, like Singapore and Thailand. Thus, great experience at launch is the next key outcome measure as shown in Figure 88. To achieve this, KPIs in this category focus on improving the overall experience, i.e., (1) Net Promoter Score, and (2) the engagement index, which focuses on how well the data-driven engagement hits the mark with customers (Warden, 2019a). The costs in this category are the costs to build a great experience from the start. The downside of focusing too hard on this outcome is an annual fixed cost that becomes unaffordable.

The next category of KPIs has to do with marginal contribution, and consists of the revenue per active customer, the number (and percentage) of active customers. The drivers of marginal cost in this category are the cost to acquire an active customer and the cost to serve and operate, which has already been covered. These numbers drive the actual profit per customer and thus are important KPIs to focus on and measure to show progress in the early years. The downside of driving this outcome too hard is not enough customers, so you must balance both the quantity and quality of customers acquired.

The cost to acquire an active customer is not an easy number to calculate, and there may be reservations in using it because of the difficulty of obtaining this number and keeping it accurate. **In TMRW, I insisted that we use it to drive home the point that we were not after just any customer, but active customers**.

Despite strong emphasis and repeated reiteration, it is ingrained in human nature to focus on achievements (e.g., acquisition numbers). Member-get-member (MGM) programmes are a common method of acquiring customers. If an MGM programme does not target active customers, you can have a "successful" MGM with a high number of customers acquired but this will reduce the active customer ratio in your base. I recall an MGM programme earlier in my career which involved signing up and transacting. But the incentive attracted some customers who invited "friends" to apply and make fictitious transactions and shared the referral incentive they collected. To avoid such issues, MGM programmes should be designed carefully so that they don't lower the overall active ratio drastically.

Annual contribution = Annual fixed cost per customer

The final set of KPIs was focused on containing the annual fixed cost but yet staying ahead. The desired outcome is to have the marginal contribution negate the annual fixed cost, which would result in break-even at a total cost per customer basis. This is a fine balance. Firstly, the cost of ownership is important, and already detailed in the technology section. The focus must not only be on the total initial project cost, but also on the annual footprint required to maintain and enhance this initial cost. As a result, building the tech stack for maintainability and enhancement is as important, probably slightly more important than getting the bank launched on time. The downside of driving this outcome measure too hard is that you may under-invest in closing your NPS® gap with your nearest competitor.

The KPI measurement system should be designed so that some measures, like NPS®, revenue per active customer, and cost of acquiring an active customer, etc., are common across all members of your transformation group. These KPIs should form roughly a third to half of the total (depending on their roles), with the other half comprising specific initiatives unique to the units concerned, like new feature launch milestones met, episode-level NPS® (e.g., NPS® for payments and fund transfers), etc. This will provide a good mix of group-wide objectives but also on unit and individual-specific objectives. The complexity is getting all these measurements (number of active customers, NPS®, marginal profit, total number of customers, etc.) moving in the right direction, all at the same time.

KPIs of all units should be shown openly to all other units so that everyone knows how everyone else is measured. In TMRW, for instance, each leadership team member presented their unit and individual KPIs and also specified the co-operation needed from other leadership team members to meet their own outcomes. We then examined if the KPIs of those whose co-operation was needed were sufficient to elicit the required support. These actions helped create a culture focused on joint success that was well balanced with individual specialisation and achievement. This approach of focus on the collective that is well-balanced with focus on the individual should be a consistent theme, e.g., performance management is done by individual people managers, but the leadership team also reviews all the key roles across the board.

In TMRW, for example, the managing and executive directors would jointly review, comment and debate on the performance of the senior vice-presidents. An HR colleague recalled that this "created joint ownership, helped to break down the silos, and to be rated highly, you had to have consistently good performance in the eyes of many, not just in the eyes of a few. It gives your team a sense of one-mindedness that will encourage everyone to make it their responsibility to help others be successful, and a sense that everyone in the leadership team must collectively own the talent pool. And because the KPI-setting and communications were robust, the performance management discussions were robust, and the people development discussions were also robust, there was a huge focus on continuously improving the standard of talent and performance."

There was also a collective KPI for the HQ-based regional leadership team on customer-centricity, where the leadership team was asked to personally get involved in an activity that would help them know more about TMRW's customers.

Leadership

We have discussed already the need for the leader to take a systems thinking approach. Any digital transformation in a sizeable company will be complex, and thus understanding how one decision affects another is the key role of the leader – one that is very hard to delegate. Besides systems thinking, the type of leaders to look for are those with three important qualities. First, the leader would have to design and morph the organisation, balancing co-ordination and depth, to provide the breadth of coverage to ensure co-ordination across units, but also the expertise to solve the problems that require technical depth. Second, the leader would have to possess the ability to spark innovation. And third, we were looking for balanced leaders to successfully navigate the complexities inherent in large digital transformation projects. Finally, we close on the topic of creating an open environment that creates a powerful feedback loop for the leader to reflect and self-correct. It isn't about being right all the time; it's about adapting your approach as the situation evolves and ensuring decision making gets better over time.

Co-ordination and depth

Many digital transformation initiatives involve the use of digital capabilities to dramatically improve customer experience. This requires a lot of co-ordination of activity across the entire customer journey to ensure a frictionless, consistent, high-quality experience. Breadth units rely heavily on methodology like design thinking, Agile-at-scale and Lean Six Sigma, project management, change management, etc., to bridge across other units. At the same time, some areas need depth or need new depth to be developed, for example in the use of data to engage customers or designing a highly responsive chat and call centre to provide great support. Figure 89 shows four possible configurations of units within an organisation charged with transformation. Technology is not depicted in the diagram but consists of two components: the Agile programme management and business-facing components in the breadth unit; and application development, infrastructure, core systems, etc. in the depth unit.

This structure provides the depth required to solve the tough problems you will encounter along the way. For example, TMRW required assembling the relevant expertise to build a self-service kiosk for authentication as no bank had done such a kiosk before; or trying to have the onboarding finished in 10 minutes in Jakarta,

Co-ordination vs Depth Matrix

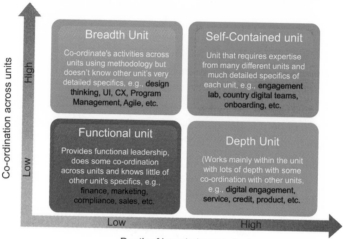

Figure 89 – Co-ordination vs depth

which required us to be able to handle bandwidth degradation as customers moved around.

However, this structure doesn't have one single owner, as there are many joint accountabilities. At times the only person who can see how all the many jigsaw puzzle pieces can fit together will be you, the overall leader. So, to attempt to alleviate this, it was necessary to co-ordinate the activities across all units. In the design-heavy phase, split weekly discussions into process and content meetings. Innovation requires both, and simply focusing on the content and ignoring the process won't result in a successful innovation outcome. "Innovation almost never fails due to a lack of creativity. It's almost always because of a lack of discipline" (Keeley et al., 2017). It is therefore essential that the leader ensures that the balance of content and process – using the co-ordination vs depth element – is well embedded in the fabric of the people & leadership dimension.

These meetings in TMRW were originally all-hands meetings; after the launch, we relaxed the requirement for all staff to attend. I insisted that everyone involved attend the meetings, and there was pushback for making so many people attend, but they served the purpose of breaking barriers between teams and helped in understanding one another's pains. It also served to keep us focused on the big picture. And I requested staff not to do their own work at these meetings, so everyone had to huddle together to discuss. The younger members of the team enjoyed these meetings as they got to understand the thinking behind the decisions we made, something they felt they rarely got to witness. The senior staff did voice concerns over the time taken, as some discussions could stretch to 3 hours.

The need to synchronise and co-ordinate in the build phase will outweigh the productivity loss of wide attendance. So, persist in greater involvement across meetings, because staff can't be motivated if they don't understand the impact of their work on the overall outcome. And because you will have many streams of work running in parallel, only by bringing everyone together can they see how their actions drive the overall performance of your transformation. These meetings are also an opportunity to communicate your thoughts, to inspire the team, to get them to ask why, so that you can pique their curiosity, and challenge them to come up with better ways to improve the overall performance.

Fostering innovation

Fostering innovation is a key task of the accountable executive that is very hard to delegate. In my view, the are three important ingredients – **people, process and leadership** – required to create a great environment that fosters innovation, as illustrated in Figure 90.

Figure 90 – Innovation requires people, process and leadership

People

You naturally can't deliver any innovation without people. We cover a lot of the attributes you should look out for when hiring in the section on "How to Hire?" later in this chapter. Here, I would like to focus specifically on two attributes specific to innovation, **high persistent** and **high experimenting**. This is part of 12 pairs of paradoxical traits that drive certain behaviours in the Paradox Graphs of the Harrison Assessment report (Harrison, 2020). A sample report is shown in Figure 95. These 12 pairs of traits appear to be opposite but are in fact complementary and synergistic.

To be innovative, there must be a good balance of persistent and experimenting. If your key staff charged with innovation are persistent but low on experimenting, they tend to use the same approach without modification, even though it is obvious that the path taken is not yielding results. On the other hand, if experimenting is high and persistent is low, people tend to move quickly to some other approach or idea they think is novel, without the persistence to see any one of them through. And so, to be inventive, your team needs to have both traits at a high level so that they are balanced and versatile in that they can use one or the other trait or both together, if needed. We will cover the paradox graphs and how they're used to develop the balanced leader in greater detail in the balanced leader section.

The other key people factor is diversity, and how to increase it. A diverse pool of talent with different experiences and domain knowledge is superior as it provides a wider collection of vantage points, resulting in more diverse views. Diversity in turn helps create divergent views that yield variance and hence a greater breadth of ideas and solutions that inject more creativity. We had a good mix of bankers and non-bankers (over 30% with non-banking experience), a good mix of nationalities (10 nationalities at the Singapore regional centre), and 50% of staff were millennials. One staff had a PhD in psychology, others worked in design, etc. In the regional centre, we tried to recruit a few staff from Thailand, Indonesia and Vietnam, so that it would be easier to bridge the language and cultural barriers with the intended countries of launch.

Process

Having a diverse team with different skillsets and expertise is one piece of the puzzle. When joined with another piece of the puzzle – having the right processes – both pieces fit neatly together and unlock a higher probability of success. Thus, process is our next ingredient, as it is crucial to innovation and can increase the probability of successful execution. One of the ironies, of course, is that creative people are often poor at process (Chamorro-Premuzic, 2013; Pisano, 2019). But innovation requires creativity because "creativity is the process of bringing something new into being" (May, 1994). To bridge this gap, the leader must ensure equal emphasis on creativity and process. Understanding key business processes helps the senior executive understand the interconnected and interrelated nature of a complex problem, innovation or transformation.

The methods and approaches introduced in this playbook – e.g., desirable-viable-feasible criteria, systems thinking, design thinking, Lean Six Sigma, Agile-at-scale, process and content meetings, stringent programme and project management methods, and 10 types of innovation – are all part of the methodologies that aid in improving process, which in turn improves the probability of successful innovation in your organisation.

These methodologies also help to ensure that properly thought through ideas make it to the next level of filter, hopefully with the most obvious and glaring mistakes caught before the launch. Thus, they help to ensure better ideas float to the top and get executed. And as **innovation is not a one-time event but a continuous process of learning and refinement,** it is also important to institutionalise the learnings and capture these observations, insights and learnings, so that you are constantly improving the probability of success. Without the right processes in place, you can still be innovative, but there is a higher likelihood that you leave things to chance, as shown in Figure 90.

Organisations that focus on people and process without significant leadership emphasis on innovation can still succeed if they focus on fundamental deep-science innovation that is bottom-up in nature. The Innovation Landscape Map by Gary P. Pisano, depicted in Figure 91 illustrates this by dimensioning innovation according to whether it leverages new or existing business models and new or existing technical competences (Pisano, 2015). On the vertical axis is the degree of business model change, while the horizontal axis is the degree of technical competency

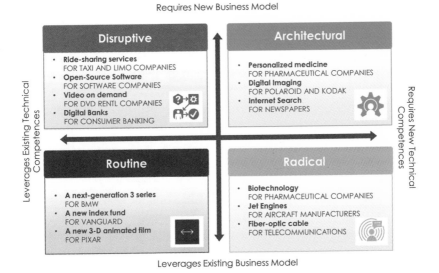

Figure 91 – The innovation landscape map by Gary P. Pisano

change. Using this framework, I would classify building a digital bank from scratch as mostly a disruptive innovation, but if you add leveraging new cloud-based solutions to lower operating costs, then it would shift a little more to the upper right, butting into architectural.

However, if what you are doing is radical, there will usually be a head of R&D or head of engineering that oversees the new technical competences. Thus, in my opinion, radical innovations as defined by Pisano could operate in a bottom-up approach and can have less involvement from the senior leadership. However, disruptive (e.g., a digital bank in an incumbent legacy bank or a digital bank in a new start-up) and architectural innovations require significant leadership participation to spark the innovation required because they involve significant changes to the business model.

Leadership

The final circle in Figure 90 is leadership. This consists of focus in 6 areas: mission, reduction of hierarchy, the right way to be accepting of failure (Figure 38), being unreasonable in goals and at the same time, being motivational and encouraging, so as to create an environment of high challenge and high support. The final factor is systems thinking, a point emphasised in abundance already.

Mission

Mission-orientation makes employees work for more than pay. **It attracts builders who want to change the world** (William, 2018). Quoting Marie-Claire Ross on mission-orientation from a 2015 article: "The reason it is so powerful is because it's the why – the emotional connection the business has to the world. Why the company exists. It's an outside-in perspective, rather than the more common inside-out approach used by most organisations. Humans are emotional beings and they buy-in to their workplace based on how much the purpose resonates with their own values. It also creates a high-performance environment" (Ross, 2015). Thus, continuously finding opportunities to remind your team of their joint purpose found in your mission is the first consideration for the leader seeking to foster innovation.

According to Imperative's research, purpose-oriented employees are 54% more likely to stay at a company for more than 5 years and 30% more likely to be high performers than those who work for a pay cheque. Employees who love their jobs are more productive, loyal and cost the company less over the long term (Ross, 2015). We discuss more about mission and its role in attracting talent in Chapter 5.4.3.

One interesting point about the mission and its impact on the right innovative culture is that your focus should first be tilted towards strong co-ordination of innovation activity to create the right customer experience. In an experience-led business, **bottom-up uncoordinated innovation doesn't help, as you can end up**

with proposals that run up against each other, e.g., an innovative way to market the product may confuse the customer about what he or she is getting.

The mandatory bundling of the debit card in TMRW was one such example. Customers had to have credentials (the 16-digit number and expiry date) that could be used to reset the TMRW password if they forgot both their password and the secure PIN[76]. In Thailand, however, there is little usage of debit cards, as there is a skew is towards credit and cash. Many customers who have a debit card can actually pay for their purchases in-store using it, but they don't. They prefer to withdraw cash from an ATM and pay cash instead. So, while the debit card was a convenient way to provide credentials, making the debit card mandatory caused confusion as customers could not understand its purpose, even when it was communicated. In addition, many users didn't even activate the debit card, and thus when they wanted to reset the TMRW PIN, they found that it didn't work as they didn't realise that they had to activate the card first. These problems were all quickly fixed but they demonstrate the need for great co-ordination.

During the build phase, it is important to set aside time to sweat the details. These details are crucial to ensure that the experience is well thought through and synchronised well across the end-to-end customer journey. Eventually when a very high NPS® is achieved, then building on that base, with the safeguards that the servicing and process units within customer experience would review all new processes, features or promotions, you can **begin to introduce initiatives that involve more ground-up innovation**, where co-ordination is still crucial but more leeway to encourage creativity can be used to foster bottom-up innovation.

One such example was the beta launch of the real-time expense tracking module in TMRW. As not all features were ready or certain, testing it with customers first in a beta provided valuable feedback as to what customers wanted before the actual launch. This helps to reduce risk of failure in an area that many have tried but most have failed. Thus, the culture of innovation is also about allowing the team the freedom to come up with solutions to the problems at hand, and to embrace greater collaboration across teams to solve problems together, which doesn't always happen in a company that is siloed into departments and where hierarchy demands a command-and-control approach.

Reduce hierarchy

Many companies are hierarchical. The point is not that a flat or zero hierarchy is always better for innovation. Many researchers into this topic have found that **hierarchy has merits in the selection of ideas for onward progress towards innovation**

---

76. Secure PIN: PIN generated by a software token within the banking app as an additional security for higher-risk transactions, which can be used to reset the TMRW password.

but is less effective in the origination of novel ideas that feed the former process (Bunderson & Sanner, 2018; Keum & See, 2017). The point about hierarchy is that it blunts challenge. And without challenge, the best thoughts don't float to the top because sufficient challenge is required for the best ideas to survive.

There is a very simple way to reduce hierarchy in your organisation. Create an environment where curiosity is valued and promote this relentlessly. For example, I constantly emphasised the need for everyone to question and ask "why". This was underscored by an unwritten rule that required the most senior person in the room to answer the most junior person's "why". This simple act reduced hierarchy, as it signalled that no matter your seniority, your thoughts were open to challenge, which meant more robust debates and better decisions.

It is extremely important that the top leader creates an environment where everyone knows that there is no penalty for proper and well-thought views and opinions that are different from those of more senior colleagues in the discussion phase. At the same time, it is critical that the leader protect the environment from any individual whose behaviours run against the values needed for the culture to thrive. This creates a situation where highly grounded viewpoints and opinions can be sourced throughout the organisation. This is hard to achieve as the penalty for opposition of authority may not be visual but is nevertheless often perceived as fatal to one's career.

Only by repeated reinforcement and exemplification can one achieve such an environment. It does not mean that if there are two equally good arguments that the leader cannot select the argument he or she favours. It simply makes the selection of an inferior approach or position much more difficult, which helps to ensure that decisions are well-debated and considered most of the time, especially in areas that have catastrophic consequences if a wrong decision is made, e.g., segment selection.

Accepting of failure

No one takes risks if the leader is not accepting of failure. Yet the leader cannot be accepting of any failure. This topic is covered in Chapter 4.6 "Learning as a differentiator". The essence is better identification of risks and what could go wrong. The most basic risks can usually be identified either through prior experience or by checking with someone who has done it or is an expert in the area. Known risks can be extrapolated to an unknown situation. This method leaves the unexpected risk or error as a learning yet eliminates carelessness and allows for failures that have been well thought through.

High challenge and high support

Finally, being unreasonable in goals and yet highly motivational and encouraging at the same time is required to create an environment of high challenge and high support. Examples of being unreasonable in goals to create a high challenge situation in TMRW include pushing the team to create an app interface that was very different. I recall a conversation with Aurelie L'Hostis in 2019, who was the senior analyst for Forrester that examined mobile banking in Europe. After a presentation I did in Barcelona, Aurelie commented that the TMRW interface was very different from anything she had seen, and this was a great compliment given how many mobile banking interfaces she sees every year (L'Hostis, 2019). This was not by accident but by design.

The unreasonable goal was to create an app interface that didn't have any first-level menus, as menus are a sign of complexity in an interface. The other example of an unreasonable goal was to design the onboarding in Jakarta such that even when the mobile network was congested and data speed slow, there would still only be very few cases where the onboarding could not proceed. To do this, the team had to significantly reduce the bandwidth required, by making the video one-way, using the latest compression techniques, streamlining the information required during the video itself by asking for some information before the video began, etc. To balance this challenge in goals, you must be equally focused on your motivational skills and provide encouragement for the team, constantly reminding them that they are doing work no one has done, e.g., pioneering work to build the world's most proactive digital bank.

The analogy I often used throughout the journey was that of the builders of the great pyramids. The builders are cutting, hauling and fitting stone blocks all day, day

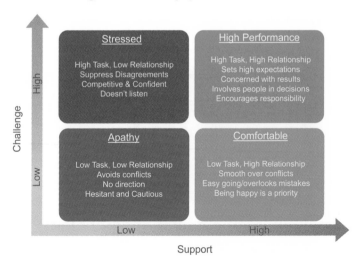

Figure 92 – Creating a high-performance environment

in and day out. You will have to find all kinds of ways to keep them focused on the belief that they are building something that will stand the test of time, as when they are long gone, what they are building will still be there, a testimony of their conviction and perseverance. This is how you get everyone to be in the high-performance quadrant in Figure 92.

Systems thinker

By now, it must be plainly apparent that the difficulty arising from a large digital innovation or transformation initiative lies in the interconnected nature of the dimensions, elements and considerations of The allDigitalfuture Playbook™, and that these interactions produce circular loops that require many trade-offs.

Systems thinking is the last point in the repertoire of behaviours and competences needed to be a transformational leader who can spark innovation. Systems thinking is an approach to understanding interconnected systems, or in this case, dimensions and elements and how they interact with each other. We discussed the causal loop brought about by such circular interacting elements in Figure 43, when we first introduced the playbook and now it's fitting to come full circle to address this issue in the leadership dimension, as it falls on the leader to recognise the requirement for a systems approach and take responsibility for it as the chief orchestrator and integrator of the programme.

Systems thinking is difficult, as you need to consider the circular interaction and causation of multiple components. Linear thinking dominates in business, and there is a role for it because to be successful at dealing with complexity, you must be good at both linear and systems thinking.

Figure 93 summarises the key differences between linear and systems thinking (Ollhoff & Walcheski, 2006). I would clarify that there is a place for breaking things into component pieces, where circular effects are not major.

LINEAR VS. SYSTEMS THINKING	
Linear Thinkers	**Systems Thinkers**
Break things into component pieces	Are concerned with the whole
Are concerned with content	Are concerned with process
Try to fix symptoms	Are concerned with the underlying dynamics
Are concerned with assigning blame	Try to identify patterns
Try to control chaos to create order	Try to find patterns amid the chaos
Care only about the content of communication	Care about content but are more attentive to interactions and patterns of communication
Believe organizations are predictable and orderly	Believe organizations are unpredictable in a chaotic environment

Source: The Systems Thinker, Making the Jump To Systems Thinking by JIM OLLHOFF, MICHAEL WALCHESK

Figure 93 – Linear vs systems thinking

Underlying TaP is a systems approach. At first glance, it can be intimidating. The playbook's 4 dimensions lead to 19 elements, which further lead to at least 56 considerations. That's a lot of complexity, drill-down and interactions. But hey, the real word is complex, and one of the factors that determine how successful you are is your comfort with the ambiguity that these dimensions, elements and considerations cause.

The allure of a cheat sheet has a lot of appeal today, e.g., just follow these 5 tips. Articles on the internet now even tell you how long it will take to read these cheat sheets. But a cheat sheet is self-defeating in my view because with systems thinking, you are concerned with the whole rather than just breaking things down into "quick wins" that may not serve you well in the long term. Unfortunately, the ease of googling the internet and shorter attention spans have magnified the popularity of cheat sheets in business and management.

To start on the right path, you need to both break things into their component pieces but also look at how the components across your entire initiative interact with one another, and thus the trade-offs you need to make, as optimising one consideration often leads to a non-optimal state for another consideration. A simple example here is just focusing on revenue without looking at costs, or just focusing on total revenue and costs without understanding marginal revenue and costs. It may sound very simple, but lots of very experienced senior executives might be tempted to tell you not to look at things in an unnecessarily complex way. You will need to focus on both process and content. You will have to understand the root cause and not fixate on the symptoms of the problem. If you can focus on these key items, you will start well. A good way to navigate this complexity is to constantly refer to Figures 54, 64 and 83, which illustrate the circular interactions between the different dimensions.

Figure 94 – Traits that enable systems thinking

Figure 94 shows the traits that you would ideally be looking for in your top executive and the team one level below (Davidz et al., 2005; Snow, 2020). These skills when used in conjunction with TaP will be a very powerful weapon to ensure the success of your digital transformation or innovation programme. Note that tolerance for ambiguity appears in both Figures 94 and 68. Your comfort with ambiguity, and not succumbing to the need to solve problems too quickly or too slowly, is one of the keys to success.

The balanced leader

In the course of launching TMRW in both Thailand and Indonesia, one observation of the leaders I worked with stood out. There are often **seemingly contradictory traits that are needed for success in complex initiatives**. We already discussed persistent vs experimenting. Another obvious pair was organised versus flexible. In starting an initiative from scratch, there is a lot of chaos because there are no systems in place and multiple streams of work are starting at the same time. So, if the pioneers in such an environment are not organised, the situation will be compounded. However, if the team is very organised and not flexible, they will be very rigid, and this doesn't work either. As the team is doing things not done before and learning how to do it, pivoting when you are wrong is essential. Thus, someone who is both organised and flexible will do better as they are able to organise flexibly.

Until a proper means of detecting these paradoxes or "yin and yang" traits surfaced, it wasn't really actionable. The Harrison Assessment and its ability to evaluate these seemingly paradoxical traits can be a good tool for you as you build your own high-complexity digital transformation. The paradox graphs are unique in their ability to assess these seemingly paradoxical traits, and are not found in any other assessment, to my knowledge. The 12 paradox graphs in Figure 95 are organised so that the rows represent the 4 stages of doing any task.

The starting point is the concept or **initiating**, where the focus is on getting the concept correct. This involves opinions (how you form and hold opinions, including how you deal with ambiguity), decision approach (how you use logic and intuition when making decisions) and strategic (how you strategically manage risk).

Once the concept is done, the leader must motivate himself or herself and call upon others to join the team to start the execution. Harrison calls this the **motivating** stage, where self (how you manage self-esteem and self-improvement), motivation (how you deal with self-motivation and stress) and finally driving (how you manage rapport and empathy when managing the performance of others) are the key paradoxes.

Once you and the team are onboard, the **implementing** stage begins. Here, communication (how you manage directness and tactfulness when communicating

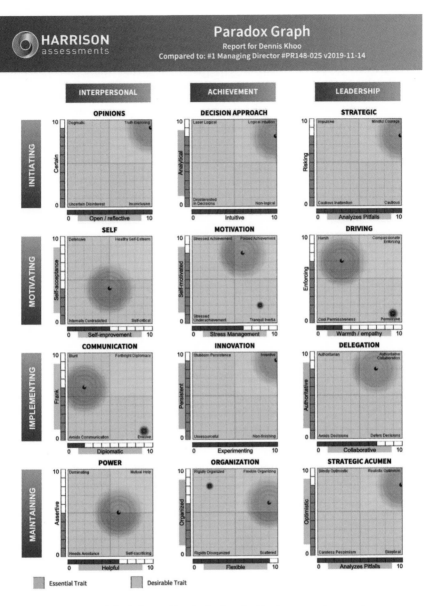

Figure 95 – "The balanced leader" using the Harrison paradox graphs

with others), innovation (how you approach trying new things and overcoming obstacles) and delegation (how you approach self-responsibility and collaboration) become important.

And finally, once implemented, you have to keep things operating smoothly. In the **maintaining** stage, power (how you approach helping others and asserting your needs), organisation (how you deal with adaptability and creating organisation or structure) and strategic acumen (how you approach opportunities and difficulties) are key.

The columns are organised into **interpersonal**, **achievement** and **leadership**. Thus, decision approach is the achievement part of initiating whilst driving is the leadership part of motivating. As there are many streams of work progressing concurrently, each at a different stage, I viewed these paradoxes not as sequential but as a repertoire of traits that leaders use concurrently depending on the discussion.

The **red traits are the aggressive traits**, and the **blue traits are the gentle ones**. Grey tornadoes appear when the red traits are much higher than the blue traits, and red tornadoes appear when the blue traits are much higher than the red ones. The greater the difference between the strength of the red and blue traits, the bigger the tornado. These tornadoes are you under stress, your bad side. Another trait, "manage stress well", determines how often a leader would flip to his stress position. The higher the "manage stress well" number, the less likely the frequency of flipping to the stress position.

This is important as in the end, the leader and his approach are intricately intertwined. Harrison may help you realise what you don't want to acknowledge, what your bad side looks like, and how you behave on a bad day. My Achilles heel is putting honesty above relationship, and this shows up in being much more frank than diplomatic. Knowing which behaviours you lack creates a greater awareness of your blind spots. And so, it's also about knowing yourself and your limitations, and those of your team so you can find people who complement you, making the team as a whole perfect vs the individuals who will always be imperfect.

I would recommend that the Harrison Assessment be used as an additional instrument in the hiring of the CEO and the entire C-suite for a complex digital transformation initiative. This will reduce the risk that the key executives tasked with the project are not sufficiently balanced. The assessment also allows you to look at the balance within the entire C-suite and see how they complement each other.

Open environment

Creating an open environment is vital for you to have a **strong feedback loop**. You may not agree with everything, but you should demonstrate that you are willing to hear things out. Consider making feedback – especially feedback about you from your team – transparent and open. Such feedback could reveal where you are a bottleneck or how you are behind the curve in adapting your approach to rapidly changing situations. This can **promote trust between you and your team** and create a powerful feedback loop that every leader needs, to adjust to the situation at hand.

It certainly does not mean you need to pander to every suggestion or feedback, and it's certainly not about being liked or popular.

As a leader, you must be both **certain and open** (Figure 95) so you minimise your mistakes. Being wrong in a senior role has a much bigger negative impact. Part of doing this is to explore divergent views in the planning stage, and in the end, consider all views that make sense, but not be afraid to make the unpopular decision, if required. The most difficult part will be the use of your intuition and judgement to decide when to slow down and diverge and when to speed up and converge. This can cause problems for those with very strong execution skills. Obviously staying too long in the planning stage is not desirable but slowing down or speeding up is necessary and extremely situational, based on whether the decision is trivial in nature or not reversible without a lot of pain.

A colleague recounts her initial frustration: "The frustration was real in that there were lots of iterations and changing requirements. Initially, we had so many long hours of very intense meetings in a room full of people. And in the beginning, we debated and explored different divergent views and decisions like, should we show all UOB products? Or should we only show TMRW products? Even the kiosks – wall mount or not? What kind of kiosks will we be building? So, it was a lot of planning. In hindsight, we didn't rush to build, and I eventually came round to the fact that it was more important to get the planning right. But for somebody with very strong execution strength like me, it was very difficult."

If someone disagreed with me, I didn't take it personally. You disagree with the idea or the proposal – and always with a good, stated reason – and not the individual. Feedback about me, like **360-degree feedback**, was always done in the open. This is one way you can create a feedback loop and obtain the input needed to reflect and self-correct, where necessary. Figure 96 shows two of many questions I asked my leadership team to provide to obtain feedback about myself. Q3 indicated that I was making too many decisions. There was probably a good reason for this, and it should be evident at this point in the book. The accountable senior executive is the conductor of the orchestra. It is only from his vantage point that he can and should see how all the dots are connected – a task often made very difficult by the lack of a map of these dots. Based on this feedback, however, maybe it was time after the design-heavy phase was over to ease off, so we held a decision-making retreat in Sentosa. It was basically a "What should be escalated to Dennis and what should not" workshop. We decided that whatever affected customers or the launch timeline would still come to me. The rest of the items would go to the programme management office.

In an initiative that requires a lot of attention to detail and co-ordination, you can overdo the degree to which you need to align activities, resulting in your team feeling that the trust level is low. The other question, Q4, was about trust and confidence.

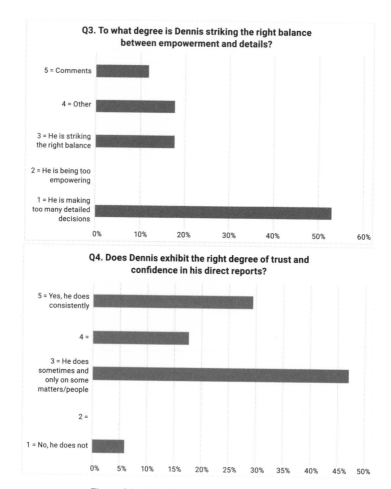

Figure 96 – 360-degree feedback in the open

I wanted to see how to improve the overall scores. So, I asked those who gave me a 4 or 5 rating to compare notes with those who gave me a 3 while I left the room, returning only when they had a recommendation. This approach didn't work out the way it was supposed to, as the team couldn't come to a conclusion or didn't want to tell me the conclusion. But based on my discussions with the participants after the workshop, more of the team who had lower executional abilities tended to be the 3 scorers. TMRW is firstly an initiative that is reliant on creating an experience from doing the small things well, and then secondly an experiment in making digital engagement through many conversations with customers a breakthrough and reality. In such a case, attention to detail is paramount, and thus those whose executional details were weaker often faced tougher scrutiny, leading them to conclude that the trust level was lower, whilst those whose executional abilities were very strong often got to execute with very few questions asked. Still, it made me reflect what I could do to give this message in a way that motivated rather than demotivated the team, and I started to put that into practice.

An HR colleague, who worked closely with us, reflected on my leadership style: "I would say Dennis is the stoic leader. He is a person who can endure pain or hardship without showing much feelings or complaining. He's not the warm and fuzzy type, but he can make fun of himself, and takes the time to write personal notes to his team to thank them, and not just a thank you, but a personalised note to everyone. Very few leaders do that. And as you get to know him, you begin to feel comfortable because of the safe environment he creates in his consistency of values and behaviours. It's in the simple things like texting you when he remembers something in the weekend, so it doesn't escape him, but realising that it's the weekend, being very understanding if you don't get back till Monday."

"When TMRW's Indonesia digital head joined, Dennis made it a point to fly down and spend the day orienting him and making sure he started well. When one of the country marketing heads was frustrated and wanted to quit, Dennis called her from halfway round the world to speak to her personally. Then there was the constant encouraging of those who disagreed to speak up, to challenge and to make the right mistakes. The consistency showed again in that there were no repercussions for those who had a different viewpoint and debated them well. Not being a natural in quickly getting people comfortable, Dennis nevertheless held a lot of skip-level meetings to get to know the people better, even though it was very time-consuming. And the constant reflection along the way, to celebrate success, to understand what brought us this far. The willingness to be a coach and focus on developing each individual leader even if they didn't work directly for him."

As an INTJ[77] (The Myers-Briggs Company, 2020), I am at once surprised I have made it so far and dismayed occasionally that I have not made it further. Small-talk, making others feel comfortable and warmth-empathy are not the strong suit of the INTJ. We find it hard to understand why people associate kindness with niceness, when sometimes the worst kinds tend to be the nicest. But over the years, I have come to recognise that the INTJ is easily misunderstood, and have adjusted my behaviour, and remind myself of this all the time.

Here's Gemma reflecting on her experience in the 3 years she was involved in TMRW: "What made a huge difference was that as a leader, Dennis took great pains to understand his one-downs and made sure we all understood the intent, in order for us to bring that message to our own teams. The message from him was always, 'Please update the teams and be transparent with them'. If we could convince our

---

77. INTJ (introverted, intuitive, thinking, and judging) is one of the 16 personality types identified by a personality assessment called the Myers-Briggs Type Indicator (MBTI). Sometimes referred to as the Architects or the Strategists, people with INTJ personalities are highly analytical, creative and logical. Source: verywellmind.com

own team, then it would make everyone understand and follow the vision and mission diligently. It always starts from the top. The leader needs to understand the strengths that each one of us brings to the table. Only when leaders take sincere interest in the development of their teams can people shine. For Dennis, he would go to great lengths to upgrade our knowledge, our leadership style, coach us and remind us to look at the big picture. When that kind of leadership is in place, the rest of the staff will follow suit. This drove a healthy culture for the good of the entire TMRW digital team. Being happy at work brings more joy to the workplace and to those working with us."

Talent gap

You need the people to work the plans you have now created. Product managers, developers, programme managers, project managers, customer experience staff, user interface designers, data analysts, developers, scrum masters, Agile coaches, marketing, etc. Initially when we started, we had fewer than 10 staff in the TMRW team. Contrast this to the peak of the build, when we had a few hundred staff, both permanent and contracted headcounts. This was a massive growth and hiring exercise!

The ability to **draw talent by telling a great story about how you plan to change the world** is our starting point. The secret is your story, your conviction and your personal reputation. I've found that if all are strong, it is very possible to attract the right talent to fill the most difficult roles. Thomas Davenport and Thomas Redman, experts in the field of digital transformation, recommend that you pay particular attention to 4 key areas: **organisational change, process, data and technology** (Davenport & Redman, 2020). They describe very aptly their thinking in this interesting analogy: Technology is the engine of digital transformation, data is the fuel, process is the guidance system, and organisational change capability is the landing gear. You need them all, and they must function well together. The lack of talent in these 4 areas is one of the contributing factors in failed digital transformations.

Even if you find the right talent, there is a constant need to grow and develop them to keep pace with changes. There was a lot of focus on developing individuals by understanding and strengthening the competences for the role and aligning the values-behaviour of each of the leadership team members. Using Gallup StrengthsFinder for role competences and Harrison Assessments for role and values-behaviour alignment allowed us to tailor development plans for specific individuals, whilst constantly improving how the leadership came together as a team.

Current vs needed

Once your core competence gaps have been derived and with your key design considerations as a guide, you are ready to start drafting a bill of roles that would be needed. You must clearly specify the roles and responsibilities of each position in a properly written job description. The job description is then used to derive the qualities needed. For example, customer process designers design the end-to-end business process to support the desired experience for your customers (role). This position requires immense attention to detail (traits or attributes). The interview guide must contain a question that seeks to determine the presence of this attribute, e.g., "Tell us about a time you helped create a complex customer journey. How did you keep track of all the little details? How did you recall things that were discussed and debated? How did you ensure that the experience was smooth?" We also sent all the managers who needed to hire a lot of staff to interview trainings again to refresh them on the best ways to match a candidate's technical and cultural fit for the role.

A weekly tracker of jobs that needed to be filled versus the actual number filled was created, and weekly meetings on the gap in the hiring traction were carried out with all stakeholders. We painstakingly went through each hiring requirement, to understand the challenges (if any) and how we should tackle them. These robust and regular discussions helped correct any shortfall in hiring. In senior hires (senior vice-president and above), we had only two people we parted ways with and one person who resigned because he found he wasn't a good fit.

Gemma remembers she had to keep updating the weekly hiring tracker spreadsheet, chasing the countries and various COE units to update the people tracker. We had a discussion early on about the delays in hiring, and we did an analysis into how candidates were funnelled into the system to find out all the bottlenecks. To make things happen faster, we tracked the candidate pipeline, which part of the process the candidates were in, and how long they stayed there. With this regular tracking, and identification of the bottlenecks (i.e., was it in getting the suitable pool of candidates to interview, or difficulty in securing the interviews, or uncertainty around the fit, etc.), it was very clear if you were behind on your hiring, and what help was needed.

Hire vs buy

One of the issues you will encounter is that there is a point in the project where you will need peak resourcing to deliver the initiative. This usually happens at the end of the design and build phase. You won't need as many resources later, and hence determining where you have contracted help, and where you tap in-house permanent hires is crucial, so as not to over-hire and either have too big an annual fixed cost or have to let many staff go at the end of the build phase. Much of this variance between peak and run-phase resources is likely to be in the software development, software development support, testing and release teams.

If your new digital unit is not a separate company but a start-up within an incumbent entity, then you will need to manage a situation where not everyone reports to you directly. So, your structure[78] is likely to consist of direct staff whose cost and reporting lines are to you (e.g., business, product, partnership, marketing, etc.), direct staff whose costs are with you but cannot report to you because they are part of a control function that oversees what you do (e.g., compliance, legal, credit, etc.) and third, indirect staff with no formal reporting, whose cost you don't carry directly but are billed to you indirectly (e.g., technology and operations). Finally, there are contracted staff through third-party agencies that may be billed directly to your costs (e.g., testers, temporary help, administrators, etc.), and contracted staff not reporting formally that are part of indirect costs (e.g. software developers, tech analysts, Agile coaches, etc.).

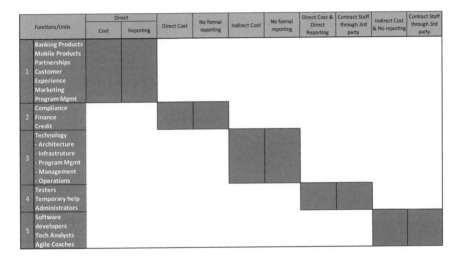

Figure 97 – Cost and reporting alignment to TMRW across various units

Figure 97 shows these 4 categories of staff. For the staff whose direct and indirect costs are billed to you but there is no formal reporting, this structure allows you to leverage staff and obtain support within the mothership, which might lower the overall cost burden in exchange for higher complexity. Some of these senior staff will be part of your management committee, but they will be the ones who are going to miss some meetings because they don't report directly to you. Thus, positional authority can only go so far, and the ability to influence them personally is critical to your success. This may mean going out of your way to establish a personal relationship with them.

If I were to go back to the time we started, the only thing I would change is to

78. This assumes you are an "independent" unit within a larger company. Naturally, if you are a separate company, all reporting lines would be to the CEO, simplifying this consideration significantly.

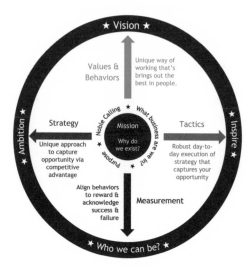

Figure 98 – How to inspire and attract talent

have some of the third group of resources (#3 in Figure 97) in my direct costs rather indirect costs. A lot of time was spent discussing headcount costs, which tended to drag things out without much accomplished. Everything else worked well and I don't think they require any additional tweaking.

Internal vs external

Building a start-up bank, Fintech or any other from-the-ground-up initiative has the issue that everything needs to be created, and thus the chaos that ensues, the learning curve, the additional costs, are all higher if there isn't leverage from an existing mothership. Also, there are roles that need to serve as interface to the mothership organisation. This is crucial as the support for your programme from the mothership will be important. Therefore, for the programme management role, marketing role and customer experience role, which required significant interfacing with the incumbent organisation, I handpicked internal staff who knew their way around the incumbent organisation.

For the banking product role, I had hoped I would be able to source internally, but there were no takers, so I rehired an ex-staff and brought in an experienced senior product manager. I recall trying to hire a head of products, and thought I found one, but when these two product managers interviewed him, they didn't feel a connection, so I decided not to proceed and just manage it directly, until I was able to promote the senior product manager into the head role. Partly because it was difficult to convince internal UOB candidates to join, as a lot of them wanted roles

#	Attribute	Description	Question to detect	Rating 1	2	3	4	5
1	Persistence	Comfort in an environment of change. Takes ambiguity in stride. Tenacity to move on with positivity, when there is a change in direction. Does not give up easily.	1. Tell us about the most chaotic time in your career. What was the situation and how did you manage. 2. What was ambiguous? How did you feel? How did you cope? 3. When there was a change in direction, how did you feel? How did you cope? 4. Describe a time when your sheer persistence paid off in a difficult situation.	Could not articulate clearly	Did not demonstrate tenacity in the face of difficulty	Had difficulty coping but survived	Demonstrated ability to work with ambiguity, and was tenacious in handling the situation	Demonstrated mastery in resilience on multiple occasions
2	Continuous Learning	Curious and interested in area of domain but also outside. Has a thirst for knowledge and insight that brings fresh ideas and perspectives	1. When was the last time you read something that made you curious to know more? 2. If you are given an assignment you don't know anything about, what will you do? 3. Tell us about the last time you brough a fresh idea to the table.	Could not articulate clearly	Sticks to familiar ground. Interest range is narrow. Seldom brings something fresh	On occasion has the spark but would not be considered someone that is curious and willing to go for the unfamiliar	Curious and willing to learn but to a limit. Very unfamiliar territory scares this candidate.	A curious, enquiring mind. Constantly hungry to learn. Very willing to accept new learning challenges
3	Bold	Not afraid to respectfully disagree or be the lone voice of dissent when appropriate. Able to challenge status quo without putting others down.	1. Think back to a time when you had a view different from everyone else. Tell us about the situation and what you did. 2. When's the last time you challenged the status quo? Tell us what happened. 3. Think back to a difficult conversation with your staff. Why was it difficult and how did you handle it? 4. Think back to a difficult conversation with your boss. Why was it difficult and how did you handle it?	Could not articulate clearly	Generally will go with the crowd. Could not articulate any really difficult situations	On occasion has expressed dissenting voice on an area that is safe. Generally plays the safe game.	Able to provide examples of difficult conversations but either immature in approach or backed down when challenged further	Demonstrated mastery in ability to speak up even if everyone one else doesn't. Mature in approach when disagreeing.
4	Team Work	Collaborative, shares ideas, celebrates others' success, builds effective working relationships, not afraid or jealous of the success of others	1. Tell us the last time you worked in a group. What was the assignment? Describe who was in your team? What were they like? How did you connect with them? Strengths and Weaknesses of the group. 2. Describe how you build on others ideas to make them better. 3. Describe a time when someone in your workgroup was recognised instead of you.	Could not articulate clearly	Focuses on himself or herself. Does not give credit when due, mostly complains about others	Participates but does not stand ground in controversial topics. Prefers to play it safe to maintain relationships	Builds on others ideas. Willing to concede points where ground is not as solid as opposing viewpoint. Challenges in tactful way.	Willing to let others shine and take the limelight. Able to handle disagreements tactfully. Knows when to lose the battle to win the war.
5	Communicates Succinctly	Gets points across clearly and succinctly. Approachable and engaging. Discussions are two-way. Listens actively to points of view different from your own.	1. Pick a topic of interest to you, and tell us the most salient points that we need to know about that topic in the least number of words so that we know a lot about it. 2. How do you listen to understand rather than listen to rebut?	Could not articulate clearly	Tends to be very long winded and veer off the point. Shows signs that he or she is not confident.	Does not get to the point quickly enough. Not listening intently enough to understand clearly	Articulate but isn't as succinct as can be. Mostly confident but at times seem to lose it.	Engaging, confident but not over-confident. Able to use the least amount of words to express a complex idea.
6	Responsible and Accountable	Takes ownership to ensure quality and timely delivery, proud of outputs, explores all options for a quality solution, detail oriented, balances strategy and execution	1. Tell us a time time you were accountable for an initiative and how you went about managing it? 2. What did you do when things went offtrack? 3. How did you ensure that things would run smoothly? 4. When do you look at the big picture and when do you look at the small details?	Could not articulate clearly	Was not able to demonstrate that he or she was on top of the situation and was able to get things under control	Does know the details as much as he or she should. Ownership seems spotty and isn't the driver or champion he could be.	Appears to know most of the details but there are gaps. Not equally focus on the strategy and tactics, preferring one or the other.	Demonstrates responsibility and accountability across all aspects of delivery. Able to articulate the details clearly and has spent time on both the strategy and tactics.
7	Systems Thinking	Seeks to understand the big picture, identifies and understands circular interactions in complex systems, thinks ahead, can see things at a macro level as well as micro level	1. What's the most complex work related initiative you have been involved with? 2. What were the moving parts? 3. How did you understand the interrelated impact each part had on another part?	Could not articulate clearly	Tends to look at things in a siloed and compartmentalised way.	At times able to connect the dots, but mostly overwhelmed by complexity, and unable to link cause and effects across the entire system	Most times able to connect the dots and see the bigger picture and understand the system. But, doesn't think ahead sufficiently.	Proven ability to connect the dots and see the forest for the trees, yet able to single out the tree if needed. Thinks ahead. Equally adept at the micro

Figure 99 – Important core attributes

that were more certain, and partly to infuse staff that had a difference perspective, we ended up with 85% external hires.

How to hire?

There will be a shortage of talent. However, it doesn't mean you can't hire. It's all about your story. The first rule I have discovered is that the builders you need in the build phase care more about your purpose (mission) and your ambition (vision). They will be moved by it, and by your values and how you want to create a conducive environment for them to thrive. If it's just about making money or you're just narrowly focused on your business, you severely handicap your ability to attract them.

Figure 98 shows one approach to get better at inspiring and attracting the talent you need. We covered most of this construct in Chapter 5.4.1. We put it to good use here by using it as your platform to attract the new hires you need. We start at the centre, your mission. The key is to make it a noble calling that will serve the greater good, e.g., to proactively help future generations of young men and women manage their finances better so that they can lead purposeful lives. The next step is your ambition, depicted in the outer circle. It answers the question, "If we serve our purpose extremely well, who should we aspire to be?" – e.g., to be the world's most proactive bank for millennials everywhere.

If you articulate your mission and vision well enough, you should get the attention of the candidate who answers to this calling to do something different and meaningful. If not, then maybe he or she isn't the right person. You then need to follow up with how you plan to get from your purpose to your ambition. To do this, articulate the values and behaviours you will foster to create an environment that will be very conducive to achieving that aim, your strategy and key tactics, and how you will measure your success along the way.

If you are part of a much bigger company, you may need to short-circuit the typical hiring processes that many companies have. An HR colleague recalls a time when we were discussing a particularly difficult role to fill, because of the unique talent required: "I remember attending a meeting to discuss the difficulty in filling a certain role with my talent acquisition colleague. We were discussing the traditional channels when Dennis whipped out his iPad and there and then started looking at LinkedIn profiles that he thought might be suitable and projected it on the meeting room's screen. We immediately started targeting potential candidates and got to work. It's hard to explain, but both my colleague and I were feeling super charged after the meeting. There was this sense of enthusiasm, persistence, a never-give-up attitude that rubbed off on us and created this collective excitement."

Once you have a candidate in sight, how do you link what success looks like to the core attributes needed for that success. Figure 99 shows a possible core attributes list for your digital transformation that you can leverage. It has been created from scratch from my experience looking for the right qualities for hiring change agents over the years. I looked at candidates that didn't make it and I had to let go of, and those that excelled, and I distilled the **attributes which made some hires more successful than others**. This is an important codification of the kind of talent you want to attract, and time and time again, I found that I could attract them if we had a great and inspiring story to tell.

The dynamics of the pioneer team were such that they were close-knit and thus it was crucial to bring in the new talent we needed fast but also to ensure they didn't damage the camaraderie and existing culture that was powerful and infectious. So, interviews included other leadership team members even if the candidates didn't report to them to get wider views across the board, and to size them up for competence, attributes and cultural fit. During lunch after the interviews, the interviewers would debate and decide on the final candidate. This allowed TMRW to hit the nail on the head for hiring most times.

Another colleague involved in a lot of TMRW's hiring reflected on the difficult positions to fill: "We ran a market mapping exercise for Head of Digital Bank in Vietnam and Indonesia, using a market mapping company. This created a wide list of eligible candidates within and outside the usual candidates and industries. We did a briefing session with them and narrowed the long list down to a shortlist. Dennis flew down to interview the candidates and found that broadening the pool of candidates greatly helped in identifying the right candidates."

Gemma was always better than me at reading people, having significantly greater warmth and empathy. After making a few hiring mistakes, I would always try and bring her into a senior hire meeting to ask her for her feel of the person. She recalls the difficulty of getting the right people for the job: "Dennis decided to relook at the way we interviewed potential candidates and that was to include other leaders or team members that were not the direct reporting manager. After all, we were a high-functioning team with strong cross-collaboration and the new hires would definitely interact with others. So I was roped in to be part of the new process. With this change, I felt there was improvement in candidate selection."

"The questions we asked were also quite challenging and diverse. We would question them about failed experiences and how they managed it. We were not just focused on success stories. That's the easy part, as one can go on about how good they are. We asked questions that made the candidates open up about themselves. For example, "What were your last appraisal review comments and improvement points from your boss and team members? Tell us about a time when you made mistakes? How would your friends describe you? What about your co-workers?" And the list goes on. With a diverse group coupled with a roundtable interview format, we could cover more aspects of the candidate's profile and suitability compared to if it had been only the hiring manager or HR. After that, we would review and have an open conversation about the candidate's profile, especially if he/she had the values that the digital team advocated. That was an important aspect. Afterwards, we would all come to a decision. This process did not take very long and it gave all of us an insight not just about who we were hiring but how we came together as a team to cover what the others may not have picked up."

When it came to attracting candidates, the team developed a microsite listing all the jobs available. All open requisitions for the digital bank would be reflected on this page. Any social media marketing (through Facebook or LinkedIn) would reference this page, and as a call to action, all TMRW roles would be directed there. The hiring process and approval were streamlined, and if the salary fell within the range, approvals were accelerated. This sped up the approval process significantly.

Structure

The final element is structure and environment. This is something very close to the hearts and minds of your staff. It's what affects them day-to-day. Dress down was the standard for TMRW. It was a first for UOB and we set the trend for a more casual environment to eliminate the hierarchy. We wanted to increase consideration for others when we relocated to the SGX building, so there were no personal dustbins for each workstation; instead, all trash was to be placed at the common pantry. All workspaces were shared, so we had to have clean desks. The increased general cleanliness of the office helped to create a sense of belonging. People stopped eating at their desks and cleaned up meeting rooms after meetings and focused more on the thoughts and concerns of others.

Our starting point is the structure to put in place that will ensure a high degree of alignment between your team and the organisation at large. If you are an intrapreneur operating within a large traditional company like a bank, this organisational alignment is extremely crucial. The organisation will tend to reject the "mutant children" of the start-up units as they look different, speak different and, in fact, *are* different – otherwise it defeats the whole purpose.

Organisational alignment

If you are building something with a very different business model in a larger organisation, you are going to be misunderstood. This issue was so prevalent that I used Jeff Bezos' quote very often: "One thing that I tell people is... if you're going to do anything new or innovative, you have to be willing to be misunderstood" (Clifford, 2018). There will be lots of people who won't be able to understand what you are doing. There is certainly no debate that it must be a separate unit not reporting to the current owner of the business, unless this person is mature enough to see the future and wants to do something about it. Such transformations are for the long term, to protect the future when it is still possible to do so.

Most digital transformations are likely to be multi-year, so things can change quickly if the organisation comes under revenue pressure. Such pressures often lead to shorter-term thinking. Even if it is agreed upfront that the goal will only be achieved long-term, and that the profit and loss for the unit is going to look bad as costs more than outweigh revenue initially, people have short memories when the red ink starts coming in. In a traditional bank, there is also likely to be a high capitalised expenditure cost, as internal technology costs are high.

I knew this, so I was a big advocate of using managerial accounting to track and measure marginal cost per customer first. This focuses the larger organisation on the right measures and allows the internal start-up venture to show progress over time. The mothership may not be used to seeing losses over a sustained period and hence ensuring that the right key measures are agreed in advanced and reinforced constantly is vital for good alignment. This position, however, isn't one the mothership business units are used to, and so there will potentially be a lot of dissonance. Sometimes it will feel like a thankless task – after doing everything you were asked to do, and doing it well, the whole premise can still come under attack.

There has to be a senior defender of such bold, long-term initiatives, and it must be the CEO or a very senior C-1 that works for the CEO who is long-tenured and highly respected. No one else will do. There will be many occasions when your team will be depressed by what others say about them. It is human nature to compete, and your new unit with its large investments and small initial revenues may be in the spotlight or crosshairs of others. Disparaging comments may circulate through the grapevine. Such comments can be very disheartening for your team, and you have to shield them as much as you can, but also cheer them on whenever you can.

A strategic, selfless leader who will put the company and the team ahead of himself or herself is a rare commodity. Therefore, having a separate unit reporting to one of the executives I mentioned in the prior paragraph is what you must insist on. It is difficult for some to accept that without the right leadership and culture, the digital bank that I am describing in this book cannot be brought to life. Thus, you must convince your own seniors that **the most crucial starting point is to create a new culture**, one that is innovative, non-hierarchical, focused on customers, etc. It is my belief that the way of working is more important than the savings from having one unit. It is the way of working that attracts the talent and competence needed. In other words, if you just look at output, you can combine for synergy but will lose the right people needed for innovation, as to most builders, the way of working is more important than the output. The traditional bank is not worried if the digital banks fail, but they must be very worried if they succeed.

If you made it this far in the book, I hope I have convinced you that if you are running a traditional bank or any other incumbent facing a digital threat, you can only succeed if you make a radical switch in your proposition and focus, one that is very different from what your traditional competitors offer. And this can only happen if there is a culture that allows this new proposition and focus to be created, to grow and to thrive. So, if you view it this way, then there is no other way but to separate the unit and protect it so it can survive. For an incumbent bank, it is an insurance. All boards should ask for that insurance against a future where a few successful digital banks that get the formula right begin to capture share with a great experience built over the years when they were small and ignored.

That is not to say that all incumbents need to set up a separate company, as that involves higher costs and increases reasons why the incumbent might not want to support the subsidiary. In retrospect, I feel that being a unit within an incumbent can work if there is strong support from the top to protect, nurture and guide it. The benefit of staying within is the ability to leverage capabilities that are not core enough to have within the start-up unit, e.g., treasury, balance sheet management, finance, etc. The downside can be managed by the degree of autonomy accorded to the executive in charge to do what's right.

One of the areas we did well was the clarity of TMRW's approach and the regular updates along the way. The senior management team was regularly updated from the time we started in January 2017 till the launch of TMRW in Thailand on March 2019. These regular updates did a lot to ensure alignment and coherence between TMRW and the mothership. The tech development took about 14 months. The other 10 months were taken to plan it out properly. This alignment around not rushing to launch but to build something truly breakthrough came from the top and turned out to be a great piece of advice. This allowed us the time to think through thoroughly what we needed to build.

Grouping transformational projects like TMRW under a **strategic change programme** is recommended as this means separate budgets, which allows you to be more responsive to the market in hiring, retention, etc., and more flexible in your ability to create a slightly different work environment and subculture.

Organisational structure and design

How you design your organisation is crucial to success, and often not enough thought is put into **how you can design an organisation that supports the strategy you have chosen**. The path TMRW took was one of great customer experience and the use of data to engage customers vs simply relying on the frictionless excellence of the hygiene transactional capabilities. This meant that the requirement was for people to be very fussy about small details, to be able to bring in people with experience in data, databases, and how to leverage data for insight generation. This can be discerned from the 6 key design considerations found in Figure 69. This is a key step in understanding the gaps in the talent needed to execute on these design considerations and bring them to life.

Organisational role design should not be just left to HR. It should be a joint exercise between the senior executive accountable for the initiative and a senior HR executive.

Figure 100 explores the relationship between employee motivation and key company processes (Doshi & McGregor, 2015). Note that Doshi and McGregor found that **role design had the highest probability of being extremely demotivating when done poorly or extremely motivating when done well.**

Figure 100 – Employee motivation vs company processes
(Source: Primed to Perform)

We started with a simple functional model on day one. The existing digital banking team and a handful of other staff moved over, and we continued to support digital banking while building the digital bank from 2017 to mid-2019.

One of my first realisations was that the customer onboarding experience, service and process would be a very difficult set of competences to gain. Traditionally, onboarding, customer experience and service were part of an integrated digital mobile products team. I decided to pull them out as a separate unit, under customer experience. This was long before I was certain that creating advocates through high NPS® and customer experience would be critical measures.

My team had expected onboarding to be part of the mobile digital products team, a more traditional product structure. The lesson here is that it is crucial to go back to the fundamentals and examine what core competences you need from the business dimension, and not be constrained by how things were done before. It is also important to have the right people for the right roles, who understand the different objectives. In those early days, very few knew what customer experience really did. I made the decision despite this, and it turned out to be a very good decision.

This was one of the crucial decisions made early in the programme to build a strong competence in process design, and the fussiness and attention to detail required to design and execute great processes. In TMRW, as a standard, for any product, partnership or onboarding design, the service design team within customer experience would review it so that the design would not create downstream servicing impact.

The organisation was also kept very flat. The maximum span from myself to the most junior person was 3. This helped to ensure that there was a minimum of bureaucracy, and an ability to communicate directly with me if needed. My original concept was to identify areas that would need a lot of depth, and those that would need a lot of co-ordination. It's not to say that there is any unit that doesn't need both to some degree, but I wanted to identify those that needed a lot of either or both to an extent that we never had in the past. I already shared this delineation in Figure 89. The engagement lab, for example, was clearly in the self-contained quadrant, and the onboarding unit as well.

Once the design stage became sufficiently granular, it was time to structure the streams of work. Not having much hindsight at the start, we did what was obvious. By this time, we had 12 workstreams: banking products, onboarding, partnerships, usage, credit, marketing, transactional banking, servicing, engagement, app creation, regulations and compliance, and tech infrastructure, architecture, DevOps as the last stream. So, we structured the build teams around these workstreams. They reported their progress weekly.

The drawback of this approach quickly became evident. The streams of work didn't cater sufficiently to interdependencies and were too siloed. We added dependencies – like who or what you were affecting, and who or what was affecting you – as standard reporting. This helped, as some didn't want to call their colleagues out; doing it this way institutionalised the approach and made it acceptable.

Eventually, I enhanced the workstreams into Centres of Excellence, or COEs, to better balance the co-ordination effort across streams of work, and the depth of expertise and knowledge needed in some streams of work. In doing so, I had the aim of breaking away from the traditional siloed nature of the departmental unit to an organisational design that had the best of both depth and co-ordination.

One good example to illustrate this was how the COE structure transformed the way the UI design was done. Prior to the COE structure, the UI design team was mostly at the tail end of the process, taking instruction from the rest of the units on what screens were needed. This produced work that was sometimes reactive and not properly thought through. For example, after the fifth digit of a password, the keyboard did not automatically retract, and the user had to hit Enter again. By defining UI as a co-ordinating COE, it became the UI team's role to look at the end-to-end process required to create well-designed, frictionless user interfaces that were clear, efficient, and intuitive.

Country vs HQ

The situation was further complicated by the fact that we were launching in Thailand and Indonesia first, with the regional HQ in Singapore. This increased the magnitude of difficulty significantly. I wanted to maintain as much regional code as possible to prevent things eventually degenerating into two completely different applications for Thailand and Indonesia, which would reduce TMRW's ability to produce continued enhancements down the road. The country had to take care of marketing due to cultural and language issues. Many of the operational processes were local, so we had to have some capability to provide input and refinement of the processes to cater to country-specific ones that we could not standardise.

From the beginning, it was vital to make the countries feel that this was not a Singapore design intended for Thailand or Indonesia. For a bank headquartered in Singapore, many things are first tried out in Singapore, and in the process, you can lose sight of the fact that countries are different. Yet, if you have every entity run as a separate country entity with little in common, it can't work, because to benefit from multi-nationality, you need to be able to bring certain firm advantages across the border, like your management and business processes or your intellectual property.

In fact, internationalisation is not the driver of firm performance (Khoo, 2012). The drivers of firm performance are the firm advantages that can cross borders, and then internationalisation or multi-nationality can vary the degree of impact. So, you must balance the catering for local needs and the drive for regional standardisation, and I repeated this very frequently to the country teams. The country had to prove that it was really needed, otherwise it would not be incorporated into the build. This proved harder to achieve than we imagined.

In Singapore, there is already quite a majority that may not voice their views against those of a more senior person or authority. Outside Singapore in ASEAN, it is compounded. The more junior country teams don't like to disagree. This was especially key in the first launch in Thailand. Thailand's standards of digital banking are very high, and to be a credible alternative, we had to equal or better KBank's digital banking standard.

There will also sometimes be the issue of scepticism initially in the countries vs the HQ. For TMRW, this was the first time an initiative as major as this started without road-testing in Singapore first, but this was also very powerful as the countries knew that the large investment could benefit them. It took a lot of constant effort and communication to win the countries' support and make them believe that we could do it and be successful. This for me was one of the **highlights of my journey with TMRW, to experience strong support from the countries, and working closely with them to successfully achieve TMRW's ambition together**. It required a deft approach, knowing when to step back and let the countries decide (e.g., local issues based on language and cultural norms that we would not be able to add value) and when to insist (e.g., a big departure from the agreed strategy or directions that would lead to a fork in the code).

Physical environment

The physical workspace, although playing a backstage role in the current pandemic, is one of the levers you can use to help ensure teams work together to solve the circular interactions that complex digital transformations pose. In addition, breaking down the barriers that have traditionally separated the ranks, so that it creates a sense of openness that reduces hierarchy, is one of the factors that fosters innovation, as discussed previously. Innovative ideas often require different inputs. When you are stuck with a problem that you are having difficulty solving, talking to a more diverse group of people is often more useful than staying within your own team or function. In a study by the University of Exeter that examined "an agile workspace against an enriched one", it was found that "just adding plants, art and colourful surroundings drove up productivity by 17%. A further study showed organisations that empowered employees to take part in the design of their workspace saw this figure nearly double, to 32%" (Clark 2015).

TMRW moved from a traditional bank office layout in UOB Plaza into the SGX building, which used to be a UOB branch, in December 2018. It had a high ceiling with a mezzanine level that looked onto the first floor where there was a tree planted in the old banking hall. That added a touch of difference to the space. But the biggest difference was the setup, with **no cubicles for management and an entirely open-plan seating office**.

At the time of the move, I was concerned about the COE units we had built up: Banking Products, Mobile Products, Customer Experience, Partnerships, Digital Engagement and Engagement Labs, Marketing, and the Compliance and Technology team that sat with us but had a different reporting line. Within some of these units, you had more sub-units like onboarding, process and servicing within customer experience. Functional units are needed because they create specialisation and depth but the moment you create functional units, working across those units may start to have co-ordination issues. So, instead of traditional siloed seating arrangements, we opted for an agile work environment, with many discussion rooms to support the daily stand-up meetings, and reconfigurable layouts to support interaction.

Gemma was in charge of the move and she recalled: "We tested different seating arrangements with the team. The intention was to enhance collaboration across the teams. Then an idea came up that we should sit with the technology folks. I thought that was crazy, because they had a lot more people than we do. But Dennis was quite adamant. He believed in achieving the collaboration we needed by being physically next to each other. Another reason was that TMRW's technology colleagues were seated across various office locations. We actually had a hard time convincing the rest of the leadership team that this was something we had to try out."

"As a result of this arrangement, we became a lot closer to our technology colleagues. We would see them all the time and expanded our interaction across various teams. It helped with many of the issues that we were facing, especially when we first started out. That to me was the pivotal point that convinced everyone we made the right choice. We saved a lot of time from running across the island to different offices, and we didn't have to arrange for telecalls. The beauty of it is they are literally next to us! No more excuses of being unable to find our colleagues because eventually they will need to come back to their desk. This arrangement was the first of its kind in the bank (not a temporary arrangement but a permanent one). This caught the attention of the rest of the business units as they looked at us as examples."

One of the thoughts I had was to have the units mixed up when we moved to SGX to promote more communication across teams. And since team heads will always tend to be closer to the team they manage than the team they are part of, I decided to do an experiment to have all my direct reports sit together in the hope that if they did, it would increase awareness and collaboration. It was a controversial decision. Some people hated the idea and wanted to be with their teams, but some seemed open to try it out. I put this to a vote – actually one of the few times I made a vote by consensus – because where people sat was personal, and we had already asked a lot of them by asking senior staff to give up their cubicles. It was a tie: half wanted to sit with their teams, and half were ok to try out my idea. So, I had the tie-breaking vote and I voted to have all my direct reports sit together and promised to review it in 6 months if they were not happy with it. And we went ahead with it.

As Gemma puts it: "There was already resistance due to splitting teams across two floors, but this arrangement made a difference towards better teamwork, as we were all forced to work together and spend more time with other teams rather than our own and be cliquish. We also wanted to do away with cubicles, regardless of rank. So, whether you are MD, ED, you're not going to have a cubicle. It will be an open concept. Some of the team members were not happy with the idea. Some leads started telling me where they wanted to be seated (window, aisle, etc.), or who they wanted to sit with. To decide who would sit where for the leadership team, I came up with the solution of drawing lots. In this way, I wouldn't be seen as biased, and it was down to luck. It worked quite well! The leads got their seats, and if they wanted to do a private trade with somebody else, I left it to them. With all senior leaders seated together, I noticed that if there were any issues, they would turn around and sort it out as leaders. This helped to bring the team closer together to discuss problems that otherwise would have not been so quickly resolved. Even Dennis sat with us in the same open area, and he became a lot more approachable to the junior staff, who saw him so much more often as opposed to when he was in a room. This broke down the hierarchy culture that TMRW digital bank wanted to avoid."

TMRW has been the most complex initiative in my 30-year career. In my farewell to my team, I recalled the sheer scale of what we had done: "When we started, we had but a dream, a dream that we could build the world's most engaging digital bank. Whilst we have yet to finish, we are well past it being just a dream. Being an experience company is very hard, but our high NPS® scores are a testimony to what we have done in such a short period of time. When I think back, we were just so busy that I never had time to think about what if it didn't work. But deep down I also know we achieved it against all odds. I am extremely grateful to all of you for coming together like you did when it was most pivotal, back in 2018, and once again in 2019, when we found that despite our best efforts, our NPS® was not up to mark. Our NPS® today is +42 and +52 in Thailand and Indonesia, respectively. You can buy customers, especially dormant customers. You can't buy high NPS®! It's a very tough measure. You have to rate 9 and 10 out of 10, and still subtract it from customers who rate 0 to 6. I have been a demanding boss. Exacting expectations, ever higher standards, robustness, design principles, focus on detail, and constantly pushing you to be better. For those who relished it, you're most welcome! For those who hated it, my apologies for the tough training you had!"

Key takeaways

- It is mandatory and essential to success to require the hiring manager to write a job description with the qualities needed, and how to detect them.

- Your mission statement defines why the company exists and serves to coalesce your team, resulting in a clear, compelling and common purpose.

- When you constantly remind your employees of their mission, a sense of purpose, resulting in higher engagement and positive work culture, occurs.

- Your vision statement serves to ignite an ambition that will inspire your team to reach for the stars.

- Your values statement is the glue that holds the team together by specifying the right behaviours needed to bring out the best in everyone.

- The builders you want to hire are most attracted by your mission, vision, values and behaviours you expect.

- It is vital to put together a set of activities and programmes dedicated to keeping the team inspired over the course of your transformation journey.

- Companies spend a lot of time crafting and refining their strategy but afterwards spend little time discussing what KPIs they will measure.

- Focusing on measures doesn't necessarily make them better but focusing on the drivers of those outcomes or measures will.

- A new holistic scorecard ensures that you launch well, focus on marginal profitability and contribution, and annual fixed cost recovery.

- The most basic measurements are profit and loss. They are also the worst measures to use to measure a digital bank's success.

- If your target segment has low current revenue potential but high future revenue potential, managing costs is critical.

- Focus on minimising 3 types of cost measures: the cost to acquire and transact, the cost to serve, and the cost to innovate.

- It is easy to get the overall acquisition numbers up at the cost of a lower and lower active ratio. Drive home the point that it has to be active customers.

- The complexity is getting all the key measures (number of active customers, NPS®, marginal profit, total number of customers, etc.) moving in the right direction, all at the same time.

- The focus must not only be on the total initial project cost, but also on the annual footprint required to maintain and enhance this initial cost.

- As a result, building the tech stack for maintainability and enhancement is probably slightly more important than getting the bank launched on time.

- Some KPI measures should be common across all staff (e.g., NPS®, revenue per active customer, cost of acquiring an active customer, etc.) and form roughly a third to half of the total, depending on their roles.

- The other half can be focused on specific initiatives unique to the units within the group, e.g., new feature launch milestones, episode-level NPS® (e.g., NPS® for payments and funds-transfers), etc.

- This will provide a good mix of focus on group-wide objectives but also on unit and individual-specific objectives.

- Ensure that all teams know their organisation, unit and individual KPIs and also those of other teams which they depend upon to succeed.

- Three areas of leadership are paramount: designing and morphing the organisation over time, ability to spark innovation, and balanced leaders that can successfully navigate the complexity.

- Breadth units rely heavily on methodology to bridge across units to ensure great co-ordination, whilst depth units bring the specialised skills to bear to solve tough (usually technical) problems.

- Having the right blend of both depth and breadth is crucial to success.

- Innovation requires both process and content, and simply focusing on one and ignoring the other won't result in a successful innovation outcome.

- Contrary to popular belief, innovation almost never fails due to a lack of creativity. It's almost always because of a lack of discipline.

- Staff can't be motivated if they don't understand the impact of their work on the overall outcome.

- Three important ingredients – people, process and leadership – are required to create a great environment that fosters innovation.

- To be innovative, there must be a balance of persistent and experimenting.

- A diverse pool of experience and domain knowledge is superior as it provides a wider collection of vantage points, resulting in more variance.

- Variance results in a greater breadth of ideas and solutions.

- Process knowledge helps the senior executive understand the interconnected and interrelated nature of a complex problem.

- Disruptive and architectural innovations require significant leadership participation to spark the innovation required because they involve significant changes to the business model.

- Where innovations require significant changes to the business model, co-ordination is key, so you don't end up doing things that are contradictory.

- Mission-orientation is powerful because it gives an outside-in perspective; it is the "why" that creates the emotional connection the business has with the outside world.

- Hierarchy has merits in the selection of ideas for onward progress towards innovation but is less effective in the origination of novel ideas that feed the former process because it tends to blunt challenge.

- Without challenge, the best thoughts don't float to the top. To promote this, constantly emphasise the need for everyone to question and ask "why".

- Challenge makes the selection of an inferior approach or position much more difficult, which helps to ensure that decisions are well-debated and considered most of the time.

- The known-unknown method of accepting risk leaves the unexpected risk or error as a learning yet eliminates carelessness.

- Being unreasonable in goals and yet highly motivational and encouraging is required to create an environment of high challenge and high support.

- Systems thinking is an approach to understanding interconnected systems or how the TaP dimensions and elements interact with each other.

- As a leader who is a systems thinker, you will have to understand the root cause and not fixate on the symptoms of the problem.

- Your comfort with ambiguity, and not succumbing to the need to solve it too quickly or too slowly, will be one of the keys to success.

- Seemingly contradictory traits are needed for success in complex initiatives, e.g., certain yet open, persistent yet experimenting. Together they represent how balanced a leader is or should aim to be.

- Even if you are certain, there is always the possibility you could be wrong, and being wrong in a senior role has a much bigger negative impact.

- You disagree with the idea or the proposal – and always with a good, stated reason – and not the individual.

- The accountable senior executive is the orchestra conductor. It is only from his vantage point that he can and should see how all the dots are connected – a task often made very difficult by the lack of a map of these dots.

- Creating a list of core attributes distilled from the difference between hires that excelled and hires that didn't creates an important codification of the kind of talent you want to attract that is linked to directly to your success.

- If you are an intrapreneur operating within a large traditional company like a bank, organisational alignment is extremely crucial. The organisation will tend to reject the "mutant children" of start-ups as they look different, speak different and, in fact, are different – otherwise it defeats the whole purpose.

- If you are building something with a very different business model in a larger organisation, you are going to be misunderstood.

- There has to be a senior defender of such bold, long-term initiatives, and it must be the CEO or a very senior C-1 that works for the CEO who is long-tenured and highly respected. No one else will do.

- You have to convince them that the most crucial starting point is to create a new culture, one that is innovative, non-hierarchical, focused on customers, etc.

- There is no other way but to create a separate unit and protect it so it can survive and thrive.

- All boards should ask for that insurance against a future where a few successful digital banks that get the formula right begin to capture share with a great experience built over the years when they were small.

- Organisational role design has the highest probability of being extremely demotivating when done poorly or extremely motivating when done well.

- Onboarding, process, service and customer experience are areas where the fussiness and attention to detail required to design and execute great processes are paramount.

- As a leader, you must be both certain and open so that you can minimise your mistakes. Part of doing that is to explore divergent views in the planning stage.

- The most difficult part will be the use of your intuition and judgement to decide when to slow down and diverge, and when to speed up and converge.

- It is vital to maintain as much regional code as possible to prevent things eventually degenerating into completely different applications for each country of launch, which would reduce your ability to produce continued enhancements down the road.

- It will require a deft approach, knowing when to step back and let the countries decide (e.g., local issues based on language and cultural norms that we would not be able to add value) and when to insist (e.g., a big departure from the agreed strategy or directions that would lead to a fork in the code).

CHAPTER 6

Beyond banking

This chapter wasn't in the original design of *Driving Digital Transformation*. I added it after an ex-colleague from Hewlett-Packard suggested that I close with a chapter on digital transformation across industries. I was intrigued by the suggestion and decided to do some research into how I should go about it. I immediately realised that it would be an extremely difficult chapter to write. Where would one even start? What's causing such disruption across industries? Where is this leading us, and how is TaP applicable? After much research and thinking through how best to encapsulate such a broad topic in the last chapter, I decided to use three lenses:

1. The first lens pinpoints the drivers of the digital revolution powering the fourth industrial revolution;

2. The second is the lens on types of digital transformation vs complexity;

3. And the final lens is that of current and future anticipated disruption by industry.

Taken together, these three lenses form a powerful scope to understand the fundamental changes taking place in all industries globally.

Lens 1: The drivers of the digital revolution

Let's start with the fundamental drivers of the change we are witnessing. One of the key drivers of change is clearly the increased processing power we have experienced over the past 30 years. "Computers then did an OK job and cost a couple million dollars. Now what used to be thought of as supercomputers are inside smartphones. They cost a million times less, are a million times faster and have a million times as much memory" (Meek, 2018). Coupled with the ubiquity of the World Wide Web, this has made communications and computing power cheaply and readily available.

Figure 101 illustrates the profound impact that these developments have had, by making it possible for the first time to reach billions around the world, and enabling business to rent all manner of infrastructure, from the most basic tools like email to their data centre (and software) with the advent of cloud computing, offering software-as-a-service and platform-as-a-service[79]. This has allowed companies whose products and services are fully digital – like new media firms, social media firms, instant messaging, video streaming, matching platforms, in fact any offering that isn't physical and can be delivered via software – to have lower start-up costs and greater reach.

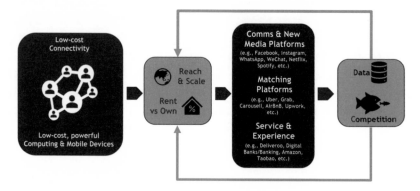

Figure 101 – The digital revolution

Entire new industries were created on the back of the reach and scale of this revolution, allowing an unprecedented degree of constant global communications. Communications platforms such as Facebook, Instagram, WhatsApp, WeChat, Twitter and YouTube developed as a result. The rise of online influencers and massive sharing of information round the clock ensued. Facebook has almost 2B daily active users. These communications platforms are facilitating the creation, storage and sharing of an unparalleled amount of data.

The World Economic Forum estimates that by 2025, 463 exabytes of data will be created each day globally – that's the equivalent of 212,765,957 DVDs per day (Desjardins, 2019)! If you are in an industry whose nature allows it to be purely digital, Figure 101 is sufficient to create untold growth if you are a start-up, or untold misery if you are an incumbent, as many of the traditional media and print companies have discovered. The magazine industry in the US has taken a nosedive, for example, down from US$46B in 2007 to around US$28B in 2017. It has enabled new media companies like Netflix and Spotify to serve multilingual content to a global audience.

The sheer ability to connect the world's population has also resulted in the creation of matching platforms like Uber, eBay, Airbnb, Upwork[80], etc., who don't

---

79. Primarily useful for developers and programmers, PaaS allows the user to develop, run, and manage their own apps without having to build and maintain the infrastructure or platform usually associated with the process. Source: redhat.com

80. Upwork is a legitimate freelance marketplace that connects clients and freelancers.

own any infrastructure of their own. These platforms match the needs of one side of their platform (e.g., people who need a ride) to those on another side of the platform (those who can provide a ride). And finally, companies of all shapes and sizes have leveraged low-cost connectivity and powerful mobile devices to personalise individual experiences, remembering your preferences, offering recommendations based on past preferences and transactions. These new digital companies create more data than ever before in the history of mankind, and combined with the fact that it is now easier than ever before to start a software company, this is creating even more competition in this space.

In Figure 102, with the exception of Tesla and Xiaomi, all the others are software companies. The insight here is that it shows the reach and scale of a global business at work, and explains why these industries (software, media, entertainment, communications) are most susceptible to digital disruption and hence are experiencing the highest degree of disruption, as illustrated later in Figure 104. The global businesses (e.g., software) that can leverage the drivers of the digital revolution and thus reach a scale not possible before in a timeframe much shorter than before, have thus grown significantly in size.

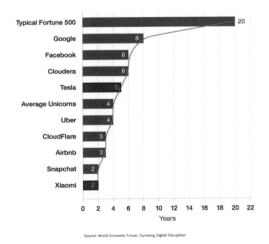

Source: World Economic Forum, Surviving Digital Disruption

Figure 102 – Years to reach a valuation of $1B or more

Lens 2: Types of transformation vs complexity

Let's change the lens of analysis to understand what types of transformation there are, and how they vary in complexity. Figure 103 shows the 6 different types of digital transformation a company can pursue, in order of increasing complexity as we move from left to right. They are not mutually exclusive, and so a company could pursue one or more of them in combination. The business model digital transformation is the most complex, potentially encompassing all of the prior five, as fundamental changes in the customer proposition, revenue and profit generation and in the way the firm competes are all put into play. The key enabler in all this is the backend operations of the firm and leveraging process re-engineering techniques to continuously improve the throughput and quality whilst reducing costs and exposing the inputs and outputs of the process to customer-facing systems to bring out enterprise-wide changes that have huge impact on cost and the way business is done.

	Type I Selling Online	Type II Servicing Online	Type III Engaging Online	Type IV Robotics	Type V Data-driven Decisions	Type VI Business Model
What?	1. Pure Online 2. Offline to Offline & Online	1. Troubleshooting and resolving problems with customers online 2. Enabling staff to do their service jobs better and faster	1. Personalise the online experience. 2. Proactive anticipation 3. Influence Decisions	Replace human action	1. Make better business decisions using data 2. Replace Human Decisions	
	Change the way value & profit is generated, and how you compete.					
Examples	Online retailers: Amazon, AliExpress Department stores: Online to Offline	Banks, Computer Manufacturers, Networking Hardware Vendors	Recommendation engines: Netflix, Spotify, Amazon, etc Automated CV scanning, e.g. Filtered, monster.com, etc	Smart Vacuum robots: Roomba. Household Assistant: Samsung Bot Handy	Driverless cars: Telsa X-ray interpretation: CheXpert	Netflix vs Blockbuster, AirBnB vs hotel chains, Challenger Digital Banks vs Legacy Banks, New Online media vs Traditional media, etc
Key Enabler	Digitalising and Automating Operations 1. Improve efficiency of operations by streamlining processes and reducing or eliminating human involvement and wastages. 2. Exposing your core transactional capabilities 3. Technology & Data					
Relative Complexity	Low	Mid	Mid-High	Mid-High	Mid-High	High
Probability of Success	Higher		Medium-Low		Low	

Figure 103 – Types of digital transformation

The most basic form of digital transformation, Type I, has been in existence since the dot-com days, and Amazon has parlayed this into a multi-billion-dollar business and a market cap of US$1T. Naturally, in its journey to the top, it has along the way implemented all the 6 types shown in Figure 103. Successful Type I transformations are tightly coupled with the warehousing, ordering and logistics core systems found in the key enabler layer, and successful firms have had to gain both the ability to be extremely customer-centric in their online distribution experience as well as extremely adept at streamlining their logistics and operations processes to ensure that the goods are delivered and tracked for on-time performance. In the course of doing this, they have also implemented Type II capabilities to serve customers online, as well as implementing robotics at their warehouses to achieve lights-out operations, round the clock.

Lens 3: Disruption happens at a different pace in different industries

Accenture studied 18 industry sectors and 106 industry segments within these sectors and analysed 10,000 of the largest listed companies based on revenue between 2011 and 2018 to derive their disruptability index, which measures an industry's current level of disruption as well as its susceptibility to future disruption (Accenture, 2018). Note that Accenture has two versions of their index, and I am using the version that uses the median[81] rather than a weighted average. The result is shown in Figure 104. The disruptability index splits the industries into 4 quadrants based on their current and future levels of disruption:

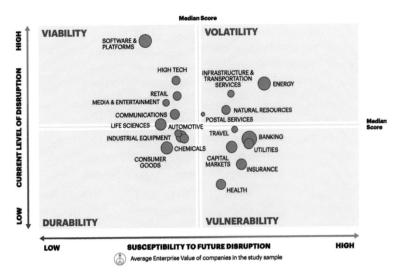

Figure 104 – Accenture's disruptability index by industry
(Source: Accenture)

A. **Industries in the durability quadrant face low current and future levels of disruption.** The 4 industries listed in this quadrant are automotive, chemicals, consumer goods and industrial equipment, which we can broadly categorise as manufacturers. Note that these manufacturers are at the border with the other 3 quadrants and thus the implication is clear that although more resilient to the forces of current and future disruption, the levels of disruption are not necessarily low. Whilst these industries may not have been as affected by the twin

---

81. In statistics and probability theory, the median is the value separating the higher half from the lower half of a data sample, a population, or a probability distribution.

forces of mobile computing power and ubiquitous bandwidth, a robotics rev-olution has been taking place in manufacturing. Robotics-oriented production processes are most obvious in factories and manufacturing facilities; in fact, approximately 90% of all robots in operation today can be found in such facil-ities (Inc., 2006). Robots in the manufacturing industry now perform welding, painting, pick & place, packaging, assembly, disassembly, and so much more (Profozich, 2021). The increasing use of instrumentation to send back data over the internet is also revolutionising the ability of manufacturers to collect data and monitor the performance of their products in real-time use.

B. **Industries in the viability quadrant face high current levels of disruption but are less susceptible to future levels of disruption** as they are already operat-ing in an environment where technology is enabling high levels of innovation, and thus competition and the forces of creation and destruction are accepted as the industry norm. These industries either have products and services that are easily digitisable, for examples, media and entertainment, communications, or are involved directly in enabling digitisation, like high tech and software. Disruption is the norm in technology, and so no one is surprised that high tech and software are in this quadrant. The media and entertainment industries have found it very difficult to adapt to a world where sharing is the norm, made possible by the forces described in Figure 101. In the past, sharing was only possible with those in your proximity and close circle. Today, the internet has made sharing ubiquitous, and a generation has grown up not knowing about subscriptions for magazines, and not paying to own songs. This, together with an increasing trend to forgo reading for browsing online content, has led to shrinking subscribers of paid media, and shrinking advertising revenue as more and more advertising shifts to online media. At the same time, however, with high-bandwidth fibre now available in many major cities globally, Netflix, founded in 1997, has taken advantage of it to offer low-cost subscriptions for access to thousands of movies to grow their video streaming service globally. As of April 2021, Netflix has 208M subscribers globally (Zeitchik, 2021).

Retail is in the viability quadrant, and since the dot-com era of the 2000s, physical distribution in retail has been continually disrupted, and the final nail in the coffin may just have been delivered by the Covid-19 pandemic[82], with J.C. Penney, Niemen Marcus and other storied names filing for bankruptcy, hasten-ing a 20-year decline in sales from their traditional brick-and-mortar distribution format. Amazon, as well as other major online distributors, has leveraged the

---

82. The Covid-19 pandemic, also known as the coronavirus pandemic, is an ongoing global pandemic of coronavirus disease 2019 (Covid-19) caused by severe acute respiratory syndrome coronavirus 2 (SARS-CoV-2).

Type I transformation so successfully in the past 27 years that it has needed to set up stores as legacy format closures have left it with no outlets to try out products that need to be fitted or experienced before buying.

Communications has also faced the onslaught of massive disruption as data speeds went from 2400 baud modems when I was a teenager to 1Gbps speeds now at most home and office networks and in the hundreds of Mbps with most hotel WiFi. Some mobile operator plans don't even have traditional call minutes anymore, charging customers only for massive amounts of data monthly. Almost no one dials IDD anymore, as Facetime, WhatsApp, Zoom and their like now work globally, with high-resolution video to boot. Together with competition introduced by regulators globally, mobile data plans have remained very competitive and affordable, whilst revenues have been affected as traditional high-margin analog calls are cannibalised at the expense of lower-margin data services.

The education industry is an anomaly. Its products and services are all fully digitisable. What has prevented further disruption is the human touch – the need to be in the classroom and experience interactive learning face to face. And not to forget, the value of being in a storied campus in an Ivy League university. However, the Covid-19 pandemic has rapidly and radically changed things. Work from home and home-based learning are now the norm. Singapore's Ministry of Education has been distributing devices to equip students to take lessons from home. The distribution of these devices – laptops or tablets – to support this format of learning is 7 years ahead of the original plan, Senior Minister Tharman Shanmugaratnam said in June 2020 (Teng, 2021). An article in the *Straits Times* highlighted one secondary four student's experience: "Previously I would be quite shy to share my thoughts in class as I wasn't sure if my opinion was inferior. But when I see all the answers on the screen, I feel more motivated to voice my opinions." The article also reported the use of supporting apps like ClassPoint to share presentation slides and set interactive quizzes. This could signal the start of further disruption in education and the rapid development of EduTech by EduTech firms.[83]

C. **Industries in the vulnerability quadrant face low levels of current disruption, but the anticipated future disruption is high.** Capital markets, insurance and banking – collectively, we can label them as financial services – are all in this quadrant. The financial services industry's products and services are easily digitalised, since they are all intermediaries, perhaps with the exception

---

83. Educational technology (commonly abbreviated as EduTech, or EdTech) is the combined use of computer hardware, software, and educational theory and practice to facilitate learning.

of their role as the guarantor of deposits. Thus, the reason why these industries haven't faced very high levels of current disruption can likely be attributed to regulations, including the capital requirements to operate as a financial services company, and the non-global nature of some segments within financial services like banking. Since the study was published in 2018, the pace of disruption has accelerated from both Fintech competitors, and neo and challenger banks. It's likely that if this study were to be repeated today, some of these industries might now find themselves in the volatility quadrant. The utilities industry and health are also regulated industries, so one of the common themes of industries in the vulnerability quadrant could be higher barriers to entry and competition.

D. **The final quadrant, volatility, contains industries that face both high current and future disruption.** Infrastructure and transportation, energy and natural resources face the brunt of the forces pushing back against the disastrous impact of global warming and climate change as sustainability initiatives take hold. The replacement of carbon-based fuels and sources of energy with green sources of fuel and energy is already happening and the signs are that it will accelerate. The only question is whether it will be in time to avert a significant warming that would prove disastrous to living conditions.

We have briefly covered the increasing use of industrial robots in manufacturing. After many years in labs, robots are now beginning to make their way into commercial applications outside of manufacturing. Boston Robotics is unlike most other robotics companies. Founded in 1992 as a spin-off from the Massachusetts Institute of Technology, the company is famous for its highly dynamic and mobile robots. "Each time the firm shares new footage of its machines, they cause a sensation. Whether it's a pack of robot dogs towing a truck or a human-like bot leaping nimbly up a set of boxes, Boston Dynamics' bots are uniquely thrilling" (Vincent, 2019). Figure 105 illustrates the improvements Boston Dynamics robots have made in recent years, from box jumps and backflips to opening doors and running up

Figure 105 – Boston Dynamics robot improvements over time

stairs, to gymnastics and dancing. After years of R&D, Boston Dynamics finally released its first commercial robot, Spot. Spot can go where you tell it, avoid obstacles, and keep its balance under extreme circumstances – which are all crucial skills if you're trying to navigate an unknown environment (Brandom, 2019).

Pulling it all together

The key drivers of digital transformation have been driven by Moore's Law, with computing power roughly doubling every 24 months. Low-cost mobile devices that have the power of supercomputers of yesteryear have become ubiquitous, and the internet now connects the world's citizens online. This has created a global marketplace. For businesses whose products are information services like software, high tech, media and communications, they have all been hard-hit by disruption. Financial services, although similar to information services in product nature, have received some shelter due to regulatory barriers, but the forces of disruption are growing rapidly.

These drivers of disruption have created many new media businesses (e.g., Google, Facebook) and matching platforms (e.g., Uber, Airbnb) whilst vanquishing the retail giants of the past like Sears and J.C. Penney. When they are now combined with the latest robotics and instrumentation advancements, together they form a formidable combination by generating lots of useful data and also replacing expensive labour at the same time. In the future, these capabilities are likely to advance even further.

Hence complexity is likely to rise, not fall. Figure 106 illustrates this. In the most complex transformations, a company that manufactures B2C products that wants to transform itself front-to-back faces an enormous and complex task. Even the companies that are focused only on front-end transformation will face substantial complexity in integrating all the different types of transformations and making everything work holistically.

The first key difference in TaP is its focus on starting with the client or customer, and in doing so, understanding the problems they face, and what solutions are best placed to solve these problems in a manner that they are willing to put a price to the value unlocked. **Digital transformation tends to get lumped together with technology when it actually should be relabelled as business transformation through design, process, technology, data, new methodologies and change management.** Defined this way, it is actually traditional business management with a twist. Because of the more experimental bent to it, the approach and the execution have become more intertwined. This has made it much more difficult for the consultants, who tend not to have sufficient work experience to traverse this coming together of thinking and doing.

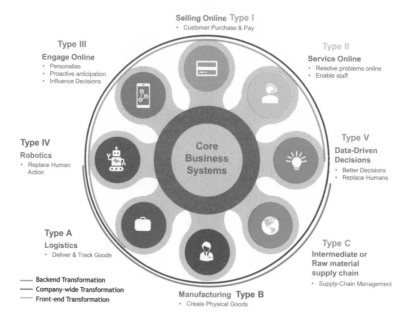

Figure 106 – Digital transformation complexity vs coverage

Industries with high technological change have long practised a solution-looking-for-a-problem approach. The root of this lies in invention and the inventor exploiting an emerging technology, at times not knowing where it could lead. The transistor was first used in amplification in transistor radios in prototypes as early as 1952, before the world's first transistor computer was built at the University of Manchester in November 1953. So invention has always been about what's possible, and the inherent risk that nobody wants the invention is always there. Some fail because the timing is too early, and the necessary supporting infrastructure and components are not ready or available, like the AT&T Picturephone, which had its first public unveiling in 1964 at Disneyland California (Hernandez, 2012). The cost was too high and the infrastructure not ready to deliver a high-quality resolution. Today, 47 years later, everyone is using video-conferencing tools such as Zoom.

Sometimes, the invention fails because there is really no market for it, like internet-based fridges. There have been many internet-based fridges over the years, none of which have seemed to generate much excitement, but manufacturers keep trying (Jaume, 2012). It's no wonder there is a phrase, "What's the killer app?", in tech – it is a challenge to the inventor to look for that application that will make the invention widely successful. Many inventions fall by the wayside because they are too early and thus not desirable, or simply there is no "killer app" for it.

When this approach is used in digital transformation initiatives in companies, money is applied to solutions that don't move the needle for the company. When these solutions don't have obvious real-world problems, the company can't pivot like a start-up can, because they aren't in it for the tech, they are in it for the benefits. Another approach is to be a fast follower of a company that appears to be on the cusp of a killer app. There isn't anything wrong with being a fast follower, but often just copying your competitor without understanding your customer as well as your competitor doesn't allow you to pivot as well as your competitor when you hit rough seas. This aspect of TaP is likely universally applicable across any industry that needs to transform.

The second difference in TaP is that technology is a capability, and to avoid putting the solution before the problem, the customer and business first need to achieve the desirability and viability criteria, and technology is one element in the capability dimension that can make the transformation successful (feasible). In many cases, process may be even more important to get right first, because technology is merely automating the process on paper, enabling it to be fast and error-free. The emphasis on process, data and design gives these three supporting elements equal weightage as technology, which is what happens most of the time in a successful transformation.

The third difference is that TaP excels in managing the complexity that is a natural outcome of the scope of the transformation as shown in Figures 103 and 106. Unless a firm is doing the most trivial type of digital transformation, e.g., building an app or web order-taking module, which is now a simple task, adding one or two more types of digital transformation quickly increases the complexity exponentially. In industries where additional disciplines are needed, e.g., automation and robotics, where the transformation is in manufacturing or activities currently undertaken by humans and a large cost decrease is desired to compete better, additional complexity is added, versus a transformation only involving products and solutions that can be fully digital. The costs are thus higher, and the risk of failure correspondingly so. So it's fairly safe to say that the complexities are the same or higher outside of where TaP was created – i.e., in financial services, where the products are all digits on computers – and hence a method to handle this complexity becomes even more crucial.

In summary, the four dimensions, customers, business, people & leadership remain relevant across industries, as the methods used and the elements and considerations are known from prior experience and body of knowledge to be highly extensible. The capabilities dimension was redesigned significantly to cater to adaptability across industries. Methodologies, technology, ecosystems and new disciplines all allow for industry-specific considerations like robotics or instrumentation. As of the writing of this book, I am actively exploring use cases in other industries, and there are some highly interesting ones that have a high probability of applying TaP. I hope to be able to update *Driving Digital Transformation* with these new cross-industry use cases in the next edition of the book.

As a final learning point, history has shown time and time again that when a tidal change happens, you must embrace it. Otherwise, when it hits your industry anyway, would you rather be prepared or unprepared? If you look at the Fortune 500 in 1955 versus 2019, you'll see that only 52 companies – about 10% – are still on the list (Perry, 2019). TaP is a discipline of thinking and implementing that can be a powerful ally in the new world we live in. A world of fleeting competitive advantage, significant ambiguity and uncertainty, but yet with technological change accelerating and forcing greater disruption than ever before. In this new era, the thinking tools alone or the implementation tools alone aren't enough to raise your probability of success. You have to combine them together so that the thinking and doing work in lock-step.

Thank you for reading, and do let me know at dennis@allDigitalfuture.com if you have a use case that could be assured a higher chance of success by leveraging TaP.

Key takeaways

- Beyond Banking uses three lenses: the first lens pinpoints the drivers of the digital revolution that is powering the fourth industrial revolution, the second is the lens on types of digital transformation vs complexity, and the final lens is that of current and future anticipated disruption by industry.

- Taken together, these three lenses form a powerful scope to understand the fundamental changes taking place in all industries globally.

- Computers that cost a million times less, are a million times faster and have a million times as much memory vs 30 years ago, coupled with the ubiquity of the World Wide Web, have made communications and computing power cheaply and readily available.

- This in turn makes it possible for the first time to reach billions around the world, and enables business to rent all manner of infrastructure, rather than own infrastructure.

- In turn, this has allowed any company whose offering isn't physical and can be delivered via software to have lower start-up costs and wider reach.

- Facebook, Google, Instagram, WhatsApp, WeChat, Snapchat, Twitter, YouTube, Uber, eBay, Airbnb, Upwork, Netflix, Spotify showcase the reach and scale of a global digital business at work, and explains why these industries (software, media, entertainment, communications) are most susceptible to digital disruption.

- The business model digital transformation is the most complex, encompassing all of the prior 5 types and more, as fundamental changes in the customer proposition, revenue and profit generation and the way the firm competes are all put into play.

- Accenture's disruptability index splits industries into 4 quadrants based on their current and future level of disruption.

- Industries are classified as either durable to disruption (durability quadrant), facing viability concerns due to disruption (viability quadrant), vulnerable to high levels of future disruption but buffered against current disruption (vulnerability quadrant), or volatile as they are facing both high current and future disruption (volatility quadrant).

- Complexity is likely to rise, not fall.

- The key difference in TaP has been the focus on starting with the client or customer, and in doing so, understanding the problems he faces, and what solutions are best placed to solve these problems in a manner that he is willing to put a price to the value unlocked.

- Digital transformation tends to get lumped together with technology when it actually should be relabelled as business transformation through design, process, technology, data, new methodologies and change management.

- Defined this way, it is actually traditional business management with a twist; because of the more experimental bent to it, the approach and the execution have become more intertwined.

- This has made it much more difficult for the consultants, who tend not to have sufficient work experience to traverse this coming together of thinking and doing.

- Industries in high technology have long practised a solution-looking-for-a-problem approach.

- The root of this lies in invention and the inventor exploiting an emerging technology, at times not knowing where it could lead to.

- Invention has always been about what's possible, and the inherent risk that nobody wants the invention is always there.

- Some inventions fail because their timing is too early, and the necessary supporting infrastructure and components are not ready or available.

- Some inventions fail because there is really no market for them, like internet-based fridges.

- It's no wonder there is a phrase, "What's the killer app?", in tech, that is a challenge to the inventor to look for that application that will make the invention widely successful.

- When this approach is used in digital transformation initiatives in companies that are not in the business of high tech, money is applied to solutions that don't move the needle for the company.

- When these solutions don't have obvious real-world problems, the company can't pivot like a start-up can, because they aren't in it for the tech, they are in it for the benefits.

- The aspect of TaP that gives customers and their problems due recognition is likely universally applicable across any industry that needs to digitally transform.

- The second difference in TaP is that technology is a capability, and to avoid solution-before-problem, the customer and business first need to achieve the desirability and viability criteria, and technology is but one element in the capability dimension that can make the transformation successful.

- In many cases, process may be even more important to get right first, because technology is merely automating the process on paper, enabling it to be fast and error-free

- The emphasis on process, data and design gives these three supporting elements equal weightage as technology, which is what happens most of the time in a successful transformation.

- TaP excels in managing the complexity that is a natural outcome of the scope and interaction of the dimensions and elements of a digital transformation.

- The four dimensions, customers, business, people & leadership, remain relevant across industries, as the methods used and the elements and considerations are known from prior experience and body of knowledge to be highly extensible.

- The capabilities dimension was redesigned significantly to cater for adaptability across industries. Methodologies, technology, ecosystems and new disciplines all allow for industry-specific considerations like robotics or instrumentation.

- TaP is a discipline of thinking and implementing that can be a powerful ally in the new world we live in.

- This is a new world of fleeting competitive advantage, significant ambiguity and uncertainty, but yet with much technological change accelerating and coming together to leverage each other to force greater disruption than ever before.

- In this new era, the thinking tools alone or the implementation tools alone aren't enough to raise your probability of success. You have to combine them together so that the thinking and doing work in lock-step.

References

Accenture. (2018). *Disruption Need Not Be an Enigma*.

Agar, M., & MacDonald, J. (1995). Focus Groups and Ethnography. *Human Organization*, *54*(1), 78–86. http://www.jstor.org/stable/44126575

Andrew, C., & Marcus, A. (1997). "What's Wrong with Strategy?" *Harvard Business Review*, *75*(6), 8. https://hbr.org/1997/11/whats-wrong-with-strategy

Andrews, E. (2018). "Pedal Your Way Through the Bicycle's Bumpy History." History.com. https://www.history.com/news/pedal-your-way-through-the-bicycles-bumpy-history

Ang, P. (2020). "Singapore to have 4 digital banks, with Grab-Singtel and Sea getting digital full bank licences." *The Straits Times*. https://www.straitstimes.com/business/banking/mas-awards-digital-full-bank-licences-to-grab-singtel-and-sea-ant-gets-digital

Anthony, S. (2016). "Kodak's Downfall Wasn't About Technology." *Harvard Business Review*. https://hbr.org/2016/07/kodaks-downfall-wasnt-about-technology

Antony, J. (2016). "Six Sigma vs Lean Six Sigma." *Purdue University*, *60*(2), 185–190. https://www.purdue.edu/leansixsigmaonline/blog/six-sigma-vs-lean-six-sigma/

Appolonia, A. (2019). "The Rise and Fall of BlackBerry." Business Insider. https://www.businessinsider.com/blackberry-smartphone-rise-fall-mobile-failure-innovate-2019-11

Asian Banking and Finance. (2020). "UOB to launch digital bank in Indonesia." https://asian-bankingandfinance.net/retail-banking/more-news/uob-launch-digital-bank-in-indonesia

Bain. (2018). "Measuring Your Net Promoter Score." https://www.netpromotersystem.com/about/measuring-your-net-promoter-score/

Bain & Co., Google, & Temasek. (2019). "The Future of Southeast Asia's Digital Financial Services." Bain and Company. https://www.bain.com/insights/fufilling-its-promise/

Baldwin, C. Y. (2019). "Design Rules, Volume 2: How Technology Shapes Organizations: Chapter 17: The Wintel Standards-based Platform." *SSRN Electronic Journal*. https://doi.org/10.2139/ssrn.3482515

Barquin, S., Vinayak H. V., and Shrikhande, D. (2018). "Asia's digital banking race: Giving customers what they want." *Global Banking* (April), 1–16. https://www.mckinsey.com/~/media/McKinsey/Industries/Financial Services/Our Insights/Reaching Asias digital banking customers/Asias-digital-banking-race-WEB-FINAL.ashx.

Baxter, D., Koners, U., & Szwejczewski, M. (2013). "Hidden needs: Comparing ethnography and focus groups." 20th International Product Development Management Conference. https://www.researchgate.net/publication/299365380_Hidden_needs_comparing_ethnography_and_focus_groups

BCG. (2020). "Flipping the Odds of Digital Transformation Success." https://www.bcg.com/publications/2020/increasing-odds-of-success-in-digital-transformation

Bendor-Samuel, P. (2019). "Why digital transformations fail: 3 exhausting reasons." The Enterprise Project, 2019–2021. https://www.everestgrp.com/2019-08-why-digital-transformations-fail-3-exhausting-reasons-blog-51164.html

Boutetière, H., Montagner, A., & Reich, A. (2018). "The keys to a successful digital transformation." McKinsey; in *Survey*. https://www.mckinsey.com/business-functions/organization/our-insights/unlocking-success-in-digital-transformations

Brandom, R. (2019). "Boston Dynamics' Spot is leaving the laboratory." *The Verge*. https://www.theverge.com/2019/9/24/20880511/boston-dynamics-spot-robot-mini-hands-on-lease-buy

Bunderson, J. S., and Sanner, B. (2018). "The truth about hierarchy." *MIT Sloan Management Review*. https://sloanreview.mit.edu/article/the-truth-about-hierarchy/.

CBNEditor. (2019). "Tencent Leads Chinese Tech Giants in Online Banking." *China Banking News*. https://www.chinabankingnews.com/2019/02/26/tencent-leads-chinese-tech-giants-in-online-banking/

Chamorro-Premuzic, T. (2013). "Seven rules for managing creative-but-difficult people." *Harvard Business Review*, 634, 1–6. https://hbr.org/2013/04/seven-rules-for-managing-creat.

Chiew, S. (2018). "UOB launches Engagement Lab to meet banking needs of Asean's booming digital generation." *The Edge, SIngapore*. https://www.theedgesingapore.com/news/startups-entrepreneurs-digital-economy/uob-launches-engagement-lab-meet-banking-needs-aseans

Choi, J., Erande, Y., Yu, Y., & Aquino, C. J. (2021). *Emerging Challengers and Incumbent Operators Battle for Asia Pacific's Digital Banking Opportunity*. Bcg.com. https://web-assets.bcg.com/53/42/92f340e345dab62aa227fd53ccd4/asian-digital-challenger-bank.pdf

Choose. (2019). "Switching Current Accounts with UK Banks: How and why?" Choose.co.uk. https://www.choose.co.uk/guide/current-account-switching-service.html

Christensen, C. M., Hall, T., Dillon, K., & Duncan, D. S. (2016). "Know your customers' 'jobs to be done'." *Harvard Business Review* (September). Harvard Business School Publishing.

Chua, M. H. (2021). "The battle between Big Tech and Big Media (with Big Govt backing)." *The Straits Times*. https://www.straitstimes.com/opinion/the-battle-between-big-tech-and-big-media-with-big-govt-backing-0

Clark, S. (2015). "Space matters: How physical environments can enhance creativity and innovation in our digital world." Changeboard.

Clifford, C. (2018). "Jeff Bezos on what it takes to be innovative." Cnbc.com. https://www.cnbc.com/2018/05/17/jeff-bezos-on-what-it-takes-to-be-innovative.html

Collins, J. (2020). "The Flywheel Effect." https://www.jimcollins.com/concepts/the-flywheel.html

Collins, J. (1994). "Built to last." In *Built to Last*. https://www.harpercollins.com/products/built-to-last-jim-collinsjerry-i-porras?variant=32117226274850

Crisanto, J. M. (2020). "Kakaobank's digital-only service wins customer vote to top BankQuality survey." *The Asian Banker*. https://www.theasianbanker.com/updates-and-articles/kakaobanks-digital-only-service-wins-customer-vote-to-top-bankquality-survey

Dalton, J. (2016). "What is Insight? The 5 Principles of Insight Definition." Thrive. https://thrivethinking.com/2016/03/28/what-is-insight-definition/

Davenport, T. H., & Redman, T. C. (2020). "Digital Transformation Comes Down to Talent in 4 Key Areas." *Harvard Business Review*. https://hbr.org/2020/05/digital-transformation-comes-down-to-talent-in-4-key-areas?registration=success

Davenport, T. H., & Westerman, G. (2018). "Why So Many High-Profile Digital Transformations Fail." *Harvard Business Review*, 2–6. https://hbr.org/2018/03/why-so-many-high-profile-digital-transformations-fail?ab=at_art_art_1x1

Davey, N. (2013). *Consumer Research: Focus Groups vs Ethnography.* https://www.mycus-tomer.com/marketing/data/consumer-research-focus-groups-vs-ethnography

Davidz, H. L., Nightingale, D. J., & Rhodes, D. H. (2005). "Enablers and Barriers to Systems Thinking Development: Results of a Qualitative and Quantitative Study." *Field Studies* (January), 1–9. https://www.researchgate.net/publication/228367934_Enablers_and_barriers_to_systems_thinking_development_Results_of_a_qualitative_and_quantita-tive_study

Deakin, J., LaBerge, L., & O'Beirne, B. (2019). "Five moves to make during a digital transfor-mation." McKinsey. https://www.mckinsey.com/business-functions/mckinsey-digital/our-insights/five-moves-to-make-during-a-digital-transformation

Delamore, S. B.-D. (2020). "The 5 Essential Elements of Modular Software Design." Medium.com. https://shanebdavis.medium.com/the-5-essential-elements-of-modular-software-design-6b333918e543

Design Council Singapore. (2019). "The designers behind UOB's first mobile-only bank." Design Singapore Council Stories. https://www.designsingapore.org/stories/the-design-ers-behind-uob-first-mobile-only-bank.html.

Desjardins, J. (2019). "How much data is generated each day?" World Economic Forum. https://www.weforum.org/agenda/2019/04/how-much-data-is-generated-each-day-cf4bddf29f/

Digital Banker. (2020). "TMRW by UOB: Best-in-class experience for the digital generation." *The Digital Banker* (Jan–Mar 2020).

Doshi, N., & McGregor, L. (2015). *Primed to Perform.* https://www.harpercollins.com/products/primed-to-perform-neel-doshilindsay-mcgregor?variant=32206672298018

Drake, J. (2012). "Understanding Insights." https://johndrake.typepad.com/advertis-ing/2012/07/insights.html

Du Toit, G., Cuthell, K., & Burns, M. (2018). "CX in Banking and Bank NPS. In Search of Customers Who Love Their Bank." https://www.bain.com/insights/in-search-of-customers-who-love-their-bank-nps-cx-banking/

Efma. 2021. "Forging your own challenger bank: TMRW by UOB." https://www.efma.com/article/16051-forging-your-own-challenger-bank-tmrw-by-uob.

Eisape, D. (2019). "The Platform Business Model Canvas a Proposition in a Design Science Approach." *American Journal of Management Science and Engineering,* 4(6), 91. https://doi.org/10.11648/j.ajmse.20190406.12

Eisape, D. (2020). "Platform Generation: Platform Business Model Canvas & digital economy." Platformgeneration.com. https://www.platformgeneration.com/en#About

Fall, F. S., Orozco, L., and Al-Mouksit Akim. (2020). "Adoption and use of mobile banking by low-income individuals in Senegal." *Review of Development Economics,* 24(2), 569–88. https://doi.org/https://doi.org/10.1111/rode.12658.

Fenn, T., & Hobbs, J. (2017). "Conceiving and applying relationship models for design strategy." *Smart Innovation, Systems and Technologies,* 66, 517–528. https://doi.org/10.1007/978-981-10-3521-0_45

Finews.asia. (2019). "UOB launches digital bank for ASEAN start-ing from Thailand." Finews.com. https://www.finews.asia/finance/28245-uob-launches-digital-bank-for-asean-starting-from-thailand.

Fintech Singapore. (2019). "UOB's Thai digital bank TMRW to enable biometrics for account opening." Fintechnews.sg.

Fisher, A. W., & Mckenney, J. L. (1993). "The Development of the ERMA Banking System: Lessons from History." *IEEE Annals of the History of Computing, 15*(1), 44–57. https://doi.org/10.1109/85.194091

Fujii, H. (2016). "Fujifilm: Surviving the digital revolution in photography through diversification into cosmetics." HBS Digital Initiative. https://digital.hbs.edu/platform-rctom/submission/fujifilm-surviving-the-digital-revolution-in-photography-through-diversification-into-cosmetics/

Futures, F. (2021). "Banking Tech Awards 2020 Winner: TMRW – Best UX/CX in Finance Initiative." Fintech Futures. https://www.Fintechfutures.com/2021/03/banking-tech-awards-2020-winner-tmrw-best-ux-cx-in-finance-initiative/

Gagua, F. (2020). "No 'one-size-fits-all' for mobile bank TMRW." Asian Banking & Finance. https://asianbankingandfinance.net/financial-technology/in-focus/no-'one-size-fits-all-mobile-bank-tmrw

Gallo, A. (2017). "Contribution Margin: What It Is, How to Calculate It, and Why You Need It." *Harvard Business Review*, 1. https://hbr.org/2017/10/contribution-margin-what-it-is-how-to-calculate-it-and-why-you-need-it

Gans, J. (2016). "The other disruption." In *Harvard Business Review* (March). https://hbr.org/2016/03/the-other-disruption

Gera, P., McIntyre, A., & Sandquist, E. (2019). "2019 Global Financial Services Consumer Study." Accenture. https://www.accenture.com/_acnmedia/PDF-95/Accenture-2019-Global-Financial-Services-Consumer-Study.pdf

GlobalData Financial Services. (2019). "Why some banks have the best net promoter scores in the UK." *Retail Banker International.* https://www.retailbankerinternational.com/comments/first-direct-nationwide-net-promoter-scores-uk/

Goh, J., & Paul Raj, A. (2019). "The South Korea Experience: How Kakao Bank forced traditional banks to buck up." *Edge Weekly.* https://www.theedgemarkets.com/article/cover-story-south-korea-experience-how-kakao-bank-forced-traditional-banks-buck

Hagiu, A. (2014). "Strategic decisions for multisided platforms." *MIT Sloan Management Review, 55*(2), 71–80. https://sloanreview.mit.edu/article/strategic-decisions-for-multisided-platforms/

Harrison, D. (2018). "Harrison Assessments: An Innovative Approach to Employee Assessments." HR Tech Outlook. https://leadership-development.hrtechoutlook.com/vendor/harrison-assessments-an-innovative-approach-to-employee-assessments-cid-410-mid-57.html

Harrison, D. (2020). "Talent Management technology: Acquire, Develop, Lead, Engage." https://www.harrisonassessments.com/

Hernandez, D. (2012). "April 20, 1964: Picturephone Dials Up First Transcontinental Video Call." Wired. https://www.wired.com/2012/04/april-20-1964-picturephone-dials-up-first-transcontinental-video-call/

Hinchliffe, R. (2020). "NatWest's Mettle gives users access to FreeAgent's accounting software." FinTech Futures. https://www.Fintechfutures.com/2020/04/natwests-mettle-gives-users-access-to-freeagents-accounting-software/

Ho, J. (2020). UOB reaches young Asean professionals with TMRW." *The Edge Singapore.*

Huang, E. (2018). "Tencent's WeBank hopes A.I. and robots can improve customer service." CNBC.com. https://www.cnbc.com/2018/11/28/tencents-webank-hopes-ai-and-robots-can-improve-customer-service.html

Inc. (2006). "Robotics – Encyclopedia." Inc.com. https://www.inc.com/encyclopedia/robot-ics.html

Insley, J. (2010). "Bank accounts: People don't want to press the switch." *The Guardian.* https://www.theguardian.com/money/2010/oct/09/switching-bank-accounts-consumer-focus

Jaume, J. (2012). "8 Tech Inventions and Gadgets That Never Took Off." Brandwatch. https://www.brandwatch.com/blog/8-tech-inventions-and-gadgets-that-never-took-off/

Jeffries, I. (2011). "Three Lenses of Innovation." https://isaacjeffries.com/blog/2016/3/9/three-lenses-of-innovation

Jiao, C., Sihombing, G., & Dahrul, F. (2012). "Sea and Gojek can target Indonesia's 83 million who lack bank access." *The Straits Times.* https://www.straitstimes.com/business/banking/sea-and-gojek-can-target-indonesias-83-million-who-lack-bank-access

Kaelig. (2016). "Design Systems Ops. Who bridges the gap between the design." Medium. com. https://medium.com/@kaelig/introducing-design-systems-ops-7f34c4561ba7

Keeley, L., Pikkel, R., Quinn, B., & Walters, H. (2017). "Ten Types | Doblin." Doblin – A Deloitte Business. https://doblin.com/ten-types

Keum, D. D., & See, K. E. (2017). "The Influence of Hierarchy on Idea Generation and Selection in the Innovation Process." *Organization Science, 28*(4), 653–669. https://doi.org/10.1287/orsc.2017.1142

Khoo, D. (2012). "What drives superior performance when large firms internationalize?"

Khoo, D. (2019a). "Engaging tomorrow's customers: The opportunity in ASEAN." *The Business Times.* https://www.businesstimes.com.sg/asean-business/engaging-tomorrow's-customers-the-opportunity-in-asean.

Khoo, D. (2019b). "UOB Corporate Day 2019: ASEAN's digital bank for ASEAN's digital genera-tion." UOB Investor Relations.

Khoo, D. (2020a). "Banking for the digital generation." Uobgroup.com Investor Relations.

Khoo, D. (2020b). "If you're an incumbent bank, here's how you can be a challenger bank." *The Nation.* https://www.nationthailand.com/noname/30390219?utm_source=catego-ry&utm_medium=internal_referral.Kim Yoo-chul, & Park, A. J. (2020). "Clear ownership to bolster Kakao Bank IPO." *The Korea Times.* https://www.koreatimes.co.kr/www/biz/2021/02/126_300081.html

Kitani, K. (2019). "Here's why GE, Ford's digital transformation programs failed last year." CNBC. https://www.cnbc.com/2019/10/30/heres-why-ge-fords-digital-transformation-programs-failed-last-year.html

Krigsman, M. (2018). "Nokia reinvented: Decline, resurrection, and how CEOs get trapped." ZDNet Online. https://www.zdnet.com/article/nokia-reinvented-decline-resurrection-and-how-ceos-get-trapped/

Kwatinetz, M. (2018). "Why Contribution Margin is a Strong Predictor of Success for Companies." Soundbytes II. https://soundbytes2.com/2018/08/29/why-contribution-margin-is-a-strong-predictor-of-success-for-companies/

L'Hostis, A. (2019). "Profiling Fintech: Q&A with Dennis Khoo, Regional Head at TMRW Digital Group, UOB." Forrestor. https://go.forrester.com/blogs/profiling-Fintech-qa-with-dennis-khoo-regional-head-at-tmrw-digital-group-uob/

Laambert, C. (2014). "Clayton Christensen on disruptive innovation." *Harvard Magazine.* https://harvardmagazine.com/2014/07/disruptive-genius

Lam, K., and Koh, J. (2020). "UOB's digital bank: TMRW investor update." UOB Investor Relations.

Lee, S., & Kim, H. (2019). "Korea's online lender Kakao Bank hits 10 mn accounts in 2 yrs."
    Pulse by Maeil Business News. https://pulsenews.co.kr/view.php?year=2019&no=514398
Lee, Y., & Ho, Y. (2020). "Gojek Buys Slice of Indonesian Bank in Biggest Fintech
    Deal Yet." Bloomberg. https://www.bloomberg.com/news/articles/2020-12-18/
    gojek-buys-slice-of-indonesian-bank-in-biggest-Fintech-deal-yet
Leung, J., & Gordon, F. (2019). "Success Virtually Assured." In Accenture Report: Success
    Virtually Assured. https://www.accenture.com/_acnmedia/PDF-109/Accenture-Success-
    Virtually-Assured.pdf
Liu, M., & L'Hostis, A. (2019). "Forrester Case Study: How WeBank Became The World's
    Leading Digital Bank." https://www.kapronasia.com/china-banking-research-category/
    webank-the-world-s-top-digital-bank.html
Liu, S. (2020). "Office suites market share U.S. 2020." Statista. https://www.statista.com/
    statistics/961105/japan-market-share-of-office-suites-technologies/
Magotra, I., J. Sharma, and S. K. Sharma. (2015). "Technology adoption propensity of the
    banking customers in India: An insight." *International Journal of Management,* Accounting
    and Economics 2(2), 111–24. http://www.ijmae.com/article_115388.html.
Making "Freemium" Work. (2014). *Harvard Business Review.* https://hbr.org/2014/05/
    making-freemium-work
Marous, J. (2020). "WeBank: Insights From The World's Top Digital
    Bank." The Financial Brand. https://thefinancialbrand.com/104213/
    digital-banking-transformed-podcast-china-webank-henry-ma/
Martinez, J. D. L. (2016). "How to scale up financial inclusion in ASEAN coun-
    tries." World Bank Blogs. https://blogs.worldbank.org/eastasiapacific/
    how-to-scale-up-financial-inclusion-in-asean-countries
Massi, M., Sullivan, G., Michael, S., & Khan, M. (2019). "How Cashless Payments
    Help Economies Grow." BCG. https://www.bcg.com/publications/2019/
    cashless-payments-help-economies-grow
May, R. 1994. *The Courage to Create.*
McGovern, G. (2013). "Why It's So Hard to be Customer-Centric." CMSWiRE. https://
    www.cmswire.com/cms/customer-experience/why-its-so-hard-to-be-customercen-
    tric-021809.php
McGrath, R. G. (2013). "The end of competitive advantage: How to keep your strategy
    moving as fast as your business." *Harvard Business Review* (June), 1–25. https://hbr.
    org/2013/08/the-end-of-competitive-advanta
McKendrick, J. (2019). "Plenty of digital transformation, but not enough strat-
    egy." Forbes.com. https://www.forbes.com/sites/joemckendrick/2019/03/23/
    plenty-of-digital-transformation-but-not-enough-strategy/?sh=4c99fe407d68.
McKinsey & Company. (2016). "The 'how' of transformation." https://www.mckinsey.com/
    industries/retail/our-insights/the-how-of-transformation
Meek, T. (2018). "The Rise In Computing Power: Why Ubiquitous Artificial Intelligence is Now
    a Reality." Forbes. https://www.forbes.com/sites/intelai/2018/07/17/the-rise-in-comput-
    ing-power-why-ubiquitous-artificial-intelligence-is-now-a-reality/?sh=505e11701d3f
Michon, B. (2021). "Why consumer insights are so important in mar-
    keting?" Mihon Creative. https://michoncreative.co.uk/news/
    why-consumer-insights-are-so-important-in-marketing/
Moed, J. (2019). "The Real Reason It's Hard For Startups To Scale Internationally."
    Forbes.com. https://www.forbes.com/sites/jonathanmoed/2019/02/28/

the-real-reason-its-hard-for-startups-to-scale-internationally/?sh=69440a575f0b

Morgan, B. (2019). "100 of the most customer-centric companies." Forbes. https://www.
forbes.com/sites/blakemorgan/2019/06/30/100-of-the-most-customer-centric-
companies/?sh=75f07d5963c3

Morris, H. (2019). "China's march to be the world's first cashless society." *The Straits Times.* https://www.straitstimes.com/asia/east-asia/
chinas-march-to-be-the-worlds-first-cashless-society-china-daily-contributor

Murray, F., & Johnson, E. (2021). "Innovation Starts with Defining the Right
Constraints." *Harvard Business Review.* https://hbr.org/2021/04/
innovation-starts-with-defining-the-right-constraints

Myre, M. (2018). "The 14 Best Wireframe Tools." Zapier Blog. https://zapier.com/blog/
best-wireframe-tools/

Newman, D. (2015). "What is the Experience Economy, and Should Your Business
Care?" Forbes.com. https://www.forbes.com/sites/danielnewman/2015/11/24/
what-is-the-experience-economy-should-your-business-care/?sh=13cec1791d0c

Newnham, C. (2020). "10 Best Wireframe Tools For UX/UI Designers in 2020." Insightful UX
Blog. https://www.insightfulux.co.uk/blog/10-best-wireframe-tools-ux-2020/

Nice, S. (2018). "NICE Satmetrix Releases US Net Promoter Score Benchmarks for 2018."
NICE. https://www.nice.com/engage/press-releases/NICE-Satmetrix-Releases-US-
Net-Promoter-Score-Benchmarks-for-2018-Revealing-Customer-Loyalty-Leaders-in-23-
Industries-622/

Nikkei. (2020). "Canon's 45.4% market share is greater than Sony, Nikon and Fuji's
combined." Digitalcameraworld. https://www.digitalcameraworld.com/news/
canons-454-market-share-is-greater-than-sony-nikon-and-fujis-combined

Obradovich, N. (2019, February 26). "The data is in. Frogs don't boil. But we might."
The Washington Post. https://www.washingtonpost.com/weather/2019/02/25/
data-are-frogs-dont-boil-we-might/

Ollhoff, J., & Walcheski, M. (2006). "Making the Jump to Systems Thinking: The Road to
Becoming a Systems Thinker." The Systems Thinker. https://thesystemsthinker.com/
making-the-jump-to-systems-thinking/

Osterwalder, A. (2017). "How to Systematically Reduce the Risk & Uncertainty of
New Ideas." Strategyzer. https://www.strategyzer.com/blog/posts/2017/12/6/
how-to-systematically-reduce-the-risk-uncertainty-of-new-ideas

Patrizio, A. (2018). "What is cloud-native? The modern way to develop applications."
InfoWorld. https://www.infoworld.com/article/3281046/what-is-cloud-native-the-mod-
ern-way-to-develop-software.html

Perkins, B., & Fenech, C. (2014). "The Deloitte Consumer Review: The growing power of
consumers." http://www.deloitte.com/view/en_GB/uk/industries/consumer-business/
research-publications

Perry, M. J. (2019). "Only 52 US companies have been on the Fortune 500 since 1955,
thanks to the creative destruction that fuels economic prosperity." https://www.aei.org/
carpe-diem/only-52-us-companies-have-been-on-the-fortune-500-since-1955-thanks-
to-the-creative-destruction-that-fuels-economic-prosperity/

Pidun, U., Reeves, M., & Schüssler, M. (2019). "Do you need a business ecosystem?"
BCG Henderson Institute. https://www.bcg.com/de-de/publications/2019/
do-you-need-business-ecosystem

Pidun, U., Reeves, M., & Schüssler, M. (2020a). "How Do You 'Design' a Business

Ecosystem?" BCG Hendersen Institute, 1–15. https://www.bcg.com/publications/2020/how-do-you-design-a-business-ecosystem

Pidun, U., Reeves, M., & Schüssler, M. (2020b). "Why do most business ecosystems fail?" BCG Henderson Institute, 1–18. https://www.bcg.com/publications/2020/why-do-most-business-ecosystems-fail

Pine, B. J., & Gilmore, J. H. (1998). "Welcome to the experience economy." *Harvard Business Review, 76*(4), 97–105. https://hbr.org/1998/07/welcome-to-the-experience-economy

Pine II, B. J., & Gilmore, J. H. (2011). *The Experience Economy.* https://www.amazon.com/Experience-Economy-Updated-Joseph-Pine/dp/1422161978

Pisano, G. (2015). "You need an innovation strategy." *Harvard Business Review, 316* (June). https://hbr.org/2015/06/you-need-an-innovation-strategy

Pisano, G. P. (2019). "Innovation isn't all fun and games. Creativity needs discipline." *Harvard Business Review.* https://hbr.org/2019/01/the-hard-truth-about-innovative-cultures.

Profozich, G. (2021). "Ready or Not, Robotics in Manufacturing is on the Rise." Cmtc.com. https://www.cmtc.com/blog/overview-of-robotics-in-manufacturing

PuReum, L., & Chung, D. (2019). "Tourists on GrabChat!" Grab Tech Blog. https://engineering.grab.com/tourist-chat-data-story

Ranadive, A. (2017). "Strong Opinions, Weakly Held: A framework for thinking." Medium.com. https://medium.com/@ameet/strong-opinions-weakly-held-a-framework-for-thinking-6530d417e364

Rodriguez, B. (2017). "The power of creative constraints." TED Talk. https://www.ted.com/talks/brandon_rodriguez_the_power_of_creative_constraints?language=en

Rogers, B. (2016). "Why 84% of Companies Fail at Digital Transformation." Forbes, 1–5. https://www.forbes.com/sites/brucerogers/2016/01/07/why-84-of-companies-fail-at-digital-transformation/?sh=59b92534397b

Ross, M.-C. (2015). "5 Reasons Why Mission-Driven Leaders are the Most Successful." LinkedIn. https://www.linkedin.com/pulse/5-reasons-why-mission-driven-leaders-most-successful-ross-gaicd

Rubinstein, M. (2021). "Tinkoff, Russia's Capital One." Net Interest. https://www.netinterest.co/p/tinkoff-russias-capital-one

Sandstrom, C. (2009). "Canon and the Disruptive shift to Digital Imaging", 115.

Schneider, J. (2017). *Understanding Design Thinking, Lean, and Agile.* In O'Reilly Media Inc. http://oreilly.com/safari

Schumpeter. (2012). "Sharper focus." *The Economist.* https://www.economist.com/schumpeter/2012/01/18/sharper-focus

Segran, E. (2017). "Three Weird Customer Insights that Led to Kick-Ass Products." Fast Company. https://www.fastcompany.com/40483379/three-weird-customer-insights-that-led-to-kick-ass-products?position=10&campaign_date=03072021

Sendingan, S. (2019). "How Kakaobank successfully cracked the profitability code two years after rocket launch." Asian Banking & Finance. https://asianbankingandfinance.net/financial-technology/exclusive/how-kakaobank-successfully-cracked-profitability-code-two-years-after

Sheppard, B., Sarrazin, H., Kouyoumjian, G., & Dore, F. (2018). "The business value of design." *McKinsey Quarterly.* https://www.mckinsey.com/business-functions/mckinsey-design/our-insights/the-business-value-of-design

Shevlin, R. (2021). "Embedded Fintech versus Embedded Finance: Jumpstarting New Product Innovation in Banks." Forbes.com. https://www.forbes.com/sites/

ronshevlin/2021/04/12/embedded-Fintech-versus-embedded-finance-jumpstart-
ing-new-product-innovation-in-banks/?sh=e0048ee5892a

Sia, J. (2019). "Joint Venture with VI (Vietnam Investments) Fund III, L.P." SGX. www.
UOBGroup.com.

Skinner, C. (2021). "Even with a bribe, no one switches their bank account." Chris Skinner's
Blog. https://thefinanser.com/2018/02/even-bribe-no-one-switches-bank-account.html/

Snow, S. (2020). "Our Leaders of Tomorrow are Going to Need These 4 Rare
Skills." Forbes. https://www.forbes.com/sites/shanesnow/2020/06/04/
our-leaders-of-tomorrow-are-going-to-need-these-4-rare-skills/?sh=5d012c1e1855

Solis, B. (2020). "When digital transformation fails, focus on the why and how of change,
not just technology and transactions." ZDNet Online. https://www.zdnet.com/article/
when-digital-transformation-fails-focus-on-the-why-and-how-of-change-not-just-tech-
nology/

"StanChart, NTUC Enterprise plan digital-only bank in Singapore." (2020).
The Straits Times. https://www.straitstimes.com/business/banking/
stanchart-ntuc-enterprise-plan-digital-only-bank-in-singapore.

Sulaiman, A., Jaafar, N. I., and Mohezar, S. (2007). "An overview of mobile banking adoption
among the urban community." *IJMC*, 5 (January), 157–68. https://doi.org/10.1504/
IJMC.2007.011814.

Sutcliff, M., Narsalay, R., & Sen, A. (2019). "The two big reasons that digital transformations fail." *Harvard Business Review*, October, 2–6. https://hbr.org/2019/10/
the-two-big-reasons-that-digital-transformations-fail

Sutherland, J., Sutherland, J. J., & Schneier, A. (2020). "2020 Scrum Guide
Changes and Updates Explained." Scrum Inc. https://www.scruminc.
com/2020-scrum-guide-changes-updates-explained/

Tabrizi, B., Lam, E., Girard, K., & Irvin, V. (2019). "Digital Transformation is Not
About Technology." *Harvard Business Review*. https://hbr.org/2019/03/
digital-transformation-is-not-about-technology

Tanimoto, T. (2018). "What is Business Design?" Medium.com. https://medium.com/
spotless-says/what-is-business-design-58d849eaefef

Tech Wire Asia. (2019). "UOB's TMRW is proof banks are making an effort to understand
customers." Techwire Asia.

Teng, A. (2021). "Schools in Singapore continue to reap benefits of remote learning."
The Straits Times. https://www.straitstimes.com/singapore/parenting-education/
how-a-virus-taught-education-in-singapore-a-lesson-in-adapability

The Myers-Briggs Company. (2020). INTJ personality profile. https://eu.themyersbriggs.
com/en/tools/MBTI/MBTI-personality-Types/INTJ

The Straits Times. (2018). "UOB sets up joint venture with Chinese Fintech firm." *The
Straits Times*. https://www.straitstimes.com/business/companies-markets/
uob-sets-up-joint-venture-with-chinese-fintech-firm.

Tinkoff, O. (2010). "Oleg Tinkov: 'I'm Just Like Anyone Else'." https://anisimov.biz/
oleg-tinkov-im-just-like-anyone-else/

Umit Kucuk, S., & Krishnamurthy, S. (2007). "An analysis of consumer power on the Internet."
Technovation, 27(1–2), 47–56. https://doi.org/10.1016/j.technovation.2006.05.002

Vincent, J. (2019). "Boston Dynamics' robots are preparing to leave the lab. Is the
world ready?" The Verge. https://www.theverge.com/2019/7/17/20697540/
boston-dynamics-robots-commercial-real-world-business-spot-on-sale

Wade, M. (2018). "Digital Transformation: 5 Ways Organizations Fail." The Enterprisers Project. https://enterprisersproject.com/article/2018/11/digital-transformation-5-ways-organizations-fail

Warden, G. (2019a). "Banking for TMRW: Head of UOB's digital bank explains engagement, advocates, Personetics." *The Edge, Singapore*. https://www.theedgesingapore.com/capital/fintech/banking-tmrw-head-uob's-digital-bank-explains-engagement-advocates-personetics.

Warden, G. (2019b). "UOB's digital future lies in serving ASEAN." *The Edge, Singapore*. https://www.uobgroup.com/techecosystem/news-insights-uob-digital-future-lies-in-serving-asean.html.

Warden, G. (2020). "UOB digital bank focuses on TMRW's customers." *The Edge, Singapore*.

We Are Social. (2020). "Digital 2020: We Are Social." https://wearesocial.com/digital-2020.

WE Online, Jakarta. (2021). "UOB presents TMRW to support financial inclusion in the digital economy era." Newsy Today. https://www.newsy-today.com/uob-presents-tmrw-to-support-financial-inclusion-in-the-digital-economy-era/.

Wei, Y., Yildirim, P., Bulte, C. Van den, & Dellarocas, C. (2014). "How Social Media Can Be Used for Credit Scoring." Knowledge@wharton. https://knowledge.wharton.upenn.edu/article/using-social-media-for-credit-scoring/

Weng, W. (2020). "Thirteen most profitable digital banks in Asia Pacific upped earnings by 49% in 2019." The Asian Banker. https://www.theasianbanker.com/updates-and-articles/thirteen-most-profitable-digital-banks-in-asia-pacific-upped-earnings-by-49-in-2019

Which MBA? (2018). "Design thinking: People first." *The Economist*. https://whichmba.economist.com/management-ideas/2018/01/10/design-thinking-people-first

Wijeratne, D., Plumridge, N., & Raj, S. (2019). "Sustaining Southeast Asia's momentum." https://www.strategy-business.com/article/Sustaining-Southeast-Asias-Momentum?gko=32ad4

William, C. (2018). "The Importance of Having a Mission-Driven Company." Forbes. https://www.forbes.com/sites/williamcraig/2018/05/15/the-importance-of-having-a-mission-driven-company/?sh=5f38fe6c3a9c

Williams, T. (2019). "Why customer centricity is crucial to your organisation." *The Economist*. https://execed.economist.com/blog/industry-trends/why-customer-centricity-crucial-your-organisation

Worthington, S. (2021). "Are neo-banks here to stay? Or just a passing phase? Bluenotes. https://bluenotes.anz.com/posts/2021/03/steve-worthington-neo-banks-Fintech-deposits-lending

Yoshino, N., & Taghizadeh-Hesary, F. (2018). "The Role of SMEs in Asia and Their Difficulties in Accessing Finance." Asian Development Bank Institute. https://www.adb.org/publications/role-smes-asia-and-their-

Zeitchik, S. (2021). "Netflix added 4 million subscribers in most recent quarter." *The Washington Post*. https://www.washingtonpost.com/business/2021/04/20/netflix-new-subscriber-numbers/

About the author

Dr Dennis Khoo is an accomplished digital business leader and speaker in innovation and leadership. Armed with dual experience in Information Technology and banking, he has a unique advantage in developing and executing strategies for the transformation of businesses in a digital world. A digital bank pioneer in ASEAN, Dennis was group head of TMRW Digital Group (UOB's millennial digital bank), where he was responsible for the strategy, growth and delivery of the TMRW Digital Bank. The first TMRW Digital Bank went live in Thailand in 2019, and the second in Indonesia in 2020. TMRW won Global Finance Most Innovative Digital Bank in Asia Pacific in 2019. Dennis also led the joint venture initiatives that focused on scaling TMRW and created Fintech like Avatec.ai and VUI Pte Ltd as part of the ecosystem to support the growth of TMRW.

Dennis was previously a senior banker who ran billion-dollar businesses as head of consumer bank for Standard Chartered Bank and UOB in Singapore. He was responsible for many of the innovations in the consumer banking industry in Singapore, such as e$aver, XtraSaver (Winner of Asian Banker Best Deposit Linked account in 2007), Retail Bonds, Step-up time deposit, Pay-Any-Card (Winner of Asian Banker Best Payment Product in 2011), 15% Dining Cashback everywhere, 2-day Mortgage Service Guarantee, UOB Income Builder, One Account and UOB Mighty App. Dennis was previously CEO-designate in one of the consortiums bidding for the digital bank wholesale licences in Singapore. Before joining the banking industry in 2001, Dennis spent 13 years in Hewlett-Packard Singapore, in many diverse roles – hardware customer engineer, application engineer, customer engineering manager, network integration manager for Southeast Asia, Asia-Pacific Marketing Manager for software services, Manager for Intel Servers for Singapore and Asia-Pacific, etc.

Dennis is a sought-after lecturer and trainer and is involved in the Managerial Communications programme (now called Lead Your Transformation) at the NUS School of Business MBA and the Enterprise Leadership for Transformation programme for SMEs in collaboration with NUS Business School and the LinHart Group. He has also taught the Corporate Strategy course for the NUS MBA programme as Adjunct Professor. Dennis holds a degree in Engineering and a Master's in Business Administration from the National University of Singapore. He also has a Master's in Business Research and a PhD in Business Administration from the University of Western Australia. Dennis was awarded a Doctor of Philosophy for his work in International Business. His thesis, "What drives superior performance when large firms internationalise?" broke new ground in the understanding that firm-specific advantages drive performance while internationalisation is a moderating factor and not a driver of firm performance.

Dennis is a WABC (Worldwide Association of Business Coaches) Registered Corporate Coach, a certified Gallup Strengths coach, and accredited in Harrison Assessment Employee Development. Dennis has mentored and coached many successful executives in his long career.

Awards

IBF Distinguished Fellow Award in 2012

Customer Experience Professional of the Year (2019) by The Digital Banker

What did you think of Driving Digital Transformation?

First, thank you for purchasing my book, *Driving Digital Transformation*. I wrote it to help companies and executives lead their complex digital transformations towards a higher probability of success.

I would be most appreciative if you could share your experience leveraging the techniques and methods you read with me, so that I can make the next edition even better with your stories and learnings.

If you enjoyed the book and found benefit in reading it, I hope that you could take some time to post a review on Amazon. Your feedback and support will make it possible for more of your peers struggling with their own transformations to discover *Driving Digital Transformation*.

Wishing you great success in all your endeavours!

Best wishes,

Dr Dennis Khoo
dennis@allDigitalfuture.com

The
allDigitalFuture
Playbook™

Step-by-Step Workbook and Guide
Available Q1 2022

If you appreciated the robust and methodical approach The allDigitalfuture Playbook (TaP) can orchestrate for your company's digital transformation, sign up to be the first to know when the TaP workbook will be available at:

https://alldigitalfuture.com/book

We will let you know as soon as the workbook is available for purchase.